Landscapes: the Arts, Aesthetics, and Education

Volume 19

Scope

This series aims to provide conceptual and empirical research in arts education, (including music, visual arts, drama, dance, media, and poetry), in a variety of areas related to the post-modern paradigm shift. The changing cultural, historical, and political contexts of arts education are recognized to be central to learning, experience, knowledge. The books in this series presents theories and methodological approaches used in arts education research as well as related disciplines - including philosophy, sociology, anthropology and psychology of arts education.

The series editor invites you to contact her with plans and ideas for books that would fit in the series. For more information on how to submit a proposal, please write to the publishing editor, Jolanda Voogd. E-mail: jolanda.voogd@springer.com

More information about this series at http://www.springer.com/series/6199

Linda Ashley • David Lines

Editors

Intersecting Cultures in Music and Dance Education

An Oceanic Perspective

 Springer

Editors
Linda Ashley
Independent Researcher
Auckland, New Zealand

David Lines
Faculty of Creative Arts and Industries
University of Auckland
Auckland, New Zealand

ISSN 1573-4528   ISSN 2214-0069   (electronic)
Landscapes: the Arts, Aesthetics, and Education
ISBN 978-3-319-28987-8   ISBN 978-3-319-28989-2   (eBook)
DOI 10.1007/978-3-319-28989-2

Library of Congress Control Number: 2016937936

Printed on acid-free paper

This Springer imprint is published by Springer Nature
The registered company is Springer International Publishing AG Switzerland

This book is dedicated to Linda Ashley, co-editor, who sadly passed away in the final stages of publication. Linda was a source of inspiration for dance and arts educators in Oceania and across the world, and this book honours her life and work.

Contents

Introduction

Linda Ashley and David Lines

Abstract Intersecting Cultures in Music and Dance Education: An Oceanic Perspective explores the interface of Oceanic cultures through the diversity, richness and critical differences encountered in their performing arts, educational paradigms and cultural worldviews. In this introductory chapter, the editors reflect on aspects of their personal histories that inform their thinking in the book. This is followed by an editorial discussion that outlines theoretical and practical contexts informing key concepts in the book including notions of culture and cultural diversity, ethnicity, identity, hybridity, indigeneity, colonialism, migrancy, multiculturalism, tradition, cultural interaction and difference with particular reference to music and dance education in the Oceanic context.

Keywords Oceania • Music education • Dance education • Cultural diversity • Hybridity • Colonialism • Cultural interaction • Critical Pedagogy

Intersecting Cultures in Music and Dance Education: An Oceanic Perspective explores the interface of Oceanic cultures through the diversity, richness and critical differences encountered in their performing arts, educational paradigms and cultural worldviews. The ways in which cultural diversity is reflected through performing arts education in the Oceania region has not been explored to any great extent. Oceania has a history that portrays different cultural intersections and a diversity of expressions of indigeneity and postcolonial life. The region covers a wide range of performing arts traditions and innovations that often coexist in both state and private education settings. With cultural diversity becoming more evident in classrooms and arts studios worldwide, this book provides a timely reminder of the need for arts educators to rethink their pedagogical ideas and strategies. To encourage this

L. Ashley (✉)
Independent Researcher, 74 Koutunui Rd., RD 1, Auckland 3177, New Zealand

D. Lines
Faculty of Creative Arts and Industries, University of Auckland, Auckland, New Zealand
e-mail: d.lines@auckland.ac.nz

© Springer International Publishing Switzerland 2016
L. Ashley, D. Lines (eds.), *Intersecting Cultures in Music and Dance Education*, Landscapes: the Arts, Aesthetics, and Education 19,
DOI 10.1007/978-3-319-28989-2_1

rethinking, the focus of the book is on critical, conceptual thinking and the opening up of ideas around teaching of dance and music from varied cultural/philosophical perspectives. Further, the book attempts to provide an inclusive view of different educational values and artistic practices, promoting an awareness of the diversity of the authors' experiences and knowledge.

Contributors to the book include educators and practitioners in dance and music education from Polynesia, Micronesia and Melanesia, including the larger 'islands' of Aotearoa/New Zealand[1] and Australia. Many writers, including the editors, are based or have been based in New Zealand. They present perspectives on their teaching approaches and the values that underpin their pedagogy in community settings, early childhood centres, state schools and in higher education. Due to practical reasons not all islands and ethnic groups in Oceania are represented in the book. While the authors recognise this limitation it is hoped that the book will serve to broaden scholarship in this area and encourage others in the wider Oceania region to publish their own perspectives on this complex topic. As both editors and many of the authors reside in New Zealand, this sense of space and place is reflected in their worldviews as academic researchers.

As editors, we wanted to provide space for different writing styles and worldviews. Consequently the chapters vary. Some include reflective narratives and others, longer theoretically informed chapters in which more conceptual, critical and philosophical descriptions are given. The varied format allows for the voices of practitioners, researchers, teachers and theorists in music and dance education in the Oceania region to be heard together. In and around the varied styles of presentation, the following approaches underpin the writing:

- Critical philosophies of pedagogical practice in music and dance
- Pluralist perspectives on music and dance
- Personal narratives on music/dance pedagogical experiences
- Accounts of intersecting music/dance learning and cultures
- Descriptions of cultural values and beliefs
- Descriptions of intercultural dance/music and pedagogy

The aim of *Intersecting Cultures in Music and Dance Education: An Oceanic Perspective* is to re-examine present day education and pedagogical practices in music and dance in the diverse cultural environments found in Oceania. Towards this end, the book also identifies a key concern underpinned by the question: how can teachers take a reflexive view of their own cultural legacy in music and dance education as they work from and intersect with different cultural worldviews? This key concern, amongst other issues that arise, positions this book as an innovative text, featuring some fresh ideas from teachers as musicians and dancers who work in educational settings and filling a gap in the current literature. The basic premise is to offer commentaries that could underpin and inform current pedagogy and

---

[1]Throughout the book New Zealand is referred to as New Zealand, or as Aotearoa/New Zealand depending on the context.

bigger-picture policy for the performing arts in education in Oceania, and in parallel ways as appropriate for other parts of the globe.

Following this introductory section, editors, Dr. Linda Ashley and Dr. David Lines present their stories about how they became involved with intersecting cultures in education; a conversation in which ideas and relevant concepts are discussed in greater depth follows. The book is thematically separated into three sections: (i) Music and Dance in Education Through Oceanic Traditions, (ii) Culturally Responsive Pedagogies and, (iii) Sharing and Constructing Identities, Meanings and Values. Each section is introduced with a brief editorial discussion outlining the theme and progression of chapters.

1   Linda Ashley: A Journey in Dance Education

Once upon a time, in a land far away from Oceania and a long time ago, I left home as a young student to begin a life of study. There were to be many encounters of the academic kind that lay ahead as I went off to join the 'Dance Education Circus'. After a time, the intellectual and physical stimulations became many. I learnt dances from the Renaissance and every folk dance known in Europe alongside Piaget's developmental psychology and experienced the alarming realities of these diverse forms on practicum, teaching dance in 1970s Liverpool inner city schools. Heady moments of dance aesthetics were juxtaposed with drama, music, anatomy, physiology, pedagogy and sociological perspectives of educational disadvantage. The dizzy heights of choreography, running alongside enlightening encounters with cultural theory, delighted and intrigued. I learnt a new word – *hegemony*. In I.M. Marsh College, University of Liverpool dance studios, amongst a group of young impressionable peers, I 'Labanesed', so to speak, my way about, thrusting and screwing from one corner to another! My fourth year dance tutor, the late Olive Carr was inspirational and formed many of my early choreographic approaches. She offered an alternative to 'Modern Educational Dance'. Choreography was assessed by way of a choreographic reflective process diary. This was a research as practice approach that was, one might say, quite advanced for the time. The emphasis throughout was on dancing as theory in action and creating dances. This was extenuated when I was acculturated by North American Martha Graham technique, as brought by a converted alumnus! Then, a whole Graham company came to visit. It was the early days of London Contemporary Dance Theatre. The Big School had really turned it on and now everyone knew, it was official: College rocked! Although we didn't actually use those words back then. It was somewhat ahead of its educational time and a milestone intersection for me. There was so much to learn about and it all seemed important so I studied with vehemence, because one never knew when it would be handy. In my dance education, I was always aware of a pedagogy that infused theory with practice and *vice versa*, albeit at that time through somewhat mono-cultural spectacles.

My B.Ed. (Hons) was awarded in 1974 and a life of itinerant, peripatetic dance and education began, to be further embodied and embedded in Masters studies at Goldsmith's College, University of London in association with The Laban Centre. It has underpinned my dance-life as an educator, dancer, choreographer and writer ever since. As a dancer-academic my dance practice over the years has been fairly broad, but at the same time I am particularly wary of teaching specific dance genres from cultures other than my own, even though I have attended many classes over the years in a wide variety of genres. In the 1980s having been a frequent participant in African and Indian classical codified technique classes, I was injured and forced to observe. I began to wonder about the purpose and effects of these classes for the dance artist/teacher and for the participants, as there was next to no explanation of the cultural significances of the dances and everyone was content to learn 'some moves' and enjoy physical exhilaration. Meanwhile, in other areas of my work, making meaningful dance as art stressed how important the individual was in providing theatre and dance education for the many.

I migrated to New Zealand in 1997, and was collecting data in 2004 for a now completed doctorate inquiry into teaching culturally different dances in New Zealand schools (Ashley 2010), when it became clear that such teaching was bringing new challenges for dance educators in schools. At that time dance first became part of *The Arts in the New Zealand Curriculum* (New Zealand Ministry of Education 2000). Collecting data from teachers in primary, intermediate and secondary schools, I investigated the challenges, dilemmas and opportunities that teachers were facing, and to some extent still are. It became obvious that the theory, the dancing and the time it takes to prepare for and to teach culturally diverse dance contextually were causing some teachers to simply not teach a culturally diverse range of dances, dancing and the associated cultural perspectives. One of the things I felt deserved further attention in the doctorate study was firstly to produce a book that represented the doctorate inquiry itself and this was published in 2012. Entitled *Dancing with Difference: Culturally Diverse Dances in Education* (Ashley 2012a), I set out to give thorough coverage of the data and findings along with some added some extra ideas that I had not included in the final thesis. From that book I moved on to consider other issues that had arisen during the research journey but deserved further interrogation.

In *Intersecting Cultures in Music and Dance in Education: An Oceanic Perspective* I pick up the threads of issues that deserve further research. My concerns include focusing on dance specialists from diverse cultures who work in educational contexts and how they could be better included in educational settings. Threads within this book weave a layering of pedagogical possibilities that illuminate how culturally responsive teaching is not just about which dances we teach but also requires thinking deeply about how we teach, who teaches, why and where.

I feel that there has been a raising of awareness about the how, what and who of teaching culturally different dances in dance education internationally. This book, in opening a window on an Oceanic perspective, attempts to take this complex topic to the next and very necessary level.

2 David Lines – Musical Intersections in Cultural Learning Experiences

In my view it is impossible to write and theorise about what happens when different cultures come together without some kind of acknowledgement of my own position as a person, writer, researcher, teacher and musician. As a middle aged, mid-career, Pākehā (New Zealander of European descent), male music educator from Aotearoa/New Zealand I am aware of the daily cultural intersections in my work at university and as a researcher in local schools and early childhood centres. As a university educator the realities of cultural intersections are lived out in my university classroom every week. In Auckland, university music education attracts a wide nexus of students; some are local New Zealanders of European descent, others are local students from Māori and Pacific island origins, and still others are recent migrants from Asian countries like India, China, Taiwan, Malaysia, South Korea and Japan. I teach music education and studio pedagogy courses that examine research, issues and practical problems in music teaching and learning. With all these students together in one learning space, each from different ethnic and national orientations, the university music classroom becomes a vibrant space and place of cultural intersection around the pedagogy of music. Invariably classroom discussions, presentations and musical interactions become spaces where individual expressions of past cultural experiences interact graphically with the more immediate personal needs of students as they cope with music in an Oceania-based, urban, intercultural setting.

From a pedagogical perspective I find the classroom dialogue and interplay in these university courses full of learning potential and discovery. With the class rich in cultural difference, the pedagogical processes become critical to the success of each learning moment. On reflection, after many years of teaching multicultural music classes (at primary, secondary and tertiary levels) I have come to think that it is 'openness' that determines whether my students are valued as people with their own, different sets of cultural experiences. By openness I mean a stance taken, as a teacher, towards students that is positively positioned to the learning opportunities they may take up—taking into account their cultural differences, and their immediate needs and responses in their music learning. This stance also brings with it an element of risk—for it is difficult to determine how each student is going to respond to the hybrid cultural mix within the class and the sensitivities of individuals.

In one postgraduate class of this kind orientated on studio pedagogy (studying research and practice in music instrumental and vocal teaching and learning) a colleague and author of a chapter in this book, Te Oti Rakena and I,[2] developed a curriculum that began with an opportunity for students to reflect on and share their own musical experiences as learners. This allowed for an intersecting cultural dialogue to emerge as students shared their reflections of what they had become and why. During the sharing sessions we heard about the experiences of learning piano or opera in China alongside learning Indian singing with harmonium and learning violin

---

[2] See Chap. 7 in this volume.

through the Suzuki method violin in a New Zealand inner city suburb. Many of these sharing episodes generated what I would call 'epiphanies' for Dr Rakena, the students, and myself. The richness of these moments of difference could have easily been lost if we had treated them with pedagogical indifference. But we nurtured and affirmed them, and they become a place of intercultural learning about difference.

As I reflect on learning to teach in this way I cannot help but acknowledge my earlier experiences as a youth in rural New Zealand. I grew up in a small town with a relatively large local Māori population. The history of Māori settlement in this area—Horowhenua—predates European settlement by centuries. One experience as a young teenager I remember was visiting a local rural marae (meeting house), staying over for the weekend with a youth group. I recall sitting on a mattress on the floor in the beautifully carved surroundings of the marae listening to the kaumātua (elder) explain the expression of genealogy embodied in the carvings, colours and architecture of the building. As a Pākehā this experience was new and in many ways spiritually invigorating. The message communicated challenged my ideas about art—that the artistic expression of the carvings not only existed in the building as art, but also in the daily life of the people who belonged there. For me, one of the most beautiful expressions of this was the admission that as visitors who were welcomed, we also become part of the genealogical trace, in the sense that what we offered through our being and participation as visitors to the marae became part of the history of the marae and its people. This experience fostered a certain interest in me of my own cultural identity; what it was and what it could become. It made me think about culture not as a fixed form but as a lived experience that could be nurtured through becoming other.

These experiences of 'culture' or 'cultural identity' have led me to new ways of thinking about music and music pedagogy. I believe that our musical experiences can bring about critical and cultural becomings that can change our individual and collective views of who we are and who we may become. My own personal identity is coloured in part by my genealogical heritage as a New Zealander of European descent—I am a descendant from migrant families that came from Europe to the other side of the world five generations ago. But cultural identity, for me, has also been a movement of becoming in and through music. This was a key theme in my own PhD study *The Melody of the Event* (Lines 2004). In my case this has arisen through activity in music and music teaching and learning, through being a performer, and a music maker and composer, improviser and as a music sharer and teacher. These collective experiences have fuelled my interest in the themes, descriptions and ideas expressed in this book.

3   Editorial Conversation

What follows is an account of our long-term sharing of ideas and respective interests in music and dance education between the editors. We began with email exchanges from July 2013 and then developed through meetings and shared editing of dialogue. As critically reflective performing arts education practitioners we wanted to document our experiences of intersecting cultural understandings. Our discussion also introduces some terminologies and concepts that are central to the book and these may enhance the readers' understanding of its aims and focus.

Linda *Intersecting Cultures in Music and Dance Education: An Oceanic Perspective* emerged as an idea for a book in 2006 after I had collected data for a now completed doctorate inquiry (Ashley 2010). Later in the thinking process I glimpsed how what was happening in New Zealand and Oceania could be of interest to educators internationally, as we all seem to be facing similar vicissitudes of increasing cultural and ethnic diversity. So David what do you think about the idea for this book and what has taken place?

David To begin, if we are talking about 'intersecting cultures', we need to be clear about what we mean by culture in the first instance. Culture is a word that carries many meanings and clarifying how we are using the word could guide readers in their understanding of the book. To what extent is culture tied to our idea of ethnicity and/or does it go beyond that? One definition of ethnicity used in music education is: "Ethnicity defines individuals who consider themselves, or are considered by others, to share common characteristics which differentiate them from the other collectivities in a society within which they develop distinct cultural behaviour" (cited in Hebert 2010, p. 94). In New Zealand we have a number of distinct ethnic groups including indigenous Māori, people from the different Pacific islands, East Asian groups, and European ethnicities among others. There's also a generational aspect associated with ethnicity here, as many groups are descendants of migrants from many decades or even centuries ago and others are more recent migrants. There is of course the added complexity of mixed ethnicities with many children coming from a variety of ethnic backgrounds here in Auckland and across New Zealand. So, notably, different ethnic groups have been 'intersecting' over long periods of time.

Linda Indeed, I think that ethnicity plays a part in determining what culture 'is', but I think of culture as also being embedded and cultivated within larger scale socio-political, economic or familial systems, as well as being affected by individual action. Culture is experienced daily in a myriad of phenomena including languages, values, relationships, sport, music, dances, stories, fashion and so forth. As cultures intersect, people may find commonalities with each other, and intersections can bind people together. However, exploring the intersections could also highlight differences between people. This understanding of culture is threaded through the underpinnings of this book, some of the writers of which are involved in dance and music genres from their own cultures as agents of change.

David Beyond the genres, methods, or patterns of music education and the distribution of ethnic groups, some researchers are now looking at culture differently, for instance at the life of the child from a cultural perspective or ethnographic point of view. The work of Patricia Campbell (2010) looks at the world of the child from a musical perspective in terms of the games, chants, songs and perceptions that form a different kind of worldview. Similarly Kathy Marsh (2008) examines the play worlds of young children from a musical perspective showing how these lived experiences form distinct and changing forms of cultural expression. This kind of work touches on the personal and nuanced musical and cultural lives of children beyond the familiar labels and conventions readily imposed on children by adults.

Linda Certainly, teaching from within a Northern-Western, child-centred pedagogical culture, teachers are in a strong position to encourage play with cultural intersections. Thinking about how cultures are made, by children and adults, also brings into question, as you pointed out, what happens at intersections of different cultures in the worlds of learners both inside and out of school settings. At such cultural intersections, educators and learners can all be players in honouring and respecting different cultures' dances and the people whose cultures we study. Such concerns receive considerable thought in the Oceania region, even if solutions are not always easy to come by. Consequently, I feel that this book is particularly timely, innovative and important for dance educators worldwide as they grapple with the demands of their students' increasingly diverse and complex cultural profiles. The chapters of this book offer opportunities for readers, whether they are teachers, researchers, curriculum developers, teacher educators, tertiary dance lecturers, professional developers, indigenous dance specialists and resource producers, to critically reflect on encounters at such intersections.

David I think we can better understand critical thinking about music and dance culture as you mention. In this respect, a critical view of culture is vital I think, for musicians, dancers and music/dance teachers. A dancer or musician may gather concepts and identities about music and dance through experience—this is normal of course. But for teachers and learners involved in educational pursuits, a simple acceptance of what is happening without critical examination is not enough. In some educational communities in the Oceania region there is a long-standing view of some cultural forms being 'high art' and others 'low art' or mass/folk art, as you found in your own thesis (Ashley 2010). A critical knowledge of cultural theory can help an educator work through these perceptions and begin to appreciate the value of a music or dance performance from a more informed position. Critical knowledge can also be transformed into pedagogical action. There is a need for teachers to adopt a more critical approach to teaching and learning music (or dance) through a pedagogy that is culturally informed, inclusive and respectful (Rohan 2011).

Linda Yes, and this book aims to reinforce recognition of all dance as 'cultural', and avoid the view that some dances are 'cultural' and others 'art'. The question of how dance educators can be more culturally responsive to different cultures is an important focus of this book, and one which could resonate as other country's ethnic mosaics are also likely to be in flux. Critical thinking of this kind is examined by some of the writers in this book as they work at educational intersections with dances such as Māori kapa haka, Sāmoan *siva* (dance), Tahitian *'ori tahiti*, and Australian aboriginal dance. I have been active in taking what I call a 'reflexive turn' (Ashley 2013a) for many years now and this critically reflective view of personal practice could be one way to support teachers as they grapple with the challenges of cultural intersections. Arguably, current dance educators could be better prepared to include dances from different cultures by understanding dance education as a culture itself. Such a reflexive position is central to this book.

David Certainly, a critical and reflexive position is necessary. Consider the situation in music where a teacher is judging the relative merits of children's music compositions. There may be a range of cultural values and practices informing the compositions and there is always the danger of teachers judging them from a monocultural perspective. This is where notions of "hybridity" (Bhabha 1994) can help an arts teacher evaluate an intersecting form with more critical judgment.

Linda I agree, but intercultural exchanges in which different cultures mix together have differing implications for different people in different places and times. A position that can be understood via the notion of hybridity, being a 'new' third space that is created when two languages or cultural consciousnesses, previously separated through time or space, are mixed. However, ethnographer of dance, Andrée Grau (1992) argues that when minority cultures are colonised the outcomes can tilt the balance of power in favour of the dominant culture. When dances from different cultures intersect, troublesome issues can sometimes arise when cultural owners resent appropriation of their dances. Equitable acceptance of different cultures is key at cultural intersections in education, and although the scope of *Intersecting Cultures in Music and Dance Education: An Oceanic Perspective* is not new, the topic is by no means exhausted.

Dance education has its roots in twentieth century modern and contemporary choreography in the seemingly benign appropriation of the dance of other cultures. Hybridity can result in the melting pot effect of intercultural fusion dance. In my research (Ashley 2010) the Western pedagogical paradigm of creative dance and its associated prioritisation of individual creativity, was widely practiced by teachers. When culturally different dances are borrowed, and there are complexities connected with who is borrowing from whom and why; a kind of hybrid 'West and the rest' whitewash can result. We might ask, therefore, how such an intercultural fusion can be culturally appropriate sometimes and yet not at others? Dancer teachers who were specialists in dances from their own cultural heritages as research participants in my inquiry laid down some clear cultural boundaries about innovation in their traditional dances. There is, I feel, considerable scope for more research into intercultural intersections and how much is at risk in terms of being marginalised or whether cultural owners prefer to prioritise their own legacies. Allowing existing cultural groups as diasporas to maintain their heritages as they see fit traditionally, from standpoints of mutual respect and acknowledgment of difference, is another consideration.

David Yes, in New Zealand we see hybridity in urban life at intersections in a network of sub-cultures on the move. There is also a media-infused global element to the reality of modern urban life which brings about other levels of change and transience. But while mobility and transience seem to be important features of different individuals and groups in a city like Auckland we get clusters of groups often wanting to retain a strong sense of their traditional music and dance cultures through regular meetings, events and performances. In the case of Pacific Island groups this might happen for instance at church. This sense of retaining tradition and collective cultural identity can be very strong—often to the degree that it is the most important part of an event. There seems to be a strong sense of cultural identity in the retention of a traditional music and dance within the context of a new space—as ethnic groups establish patterns and ways of life in new spaces and places.

Linda In my research I found that some teachers recognised how valuing the diverse cultural identities that learners bring into school from their communities can be beneficial for their well-being. As cultures increasingly intersect in the present day, however, a helpful way of conceptualising identity could be as multiple or "fluid and in the making" (Grau 2007, p. 210). A learner's identity may be poly-cultural and layered but in transit some migrant communities go to great lengths to maintain their dance heritages, as you point out. In New Zealand the policy is to encourage them to do so and it can assist new migrants to feel a part of the society in which they have recently made a new home. The dance and music of indigenous populations such as those found in Oceania, are equally important and their inter-sections with Western education are a major feature of this book. In the classroom, I quite like the image of 'creases' (Schechner 1988) to describe the intersections where the worlds of tradition and innovation, dominant and minority arts meet. This is perhaps similar to your idea of 'folds'? In my chapter I explore embodied, cultural and pedagogical creasing in greater depth.

David Yes, I now see cultural interaction in music less as two-sides coming together and rather as a "fold" (Deleuze 1993), as a movement of difference in a direction of cultural intent. I like the idea of bringing new language into this debate to help explain the complexity and nuances of intercultural interaction. New ways of describing music and dance culture are all the more important when considering the mass-mediated effects of globalisation that emerge through popular media, social networks and large-scale global production of music and video; these forms contextualise and frame local and personal expressions too. These cultural forces impact on the real and practical expressions of music and dance that people in Oceania experience daily: they go to ballet lessons, participate in haka competitions, listen to classical music concerts, perform in hip-hop groups, listen to their ipods and watch X-Factor on television. As they interact with these things they get a practical understanding and a sense of the different categories or genres, and at the same time form personal and collective identities in terms of how they see themselves in relation to media forms.

Linda I think that Raymond Williams' (1981) view of culture as being 'ordinary' brings to life the interactions between people you have just outlined. I am interested in how we can make more 'space' for developing greater understanding in dance education about the 'not so new'—for instance, the traditional forms of Sāmoan *siva* (dance). I feel that dance educators need to give greater critical consideration to how we can recognise, include and respect traditional dance forms on their terms. Without some ways to conserve intangible traditions in dance, being an especially vulnerable and somewhat ephemeral art form, it is possible that, along with a great deal of other precious flora and fauna, some dances and the dancers who maintain such heritages may be hurtling downhill to extinction. In my chapter I ponder how schools can support conservation as well as innovation at intercultural intersections. I can think of several dance educators who offer suggestions on how to include a wide range of culturally diverse dances (Nadel and Strauss 2003; Jankovic 2008; Pugh McCutchen 2006; Scheff et al. 2010; Vissicaro 2004). However, Drid Williams (2005) finds some of these texts have potential to "reduce students to the level of tourists" (p. 183). I also find some common grounds for concern with Diane McGhee Valle's (2011) thoughts about the complexities in the wide range of decisions teachers need to make when including traditional cultural heritages.

David Yes, the same kinds of issues have surfaced in music education. The idea of multiculturalism still has some purchase, but to some extent it has been downplayed due in part to a dissatisfaction with the outcomes of multicultural music practices in classrooms and the potential for lessons being reduced to musical tourism. Although curricula, schools and teachers acknowledge the value of multiculturalism in policy, the reality is that often a teacher of one cultural background will find it difficult to adequately portray cultural values of a different culture through music. And criticisms can quickly put off teachers who may have the best of intentions. So the label 'multicultural' has become, in some areas, a term with negative connotations. Recently however, there has been a resurgence of interest in the idea of "cultural diversity" (Drummond 2005; Schippers 2010), which has brought with it a revisionary perspective of multiculturalism in music education. Whereas multiculturalism is laden with the problems of postcolonialism, cultural diversity responds to the realities of mixed cultures of urban life and the real value and interest a music learner can discover through engagement with the musics that lie outside their cultural world view. In Aotearoa/New Zealand the notion of biculturalism provides yet another perspective of cultural diversity that seeks to retain a political voice for the local indigenous culture alongside the colonising culture. This brings with it strong feelings of cultural identity when it comes to performing arts teaching and learning. Music education research in this country has revealed that Pākehā early childhood music educators have much to learn from their Māori and Pacific Island counterparts who exhibit a stronger cultural voice and identity when it comes to teaching music in the classroom (Bodkin 2004).

Linda Perhaps we need to clarify terminology at this point and lend some historical background to current usefulness. Multiculturalism as a concept emerged from

Canada in 1965 in the form of a policy that would support migrant cultures to coexist whilst adopting the identity of the host nation (Giddens 2006). But some commentators see it as failed in its attempts to fight racism and promote social understanding (Sporton 2006). Indeed, Doug Risner and Sue Stinson (2010) draw attention to the limitations of well-intentioned, multi-culturally focused dance education, in which, "So much is left out: access, representation, historical and cultural context, and the systemic biases that lie beneath continued social inequity and injustice" (p. 7).

Jean-François Lyotard's (1979) identification of *différence*, on the other hand, depicts moments in which comprehending the 'other' is difficult because linguistic or cultural understandings are not shared. As one of the implied underpinnings of a curriculum such as *The Arts in the New Zealand Curriculum* (Ministry of Education 2000), *différence* flags the importance of how a postmodern agenda "promotes the concept of cultural democracy and works towards a more equitable representation that affirms the significance of dance of other cultures and traditions of both past and present" (Hong 2000).

I feel that for teachers such underpinnings can be illusive in their day-to-day teaching. Hopefully, this book can give some helpful springboards for teachers as to how they can apply culturally responsive pedagogy and engage all their students. As Earl, Timperley and Stewart indicate:

> Cultural responsiveness is much more than introducing myths or metaphors into classes. It means interacting with the students and their families to truly understand their reality; it means understanding the socio-political history and how it impacts on classroom life. (2009, p. 12)

These themes are woven throughout the book in the personal stories and the academic research.

David   In more formal educational contexts the school curriculum can be an influential factor in the negotiation process of what kinds of cultural forms will and should be expressed through learning activities. The framing of a curriculum is important here as is the process of interpretation. If there is a freedom to interpret a curriculum, then actual learning outcomes in one lesson could end up being quite different from another. A teacher will justify a certain intercultural approach in the arts in terms of their interpretation of their curriculum document or syllabus.

Linda   Indeed, and this is recognised in the pluralist and critical philosophical underpinnings of *The New Zealand Curriculum* (Ministry of Education 2007). Unlike a prescribed syllabus, the curriculum acts a set of guidelines for dance and music teachers to teach what they feel is suited to their learners. Therefore, a complex nexus of cultural understandings is likely in any single classroom. Empowering teachers to interpret the curriculum could be an issue though. I mean certainly in dance there are still huge question marks around the adequacy of teacher preparation and the support systems for teachers once they are out in schools. Dance educators in New Zealand are talking about this problem, especially as government seems to be operating an educational policy that favours the conventional definition of literacy, that is the '3 Rs'. Also tertiary teacher dance educators here are experiencing noticeable cutbacks in the amount of time they have to lecture with undergraduates, and this is an issue of deep concern. Dance was late on the scene in terms of whether it was even taught in schools, whereas music has been an established in schools for much longer. As dance remains in catch-up mode with other art forms the case for greater resources and time is strong. Meanwhile, teachers continue their ongoing struggle to establish dance as a knowledge base in schools. Nevertheless, I believe that the ideas and discussions in this book could empower teachers and raise the profile of the performing arts in schools.

David Yes it's a complex matter. New Zealand and the Oceania region in general seems to present an interesting case study of arts education in school. Along with the indigenous population we have European settlers and their descendants who represent, in part, the dominant Western colonial culture that has much influence around the world—especially in education. This cultural history has its expression in forms of music and dance education with historical pedagogies attached to ballet, jazz, and contemporary dance, and classical, jazz and popular music (with the latter two coming from Europe and America). These forms also generate different kinds of curricula that operate in external, 'out of hours' music and dance schools and private teaching or studio contexts, usually outside state school institutions (although what goes on inside schools may certainly be influenced by these external curricula) but also in universities. These external and specialist schools tend to teach music and dance through more formal and structured patterns of learning, with carefully controlled patterns of enculturation and specific historical music and dance genres. These are forms like ballet and jazz dance classes, European-centred music education methods, classical instrumental learning in music and the like. Several chapters in this book call into question colonial conceptions of these forms of music and dance education.

Linda Although the book is not so much concerned with informal education, where attendance is by choice and pedagogy aims at virtuosic performance for competitions and syllabus-style exams, its intersections with traditional dances and music of Oceania are significant. I feel *how* dances are taught is as important as which dances are taught, and pedagogical intersections are another of the features of this book. The key is not just to teach the steps in a regimented way but to find ways by which the learners can enjoy discovering the significances of the movements that they are doing. I think about this as expanding the way in which dance education understands how it can be 'creative', insofar as our legacy has been one of seeing creativity as making dances and I think we can be more creative about creativity in our teaching (Ashley 2012b, 2013b). I am not making a hierarchical case for one being superior, but rather pondering if and how we could we more fully exploit dance education and, to use Julie Kerr-Berry's (2012) term, 'rupture' the current Western hegemonic underpinnings of dance education in order that a wider range of learners and dance heritages may be included more equitably. The questions that emerge could be seen as difficult. Oceania provides a vivid context for such scrutiny because some indigenous traditional dances and music are still widely practiced.

Some of the chapters in this book enhance, inform and sometimes challenge current pedagogical thinking, for instance understanding that in some Polynesian styles, dance, music and lyrics are so intertwined and holistically linked to their cultural values that teaching them separately in dance education could be seen as nonsensical. Such anomalies remind me that increasing opportunities for qualified teachers who are part of these heritages and building greater understanding about how they could teach their dances and music as part of an inclusive, culturally pluralist pedagogical approach needs to be a priority.

In this book I think including personal narratives as well as more academically framed writing is another way of rupturing Western hegemony of thought. In providing different Oceanic perspectives the contributors give access to thinking about issues and concepts from different worldviews on what dance education could be like in the future.

David I think *Intersecting Cultures in Music and Dance Education: An Oceanic Perspective* offers both international and regional readers with a range of fresh perspectives and points of view about problems and potential creative solutions around the themes we have discussed and more. While there is a colonial history in Oceania that has brought with it a Western heritage of performance art, there is also a resurgence of traditional and contemporary concepts of indigeneity that is challenging and invigorating music and dance education. It's my hope that this book will open up ways of thinking and forms of practice that respond to the cultural needs of students in music and dance learning institutions. It's too easy to think of music and dance as just sound and movement on its own, devoid of context, and ignore the connections, meanings, folds, creases, histories and threads that make it so much more interesting, real and relevant. The book's authors have gone some way in making this process clearer, and hopefully their efforts will pave the way for other music and dance educators and practitioners to take their ideas and extend them through new intersections.

References

Ashley, L. (2010). *Teaching dance from contextual perspectives in the New Zealand Curriculum: Concerns, dilemmas and opportunities in theory and practice.* Unpublished doctoral thesis. University of Auckland, New Zealand.

Ashley, L. (2012a). *Dancing with difference: Culturally diverse dances in education.* Rotterdam: Sense Publishers.

Ashley, L. (2012b). Culturally different dances in the New Zealand arts curriculum: Understanding about fusion, tradition and making dances in context. *Te Kaharoa: The e-journal on Indigenous Pacific Issues, 1*(2), 96–138. Retrieved December 20, 2012, from http://tekaharoa.com/index.php/tekaharoa/issue/view/17

Ashley, L. (2013a). Dancing with cultural difference: Challenges, transformation and reflexivity in culturally pluralist dance education. *Dance Research Aotearoa, 1*(1). http://www.dra.ac.nz/index.php/DRA/article/view/3

Ashley, L. (2013b). Connoisseurs' eyes on teaching dance from contextual perspectives. *New Zealand Journal of Research in Performing Arts and Education: Nga Mahi a Rehia*, Edition 4. Retrieved May 3, 2013 from http://www.drama.org.nz/?cat=280

Bhabha, H. (1994). *The location of culture*. London: Routledge.

Bodkin, S. (2004). *Being musical: Teachers, music and identity in early childhood music education in Aotearoa/New Zealand*. Unpublished doctoral thesis. University of Otago, New Zealand.

Campbell, P. (2010). *Songs in their heads: Music and meaning in children's lives*. Oxford: Oxford University Press.

Deleuze, G. (1993). *The fold: Leibniz and the Baroque* (T. Conley, Trans.). Minneapolis: University of Minnesota Press.

Drummond, J. (2005). Cultural diversity in music education: Why bother? In P. Campbell et al. (Eds.), *Cultural diversity in music education: Directions and challenges for the 21st century* (pp. 1–12). Bowen Hills: Australian Academic Press.

Earl, L. M., Timperley, H., & Stewart, G. M. (2009). *Learning from QTR&D programme: Findings of the external evaluation*. Toronto: Aporia Consulting Ltd.

Giddens, A. (2006, October 14). Misunderstanding multiculturalism. *Guardian*. Retrieved January 15, 2007, from http://www.guardian.co.uk/commentisfree/2006/oct/14/tonygiddens

Grau, A. (1992). Intercultural research in the performing arts. *Dance Research Journal, 10*(3), 3–27.

Grau, A. (2007). Dance, identity, and identification processes in the postcolonial world. In S. Franco & M. Nordera (Eds.), *Dance discourses: Keywords in dance research* (pp. 189–210). London: Routledge.

Hebert, D. (2010). Ethnicity and music education: Sociological dimensions. In R. Wright (Ed.), *Sociology and music education* (pp. 93–114). London: Ashgate.

Hong, T. (2000). *Developing dance literacy in the post-modern: An approach to curriculum*. Paper presented at the Dancing in the Millennium Conference, Washington, DC. Retrieved March 100, 2016, from http://artsonline2.tki.org.nz/TeacherLearning/readings/danceliteracy.php

Jankovic, I. (2008). The quest for preserving and representing national identity. In S. B. Shapiro (Ed.), *Dance in a world of change* (pp. 17–40). Champaign: Human Kinetics.

Kerr-Berry, J. A. (2012). Dance education in an era of racial backlash: Moving forward as we step backwards. *Journal of Dance Education, 12*(2), 48–53.

Lines, D. (2004). *The melody of the event: Nietzsche, Heidegger and music education as cultural Work*. Unpublished PhD thesis, University of Auckland, New Zealand.

Lyotard, F.-J. (1979). *The postmodern condition*. Manchester: Manchester University Press.

Marsh, K. (2008). *The musical playground: Global tradition and change in children's songs and games*. New York: Oxford University Press.

McCutchen, B. (2006). *Teaching dance as art in education*. Champaign: Human Kinetics.

McGhee Valle, D. B. (2011). *Complexities of teaching world dance. Proceedings of National Dance Education Organization, 13th annual conference* (pp. 199–208) Minneapolis.

Nadel, M. H., & Strauss, M. R. (2003). *The dance experience: Insights into history, culture and creativity* (2nd ed.). Highstown: Princeton Book Co.

New Zealand Ministry of Education. (2000). *The arts in the New Zealand curriculum (12711)*. Wellington: Learning Media.

New Zealand Ministry of Education. (2007). *The New Zealand curriculum (32646)*. Wellington: Learning Media. Pugh.

Risner, D., & Stinson, S. (2010). Moving social justice: Challenges, fears and possibilities in dance education. *International Journal of Education and the Arts, 11*(6), 1–26.

Rohan, T. (2011). *Teaching music, learning culture: The challenge of culturally responsive music education*. Unpublished doctoral thesis. University of Otago, New Zealand.

Schechner, R. (1988). *Performance theory*. New York: Routledge.

Scheff, H., Sprague, M., & McGreevy-Nichols, S. (2010). *Exploring dance forms and styles: A guide to concert, world, social and historical dance*. Champaign: Human Kinetics.

Schippers, H. (2010). *Facing the music: Shaping music education from a global perspective*. London: Oxford University Press.

Sporton, G. (2006). Dance as cultural understanding: Ideas, policy and practice. *Dance Research Journal, 36*(2), 80–90.

Vissicaro, P. (2004). *Studying dance cultures around the world: An introduction to multicultural dance education*. Dubuque: Cross-Cultural Dance Resources, Inc.

Williams, R. (1981). *Culture: Selected essays*. Glasgow: Fontana.

Williams, D. (2005). Studying dance cultures around the world: An introduction to multicultural dance education. *Journal for the Anthropological Study of Human Movement, 13*(3), 171–187.

Linda Ashley Linda Ashley   (PhD University of Auckland; MA University of London; B.Ed. (Hons), University of Liverpool) is an independent dance researcher/educator with extensive academic, choreographic and performing experience, retired as Senior Dance Lecturer and Research Leader at AUT University, Auckland, New Zealand in 2011. She is an Honorary Research Fellow at the National Institute of Creative Arts Industries, University of Auckland, 2015. As well as numerous journal articles, publications include: ***Dancing with Difference: Culturally Diverse Dances in Education*** (Sense Publishers, 2012), ***Essential Guide to Dance*** (3rd ed., Hodder & Stoughton, 2008); ***Dance Theory & Practice for Teachers: Physical and Performing skills***, (Essential Resources, 2005). Linda is a member of Dance Aotearoa New Zealand (DANZ); Independent Dance Writers and Researchers Aotearoa; and Tertiary Dance Educators Network New Zealand Aotearoa.

David Lines David Lines   (PhD) is Associate Dean (Academic) at the Faculty of Creative Arts and Industries, University of Auckland. David's research interests include music education philosophy, improvisation, early childhood arts education and intercultural arts education. He is a jazz pianist and he regularly performs and records with his band in Auckland and around New Zealand. He is editor/author of *Music Education for the New Millennium: Theory and Practice Futures for Music Teaching and Learning* (Wiley, 2005) and numerous other research articles.

Part I
Music and Dance in Education Through Oceanic Traditions

The first section of the book consists of a group of chapters that examine how different Oceanic traditions of music and dance intersect with new influences, forces or ideas, and how the original culture becomes modified or reframed. Such shifts inform and transform current pedagogy as well as pose important questions about cultural traditions and cultural equity in education.

Jenny Stevenson in collaboration with Tanemahuta Gray tell Gray's personal story, tracing how he has developed a pedagogy in which Māori martial art intersects with contemporary dance and hip-hop. In *Mau Kōrari-Traditional Māori Martial Art Training Incorporating American and European Contemporary Dance Forms* the authors describe how new teaching approaches, designed for Māori language secondary school students, are also relevant for a culturally diverse range of learners. Tikanga Māori (protocols, values and ideas of Māori) are at the heart of Gray's approach and the chapter presents some refreshing descriptions of pedagogical concepts that developed in his work.

Brian Diettrich, in *Cultural Disjunctures and Intersections: Indigenous Musics and School-Based Education in Micronesia,* takes us to the tropical Northwest Pacific and the island of Chuuk to describe the engagement of music and dance in schools and the community. He examines recent cultural transformations in the transmission of music and dance there, and poses questions about the need for more collaboration between educators and researchers in the Pacific in terms of the need for a greater understanding of the cultural dimensions of knowledge and learning in the region.

In *Sāsā: More Than Just a Dance,* Robyn Trinick and Luama Sauni explore the Sāmoan dance *Sāsā* in terms of its significance and potential as a learning tool. They examine the cultural significance and history of *sāsā* and its symbiotic nature through the merging and emerging perspectives of the two authors, who are themselves from different cultural backgrounds. The aim of their chapter is to draw out the learning potential of *sāsā* which, they assert, has value for a range of different educational contexts. In short it is indeed "more than just a dance".

Katie Wilson reflects on her research, highlighting the voices of young Aboriginal and Torres Strait Islander learners and their teachers. In *"Pride and Honour": Indigenous Dance in New South Wales Schools*, Wilson argues that the current position of performance and study of indigenous dances sits on the fringe of the Australian curriculum. She puts forward a strong case for the educational benefits accruing from learning in and about Australian Aboriginal dance and culture, maintaining that such study deserves accreditation for the learners because of its potential to foster critical understanding of their personal cultural histories.

Mau Kōrari – Traditional Māori Martial Art Training Incorporating American and European Contemporary Dance Forms

Tānemahuta Gray with Jenny Stevenson

Abstract This paper describes the development of a new movement form, Mau Kōrari, unique to Aotearoa New Zealand and named for the Harakeke or flax-bush stem that is integral to its practice. Mau Kōrari's relevance and application in education has been evaluated both within the context of the New Zealand Arts curriculum in schools and through a series of public workshops presented to a broad cross-section of the community. Mau Kōrari combines elements of Mau Rākau (the traditional Māori martial art form) with contemporary dance forms including hip hop and krumping. The Mau Kōrari form was first created as a method to facilitate the teaching of basic te reo Māori (Māori language) and to enhance student knowledge about tikanga concepts (Māori protocols and cultural ideas). The paper details the benefits to learners that have been observed over many years of teaching the form and through feedback from participants and observers. Of particular interest is the silent teaching form of Mau Kōrari in which instruction is communicated to the students through physical demonstration of the movements in total silence.

Keywords Mau Kōrari • Mau Rākau • Martial arts • Flax-bush stem • tikanga Māori • te reo Māori • Silent teaching form

Mau Kōrari – Traditional Māori Martial Art Training Incorporating American and European Contemporary Dance Forms
By Tānemahuta Gray (with Jenny Stevenson)
Ko Io Matua Te Kore anake
We acknowledge Io Matua the creator of all things
Ko Rangi, ko Papa, ko Rongo, Ko Tāne Mahuta, ko Tawhirimātea
We acknowledge the sky, earth, cultivated foods, forest realm and the wind realm.
Hōmai ōu taonga matauranga, ōu taonga wairua, ōu taonga aroha.

T. Gray (✉)
Taki Rua Productions, 7 Rutherford Drive, Waikanae 5036, New Zealand
e-mail: tanemahuta.gray@gmail.com

J. Stevenson
Taki Rua Productions, P.O. Box 98, Helensville, Auckland 0840, New Zealand
e-mail: jennystevenson1@gmail.com

Pass down to us this treasure of knowledge, spirituality and love
Hōmai tō kōrari kia mātou
Pass down to us the Flax stem
Hei uru mauri me te mana wairua
To uphold the life force and spirituality that will settle within us
E manaaki ana i a mātou i tēnei wā
Protect us on this journey of training.
Rite tonu me tū mātou ki te poutoko
And let us stand like the supporting pole of the meeting house
Ki te whaiao, ki te ao marama e
Bringing us into the world of light
Tihei Mauri Ora!
Tis life and breath for us all
Karakia (invocation) to prepare for working with the Kōrari (lightweight fighting staff)

1 Introduction

For many years now, I have been developing, refining and teaching the Mau Kōrari training method which comprises the melding of a Māori martial art form with a variety of contemporary dance styles that have their origins in the United States and Europe. I have named it Kōrari after the lightweight flax stem that is used as a fighting staff when executing the form. Growing out of the strict training regime of traditional Taiaha (long fighting staff) of Mau Rākau (Māori martial arts with traditional weapons) the form has now been taught to over 7200 people since 1995.

I have not limited Mau Kōrari training to any one particular social group. It has been taught in kohanga reo (total immersion Māori language programme for young children: from birth to 6 years), primary and secondary schools, as well as to tertiary performing arts students, teachers and the general public (both nationally and internationally).

In their paper, *Indigenous epistemology in a national curriculum framework?* Macfarlane, Glynn, Grace, Penetito and Bateman discuss "theorizing from within a Māori worldview" (2008, p. 107). This description epitomises the approach that I took in creating the Mau Kōrari practice.

> In contrast to the western/European metaphors of human development and learning, a recent bicultural early childhood education document draws on a distinctive Māori metaphor of weaving together different strands (knowledge bases, beliefs, values, relationships and practices (2008, p. 108).

The inspiration to develop the Kōrari form came about initially when I was trying to find a way to teach basic te reo Māori (Māori language) and impart knowledge about tikanga concepts (Māori protocols and cultural ideas) including mihimihi (personal identity and connections) and atua (the metaphysical world). The first target group was a class of secondary school students who were just starting their journey in te ao Māori (the Māori worldview), and the challenge I set myself was to find a physically interactive way to make learning te reo Māori an enjoyable experience.

I decided on an integrated style of teaching as a way to encourage students to learn in a manner that would come easily to them. In discussing this teaching approach with regards to early childhood education, Pigdon and Woolley (1992, p. 1) state:

> An integrated approach allows learners to explore, gather, process, refine and present information about topics they want to investigate without the constraints imposed by traditional subject barriers.

This aligns with my own teaching practice which is loosely based on my experience as a student, encompassing both the rigours of the traditional training I received when studying Mau Rākau combined with my dance training in both classical ballet and contemporary dance (Martha Graham and José Limón styles) which has encouraged artistic exploration, creativity, interpretive freedom and improvisation. My own bi-cultural upbringing, (Māori and New Zealand European) has prepared me to embrace the integration of two such culturally diverse and contrasting training approaches into my own teaching practice.

The training that is received in Mau Rākau engenders an obligation to pass on the knowledge to others, but I wanted to achieve this with a format that could have relevance across the spectrum of students: to both male and female, Māori and non-Māori alike and also to provide opportunities for students to participate in creativity and experimentation which is not a salient feature of Mau Rākau (traditional Māori martial art training).

Mau Taiaha is a staff-fighting martial art-form, which includes strikes, blocks, parries and disarming movements similar to Asian weaponry martial fighting styles. It is a senior form of Mau Rākau, in which the requirements are demanding at all levels of human development. Mau Kōrari (which uses the lightweight flax stem as a "lightweight staff") is very much the teina or younger sibling of Mau Taiaha, but I saw the possibility of using it as a stepping stone to build the physical flexibility and skills that would be advantageous for further training either in Mau Taiaha or in dance, (or both) depending on the student's abilities and preferences. It also seemed to be the perfect vehicle for teaching te reo Māori (Māori language) in conjunction with the culture and history of Māori.

2 Mau Rākau Training

My formal training in Mau Rākau was undertaken through the art of Mau Taiaha, when I was tutored in two different styles of this fighting form. The first was under the mantle of Koro Mita Hikairo Mohi (Ngāti Rangiwewehi), in which most of my education took place on Mokoia Island in Rotorua, and in other training wananga (camps) around the North and South Islands. The second style which I studied, was under the guidance and leadership of Hēmi Te Peeti (Ngāti Whakatere, Te Arawa) through his training group Te Ngū o te Wheke (The Silent Movement of the Squid).

Mita Mohi and his whānau (family) taught a style that involved mastering the five strands of development before being deemed sufficiently prepared to undertake training at Kura Wero (a training school to learn the art of the formal challenge which is known as the wero within the Pōwhiri or formal greeting process). It should be emphasised that this style of martial art was taught with peaceful intentions, as the traditional cultural form has now moved into a more focused position aimed at keeping alive the art-form, the language and cultural protocols and ensuring that they are passed on for future generations to maintain into the future.

The first strand of the form taught by Mita Mohi is Ngā Āhei: the on-guard positions and fighting stances from which a trained warrior can choose to execute their strikes and blocks. These stances and placement of the Rākau (the length of wood used for Taiaha/Mau Rākau) provide the base from which all the next phases of movements stem. It also includes preparation for a Taiaha Warrior to move from Noa (a state of calm and a non-combative position) to Tapu (the sacred space where a Warrior is ready to fight or prepare for ceremonial activity, such as wero or challenge).

When executing this strand of movement, the student or warrior is brought to the position of toropaepae, the middle ground between Ranginui and Papa-tū-ā-nuku (Sky Father and Earth Mother) so that karakia (invocations) can be given to take the student into the martial realm of Tū-mata-uenga, the Māori god of warfare (as recognised throughout most of Aotearoa, New Zealand).

On attaining this spiritual and emotional state, the student is then ready to learn the fighting forms and aspects of movement of Tū-mata-uenga, and the creation myth in which Tū held the son (Akerautangi who was the physical manifestation of a weapon) passed to him by his cousin Rurutangiakau, in order to defeat his brother Rongo Maraeroa (God of Peace and cultivated crops), in their dispute over the plot of land named Pōhutukawa. The weapon that he was gifted on this occasion personified by Akerautangi had two heads and four eyes (in order to be able to see in a 360° perspective) and a protruding tongue (representing the defiant spirit of the warrior). It was the prototype for the Taiaha as we know it today, constructed from the wood of the native New Zealand Akeake tree.

The rest of the movements within the strand of Ngā Āhei are concerned with building the mana (confidence and prestige) of the warrior, so that he starts to learn about who he is, and where he comes from. This is achieved through the study of traditional stories and history, complemented by their accompanying names and movements. This aspect of the training is designed to add layers of understanding, knowledge of identity and a sense of belonging within the Māori cultural sphere.

Photo: Stephen A'Court – Ngarino Watt (pictured)
Maui – One Man Against the Gods: Te Ao Mārama Tāpui (2011)

The next three strands of training passed on by Mita Mohi were: Ngā Paoa, or the strikes that are used to inflict damage to all parts of the opposition's body; Ngā Karo, the blocking of those strikes; and the combinations, Ngā Kurua, which are taught once the warrior becomes more adept. Repetition in practising and learning these moves is paramount in the instruction, so that the body (tinana), mind (hinengaro) and spirit (wairua) can receive and process the movements, etching them into the whole being of the warrior who is working the Rākau.

The fifth strand is Nga Tā or the ceremonial movements, which include footwork and a variety of combinations of blocks and strikes that provide the more extensive range of movement necessary for the wero or formal challenge. The flexibility and strength of the warrior's wrists, arms and body together with the agility of the footwork, should by this stage be highly developed, in order for the warrior to deliver the wero. The physical movement must begin to work organically, with the warrior's focus being on entry into the spiritual realm that is required within the training of Te Kura Wero (the formal challenge training school).

Wero School is the place where all the discipline and repetition of movements are taken to the next level. This includes pushing the body to extreme levels of physical exhaustion, in order to move the mind from the physical training space, into the spiritual domain. In addition, the warrior is required to understand the moves at a much deeper level in order to develop a platform from which to develop his own combinations and figures (within a rigorous Wero movement structure) and to demonstrate an individual style.

Photo: Stephen A'Court – Ngarino Watt (pictured)
Maui – One Man Against the Gods: Te Ao Mārama Tāpui (2011)

The warrior's entry into a higher state of being on a spiritual level, entails entering into a transformed state (evoking the spirit of the War God Tū-mata-uenga and the warrior's own ancestral lineage). This facilitates the connection to ancestral whakapapa (genealogies, lineage or stories) to assist them through the tapu (sacred) state inherent in executing the wero (challenge). This training is open only to men and to those male teenagers who have passed through puberty and have demonstrated the necessary physical, emotional and spiritual maturity to be able to tackle such arduous training components and participate in such an advanced level of instruction.

The second style of Mau Rākau instruction which I was extremely privileged to learn under the mantle of Hēmi Te Peeti, includes many of the same forms described above. In addition it covers tuition in how to melee (undertake close combat scenarios) in fight training and to learn moves that are based on the movement characteristics of the animal kingdom. These actions emerge from the realm of Tāne Mahuta (the forest domain) and Tangaroa (the sea domain).

I spent a shorter period of time learning this style of Mau Rākau, yet it emphasised clearly for me the connection the form has with the elemental and natural world. Studying this practice has corroborated my own belief that we are all connected to the cycle of the elements, from which we can continue to learn.

The style of movement that Hēmi shared with his students had a more contemporary shape to the figures (even though it came from an ancient understanding of the natural world) and I found that it opened my mind to the possibility of being even more adventurous in the movement choices that Mau Rākau (stick martial fighting form) had to offer.

An aspect of the training practice that Hēmi Te Peeti shared, which was very influential on me, was the manner in which he taught new moves within Te Ngū: a silent teaching form. In this method all the instruction is communicated to the students through the physical demonstration of the movements in total silence, using the eyes and the head to drive the tuition. Following my initial induction into the form (which lasted for 2½ h), I discovered that I was able to shut down the questioning and "chattering" portion of my mind and instead, build a meditative, constructive experience.

This type of follow-the-leader process encourages a silent trust between teacher and student. The whole room slows down into a concentrated and contemplative stillness and the intensity of focused energy is palpable within the room. It is a unique experience, which I have discovered can create a very sacred space for instruction to take place.

Photo: Stephen A'Court – Ngarino Watt (pictured)
Maui – One Man Against the Gods: Te Ao Mārama Tāpui (2011)

An additional benefit of this method, which I noticed when I assimilated it into my own teaching practice of Mau Kōrari (lightweight staff), is that it gives an excellent opportunity to gauge rapidly, the concentration abilities of the group. It is possible to discern instantly, whether the group can cope with the stillness and focus that occurs when it is not possible to ask questions and when each person must discover answers through their own application, during the instruction process. This enables me to determine which students will have trouble focusing for long periods of time and those who will be able to manage the intensity of this type of instruction.

In 2013, following a class taught in Wellington to Year 9 students who were approximately 13 years old, a teacher commented in her assessment: "Learning the sequence in silence required the girls to really embrace thinking for themselves. Very positive". (Mau Kōrari Teacher Assessments 2013). Similarly, a class taught in Wellington in 2015, to Year 7 and 8 students who were approximately 11–12 years old, elicited the following comment:

> The tuition style in silence really challenged the students in their ability to concentrate for an extended period of time. The discipline of the working style really pushed the students into a new space that they had not inhabited before (Mau Kōrari Teacher Assessments 2015).

I have also discovered that this type of silent instruction engenders a really strong internal physicalisation of the movements in students, with a marked improvement in retention, for a much longer period of time. The students undergo a unique experience of instruction which is unlikely to be forgotten, due to its mysterious process. Therefore the moves tend to remain in their body memories for a lot longer afterwards. This lends credence to the notion that the silent learning experience of Te Ngū creates an internal embodiment of the movement, which goes beyond the physical and transcends into the spiritual realm. The movement becomes imprinted on the student's wairua (spirit) and therefore is much more likely to remain with the student after the lesson has been completed.

My own personal discovery has been that this process is very similar to that of learning karakia (prayers). On waking up early in the morning to start the process of learning the verses of a karakia through repetition, the body is often reluctant, remaining sluggish and in a sleepy state. Working under these conditions can create stress on the body that in turn aids the muscular memory of the words. When reciting the karakia later, the uncomfortable experience of the initial instruction is recalled and that physicalisation helps the body, mind and spirit to evoke the words and the vibrations of the karakia.

Hēmi also shared the instructional process of Te Ngao, which is a slow form of teaching, where the movement is demonstrated and practised in slow motion, to correct the line and improve the precision of the strikes and blocks. Ideally, as the student progresses, the movement will gradually speed up, with accuracy being retained, as the pace increases. This process (although frustrating for younger students who don't always have the discipline to move slowly for a long period of time), allows for faster progress in the long term, if patience is exhibited in the initial learning process.

Te Ngao also allows the teacher to ensure that the student is moving the Rākau (stick) in the correct pathways for perfect precision and "bite", so that when the moves speed up, the power, flexion and focus form good habits in the mover, by utilising the proper muscles. Te Ngū and Te Ngao are often both combined for a substantial portion of the teaching.

3   The Development of Mau Kōrari (Lightweight Staff Contemporary Martial Art Form)

Having completed my traditional martial arts training, I began to consider the feasibility of combining a more contemporary practice of movement styles and combinations with Mau Rākau (staff martial fighting form), so that it could be used to communicate ideas in a different setting, other than that of the traditional marae (gathering place of people). I realised that if I were to use Mau Rākau in a theatrical setting it would be easier to achieve using the Mau Kōrari form, as it would be less restricted by traditional protocols. I reasoned that it would also enhance the choreographic content for dance students who might be well versed in hip-hop and various contemporary movement forms as the practice would present additional challenges to their movement exploration.

The idea to use the Kōrari flower stems of the Harakeke (native New Zealand flax bush) as a fighting staff was inspired by an initiative already established among contemporary Māori weavers who have used Harakeke to develop multiple new design shapes and forms from both Te Ao Māori and Te Ao Pākehā (Māori and European perspectives). By using Kōrari to develop a new martial art movement form that integrated dance influences, it was as though I was being given permission to proceed, by following a pathway already blessed by our kuia and kaumātua weavers (Māori elders).

I soon discovered that the lightness of the flax stem allowed an extra range of movement to be incorporated into the form, that would not have been possible when using a Taiaha or full length Rākau (weapon) which has extra height and weight. Ideally, the Kōrari stick should be standing at the height of the pito (belly button) of the student, measuring from Papa-tū-ā-nuku (the ground). This references the nurturing that we received in the wombs of our biological mothers, and also symbolically represents the nurturing that we receive from the food provided by Papa-tū-ā-nuku (our Earth Mother).

The strands of movement development within the structure of Mau Taiaha (staff fighting form), inspired me to build similar strands for Mau Kōrari, creating a base from which all the movements would stem. To date I have created four such categories within the form. It is possible for all of these tiers to work within each other, as combinations are built from each of the strands, thereby allowing the choreography to develop organically.

This first tier of learning in Mau Kōrari is Ngā Tohutohu (directionals). This tier supports the learning of actions and movements for moving forwards and backwards, side to side, inside and outside, upwards and below, in order to build a dimensional sphere of movement possibilities. It is similar to Leonardo Da Vinci's famous *Vitruvian Man* drawing and creates the base from which the work can then progress down to the ground or up into the air, as it is being developed further.

Ngā Tohutohu, also encourages cohesion within the group, and develops the kapa (group) energy. Moving as one entity creates a powerful energy force, which in turn informs the movements of the group. The moves are not difficult to execute, but there is transference of weight from one leg to the other, as well as balancing. This helps to create an understanding of counter-balancing in movement.

Ngā Mihimihi is the second strand of movement development in Mau Kōrari focusing purely on the elements of the mihimihi or pēpēhā which concern identity (personal introduction). The mihimihi is linked to: the waka (vessels of ancestral migration to Aotearoa); maunga (the mountain that people connect to); awa (the river or body of water important to the health and nurturing of the people); the iwi and hapū (tribal and extended family links); tūpuna (ancestral whakapapa); marae (traditional gathering space of the tribe or hapū); and the ingoa or name of your family. These movements are much more contemporary in form and the dancers must alter their levels: combining ground work with elevation.

The third tier: Ngā Ātua Māori, consists of movements that personify the gods within a Māori world-view, and which hold a nature-based perspective. The combination of contemporary dance and Mau Rākau movements continues to evolve even further in this segment, adopting a bi-cultural choreographic voice, and producing shapes and patterns that personify the elemental potency of these Atua (gods or spirits), such as Tāne Mahuta, God of the forest and Tangaroa, God of the oceans.

The phrases in this section assume a similar role to the ceremonial movements of Nga Tā in Mau Rākau (staff martial art form): increasing the number of movements while abbreviating the length of the phrase, which encourages explorative choreography. One example of a dance work that I have developed in this context, concerns the Sky-father, Ranginui. Using a line from a Haka chant (traditional war cry and/or dance), I created movement to express a section of his story. The words from the Haka chant were "Ko Ranginui e tū iho nei", referring to Rangi who stands above us. The movement I choreographed to accompany this chant, began with Tū Haka stance (equivalent to second position grand-plié in classical ballet). The hands of the dancer are spread to the edges of the kōrari and then, via the heel of the hands, the kōrari is lifted into the sky.

The resulting image references the story of Tāne Mahuta raising the Sky-father, Ranginui into the heavens with his legs and feet, separating him from the embrace of his wife Papa-tū-ā-nuku. These actions of Tāne Mahuta brought light into the world and instigated the next stage of the earth's development, so the movements of this phrase resonate on multiple levels, (both physically and within their cultural context), thereby helping students to understand the stories and history behind Māori philosophy and mythology.

The fourth strand of Mau Kōrari: Kōmitimiti, opens up the form to encourage choreographic freedom and the merging together of movements and combinations. Group formations allow exploration of a full range of themes, ideas and processes to express any kaupapa (subject) inspirational to the choreographer. It is a form of expression that is uniquely Māori, but when combined with other dance forms to create new styles of movement, it also has the potential to relate stories and themes from divergent cultural contexts.

Students who have had previous choreographic experience obviously have more success in creating their own movement in other dance forms. I have found when teaching workshops that some students relish the freedom to explore, while others become completely frozen at the prospect of having to create their own movement phrases using a combination of contemporary and traditional dance. Quite often it is those students who have only experienced traditional Māori movement that struggle the most to express themselves through blending the different elements.

In my personal exploration of fusing Mau Rākau with contemporary dance forms, I have used elements of North American hip-hop and krumping battles (which are in turn based on African ritualistic dances) as an inspiration. I wanted to see if the combination of these elements could evolve into a style of movement which is unique to Aotearoa, while still incorporating influences from other parts of the world. Through experimenting in this way, I discovered that the high energy levels inherent in the blend of combative martial art and dance, mirrors the highly competitive nature of street-dance "battles". It demonstrated to me that indigenously-based choreography could initiate social interaction in the community, through creating dance challenges with an Aotearoa (New Zealand) flavour.

This concept was first established in the "Haka Battlez" competitions brought to Wellington in 2006 by Kereama Te Ua (https://www.youtube.com/watch?v=tMq6aw3TWfo), who perceived that this social contact and the element of challenging one another" was a good way to bring youth together. The idea was to battle it out using a Haka-influenced (traditional Māori Dance form) movement vocabulary, that differs from those dance styles traditionally seen in the World Championship dance battles.

I have also found inspiration in the movement formations of the animal kingdom, when working with dance groups onstage. A prime example would be the mimicking of the formations of the Mangopare (Hammerhead Shark) and the manner in which they fight in groups with a determination never to give up on the battle until such time as they perish. The way that this image can influence dancers to move through space, attacking and parrying in combinations, often results in new and innovative methods of constructing group formations. Whakataukī (Māori proverbs) provide the inspiration for these choreographic developments to be guided by the wisdom of ancient insights and cautions:

> Kaua e mate wheke, e mate ururoa – Do not die like an Octopus with no resistance, but die like a hammerhead shark that fights to the bitter end.

Māori design and in particular, the motifs of traditional Māori Kōwhaiwhai (ornamental painted patterning) and tā moko (tattoo body design) provide visual inspiration to bring these patterns and shapes into context. I have found this to be particularly helpful when working on choreographic forms and formations. This type of choreographic process combines both a European creative approach of using images to inspire movement, with a Māori perspective, in which traditional motifs and patterns are used to explore how the body can move through the space and also how a group can create shape and form through their onstage placement.

Contemporary Kowhaiwhai pattern of Mangopare and other designs used for tā moko.
Permalink: http://www.tattootribes.com/index.php?idinfo=1475 (Accessed 16/08/2014)

Traditional Kowhaiwhai design of Mangopare.
http://www.maori.org.nz/whakairo/default.php?pid=sp55&parent=52 (Accessed 16/08/2014)

4   Martial Arts Programmes in Schools

In recent times there has been interest in the United States in particular, in providing martial arts programmes in schools, as a key to developing self-confidence in students. At present most martial arts training is undertaken by students through after-school programmes in the States and in many other parts of the world, including Aotearoa (New Zealand). In her work *Case study: Martial arts for self confidence in schools*, Miles (n.d.) states: "Since it has been so difficult to incorporate martial arts into our public school systems, many programs are outside of the traditional classroom" (p. 6). She poses the question: "Why isn't martial arts a part of every schools (sic) curriculum? Does Eurocentricism still control our curriculum, and is it not accepted because martial arts is (sic) an Asian thing?"

Miles argues for the inclusion of martial arts in the physical education pro-grammes of schools, although she does not espouse any particular form. She cites the (then) Senator Obama's "initiative in 2007 to improve standards for physical education and to include martial arts in public schools" (p. 3), although this bill never became law. She also details twenty ways that martial arts can build confidence in students, quoting the benefits as expressed by martial arts teacher Master John Matthew Klein who teaches karate to children. These benefits include:

1) Learns body postures, eye contact and other movements typical of a confident student....... and:
12) Learn to accept mistakes as a part of learning
13) Students learn limits and boundaries, because strict rules in the practice room are understood by the students for their own safety. (Miles, p. 6)

These specific benefits as cited by Miles, resonate strongly with me, as I have observed similar improvements in students, when teaching Mau Kōrari (lightweight staff contemporary martial art form). I have found this to be the case particularly with those students who have encountered challenges in concentration when studying academic subjects, but more especially with Māori students, who identify strongly and feel an affinity with the work and who often excel in the practice.

I suggest that Mau Kōrari has great potential in terms of its introduction into schools in Aotearoa, combining as it does the creativity of dance with the discipline of martial arts while teaching students not only te reo Māori (Māori language), but also the valuable life-lessons of tikanga Māori (Māori customs).

I have been fortunate to have had the opportunity through Dance Aotearoa New Zealand (DANZ), to provide Mau Kōrari workshops to numerous schools nationwide, through their LEOTC (Learning Experiences Outside the Classroom) initiative with the Ministry of Education, which enables students to work in a variety of new and challenging ways. Mau Kōrari has proved to be very successful in this respect, with a series of workshops being presented over the past decade to a wide range of students. These include those who have experienced very little Māori culture previously, as well as those who are already proficient.

Mau Kōrari has been well received by the majority of students and teaching staff and it has proved to be a great method to experience the bi-cultural connections that inform this combination martial art and dance form. I believe that documented experiences from these workshops and others I have held through my own initiative, have demonstrated categorically that there is a place for this type of training in the classroom.

References

Macfarlane, A. H., Glynn, T., Grace, W., Penetito, W., & Bateman, S. (2008). Indigenous episte-mology in a national curriculum framework? *Ethnicities*, *8*(1), 102–126. doi:10.1177/1468796807087021.

Miles, N. J. (n.d.). *Case study: Martial arts for self-confidence in school.* North Carolina: Fayetteville State University. Retrieved from: https://www.academia.edu/766189/Measuring_Selfconfidence_with_Martial_Arts_in_High_Schools

Pigdon, K., & Woolley, M. (1992). *The big picture.* Victoria: Eleanor Curtain Publishing. Retrieved from: http://www.angelfire.com/stars5/integrated_teaching/integration.html

Tānemahuta Gray is a choreographer, dancer, aerialist, teacher and producer of 18 productions and events and has worked both in New Zealand and abroad since graduating from the New Zealand School of Dance in 1994. His choreographic credits include WOW-World of WearableArt Awards, Māui – One Man Against The Gods, Arohanui – The Greatest Love, Kōwhiti Festivals 2010–2013, The Ragged and the Opening Ceremony of the Chinese World Expo. His performance credits include De La Guarda & The Beautiful Ones.

Jenny Stevenson A former professional dancer, Jenny founded and managed the Wellington Performing Arts Centre, a tertiary Private Training Establishment now operated by Whitireia New Zealand. Since 2010, she has co-produced three consecutive Kōwhiti Contemporary Indigenous Dance Festivals in Wellington with Merenia and Tānemahuta Gray and is currently working as assistant producer for Auckland-based Hawaiki TŪ Haka Theatre Company. Jenny was a dance writer and critic for the *Dominion Post* in Wellington for many years and is continuing to work as a free-lance writer in Auckland.

Cultural Disjunctures and Intersections: Indigenous Musics and School-Based Education in Micronesia

Brian Diettrich

Abstract Musical learning in Micronesian schools is characterised by a cultural disjuncture, a partition between the musical experiences that take place in educational institutions, and the indigenous musical practices in the wider community that have deep roots in the nation's peoples and cultures.

In this chapter I examine the culture of music learning in Chuuk in the Federated States of Micronesia, and I seek to understand the underlying frameworks that have supported this division in transmission. The apparent separation of traditional musical practices from school-based curriculum raises questions about the larger role of indigenous culture in education in this region of the Pacific. In this chapter I critically examine the relationship between indigenous musical practices and contemporary cultures of learning. In the last section I provide a description of and reflection on one musical event that illustrates the potential of indigenous performance within the school environment.

Keywords Micronesia • Indigenous music • Education • Schools • Colonialism • Cultural intersections

At 9:00 am on Monday morning, tertiary students gather together in a small classroom for MU 101, "Introduction to Music," a core course in the humanities at the College of Micronesia (COM), National Campus in the Federated States of Micronesia (FSM). The assembled students represent a diversity of cultures that comprise the nation—several are from Chuuk and Pohnpei, others from Kosrae and Yap, and still others from several atoll communities. The class that morning follows a set curriculum at the college that provides "a practical (applied) music course providing students with an understanding of the fundamentals of music, basic skills in note reading and instrumental performance" (College of Micronesia-Federated States of Micronesia). Sitting in rows, each in front of a small Yamaha keyboard with headphones, the students work together through the fingerings of the short notated musical examples found in the beginning textbook *Piano 101* by Lancaster

B. Diettrich (✉)
Victoria University of Wellington, PO Box 600, Wellington 6140, New Zealand
e-mail: brian.diettrich@vuw.ac.nz

© Springer International Publishing Switzerland 2016   33
L. Ashley, D. Lines (eds.), *Intersecting Cultures in Music and Dance Education*, Landscapes: the Arts, Aesthetics, and Education 19,
DOI 10.1007/978-3-319-28989-2_3

and Renfrow. Over the semester the students gradually develop skills in reading staff notation and in playing keyboard, in addition to studying in group singing. The course, like other subjects at the College, largely follows an American curriculum, in general "music" that was created within the frame of its educational accreditation status through the U.S. Music in many ways parallels language at the COM, where English is the primary means of education.[1] A popular choice among students, the music curriculum at College, however, does little to engage with the indigenous cultural practices of the nation. The situation at the COM is not unique; across the FSM musical learning in schools is characterised by a cultural disjuncture, a partition between the musical experiences that take place in educational institutions, and the indigenous musical practices in the wider community that have deep roots in the nation's peoples and cultures.

In this chapter I examine the culture of music learning in Micronesia, and I seek to understand the underlying frameworks that have supported this division in transmission. The apparent separation of traditional musical practices from school-based curriculum raises questions about the larger role of indigenous culture in education in this region of the Pacific, and in this chapter I address the historical and cultural factors that have contributed to this divide. I limit the examples to the islands of Chuuk, the most populous state in the FSM.[2] My perspectives come from my close involvement in Chuukese communities over the past 15 years, and as a past teacher in music at the secondary and the tertiary levels in Chuuk in addition to time spent teaching music at the national level on Pohnpei. More recently I have advised for the cultural work of the Akoyikoyi Center, a new initiative in early education on Chuuk's main island of Weno. In exploring these issues for Chuuk, my intention is not to locate practical methods for the incorporation of cultural content within schools—a long-term project that can only be organized by educational institutions within Chuuk. Instead I wish to examine critically the relationship between indigenous musical practices and contemporary cultures of learning. In the last section of this chapter I provide a description and reflection of a musical event that illustrates the potential of indigenous performance within the school environment.

Researchers have examined the intersection of culture and learning for the Pacific in a growing body of work that has considered indigenous frameworks of transmission and the role local culture in formal education (Thaman 2003a, b, 2007; Teasdale and Rhea 2000; Smith 2005). Past research on education in Micronesia has focused on the historical development of schools (Hezel 1984; Peacock 1985, 1990), traditional knowledge (Falgout 1992), and more recently the critical study of decolonization

---

[1] The College of Micronesia-FSM is accredited by the Western Association of Schools and Colleges in the U.S.

[2] The Federated States of Micronesia is a diverse Island nation of just over 100,000 people in the northwestern Pacific (FSM 2009). Chuuk State has 41 islands, several regional dialects, and its population is just over half that of the total of the FSM. Chuuk and the FSM more generally are characterized by a consciousness of American culture, stemming from the current neocolonial agreements between both nations and a large outward migration. The American colonial mark on the FSM today traces back to 1945 when the U.S. administered the region of Micronesia until 1979, when the congress of Micronesia negotiated the resulting FSM nation. Outward migration has resulted in large and quickly growing populations on Guam, in Hawai'i, and in the continental US.

(Kupferman 2012). In considering learning from within Chuukese culture, Sachuo (1992) has previously examined the consequences of colonial-derived education in Chuuk's schools, while Margarita Cholymay (2013) has recently called for a renewed and critical assessment of education in the state. Both Sachuo and Cholymay outline frameworks that are both community-centered and culturally determined, and in seriously considering indigenous cultural values they offer significant challenges for current education in Chuuk. While other Pacific states have foundations of engagement with local culture and traditions through education, the FSM by comparison is still largely anchored within the process of decolonisation (Kupferman 2012). International guidelines in Pacific education continue to call for a renewed focus on cultural practices, but the incorporation of indigenous culture remains an emerging challenge for schools and communities in Micronesia.[3] It is not my intention in this chapter to search for an essentialised notion of indigenous culture in Micronesia, nor to brand education as merely a "Western" institution. Despite a widespread feeling that culture and traditions are being "lost" in the FSM, it is revealing that the nation has rarely viewed contemporary education as a response to this anxiety.

The examination of learning in Chuuk and elsewhere in the FSM brings critical attention to cultural ideas of schooling (*sukun* in Chuukese) as an institution that has been an essential arm of the larger project of "development" in Micronesia (Hanlon 1998; Kupferman 2012). The situation in Chuuk is parallel to that described by Kupferman (2012), and where the ontologies of *school* and *development* remain largely unquestioned markers along a pathway to increased social progress. But how might we discuss and define alternative practices and ideas of learning as separate from and outside of schools? More specifically for this chapter, how might local indigenous notions of learning in the expressive arts offer a space to explore and redefine such strategies in education? I contend that the examination of indigenous musical culture in the Pacific offers a fundamental challenge to the institution of school-based education today. The examples in this chapter afford possibilities for a critical investigation of educational futures in Micronesia, where societies are still negotiating the role of local culture within frameworks rooted in the colonial history of the region.

1   Foreign Artifacts?: Colonialism and Schools

The historical emergence of formal education in Micronesia and throughout the Pacific followed broad processes of colonialism and missionisation. Commenting on the history of school development in Micronesia, Francis Hezel has noted: "At one time schools might have been dismissed as foreign artifacts, but not today after decades of adaptation under local leadership. Formal education, once grafted from

---

[3] See for example the *Pacific Culture and Education Strategy 2010–2015* released by the Council of Pacific Arts and Culture and the Secretariat of the Pacific Community (2010). The report accompanies the Pacific Plan (Pacific World Heritage Action Plan 2010–2015), released by UNESCO.

an alien plant, has taken root in island Micronesia and bears rich fruit in at least some places" (2001, p. 15). School-based education has indeed become a social reality and an essential experience in Micronesian life, but like its former manifestations during the early colonial periods, the curriculum of schools in much of Micronesia still remain separated from the language, culture, and indigenous knowledge of local communities. While schools in Chuuk are not merely "a foreign innovation that is incompatible with island culture" (Hezel 2001, p. 14), neither are they completely rooted from within Chuukese society and culture, and their foundation traces back to the colonial projects of the late nineteenth century.

Music was central to early schooling in Micronesia and was a strategic tool in the earliest colonial enterprises in the region. The very first of these efforts for Chuuk came from missionaries: Islanders from Pohnpei trained by the American Board of Commissioners for Foreign Missions who first brought Christianity to the Mortlock atolls south of Chuuk Lagoon in the 1870s. Led by Americans until just after the turn of the century and then by the German Liebenzell mission from 1907 and during the German administration, the early Protestant mission made schooling a particular focus. The missions taught new musical ideas, including part-singing and new song repertories, and they organized community events for new recruits to present their new song knowledge to the community.[4] With only a small number of missionaries present in the islands, newly baptized islanders were instrumental in continuing both faith and school under the direction of the mission. Music as a subject in schools continued under the Japanese administration from 1914 and as the colonial government sought to "civilize the natives and make them into loyal and economically useful citizens of the Japanese empire" (Fischer 1961, p. 84).

The early work of the Americans, Germans, and Japanese began the process of a lasting influence in education of the region, but it was after the intervening turmoil of the Second World War when education took a renewed and powerful turn for Micronesia and that came once again, from America. Micronesia was officially administered as the Trust Territory of the Pacific Islands (TTPI), and education from the U.S. came in the form of teachers, military, missionaries and scores of peace corps recruits, and it brought new musical repertories and songs still remembered by elders today from this period. From 1963, and in an answer to charges of territorial neglect, the US dramatically increased its economic, educational, and teacher-training programmes in Micronesia, creating practices and discourses of knowledge that were directly based on those of US schools at the time (Peacock 1985). By 1970 the education landscape in the islands had been completely transformed, and most children of primary school age attended school, with learning often in English.

The cultural shift in education during the American administration is illustrated in a 1964 speech made by Chief Petrus Mailo, who was also the influential mayor of Weno Island at the time, and was one of Chuuk's most respected leaders of the last century (Gladwin 1960). Speaking at Chuuk High School, located at the

---

[4]Detailed information about mission schools is found in the archived letters of the ABCFM missionaries and in reports by missionaries in the journal *Liebenzell Mission*. See Diettrich (2011) for the cultural contexts of missionization in Chuuk.

historically and culturally significant site of Wunuunganata and with American colonial officials present, Mailo reminded students:

> They [ancestors] gave instruction in the subject of people, the subject of soil, the subject of things in the soil, the subject of the sea, the subject of things in the sea, the subject of voyaging on the sea, the subject of island history, and the subject of strategy and tactics in war. In subjects of carpentry, house building, canoe making—in all these they gave instruction ... But what was it that they taught? What was theirs! They didn't teach what was not theirs ... it is well that you should study first the things that are already ours. (Goodenough and Efot 1992, pp. 269–70)

As early as 1964 Mailo recognised the need for a cultural balance in Chuukese education, and in the full speech he asks students to keep an understanding of Chuuk's indigenous knowledge. Over the subsequent decades and through FSM independence, education in Chuuk continued to "develop" within a largely American framework, and with little educational emphasis on indigenous music and dance.

Today Chuuk has elementary schools in most of its villages, several intermediate and high schools, and a total of 154 schools spread out over its many islands (Levine 2010, p. 9). The College of Micronesia maintains a state campus in Chuuk and is the main body for tertiary education. Music as a curriculum subject is largely absent within these institutions. Singing is common as a social activity in primary schools, but is rarely incorporated fully into the larger curriculum. Music is also absent in the curriculum of secondary schools, although group song is emphasised at religious schools, as a primary means of engaging with Christian knowledge. While music is a part of the humanities curriculum at the College of Micronesia, the curriculum is organised around priorities of international general music and without engagement of indigenous practices. As part of education in Chuuk, "music" in school, like the use and knowledge of English language, is part of a larger thread of knowledge that extends from outside of Chuuk.

2 Learning at Home, in the Village, and on the Mat

Learning in music reaches well beyond the emergence of the colonial administrations and school-based education in Micronesia. In Chuuk, songs, dances, sayings, expressions, and stories all transmit cultural knowledge in society in both informal and formal contexts, but they do so outside of school-based contexts. Writing about his home culture, Sachuo (1992) organised indigenous practices of learning in Chuuk following two separate social domains: (1) *choon neesening* ('copra in the ear', i.e. the sound of liquid inside a coconut): learning by careful aural and oral means in the home among family (Sachuo 1992, pp. 107–109), and (2) *wuut* (village meeting house): learning through public discourse (Sachuo 1992, pp. 111–113).[5] These two domains of learning—one private (in the home) and one public (in the village)—also frame the transmission of songs. The song below, for example, is

---

[5] My use of Chuukese language throughout this chapter generally follows Goodenough and Sugita (1980).

sung at community gatherings and is a valuable means of public social learning, in both informal contexts and formal performances.

Tirow wóómi ami meyinisin,	Pardon me everyone,
éwúse mwechen omwusóónó ááy ttipis,	please forgive my sins,
sapw minen namanam tekiya	it is not meant to be insolent,
pwe ii fókkun iyeey	because this is real,
wusun fowutach aramas.	the hospitality of the people.

Sung to an accessible diatonic melody with regular phrases and with an accompaniment of handclaps, the song delivers a group engagement and community solidarity during performances. The text gives particular attention to ideas of cultural respect, and it sets a culturally appropriate 'feel' for listeners. This short song encapsulates important cultural values and social knowledge (*sineey*) that Chuukese emphasise among themselves and in welcoming others, and which are transmitted socially in public.

Older repertoires of songs contain cultural and social values, but they also contain specialist knowledge in history, politics, and lore—ideas that are removed from everyday experiences. Song knowledge in this context involves learning in the home and among family as Sachuo describes, but it also exists for some knowledge in a third domain: *noos* (woven mat), and referring to a traditional and formal learning environment that is restricted and occurs with a master-teacher. Specialised traditional song knowledge in Chuuk is sometimes described as *masowen noos* (contents of the mat), a phrase that encompasses performative lore termed *roong*, and includes particular domains such as history, lore, and warfare, and open-ocean navigation. The reference to *noos* (woven mat) denotes the formal learning environment, through which knowledgeable men and women pass on especially important cultural and historical information.[6] This knowledge is separated from general societal knowledge through its connection to *manaman* (spiritual power).[7] The careful repetition of the words of songs and rhythmic recitations is the primary method of learning the power of words (*kapas*). Sachuo emphasised the importance of words and language in Chuuk when he wrote, "a person should not only eat food but also partake of words in order to become a complete human being ... words must always be in the body and must always be expressed in community arenas for effective communication" (1992, p. 406). This embodied orientation towards language plays an important role in the discourse surrounding music learning in Chuuk, where people emphasise the memorisation abilities of former generations.

While some songs may transmit small threads of specialist information broadly in society, most song repertoires associated with specialised practices are too

---

[6] See Metzgar (1991) for a detailed review of indigenous education and traditional schools in Micronesia.

[7] In formal learning, either as part of navigation or historically part of *itang* (warfare and island lore) an actual mat is sometimes employed for teaching with stones, shells, and other objects used to instruct learners (about star locations for example in the case of navigation).

valuable to be distributed and widely learned, and thus they are carefully restricted and managed through knowledgeable individuals, lineages, particular islands, and by gender and age. Chuukese communities consider specialist song knowledge as very useful communal property, and many hold the customary view that its wide distribution will diminish its power as well as those that hold it. It is thus common practice to protect, conceal, and otherwise withhold knowledge.[8] In some cases, the texts of songs may be poorly understood except by very knowledgeable individuals, or interpreted with very divergent understandings. Stories abound in Chuuk wherein a father, mother, grandfather, or grandmother passed away without handing on his or her *roong* to the next generation.

In order to retain such songs associated with *roong* for the survival of the community, a person's education in *roong* takes place ideally within the clan hierarchy, thus though the mother's line, although in practice transmission can occur by other means. Usually a practicing specialist determines that a specific person is competent to learn and teaches him or her over several years. Although *roong* appears in the literature to be mostly associated with men, women hold and transmit knowledge, as well as specific information not undertaken by men such as types of healing and medical massage. People can also gain specialised knowledge outside of the clan system through payment, and for very valuable knowledge compensation can include land and money.[9]

Indigenous learning in song in Chuuk is a managed process shaped by a hierarchy of social relationships (Falgout 1992) that governs transmission to individuals, rather than widespread access to knowledge. Learning is specific, personal, and selective and dependent on whether a teacher decides to share his or her knowledge. This model of learning offers a significant contrast with that of school-based educational institutions in Chuuk, and remains one of the main boundaries that separates and differentiates the learning of indigenous musical knowledge from that in schools. In the following sections I explore some of the cultural frameworks that have maintained and shaped this disjuncture.

3   "Never Written Down": Learning Resources

The culture of indigenous musical learning and knowledge in Chuuk has significant ramifications for educational resources. Although a primary means of engaging with indigenous culture in some Pacific classrooms, there has been little sustained effort at generating such resources in Chuuk or elsewhere in Micronesia. On the popular internet forum *Micronesia Forum*, where users publicly discuss a variety of cultural issues, one user responded to a request for information about traditional

---

[8] It is common for example for young men and women to not fully understand the words of traditional dance songs due to the specialized nature of the content.

[9] A frequently discussed example is how Petrus Mailo apparently became powerful by purchasing aspects of his knowledge.

knowledge by stating that such restricted information was "never written down," promoting another user to request that the discussion thread be closed. The implicit meaning is that such knowledge is too valuable to be publicly distributed. The powerful caution of "never written down," however, is also contrary to the use of writing in Chuuk for decades. People do write down and compile indigenous knowledge including song texts, but they undertake this work mostly within the same restricted bounds that characterise traditional cultural practices. The statement encapsulates the disjuncture between traditional musics and school-based education.

Elders and new learners take full advantage of written language in order to preserve and transmit local knowledge in books (*puken roong*). Those knowledgeable about culture keep these valuable books locked away and they are given only to a chosen relative who will inherit the valuable knowledge contained within them. Recordings are also used in the same way and are significant factors in the teaching and learning of songs among families. While many studies still place such traditional Pacific knowledge within the realm of so-called "oral traditions," in Chuuk the "contents of the mat" is found increasingly in carefully guarded written and recorded media. But this media is not to be shared widely for broad educational purposes; like *roong* itself, it is restricted, protected, and passed on selectively.

Educators in Chuuk have undertaken some past projects aimed at codifying indigenous resources for schools, but very few of these materials engage with culture practices in depth and fewer still are accessible today. Perhaps the biggest such project was a text compiled and organised by the Chuuk Department of Education in the 1970s. The book is called *Uruon Chuk* (History of Chuuk), and it contains traditional vocal poetry recitations, as well as stories, histories, and cultural information (Chipen 1979). The text was published in 1979, in a joint effort between the Trust Territory Education Headquarters and the Chuuk Education Department, with the purpose of bringing a greater public awareness of indigenous culture. Takashy Chipen and staff compiled the information in Chuukese from 1972 to 1975 after interviewing elders and chiefs from all island regions. The project was originally organised together with recorded sound, and the text indicates this information at the end of each section, with the names of the informant speaker (*chóón aporous*), the recorder (*chóón tape*) and the transcriber (*chóón makei*). With over 400 pages, *Uruon Chuk* is a massive compilation of cultural information. The written text does not convey aspects of performance practice, but as written texts for originally intangible poetry, it raises many issues. Many people with whom I've discussed the book see it as political, setting down and thus standardising one version of diverse stories and poetry. Secondly, when the book's recitation poetry is compared with other recorded versions, the transcribed texts appear to be abbreviated from much fuller examples. I speculate that this was most likely the result of purposeful withholding of knowledge, a phenomenon that is regularly practiced. While I encountered many elders who knew of "the book," *Uruon Chuk* is not distributed widely in Chuuk, not accessible, and not used in schools, and while this may stem from its age, I speculate that the information is considered too valuable to be distributed widely in public environments. Educational resources such as *Uruon Chuk* sit at an uncomfortable space between the tangible and intangible, between democratic dissemination of musical and cultural knowledge through education and indigenous Chuukese practices of transmission. In Chuuk today, all knowledge is highly contested and people continue to value it through traditional social protocol, regardless of the medium.

Today, the absence of cultural resources has meant that indigenous practices remain largely within families, at home, and in the village. While other factors have also prevented the development of cultural materials, such as a lack of a standard and statewide orthography and regional differences in cultural practices, I contend that one of the main factors that has largely checked the development of indigenous resources in schools is the cultural disjuncture between the grounded place of this knowledge within the community, and the space of schools with their connections to a broader range of knowledge and experiences.

4 "When the Evil Spirits Ruled Our Islands": Cultural Ideology

Still another factor that plays a powerful role in the culture of learning in Chuuk is cultural ideology. Knowledge about indigenous music and performance is especially entangled in strongly held ideas of Christian practice, and which is often—though not always—at odds with the deeper past. Because traditional song knowledge is associated with *manaman* and thus involves spiritual practices that may conflict with contemporary Christian ideas, many traditional song repertories lie just under the surface of everyday culture and experience. Individuals in Chuuk hold a range of opinions about the nature of these repertories and ideas about their place in society and education. As a result of religious, social, and cultural factors, some communities in Chuuk characterise *roong* negatively and as obsolete or heathen; but at the same time, most people would identify it with a power that is vaguely understood and perhaps dangerous. Indigenous music, because of these associations and this inherent power, is something that should be withheld from public view by those who know about it.

Many of the most successful schools in Chuuk are also private religious schools, associated with the Protestant, Catholic, or Mormon churches, and thus these ideologies play an important role in regulating culture. For example, the Catholic schools in Chuuk hold annual 'Culture Day' events, where students and the community come together around the celebration of indigenous culture, but these events are absent in Protestant run schools, which focus instead on large spiritual retreats for students. At the same time, the culture days of Catholic schools includes general activities such as coconut husking and relay races that sometimes provide a rudimentary perspective on culture that is put away and brought out once a year. Some of these events may begin with a chant and include performances of a stick dance or sitting dance, learned from knowledgeable students with assistance from the community. However, music and dance activities at culture days take on a role of annual entertainment and are largely outside the regular school curriculum.

The College of Micronesia, the primary tertiary institution in the nation and which maintains a state campus in Chuuk does not adhere to any one faith or denomination, and tensions over the role of culture at its 2006 dedication ceremony underscore how ideology has shaped anxieties about traditional performance in education. A few faculty members wanted to include some especially important aspects of traditional culture to mark the event, which led to disagreements about the value, meaning, and place of traditional heritage within the institution. Especially prominent in the tension was the idea of beginning the day with a hauling chant (*emweyir*) as students and faculty processed onto the campus carrying a ceremonial wooden bowl. One faculty member who encourages cultural appreciation scheduled the procession to begin before the opening prayer. While others saw this as simply bad planning, some viewed it as completely unacceptable. In an email exchange that followed, one man, after referring to local Chuukese cultural practices as "dangerous," said, "[Chuukese] cultural beliefs and practices are rooted and associated with ... evil spirits that were exercised in the old and dark days when the evil spirits ruled our islands" (Diettrich, field notes). The disagreement over cultural ideology at the ceremony presents one of the main points of tension with traditional performances in Chuuk—the association with indigenous spiritual practices. The notion that indigenous practices are powerful, can be dangerous, and from some perspectives, are from the time of *rochopwak* (darkness), underscores the cultural disjuncture that exists within formal educational contexts. The exchange that took place at the College of Micronesia further demonstrates that these viewpoints are part of an ongoing dialogue about culture within Chuuk today.

5   Cultural Intersections: An Autoethnographic Account

Having explored the cultural tensions within school-based education in Chuuk, I now turn to a specific case where indigenous musics have intersected with the school environment. The example comes from a 2007 project at Chuuk High School in which I took part. In writing of my involvement with education in Chuuk, I struggle to find the best means of representation for lived musical experiences that are "dynamic, relational, embodied and highly subjective, they are difficult to express, particularly from a musical perspective where words are not the primary form of communication" (Bartleet and Ellis 2009, p. 9). As a genre, autoethnography "connects the personal to the cultural, social, and political" (Bartleet and Ellis 2009, p. 7), and in accordance with current practice that asks for reflexive accountability in research, I fully incorporate my voice in the narrative below (Bartleet and Ellis 2009; Ellis et al. 2011). The example also intersects with a growing body of scholarship in music studies that has queried the applied relevance of research projects (Harrison et al. 2010). In writing about Chuuk High School I reflect on the cultural advocacy of research within learning communities, and I consider the role of performance in particular as an agent of social transformation and education.

In mid 2007 an opportunity arose at Chuuk High School (CHS) to engage a large body of secondary students with indigenous music. At the time I was completing my doctoral research and teaching at the College of Micronesia, and I was also a volunteer music teacher for a semester at Chuuk High School (CHS) at the request of head principal Bill Sewel. CHS is the state's main public and largest secondary school, along with Weno High School and various church-affiliated schools. CHS is widely known as an educational institution of many challenges, and it has been located at the opposite end of the educational spectrum in the FSM from the highly praised and Jesuit-run Xavier High School that draws students from throughout Micronesia. I am uneasy in describing the issues at CHS, not wanting to add weight to the long list of negative depictions of education in Chuuk but also from the positive memories that remain with me as I write. The issues that CHS faced at the time are perhaps indicative of those that currently impede public education throughout Chuuk, as Hezel has summarised:

> For years people have pointed out the poor condition of the school facilities–the leaky roofs, broken windows and torn screens, the shabby condition of the classrooms, and the lack of clean water and toilets–but this is merely scratching the surface … The run-down facilities would seem to be a symptom rather than the cause of the educational malaise. In recent years, people have been hired on as teachers because of political pressure—often without credentials, but more importantly without any real interest in teaching. Failed teachers are often forced on the state education department, thus lowering morale even more … Teacher attendance, while officially reported at 97 %, is far lower than this, as everyone in the communities and at the state education department well know. Yet, no accurate record of teacher attendance can be maintained, since teachers who do not show up for work are not reported for their absences. Meanwhile, good teachers are understandably demoralized by this course of events. Some simply shrug and take the attitude: "If the teachers who never show up are getting paid, why should I come to teach every day?" (Hezel 2010, p. 1–2).

Likewise, an alarming 2010 report on education in Chuuk organized by the FSM government and the Asian Development Bank notes the many obstacles to effective learning and calls for "emergency" responses and "urgent" reforms. In 2007, and despite the efforts of a small group of concerned and hard-working staff and teachers, I found CHS a place where students mostly spent idle time outside of classrooms, but I also found a campus of inquisitive learners.[10] Like other schools in the state, music was ever-present but not a regular part of the curriculum. My experiences in the classroom at Chuuk High School were challenging and rewarding, but that semester an event presented itself that brought together the full school.

In March the Hawaiian vessel *Hōkūle'a* was voyaging through the western Pacific to the island of Satawal, and it made it a short stop in Chuuk on the island of Weno.[11] The celebrated double-hulled voyaging craft is known throughout the Pacific as a symbol for the re-establishment and revival of traditional navigation. The vessel *Alingano Maisu*—newly crafted as a gift for the renowned navigator

---

[10] During a visit to Chuuk in December 2014 and at the time of writing this chapter I learned that Chuuk High School has recently undergone a very positive revitalisation and has a growing reputation now in the FSM for the quality of its programmes.

[11] This event is briefly mentioned in Diettrich et al. (2011, pp. 153–54).

Pius Mau Piailug—accompanied *Hōkūleʻa* on its voyage. When it was announced ahead of time that members of the crew would visit CHS, a small group of teachers and students began to plan how to arrange the visit and welcome the guests, and I was fortunate to be included in these talks. The idea of a welcome performance was quickly agreed upon, but a more difficult question was *what* specifically the students would and could perform. Some suggested that the students could sing the FSM national anthem, a song in English and arranged to a German folk tune, while others wondered about how to incorporate traditional repertory for the cultural context of the occasion. It was generally agreed that the Hawaiian navigators would greet the school with a traditional performance and discussion turned to whether students could meet the crew with something culturally appropriate. A complication was that the students at CHS came from the range of cultural backgrounds that characterises Chuuk, and while students from the western atolls were easily able to arrange a traditional performance, students from elsewhere in the state had little or no background in traditional music and dance.

As an outsider and an American in Micronesia I was and continue to be critically aware of my positionality and prefer to remain in the background of discussions such as those at CHS. As a researcher I was keenly interested in the conversations and the questions that they raised. As the music teacher at CHS and COM, however, I was expected to contribute more, to go beyond these sheltered positions—I was expected to help and to contribute a suggestion about the performance that involved the full school. Situations such as these continue to prompt questions of ethics and interventions in ethnomusicology, of which Dirkson (2012) cautions that "when one consciously intervenes, the stakes are often higher, the margin of error is often larger, and the ramifications and responsibilities are often bigger." Likewise, the possibility of not intervening in such situations also raises questions of ethics, and especially where the experiences that we hold as researchers are vital and purposeful for local advocacy (Seeger 2008). The song knowledge that I had previously learned became useful at CHS "to produce more knowledge" (Seeger 2008, p. 271) and emerged as part of the "circle of cultural work [where] the divides between scholarship, social transformation, and performance become less meaningful, less clear" (Wong 1998, p. 95).

Years before I had learned to sing from a traditional repertory of songs from John Sandy, a respected educator and cultural leader from Pollap atoll. One particular genre called *engi* and that also comprises seated celebratory dances called *éwúwénú*, was iconic from Chuuk but is also performed on the western atolls. Its slow, rising, and deliberate melody seemed sonically appropriate for the event, and I felt it could be taught to a large group of students in short time. I sang an example that I knew as a demonstration, and those present commented on the importance of the traditional genre for Chuuk. The song poetry that I knew from the genre, however, was either community specific or more frequently about romantic encounters, and we laughed about how to make such texts fit into the event. A small group of students volunteered a solution, and agreed to recompose the text, to be appropriate as a welcome song (*kéénún etiwetiw*). Reusing melody but altering the words to fit new contexts is a widespread practice in Chuuk, and composers frequently transform love songs into church songs and vice versa. The altered example, called *Hōkūle'a, Alingano Maisu*, offered a sound that exemplified Chuuk, but it was also a very personal tribute to the navigators from Chuuk High School. Principal Sewel agreed to gather the full school for practice. Later at rehearsals in the school gymnasium and while standing on a chair in order to keep the group in time, I taught the song to roughly 500 students and staff. As an addition to the performance, we choreographed a percussive gesture used in dance and known as *óónu*, to mark the end of each verse.

Standing in compact rows across the space of the gymnasium the CHS students sang *Hōkūle'a, Alingano Maisu* together in unison and in full voice at the arrival of the Hawaiian delegation into the gym. A young man from the western atolls and who was competent in traditional dance performed standing in front of the group as an embellishment. Several members of the surrounding community stopped by for the occasion, and one elder commented on the tune, which he had "not heard for many years." After the performance, a small group of young women from the western atolls performed a sequence of seated dances (*éwúwénú*), and this was followed by speeches from the Hawaiian delegation and an explanation of their voyage.

Hōkūle'a, *Alingano Maisu*	Hōkūle'a, Alingano Maisu
seni Hawai'i tori nómwun Chuuk—oo.	from Hawai'i to Chuuk Lagoon.
Aloha, Nainoa Thompson, Shorty Bertelman	Aloha, Nainoa Thompson, Shorty Bertelman
tori Chuuk High School, péllúalap—oo.	to Chuuk High School, you great navigators.
Mataw, matawen wenipwunon	The sea, the great sea
Ochuffengengeniiy kich me mahalo—oo.	brought us together, with thanks.

Example 1 Transcription of "*Hōkūle'a, Alingano Maisu*" showing verse one

The performance by the full student body at CHS was a fleeting experience but in its short space of time it brought the full school together in one performance in celebration of local culture, something that one witness commented to me was "rare at CHS." The experience offered a means of directly engaging students with a small example of indigenous musical practice, but importantly it did not merely perpetuate a fossilised or essentialised perspective of culture. The performance at CHS was successful in particular from the innovation brought to the traditional content, through re-composition and choreography, and from the engagement and collaboration of the students and the sanction of the staff. For me personally, the experience was a means of locating an education centered outcome from the musical knowledge that I had gathered during research, and the *Hōkūle'a* visit created a space for transmitting knowledge beyond the academy. The brief and momentary example from CHS alone does not offer an answer to broader questions about music content in schools, but I believe the experience raises the future potential of the intersection of indigenous culture in public educational contexts in Chuuk. Performance provides students with a means to directly engage with indigenous knowledge, and this may allow space for reconsiderations about the role of music and dance in formal education in Micronesia.

6 Reflection

In this chapter I have explored issues and questions that surround education and music in Chuuk, and I examined a general disjuncture between the learning environments of schools, and indigenous musics. This chapter has suggested that this divide in education has its roots in the historical emergence and contemporary culture of schools in the region, but it is shaped further and supported by local ideas about indigenous musics and culture. This disjuncture is culturally determined and enacted, and it holds deep implications for both the future of education in the state and the future sustainability of musical and cultural practices. The disjuncture in education in Chuuk presents a challenge to the institution of schooling as found in the state, and it poses critical questions about the development of curriculum through the process of decolonisation. Chuuk has witnessed a number of government-led reports and evaluative studies that concern education, but these documents have concentrated on inadequacies of the physical institutions in terms of facilities, land ownership, finances, staffing and leadership, and administration. They have mostly ignored, however, fundamental questions about curriculum and content and the social and cultural possibilities that a renewed emphasis on music might bring. A critical reconsideration of the place of music and the expressive arts in Chuuk's education system, and indeed for the FSM, might offer possibilities for a closer intersection with the people and place of Micronesia.

Acknowledgements I thank the people and communities in Chuuk and more widely in the FSM for sharing in discussions about the ideas in this essay. In particular I thank students and staff at the College of Micronesia—FSM, both the Chuuk and National Campuses, as well as Chuuk High School for welcoming me into their educational spaces and assisting over the years in my education about Micronesia. Past research has been generously funded by the Wenner-Gren Foundation, The University of Hawai'i at Mānoa, Victoria University of Wellington, and the New Zealand School of Music. My thanks to Inge van Rij for assistance with notating the musical example, and to David Lines and Linda Ashley for organising this volume and for valuable feedback on earlier versions of this chapter.

References

Bartleet, B.-L., & Ellis, C. (2009). Making autoethnography sing/making music personal. In B.-L. Bartleet & C. Ellis (Eds.), *Music autoethnographies* (pp. 1–13). Brisbane: Australian Academic Press.

Chipen, T. (Comp.). (1979). *Uruon Chuk. A resource of oral legends, traditions and history of Truk*. Saipan: Trust Territory of the Pacific Islands.

Cholymay, M. (2013). *Way finding: Envisioning a culturally responsive educational system for Chuuk State,* Federated States of Micronesia. PhD dissertation, University of Hawai'i at Mānoa.

Council of Pacific Arts, and Culture and the Secretariat of the Pacific Community. (2010). *Pacific culture and education strategy 2010-2015.* Noumea: Secretariat of the Pacific Community.

Diettrich, B. (2011). Voices from 'under-the-garland': Singing, Christianity, and cultural transformations in Chuuk, Micronesia. *Yearbook for Traditional Music, 43,* 62–88.

Diettrich, B., Moulin, J., & Webb, M. (2011). *Music In Pacific Island cultures: Experiencing music, expressing culture (book and CD).* New York: Oxford University Press.

Dirksen, R. (2012). Reconsidering theory and practice in ethnomusicology: Applying, advocating, and engaging beyond academia. *Ethnomusicology Review,* 17. http://ethnomusicologyreview. ucla.edu/journal/volume/17/piece/602

Ellis, C., Adams, T. E., & Bochner, A. P. (2011). Autoethnography: An overview. *Forum: Qualitative Social Research,* 12(1). http://www.qualitative-research.net/index.php/fqs/article/view/1589/3095

Falgout, S. (1992). Hierarchy vs. democracy: Two strategies for the management of knowledge on Pohnpei. *Anthropology & Education Quarterly, 23*(1), 30–43.

Federated States of Micronesia, Office of SBOC, Statistics Division. (2009). *Population estimates.* Retrieved from http://www.sboc.fm/index.php?id0=Vm0xMFlWbFdTbkpQVm1SU1lrVndVbFpyVWtKUFVUMDk

Fischer, J. L. (1961). The Japanese schools for the natives of Truk, Caroline Islands. *Human Organization, 20,* 83–88.

Gladwin, T. (1960). Petrus Mailo, chief of Moen. In J. B. Casagrande (Ed.), *In the company of man: Twenty portraits by anthropologists* (pp. 42–62). New York: Harper and Brothers Publishers.

Goodenough, W., & Sugita, H. (Comp.). (1980). *Trukese-English dictionary.* Philadelphia: American Philosophical Society.

Goodenough, W., & Efot, B. (Ed., trans.). (1992). On education in Chuuk: Address by Petrus Mailo to the students, Chuuk high school, October 1964. *ISLA: A Journal of Micronesian Studies, 1*(2), 261–275.

Hanlon, D. (1998). *Remaking micronesia: Discourses over development in a Pacific territory, 1944–1982.* Honolulu: University of Hawai'i Press.

Harrison, K., Mackinlay, E., & Pettan, S. (2010). *Applied ethnomusicology: Historical and contemporary approaches.* Newcastle upon Tyne: Cambridge Scholars Publishing.

Hezel, F. X. (1984). Schools in Micronesia prior to American administration. *Pacific Studies, 8*(1), 95–111.

Hezel, F. X. (2001). Islands of excellence. *Micronesian counselor,* 34. Kolonia, Pohnpei.

Hezel, F. X. (2010). Make me be good: Education reform for the islands. *Micronesian Counselor,* 82. Kolonia, Pohnpei.

Kupferman, D. W. (2012). *Disassembling and decolonizing school in the Pacific: A genealogy from Micronesia.* New York: Springer.

Levine, V. (2010). *Federated States of Micronesia: Strengthening public sector performance. Technical assistance consultant's report.* Honolulu: Asian Development Bank.

Metzgar, E. (1991). *Traditional education in Micronesia: A case study of Lamotrek Atoll with comparative analysis of the literature on the Trukic Continuum.* Ph.D. dissertation, University of California, Los Angeles.

Peacock, K. (1985). The Maze of schools: American education in Micronesia. In K. Knudsen (Ed.), *History of the trust territory of the Pacific Islands: Proceedings of the ninth annual Pacific Islands conference* (pp. 83–103). Honolulu: Hawai'i: Pacific Islands Studies Program, Center for Asian and Pacific Studies, University of Hawai'i at Manoa.

Sachuo, S. (1992). *Cultural and educational imperialism: An examination of the consequential impacts of eternally designed and imposed educational systems on the children of Truk and the Trukese culture.* PhD dissertation, University of Oregon.

Seeger, A. (2008). Theories forged in the crucible of action: The joys, dangers, and potentials of advocacy and fieldwork. In G. F. Barz & T. J. Cooley (Eds.), *Shadows in the field: New perspectives for fieldwork in ethnomusicology* (pp. 271–288). New York: Oxford University Press.

Smith, L. T. (2005). Building a research agenda for indigenous epistemologies and education. *Anthropology & Education Quarterly, 36*(1), 93–95.

Teasdale, B., & Rhea, Z. M. (Eds.). (2000). *Local knowledge and wisdom in higher education.* Oxford: Pergamon.

Thaman, K. H. (Ed.). (2003a). *Educational ideas from Oceania: Selected readings.* University of the South Pacific, Institute of Education. Suva: Institute of Education in Association with the UNESCO Chair of Teacher Education and Culture.

Thaman, K. H. (2003b). Decolonizing Pacific studies: Indigenous perspectives. *The Contemporary Pacific, 15*(1), 1–17.

Thaman, K. H. (2007). Acknowledging indigenous knowledge systems in higher education in the Pacific Island region. In V. Lynn Meek & C. Suwanwela (Eds.), *Higher education, research and knowledge in the Asia Pacific Region* (pp. 175–184). New York: Palgrave Macmillan.

Wong, D. (1998). Ethnomusicology and critical pedagogy as cultural work: Reflections on teaching and fieldwork. *College Music Symposium, 38*, 80–100.

Brian Diettrich Brian Diettrich (PhD) is Senior Lecturer in Ethnomusicology at Victoria University of Wellington, New Zealand. His research focuses on Pacific Island music, and especially that of the Federated States of Micronesia. He is a co-author of *Music in Pacific Island Cultures: Experiencing Music, Expressing Culture.*

Sāsā: More Than Just a Dance

Robyn Trinick and Luama Sauni

Abstract The traditional Sāmoan dance, *sāsā*, is familiar to many children and teachers in Aotearoa/New Zealand who have participated in or attended Pasifika cultural festivals and other school and community events. While *sāsā* may be regarded as a source of entertainment with great audience appeal that integrates dance and music, its significance and potential as a multi-literacy and sociocultural learning context is often overlooked. As the authors of this paper, we argue that cultural experiences such as *sāsā* are educational as well as artistic. This chapter explores the potential of *sāsā* in education, informed by the merging and emerging perspectives of two authors from different cultural backgrounds who reflect on their own experiences and understandings. This paper also draws on narratives of a Sāmoan school principal and two pre-service education students. Some of the deeper social and historical features are discussed with a view to considering the *sāsā* as a means of enhancing artistic, sociocultural and affective benefits for learners. We found that as students from different cultures engage in the process of creating and performing *sāsā*, they construct their own meaning from the experience, bringing stories and characters to life through interplay of all the arts, particularly dance and music. However, before introducing cultural activities such as *sāsā* to the classroom, it is important to determine how both cultural and educational practices can be honoured simultaneously. The authors draw on Bronfenbrenner's (The ecology of human development: Experiments by nature and design. Harvard University Press, Cambridge, MA, 1979) *ecological model* to promote the idea that *sāsā* has educational benefits for both Sāmoan and non-Sāmoan children, and that it is 'more than just a dance.' We pose a series of questions to challenge educators to consider how they might integrate cultural practices into their teaching and learning pedagogy.

Keywords Sāsā • Dance • Music • Culturally responsive pedagogy • Samoan culture and identity

R. Trinick (✉) • L. Sauni
School of Curriculum and Pedagogy, Faculty of Education, The University
of Auckland, Private Bag 92601, Symonds St., Auckland, New Zealand
e-mail: r.trinick@auckland.ac.nz; Luama.Sauni@whitireia.ac.nz

© Springer International Publishing Switzerland 2016
L. Ashley, D. Lines (eds.), *Intersecting Cultures in Music and Dance Education*, Landscapes: the Arts, Aesthetics, and Education 19,
DOI 10.1007/978-3-319-28989-2_4

1 Introduction

Pasifika cultural groups are common in a number of schools in New Zealand-Aotearoa, particularly in Auckland where there are large Sāmoan communities who are either New Zealand born or are immigrants from Sāmoa (Macpherson 1999). Irrespective of their origins, it is customary for cultural groups to include a *sāsā*, or Sāmoan group dance, in their performance repertoire, an art form that has become increasingly familiar and popular with local New Zealand audiences. *Sāsā* is considered by many to be highly entertaining because of the high energy and exuberance shown by the performers. While this is a factor to be celebrated, our thinking as educators is that the process and performance of *sāsā* should be regarded as more than just entertainment. Our aim in this chapter is to show the multiplicity of meanings of *sāsā* where on one level, the dancer's movements reflect activities from daily life and on another level, there are complex underlying layers of human relationships and interactions. If we delve further into the sociocultural significance and educational value of *sāsā*, we develop a better appreciation of this art form and its contribution not only to maintaining the identity of Sāmoan children living in New Zealand-Aotearoa, but also to celebrating cultural and linguistic diversity in our schools, centres and communities.

The chapter opens with a brief narrative from each of the authors about their respective experiences with *sāsā*. This is followed by an outline of the theoretical framework underpinning this paper. A description of *sāsā* is then provided. Next, the discussion explores points and issues relating to two main areas – the sociocultural significance of *sāsā*, and the educational value of *sāsā*. Subsequently, key challenges for educators to consider are identified. The chapter concludes with a discussion about *sāsā* in contemporary education settings and the need for ongoing research to support our communities of practice.

2 The Authors

We, the authors of this chapter, have worked collaboratively on a number of different integrated arts projects, and share common views about the important role of the arts in education at all levels. We originate from contrasting cultural and ethnic backgrounds, and have had different experiences with *sāsā*. Luama is Sāmoan, and the focus of her teaching has been in the early childhood context. Robyn is *Palagi* (European), with a background in primary education. We have both taught in schools and early childhood centres in South Auckland, where there are large communities of Sāmoan families. We have also worked in the field of tertiary education for a considerable amount of time, and our work with adult students is informed by our early teaching experiences. It is the intention of this chapter to acknowledge our different experiences and perspectives, and also to identify intersecting viewpoints.

3   Luama's Story

*I have been involved with music and dance professional development workshops
with teachers and students in schools. Teaching the sāsā has been the most enjoyable and exciting of my repertoire of cultural dances. I think it provides the space
necessary for the performers to explore simple movements and to transform these to
more complex ones. My approach towards teaching and learning the sāsā is to
firstly respect and preserve the integrity of the learners while at the same time,
facilitate their prior knowledge, experiences and skills. I think this is crucial in
preparation for an equitable and reciprocal platform to establish collaborative
relationships, mutual trust and positive engagement.*

*In my role as a performing arts teacher at the Faculty of Education, I have
focused on facilitating the students' learning through an integrated model of teaching. The students are provided with opportunities to work in collaborative groups
that allow them to interact and communicate their holistic exploration of ideas,
problem solving skills and creativity using sāsā as a context for learning.*

4   Robyn's Story

*My first experience with sāsā was in my second year teaching in the early 1980s, in
a primary school in South Auckland. The population of the school and the local
community was predominantly Pasifika, with a large Sāmoan community. The cultural group in the school was somewhat of a tradition, and viewing a performance
of a sāsā for the first time was awe-inspiring. I watched 'my' children performing
the sāsā, and saw them through a different lens. I realised that these children brought
with them a whole different set of experiences and cultural understandings that were
different from my own. As an observer, I could see that the Sāmoan children performing were really proud of their cultural heritage. Years later, I read this poem,
and it reminded me of those early experiences, and how, in fact, at the time, I was a
learner as much as I was a teacher:*

> *Listen Teacher*
> *Listen to me*
> *Don't look away*
> *See my eyes, they hold messages*
> *that can make you understand me*
> *Hold my hand and your heart*
> *will warm towards me*
> *Let me dance and sing you*
> *my own songs which you don't know*
> *and you might smile as you have*
> *never smiled before*

Hear me tell you a story
of my ancient past
and then, maybe, you can see another person in me. (Emma Kruse Va'ai 1996)[1]

5   The Theoretical Framework

This chapter argues that sociocultural activities such as *sāsā* play an important role in the education of our children. This is inclusive of family and community contexts, and enables children to make connections between all aspects, or layers, of their worlds. It is useful, then, to draw on Bronfenbrenner's (1979) *ecological model* to consider a theoretical framework to examine the impact that culture has on children's social practices and experiences. Bronfenbrenner's model is a central focus in the current New Zealand early childhood curriculum statement, Te Whāriki (Ministry of Education 1996), and is still used as a theoretical framework for recent research in a range of domains, including the arts (Abril and Bannerman 2015; Magro 2014; Mitchell 2014). The model acknowledges the inextricable relationships existing between people and their surrounding environment on three socioecological levels: (a) micro, (b) meso, and (c) macro (Bronfenbrenner 1994).

The micro level consists of factors that directly impact on childrens' daily lives and involves "human agency and choice and small-scale social systems of various types" (Johnson 2008, p. vi). The meso level relates to the child's immediate learning environment and the relationships between them, involving home, family and school or early childhood settings. For many Sāmoan children living in Aotearoa/New Zealand, *sāsā* provides an opportunity to bridge learning environments and acknowledges "the unseen and subtle cultural spaces that students are armed with when they reach the classroom" (Sauni 2014, p. 135). Thus, it is at the meso level that *sāsā* plays an important role in helping children to make connections between home, school, and culture. This connection is important because historically there has been a recognised disconnect between Pasifika families and the school (Valdez et al. 2007). Part of the disconnect can be attributed to Sāmoan traditional perspectives of schooling. Valdez et al. (2007) claim that Sāmoan parents have historically separated academic matters that are perceived to be the responsibility of schools from spiritual and cultural matters that are considered to be the responsibility of families. On the other hand, schools in New Zealand, have tended to be very monolingual and monocultural European. Therefore, *sāsā* is an example of a culture-specific experience that may help to address some of the perceived barriers for Sāmoan families, such as English language abilities and protocols (Edwards and Danridge 2001; Vincent and Martin 2002). Sāmoan parents "generally feel more

---

[1] Letuimanuasina Dr Emma Kruse Va'ai is Professor of English and Linguistics at the National University of Samoa. She is a strong advocate for retaining and strengthening Pacific languages as well as using English and other introduced languages of the region. Many of her stories have also been translated into other Pacific languages.

comfortable participating with someone who has adopted some aspects of Sāmoan culture, thereby creating more of a mutual context for the relationship" (Valdez et al. 2007, p. 61). Such issues are related to societal attitudes and are therefore considered to be at a macro level of Bronfenbrenner's ecological model. While macro-level factors such as wider societal attitudes will impact on classrooms and individuals, they may not be as visible because of the filtering process that occurs through different levels before directly impacting on children's daily lives (Abril and Bannerman 2015).

6 What Is *Sāsā*?

Sāsā is a category of '*siva*', which is the generic Sāmoan word for 'dance'. *Sāsā* is considered to be "extant", or in current and consistent use, as opposed to other traditional Sāmoan dances that are obsolete (Radakovich 2004, p. 8). '*Sāsā*' literally means 'to strike', and is a dance performed by both genders of all ages, often in large groups. One of the distinctive and recognisable features of *sāsā* is that it is usually performed in a seated fashion. It involves clapping rhythms with hands and slapping chests, with legs and arms moving in unison and in various combinations. Both performers and viewers are inspired by the energy and force of repetitive hand movements, complemented by driving rhythms played on a range of percussion instruments including drums or empty biscuit tins. *Sāsā* is considered by many to be one of Sāmoa's most interesting dances, because of the precision of movement in synchronisation with accompanying drum rhythms.

There are different forms of *sāsā*, and the dance has evolved over time. Distinctive features have not been well documented by researchers, making it difficult to pinpoint when changes have occurred over time (Radakovich 2004). While recognised as a traditional Sāmoan dance, *sāsā* has undergone, and will no doubt, continue to undergo incremental changes in its features as performers seek to connect it to their experiences and as new ideas come to the fore. The innovation and evidence of cultural cross-fertilisation in *sāsā* design and performance are evident in performances of *sāsā* at the Auckland secondary schools Māori and Pacific Islands cultural festivals, commonly referred to as "Polyfest" (Kornelly 2008, p. xvii). Taouma (2014) suggests these changes can be seen back in the 1970s cultural festivals when *sāsā* began to reflect a cross-fertilisation of cultures as Pasifika immigrants were "looking back to their island homes and their remembered art-forms whilst looking forward with the view that Aotearoa was their new home" (p. 30).

There are some defining common characteristics that distinguish *sāsā* from other Sāmoan dance forms. *Sāsā* will often begin with the *fa'aluma* (chorus leader) calling *tulolo*, a command for the group to bow their heads, then *nofo* as a command for the group to sit up again. It has become common practice for the group to use greetings such as *talofa* (hello) at the beginning of the dance, and *tofa* (farewell) at the end. The movements and gestures used in *sāsā* represent Sāmoan histories, lands, and people, and depict actions from everyday life such as slapping off mosquitos, cooking, cleaning house, or paddling canoes. *Sāsā* will sometimes include actions depicting the gathering and preparation of coconuts for the *'ava* ceremony, a solemn Sāmoan ritual where a ceremonial beverage is shared to acknowledge important events such as the bestowal of chiefly titles. Our belief is that by increasing the understanding of the significance of gestures used in the *sāsā*, both audience and performers gain a deeper appreciation of Sāmoan cultural heritage, language and values through collaboratively creative experiences.

Despite commonalities, each *sāsā* performance is unique. Distinctions may be characteristic of the specific choreography or style of a particular tutor, or there may be variations in rhythmic accompaniments or dance formations. For example, dancers may all be seated in rows, or, alternatively, in a three-tiered organisation with the front row seated, the middle row kneeling, and the back row standing (Radakovich 2004). There are many choices to be made in the design of *sāsā*, exemplifying the dynamic and creative nature of this art form.

7   The Sociocultural Significance of *Sāsā*

It is argued that educators are not able to effectively nurture individual children without acknowledging the set of values and the life experiences that the children bring with them to the learning environment (Carpenter et al. 2000). One way to do this is to share in cultural experiences such as *sāsā* that reflect children's own and others' values, traditions and identity. By experiencing culturally diverse music and dance, children develop a positive sense of self, and an awareness and acceptance of others (Paquette and Rieg 2008).

While it should not be assumed that all children of Sāmoan descent in Aotearoa/ New Zealand have had the same life experiences, there is a common belief that Sāmoan children have a natural love for music and dance, often attributed to early socialisation experiences associated with music and dance activities involving both family and church (Trinick et al. 2010). When children encounter similar cultural experiences, such as *sāsā*, in centres and schools, they are more likely to make connections, enabling them to perceive their worlds are connected by their "personal collection of experiences" (Wiggins 2004, p. 88). An understanding of the relationship between children's own cultural resources and school or centre culture enables them to make sense of their social and cultural milieu and to construct their own reality through experiences and interactions (Gregory et al. 2004).

Considering the changing identity of New Zealand born Sāmoan, we need to be cautious about oversimplifying an individual's sense of self, based purely on ethnicity. In some cultures, a sense of self is relationally constituted and "not predicated on any notion of individual uniqueness but on one's ability to maintain harmonious relationships with others" (Hoffman 1996, p. 560). This is particularly so for "the Sāmoan self" that "cannot be separated from the *va* or relational space that occurs between an individual and parents, siblings, grandparents, aunts, uncles and other extended family and community members" (Tamasese et al. 2005, p. 303). When we consider the individual's layers in Bronfenbrenner's (1979) ecological model, we can begin to understand the complexities relating to cultural regularities and variables for individuals and groups, from a point of 'difference' rather than 'deficit'.

Sāsā provides ways to acknowledge the cultural capital (Bourdieu 2011) that Sāmoan children bring to the classroom and for all children, is a way to celebrate diversity. While different cultures of immigrants from the Pacific share some similarities, the uniqueness of the Sāmoan worldview should not be overlooked. "Young people may regard themselves as 'Pacific Islanders' but they come to develop a secure Sāmoan identity as adults" (Levine 2003, p. 2). Thus, *sāsā* gives many Sāmoan children a context to learn in ways that are meaningful to them because it contains important messages and stories that are integral to their culture, fostering a sense of status and pride. *Sāsā* involves a spiritual dimension that may not be recognised or understood by non-Sāmoan educators, and enables Sāmoan children to develop a highly tuned sense of *lagona*, or faith and intuition. *Lagona* is an indigenous way of knowing and learning that is authentic and time-validated (Phillips et al. 2014). "When *Lagona* learning is deliberately validated alongside the strict academic rigour of curriculum and the expectations of Western teaching and learning, it significantly accelerates the chances of Pasifika students to reach educational success and to enjoy the good things in life that this may bring to them and their families" (Sauni 2014, p. 146).

The New Zealand early childhood curriculum document, Te Whāriki (Ministry of Education 1996) promotes the idea of "noticing, recognising and responding" to children's cultural and artistic interests. Therefore 'success' is not just measured in terms of a child's content knowledge – it is also the acquisition of elements considered important in a cultural sense. *Sāsā* provides Sāmoan children with an opportunity to shine in a cultural context where their culture is the norm. While it could be argued that other artistic and cultural experiences offer similar benefits and outcomes, the authors consider *sāsā* to be a worthy example of an experience that according to researchers reflects "culturally pluralist pedagogy" in practice (Ashley 2014, p. 1).

As educators, we should endeavour to actively seek out opportunities to contribute to children's spiritual, physical, emotional, intellectual, social and cultural development, and the potential for *sāsā* to do this should not be overlooked as we prepare them to be life-long learners. If we, the teachers, do not have the cultural knowledge ourselves, learning experiences such as *sāsā* provide an opportunity to collaborate with others who may be more expert than ourselves. *Sāsā* encompasses collaboration and reciprocity at a number of different levels, and involves communities of dancers, musicians, teachers and audience. Some researchers argue that successful learning contexts are those which focus on a sense of community more than individualism (Scheurich 1998). This is certainly consistent with Sāmoan values of community and family (Sauni 2014). Rubie et al. (2004) have added that an effective community is reliant on collaboration which involves alliance, partnership and co-operation, and where valued elements and activities that represent the culture of the learners are central to the curriculum.

From our experiences as arts educators, we have acquired knowledge of the importance of teamwork in any group performance. *Sāsā* exemplifies collaboration between musicians and dancers and brings together causality between movement and sound. While the synchronised nature of *sāsā* performance is considered a collective activity, the individual's performance within the group is also highly valued, and if a particular performer is absent, it may change the dynamic of the group. In this way, both group and individual performance is acknowledged.

In *sāsā*, collaboration is manifested not only amongst dancers and musicians, but is also inherent in the two-way relationship that exists between performer and observer. The energy, skill, and sense of spectacle and occasion evident in a *sāsā* performance captivates the audience. This links to Leigh's (2010) view where she considers that the relationship between performer and viewer of dance involves empathy, and where observers might visualise themselves as performers, re-enacting the same moves. Kwakwa (2010) also deems empathy to be inherent in dance performance in her discussion of communal African dance, and she talks of "the unifying and sustaining dynamics of the interactions between dancers and musicians and between dancers and local audiences" (p. 54). The same could be said of *sāsā*.

Another level of collaboration occurs between teacher and student when working with dance (Sansom 2009). In our view, the strength of the teacher-student relationship is a factor that is emphasised in the arts, and enables the personal, emotional and psychological world of the child to be explored in holistic ways. When the expertise required to teach *sāsā* is not found in the teaching staff in schools or centres, it is common practice to invite experts from the community to do the teaching. This adds another layer of collaboration into the mix, and provides opportunities to develop a sense of connectedness for the child at the centre of the learning where family can play a genuine role as educators at the first level of Bronfenbrenner's (1979) ecological model.

8 The Educational Value of Sāsā

While educational and sociocultural contexts are inextricably connected, the many and varied purposes of *sāsā* in educational settings are worthy of specific mention. One of the educational values of *sāsā* as a learning experience is that it helps celebrate diversity and offers all students opportunities to engage in positive learning experiences in the arts. We argue that the interplay between music and dance in *sāsā* is more complex than it may first appear. In *sāsā*, symbols are sung, viewed, played and embodied, rather than spoken or written, thus providing a different approach to learning and communicating. While there is a wide range of literature relating to the transfer of learning from the arts to other areas of learning, it appears that there is little research done on the transfer within the arts themselves, particularly from music to dance and from dance to music. "It seems plausible to suppose that certain capacities or ways of thinking may be situated within the arts themselves... in other words, it may be that learning in the arts is both continuous with, yet distinct from, other subjects…" (Burton et al. 2000, p. 229). Unfortunately, in our view, *sāsā* is still considered by some to be an 'extra-curricular activity,' despite clearly stated achievement objectives relating to music and dance education in the New Zealand Curriculum statement (Ministry of Education 2007). We argue that it should not be seen as separate from the 'main' curriculum. Rather, it should be ongoing and contextualised, and we believe that one of the most effective ways to teach children about culture is through song and dance. The alleged freedom in delivery offered by the New Zealand Curriculum is somewhat of a paradox when choices made by teachers are seemingly "curtailed by the assessment industry that seems to operate in a paradigm of easily measurable objectives" (Begg 2006, p. 1). Children need opportunities to develop a "widening range of resources for creative expression, symbolising and representation" (Ministry of Education 1996, p. 26). The inherently multimodal and multiple symbolic nature of *sāsā* allows students to develop not only dance and music literacies, but also to transform these experiences within the practice and understandings of a range of skills in other disciplines and domains.

In *sāsā*, music and dance are interwoven in a rich weave of rhythm and movement. On the surface, it may appear to the audience to be a highly structured and choreographed piece of work, but one of the distinguishing features of *sāsā* that is not always evident to audiences is that much of it is improvised and individualised according to the concept, idea or activity that is being illuminated.

While the movement aspects of *sāsā* are the predominant attraction for the viewer, the accompanying music incorporates a range of percussive sounds, including body percussion and a variety of drums including *tu 'itu 'i*[2] and *pātē*[3] each with their own particular tone colour within a texture of sounds, creating a dynamic rhythmic effect. Sometimes a kerosene tin or a large biscuit tin is used as a drum to create an interesting rhythmic texture (Kaeppler 1978). The drumming drives the beat and provides rhythmic cues for changing actions, dividing the music and dance into clear sections, giving a strong sense of form. Accents shift around to create a syncopated feel, and rhythmic improvisation is a strong component. Although, in modern times, recorded drumming is used in the absence of live musicians, *sāsā* gives listeners and performers an opportunity to be immersed in live, acoustic music.

Sāsā involves movement of all body parts in a synchronised fashion developing an understanding of dance elements including body awareness, time, energy, space and relationships through thinking, moving and feeling. There is intent, purpose and form in both process and product, and children develop dance literacy as they refine skills and understandings about *sāsā*. "The degrees to which a dancer's awareness is refined, the physical activity articulated and the embodied knowledge universal, will define the development of the dancer's literacy" (Jones 2014, p. 111). Through *sāsā* experiences, young children are given opportunities to "become more aware of

---

[2] A *tu 'itu 'i* is a drum made from a rolled mat (*fala*) with resonators inside such as pieces of bamboo or empty bottles (Radakovich 2004, p. 85).

[3] A *pātē* is a small wooden slit drum.

the movements they see in their world and make meaning from their own encounters and interactions" (Sansom 2008, p. 26).

Sāsā provides opportunities to strengthen some learners' capabilities, and, for others, to take risks and to push personal boundaries. Much of the educational discourse relating to cultural performances is centered on 'doing' the *sāsā*, which has a tendency to undermine its status and learning potential. Dance involves incidental assimilation of memory, attention, and abstraction. As well as developing social, cultural, affective and cognitive functions, *sāsā* also contributes to learning in specific domains of learning, for both Sāmoan and non-Sāmoan learners.

> *Throughout my years as both a teacher and a Principal, we have practised performances in sāsā in the following ways: Physical Education/Health: expanding Te Reo Kori (the language of movement) to include rhythmic movement – after teaching a basic set of sāsā moves, children then created their own. Literacy – when learning about different cultures, we have gone into the ways different cultures tell stories through movement. Social Sciences – Pasifika migration – beliefs and practices of Pasifika nations – what tribes and villages hold tight to – Sāsā forms the basis of villages sharing entertainment and in these days, it is a way keeping these practices alive* (C. Hansell, School Principal, personal communication 15/08/2014).

Sāsā has its own form of literacy, both verbal and non-verbal. Meaning is conveyed through gesture, expression, sound, and rhythmic movements as performers embody the text. Performers of *sāsā* interact with the audience, telling stories and painting pictures without words. While movement and sound are important modes of communication, understanding the use of the body as a voice or as a conduit of expression is not prevalent in education circles (Sansom 2008). *Sāsā* is dynamic and interactive – "going with the moment" and sometimes involves audience participation. A long line of research into cognition suggests that where tasks share common cognitive or symbolic elements, or underlying abstract structures, transfer is more likely to occur (Singley 1989). Much of this meaning may be missed as audiences respond to the driving rhythms and visual spectacle of *sāsā*, and as educators, there is a need to encourage viewers to enjoy the artistic aspects, but also to capitalise on the learning potential that *sāsā* offers.

Sāsā builds self-efficacy which involves motivation, persistence and emotional reactions (Zimmerman 2000). It is believed that students with high self-efficacy enter into learning situations where they believe they will succeed, enhancing motivation and building personal agency, pride and self-esteem (Bandura 1977). Hoffman (1996) maintained that we should also take into consideration the cultural and individual perceptions of what self-esteem means, and acknowledge that while increased personal agency is considered to be a precursor to academic achievement, this may not necessarily be the motivating factor. An example of this is seen in the findings of Rubie et al. (2004) who suggest that students involved in Māori cultural groups developed more positive self-esteem and a stronger sense of internality over a one year intervention compared to students, both Māori and non-Māori, of similar age, who were not involved in the cultural group. Rubie et al. (2004) considered the key factors that contributed to increase in self-efficacy were "cooperation, family, explicit recognition of culture and its values in the school, and behaviours believed to enhance self-efficacy." (p. 155). While it is difficult to draw conclusions, recurring patterns and trends in research results will strengthen teachers' beliefs about the impact of cultural performance on self-efficacy. It would be interesting to carry out further research, from a sociocognitive perspective, to find out if the impact of involvement in a Pasifika cultural group has similar outcomes for Sāmoan and other children.

While most of the discourse relating to self-efficacy is to do with individuals, acknowledgment of children's cultural capital provides individuals with a confidence to learn which, in turn, contributes to "collective Pasifika benefit" (Sauni 2014, p. 136).

> *One thing that I noticed about our children when they were learning and performing the sāsā was the increased level of engagement. I could see the pride on the faces of the Sāmoan children as they shared their cultural capital, and were seen by other children as 'the leaders'. I have found that over the years, the leaders are often the 'cheeky' ones, with lots of energy, and it is great to see this energy and motivation channelled in the direction of sāsā* (C. Hansell, School Principal, personal communication 15/08/2014).

9 Considerations for Educators

Despite all our affirmative support of *sāsā*, Sāmoan children, like children from other cultures, are not homogeneous. As noted earlier, there may be an assumption that all Sāmoan children are familiar with *sāsā* and that they are willing participants. A word of caution is given by MacPherson (1999) who argues that "Sāmoan identities constructed at various times for particular purposes may have given an impression of ethnic unity which masked considerable internal divergence" (p. 50). Additionally, Hoffman (1996) claimed that although it is wrong to ignore the existence of the variety of cultural backgrounds students bring into a classroom and to teach insensitively and blindly, it is equally misplaced to assume that all students want or need aggressive affirmation or exploration of their cultural identity and self-esteem" (p. 562).

While, in theory, it is easy to celebrate the potential of *sāsā* for educational and socio-cultural purposes, in practice, there are challenges to be faced, and questions to be asked.

(a) Should non-Samoan teachers teach the *sāsā?*

The challenge for educators is to be responsive to cultural diversity. However, like all forms of teaching, *sāsā* requires appropriate pedagogical content and cultural knowledge. For non-Sāmoan educators, this is a challenging, but for some, a desirable goal in itself (Rohan 2011). The virtues and values of fortitude, commitment and initiative are not unique to learning *sāsā* but are dispositions needed to find practical ways to work across habitus, or in cultural contexts outside of our own.

The learning and teaching of a sāsā, or any other part of the curriculum, is a collective responsibility – so we would expect teachers to source expertise and increase their own personal understandings of the WHY in teaching any part of the curriculum. (C. Hansell, School Principal, personal communication 15/08/2014).

Finding a balance between ideals and realities requires "praxial wisdom" (Regelski 2002, p. 107). This requires educators to engage in a cycle of looking, thinking, acting, reflecting (Stringer 2004), while considering the political and social aspects of teaching *sāsā* and, indeed, the students they teach (Hastie et al. 2006). Teaching *sāsā* without the depth of knowledge and skills required to teach any art form out of our comfort zones raises issues of hybridisation, fusion and intercultural appropriation (Ashley 2012). While professional development opportunities can provide educators with some content knowledge, there may still be "uneasiness" associated with delivering content that may be perceived to belong to others (Hastie et al. 2006, p. 303). In practical terms, teachers can only do their best, and may choose take on the role of facilitator rather than provider of direct instruction, and children can draw on their own knowledge to create their *sāsā* inspired dances.

Sometimes doing our best brings out skills, knowledge and talents that we never knew we had, but it is not until we are pushed out of comfort zones that we recognise our own potential (C.Hansell, School Principal, personal communication 15/08/2014).

(b) How can *Palagi*, or teachers not knowledgeable about *sāsā*, find support?

Clearly, experts in teaching *sāsā* in authentic contexts are most likely to be Sāmoan, although there may be non-Sāmoan educators with knowledge and skills who could work collaboratively with others. Ideally, expertise may come from teaching staff or from the children in the school. However, caution should be taken to avoid making assumptions about expertise and/or willingness based purely on ethnicity.

We would never expect that just because a teacher is Sāmoan, that they would automatically take the 'sāsā. However, a Sāmoan teacher recently offered to work with the whole school to teach a sāsā. This raised the level of her status and mana in the school. (C. Hansell, School Principal, personal communication 15/08/2014)

Where expertise is not found on the staff, it is common practice to invite family and community members to share their expertise in teaching *sāsā* in collaboration with key teachers. While this is a positive and constructive way of involving community members in the school, this practice is generally reliant on goodwill, and there is a danger that expertise will be taken for granted. We argue that schools will willingly employ professionals to teach in specialist subject areas, and this same practice should also be a consideration for teachers of *sāsā*. These experts should also be regarded as specialists, and there should be consultation and awareness of partnerships in order to avoid cultural assumptions and frames of reference taking over. All parties involved have roles to play, including advocacy and facilitation to ensure that the experts are given the required level of support and respect.

(c) Should only children of Sāmoan descent learn *sāsā?*

While essentialist theorists of ethnic identity argue that cultural experiences such as *sāsā* are for Sāmoan only (Keddell 2006), others believe that this experience should be accessible to all children. MacPherson (1999) cautions, "categories based on descent will not necessarily reflect sociocultural realities" (p. 51). Cultural misunderstandings and assumptions often stem from the best of intentions, and some educators may feel that it is better to do nothing than to 'scratch the surface' and appear tokenistic and superficial. Contrived artistic selections can be "as insidious as not considering culture at all" (Abril 2013, p. 7). We consider that while these are valid points, it is important to bear in mind that this attitude may, in fact, be masking apathy, and there is a risk of producing teachers who "continue to present content and pedagogy that is either not relevant or contributes to sustaining the Western hegemony" (Hastie et al. 2006, p. 305). While there are substantial issues of hegemony that need to be dealt with at the macro level of Bronfenbrenner's (1979) ecological model, for some children, involvement with *sāsā* may be a rare opportunity to celebrate being Sāmoan, and for others, an opportunity to be part of a Sāmoan cultural activity at the micro level. The impact of this is evident in the reflections of two adult Sāmoan students who recall experiences with *sāsā* in their primary school years:

> *It felt good doing the sāsā. I knew how to do it. My peers would ask me to teach them, so I felt confident in this area. My aiga*[4] *could relate to this whole environment of being surrounded by Sāmoan people.* (P. A. Lautaki, personal communication, September 01, 2014).

> *Sāsā was our time to shine. While other students dominated in other areas, this was our time to shine.* (B. T. Tafa, personal communication, September 01, 2014).

Clearly, there are issues relating to the teaching of *sāsā* that need to be carefully considered and there is no one solution. As educators, we all have roles to play and we need to consider the options carefully. It is not about finding the easiest and most comfortable option, it is about choosing the option that best meets the needs and interests of the children we teach.

10 Conclusion

In our view, *sāsā* should be regarded as both educational and artistic. Educators need to find ways to demonstrate their support for artistic experiences that foster cultural values and take an active role in promoting structured activities that provide successful and valued ownership of learning for minority students. It is recognised that children achieve greater educational outcomes when they learn in a setting that embraces their language and culture, however challenging that might be (Carpenter et al. 2000). While *sāsā* supports many of the goals and objectives identified in our

---

[4] *Aiga* is the Sāmoan word for 'family'.

New Zealand curricula, Black (2000) reminds us of the need to include the living curricula on our doorsteps.

One of the challenges for us as educators, is that while we should continue to embrace diversity and endeavour to preserve traditions, we should also strive to achieve a balance between continuity and change. Despite adaptations that reflect the new environment of Aotearoa, we suggest the method of teaching *sāsā* is still very traditional. We believe it is time to take a fresh look at *sāsā* in terms of status and pedagogical approaches. How can the delivery of *sāsā* could be approached with a fresh perspective that retains cultural integrity while reflecting current educational developments? How can we use a more co-constructivist approach to the teaching and learning of *sāsā* and give our learners "voice and choice" in the learning process (Hastie, et al. 2006, p. 302)?

Educators need to think beyond curriculum and pedagogy and be cognisant of the "political under-pinnings of any multi-cultural content they teach" (Hastie et al. 2006, p. 305). While it is important for educators to find their own voice, they should also be aware that their voice is not necessarily that of the children they are teaching. Educators, as agents of change, are "on the front line" to be agents of change (Ashley 2012, p. 240). However, it would be naïve of us to think that including opportunities for Sāmoan children to be involved in *sāsā* is going to address all the complex issues of hegemony and hierarchy in education, and we should be cautious about merely 'ticking the cultural box'.

Historically, research that has considered the educational challenges of Sāmoan students has tended to focus on deficits (Carpenter et al. 2000). While more recent research points to the notion that culture counts – this in itself will not ensure change happens. We argue for a fresh approach – one that helps our community of practice to be inclusive of culture-specific experiences. There is clearly a need for further research in this area, to develop frameworks and programmes so that significant cultural activities such as the *sāsā* can be integrated into our learning spaces. In this way, schools and early childhood centres can draw on well-informed research to support the evaluation of their school-based curricula and look for ways to positively integrate the cultural knowledge of their families and communities.

References

Abril, C. R. (2013). Toward a more culturally responsive music classroom. *General Music Today, 27*(6), 6–11.

Abril, C. R., & Bannerman, J. K. (2015). Perceived factors impacting school music programs the teacher's perspective. *Journal of Research in Music Education, 62*(4), 344–361.

Ashley, L. (2012). Difference matters: The journey. In L. Ashley (Ed.), *Dancing with difference: Culturally diverse dances in education* (pp. 235–249). Rotterdam: Sense Publishers.

Ashley, L. (2014). Encountering challenges in teacher education: Developing culturally pluralist pedagogy when teaching dance from contextual perspectives in New Zealand. *Research in Dance Education, 15*(3), 1–17.

Bandura, A. (1977). Self-efficacy: Toward a unifying theory of behavioral change. *Psychological Review, 84*(2), 191–215.

Begg, A. (2006). What matters in the curriculum? *Curriculum Matters, 2*, 1–5.

Bourdieu, P. (2011). The forms of capital (1986). In I. Szeman & T. Kaposy (Eds.), *Cultural theory: An anthology* (pp. 81–93). Malden: Wiley-Blackwell.

Bronfenbrenner, U. (1979). *The ecology of human development: Experiments by nature and design.* Cambridge, MA: Harvard University Press.

Bronfenbrenner, U. (1994). Ecological models of human development. In T. Husen & T. N. Postlethwaite (Eds.), *The international encyclopedia of education* (pp. 37–43). Oxford: Pergamon.

Burton, J. M., Horowitz, R., & Abeles, H. (2000). Learning in and through the arts: The question of transfer. *Studies in Art Education, 41*(3), 228–257.

Carpenter, V., McMurchy-Pilkington, C., & Sutherland, S. (2000). "They don't look at me and say you're a palagi": Teaching across-habitus. *ACE Papers, 8*, 29–52.

Edwards, P. A., & Danridge, J. C. (2001). Developing collaboration with culturally diverse parents. In V. J. Risko & K. Bronley (Eds.), *Collaboration for diverse learners: Viewpoints and practices* (pp. 251–272). Newark: International Reading Association.

Gregory, E., Williams, A., Baker, D., & Street, B. (2004). Introducing literacy to four year olds: Creating classroom cultures in three schools. *Journal of Early Childhood Literacy, 4*(1), 85–107.

Hastie, P. A., Martin, E., & Buchanan, A. M. (2006). Stepping out of the norm: An examination of praxis for a culturally-relevant pedagogy for African-American children. *Journal of Curriculum Studies, 38*(3), 293–306.

Hoffman, D. M. (1996). Culture and self in multicultural education: Reflections on discourse, text, and practice. *American Educational Research Journal, 33*(3), 545–569.

Johnson, D. P. (2008). *Contemporary sociological theory: An integrated multi-level approach.* New York: Springer.

Jones, E. (2014). Dance literacy: An embodied phenomenon. In G. Barton (Ed.), *Literacy in the arts* (pp. 111–129). New York: Springer International Publishing.

Kaeppler, A. L. (1978). Dance in anthropological perspective. *Annual Review of Anthropology, 22*, 31–49.

Keddell, E. (2006). Pavlova and pineapple pie: Selected identity influences on Sāmoan-Pakeha people in Aotearoa/New Zealand. *Kōtuitui: New Zealand Journal of Social Sciences Online, 1*(1), 45–63.

Kornelly, S. (2008). *Dancing culture, culture dancing: Celebrating Pasifika in Aotearoa/New Zealand.* Doctoral dissertation, Temple University, Philadelphia, PA, USA. Retrieved from http://books.google.co.nz/books?hl=en&lr=&id=LU5V_QQ4Vb8C&oi=fnd&pg=PR4&dq=kornelly

Kruse-Va'ai, E. (1996). *House: A collection of poems.* Apia: Pacific Printers and Publishers.

Kwakwa, P. A. (2010). Dance in communal life. In R. M. Stone (Ed.), *The Garland handbook of African music* (pp. 54–62). New York: Routledge.

Leigh, F. S. (2010). *Choreographing empathy: Kinesthesia in performance.* London/New York: Routledge.

Levine, H. (2003). Some reflections on Samoan cultural practice and group identity in contemporary Wellington, New Zealand. *Journal of Intercultural Studies, 24*(2), 175–186.

Macpherson, C. (1999). Will the 'real' Sāmoans please stand up? Issues in diasporic Sāmoan identity. *New Zealand Geographer, 55*(2), 50–59.

Magro, K. (2014). Encouraging the artistry of teaching and learning: Working toward social justice and creativity for all. *International Journal for Talent Development and Creativity, 9.*

Ministry of Education. (1996). *Te Whāriki: He Whāriki Mātauranga mō ngā Mokopuna o Aotearoa, Early Childhood Curriculum.* Wellington: Ministry of Education.

Ministry of Education. (2007). *The New Zealand curriculum.* Wellington: Ministry of Education.

Mitchell, M. A. (2014). *Mission statement clarity and organizational behavior at an art-focused high school.* Doctoral dissertation, Walden University.

Paquette, K. R., & Rieg, S. A. (2008). Using music to support the literacy development of young English language learners. *Early Childhood Education Journal, 36*(3), 227–232.

Phillips, H., Cram, F., Sauni, P., & Tuagalu, C. (2014). Whaia I Te Maramatanga–seek knowledge. *Diversity in Higher Education, 15*, 1–19.

Radakovich, J. (2004). *Movement characteristics of three Sāmoan dance types: Ma'ulu'ulu, Sāsā And Taualuga.* Unpublished master's thesis for master's degree, University of Hawai'I, Hawai'i.

Rohan, T. J. (2011). *Teaching music, learning culture: The challenge of culturally responsive music education.* Unpublished doctoral dissertation, University of Otago, Dunedin, New Zealand.

Rubie, C. M., Townsend, M. A., & Moore, D. W. (2004). Motivational and academic effects of cultural experiences for indigenous minority students in New Zealand. *Educational Psychology, 24*(2), 143–160.

Sansom, A. (2008). The interrelationship between dance and the young child. In P. Smith (Ed.), *The arts in education: Critical perspectives from teacher educators* (pp. 25–39). Auckland: The University of Auckland.

Sansom, A. (2009). Mindful pedagogy in dance: Honoring the life of the child. *Research in Dance Education, 10*(3), 161–176.

Sauni, P. (2014). My sixth sense tells me…. Māori and Pasifika higher education horizons. *Diversity in Higher Education, 15*, 135–146. http://dx.doi.org/10.1108/S1479-3644_2014_0000015025.

Scheurich, J. J. (1998). Highly successful and loving, public elementary schools populated mainly by low-ses children of color core beliefs and cultural characteristics. *Urban Education, 33*(4), 451–491.

Singley, M. K. (1989). *The transfer of cognitive skill* (No. 9). Boston: Harvard University Press.

Tamasese, K., Peteru, C., Waldegrave, C., & Bush, A. (2005). Ole Taeao Afua, the new morning: A qualitative investigation into Sāmoan perspectives on mental health and culturally appropriate services. *Australian and New Zealand Journal of Psychiatry, 39*(4), 300–309.

Taouma, A. (2014). Pacific dance in Aotearoa: A tale of the last 20 years. *DANZ Quarterly: New Zealand Dance, 34*, 30–31.

Trinick, R. M., Sauni, L., & Allen, E. (2010). Waiata, Pese, Song: A synthesis of cultural perspectives on the value of song for language learning. In C. A. Shonerigun & G. A. Akmayeva (Eds.), *Society, London international conference on education 2010 proceedings September 6–8, 2010* (pp. 129–133). London: Infonomics Society.

Valdez, M. F., Dowrick, P. W., & Maynard, A. E. (2007). Cultural misperceptions and goals for Sāmoan children's education in Hawai'i: Voices from school, home, and community. *The Urban Review, 39*(1), 67–92.

Vincent, C., & Martin, J. (2002). Class, culture and agency: Researching parental voice. *Discourse, 23*(1), 108–127.

Wiggins, J. (2004, Spring). Letting go—Moving forward. *Mountain Lake Reader, 3*, 81–91.

Zimmerman, B. J. (2000). Self-efficacy: An essential motive to learn. *Contemporary Educational Psychology, 25*(1), 82–91.

Robyn Trinick began her career in education as a generalist primary teacher, working mainly in South Auckland primary schools. She came to the Auckland College of Education as a lecturer in primary music education in 1989 and is currently employed as a lecturer in music education. Robyn has published several journal articles, presenting at local and international conferences, and is currently carrying out a second research project relating to Sistema Aotearoa, an orchestral programme operating in South Auckland.

Luama Sauni has been a senior lecturer in the Bachelor of Education (Pasifika specialisation) programme at the Faculty of Education, University of Auckland for the past 17 years. She is currently working as an independent consultant and is involved with New Zealand Ministry of Education contracts that offer professional development for Pasifika teachers and parents in Pasifika early childhood education services in the Waikato, Wellington and Auckland regions. Her research interests and publications have focused on research methodology from a Pasifika perspective, Pasifika males in early childhood education and the enhancement of literacy and numeracy for Pasifika students through an integrated model using music, song, drama and dance.

"Pride and Honour": Indigenous Dance in New South Wales Schools

Katie Wilson

Abstract In this chapter, I discuss the positioning of Indigenous dance performance in Australian school education where European knowledges and beliefs dominate educational policies and practices. The discussion about the role and the integration of indigenous dance within curriculum takes place in the context of research with Aboriginal and Torres Strait Islander students in schools in a regional area of the state of New South Wales. More than two centuries after colonisation, dispossession and attempted deculturation of Aboriginal and Torres Strait Islander peoples, the positive value of cultural learning and practices in education is acknowledged in policy and included in curricula as a means of engaging Indigenous students with dominant education. However, while schools welcome and acknowledge the significance of Indigenous students' participation in dance performance, this activity and related acquisition of skills and knowledges by dancing students are not accredited academically.

Keywords Aboriginal and Torres Strait Islander students • School education • Indigenous dance • Curriculum

1 Introduction

In this chapter, I discuss the performance of Indigenous dance for Aboriginal and Torres Strait Islander (the Indigenous peoples of Australia) school students in educational contexts in New South Wales (NSW), Australia. My observations emerged from doctoral research in which Aboriginal and Torres Strait Islander students shared their experiences of cultural learning in schools. Although I am not a dance educator, the positioning of Indigenous dance in some school discussions illustrates the difficulties of achieving an inclusive, culturally responsive curriculum where the cultural knowledges, skills and intangible heritage of non-dominant, indigenous

K. Wilson (✉)
Victoria University of Wellington, PO Box 3438, Wellington 6140, New Zealand
e-mail: katie.wilson@vuw.ac.nz; http://works.bepress.com/katie_wilson

© Springer International Publishing Switzerland 2016
L. Ashley, D. Lines (eds.), *Intersecting Cultures in Music and Dance Education*, Landscapes: the Arts, Aesthetics, and Education 19,
DOI 10.1007/978-3-319-28989-2_5

peoples are recognised and integrated equally with dominant practices and knowledges.

I consider the role of indigenous dance performance in colonised societies such as Australia within Indigenous peoples' cultural learning, education and the place of Indigenous dance in contemporary society. Through the perspectives of some Aboriginal students and staff in three schools, I discuss the positioning of Indigenous dance at the intersection of cultures within the NSW educational curriculum.

A note about terminology: The term indigenous refers to broad discussions of indigenous issues; Aboriginal and Torres Strait Islanders and Indigenous are used in the Australian context; Aboriginal is used when discussing New South Wales education policy as specified in policy documents, and as preferred by the NSW Aboriginal Education Consultative Group.

2 Background

I was born in Aotearoa/New Zealand from Māori (Te Ātiawa, Taranaki) and Pākehā (non-Māori) ancestry, and I have lived the latter half of my life in Australia. Recently, I undertook doctoral research with Aboriginal and Torres Strait Islander students in the state of New South Wales regarding their cultural learning in schools. I held discussions with primary and secondary students, and interviewed principals, Aboriginal support staff, and teachers in six schools within the land of the Gumbaynggirr nation in the mid-north coast of NSW. From discussions with students and some staff in three schools, questions emerged about the educational role and positioning of Indigenous dance within a curriculum where Aboriginal and Torres Strait Islander cultures and the dominant Euro-Western culture intersect.

Aboriginal Australians are the First Nations peoples of the land colonised by the British in 1788, later federated as Australia in 1901. Aboriginal peoples, a generic term that describes many nations of peoples, identify by land and language and live in all Australian states and territories. Torres Strait Islanders are the original inhabitants of the Torres Strait Islands north of Australia, annexed by the British colony of Queensland in 1879 (Torres Strait Island Regional Council 2014), later becoming part of a federated Australia. Aboriginal and Torres Strait Islander peoples comprise the Indigenous populations of Australia. Through colonisation, Aboriginal and Torres Strait Islander communities were displaced and dispossessed of their lands. Deliberate policies of assimilation in the twentieth century disrupted education and knowledge learning customs, and separated many Aboriginal and Torres Strait Islander children from their families and cultures, forcing them into British lifestyles, foster families and institutions. The thousands of people affected by this practice are known as the Stolen Generations (Human Rights and Equal Opportunity Commission 1997). Further, inequitable policies and practices denied the rights of Aboriginal and Torres Strait Islander peoples to access and participate in a full education and to learn and practice their languages, cultures and knowledges. The exclusion of Aboriginal and Torres

Strait Islander peoples and histories from Australian education curricula and text books until the 1980s (Reynolds 2000), together with assumptions of cultural superiority and prejudice, has contributed to ignorance and misunderstanding within the dominant, non-Indigenous Australian population.

The recovery of dance and performance among indigenous peoples living in colonised nations, along with visual and performing arts, is part of an ongoing assertion of indigenous rights to history, language and culture. In societies where indigenous peoples have been subjected to colonising practices, such as Africa, Aotearoa, Australia, Canada, the Caribbean and the United States, performance of indigenous dance was forbidden through the oppression of people's ways of life, languages and cultures. Cultural dance, integral to heritages, communicated and "embodied knowledge" (Cruz Banks 2009, p. 360), and the denial of dance performances was instrumental in the subjugation of indigenous knowledges and cultures. Within Aboriginal and Torres Strait Islander communities, dance functions as ceremony and as entertainment. Dance performances embodying deep knowledge and skill have continued as an integral part of practised culture and custom in some communities, particularly in northern Australia and the Torres Strait Islands. In other areas, as a result of the assimilative and forced movement practices discussed above, Aboriginal and Torres Strait Islander peoples' regular connection with cultural dance has lessened. However, contemporary Indigenous dance performance is flourishing, drawing on "historical practices" (Casey 2011, p. 54) as well as creating new dance that incorporates histories, political and social issues of concern to Indigenous peoples, and landscape.

The praxis and critical pedagogy of dance in education is recognised as a powerful embodiment of identity and healing that contributes to indigenous students' critical understanding of their worlds (Cruz Banks 2009), as well as to the knowledge of non-indigenous students (Mackinlay 2005). The recently introduced national *Australian Curriculum* recognised the "deep knowledge traditions and holistic world view" of Aboriginal and Torres Strait Islander communities (Australian Curriculum Assessment and Reporting Authority (ACARA) n.d.), and designated Aboriginal and Torres Strait Islander histories and cultures as one of three cross-curriculum priorities. Dance is one of five elective subjects in the Arts Curriculum (Australian Curriculum Assessment and Reporting Authority 2013). Throughout the curriculum and the Arts syllabus, Aboriginal and Torres Strait Islander perspectives and cultures intersect with the predominant Euro-Western culture as an optional cross-curriculum priority. As a guideline only, the Arts Curriculum refers to developing all students' understandings of Aboriginal and Torres Strait Islander cultural arts protocols and practices, but the extent of the inclusion of such cultural learning is a choice made by individual schools and teachers. However, this position is threatened. A recent government commissioned review of the *Australian Curriculum* criticised the place of the Aboriginal and Torres Strait Islander perspectives cross-curriculum priority (Wiltshire and Donnelly 2014). An arts specialist commented that there was "too much emphasis on dance from Aboriginal and Torres Strait Islander culture" and recommended the expansion of "Asian and European…cultural references" (p. 217).

By comparison, in Aotearoa, the role of Māori dance performance and movement is acknowledged and integrated within the secondary curriculum. *Kapa haka* (dance in rows) is recognised as a culturally responsive school pedagogy and dance activity that is accredited academically, as a subject contributing credits towards the National Certificate of Educational Achievement and towards a National Certificate in Māori (Whitinui 2010a). The inclusion of *te ao kori* (expressive movement) as a Māori dimension in school physical education curriculum since 1987 contributes to the strengthening of identity and self-esteem of Māori students and non-Māori students through the embodiment of Māori culture (Legge 2011).

3 Indigenous Dance in Australia

Among Aboriginal and Torres Strait Islander peoples, dance has ceremonial purposes, communicating knowledge about spirituality, heritage and culture, connecting with land, place and customary practices through stories. As a result of forcible movement and disruption of the lives and customs of many communities, the practice of dance as ceremony was interrupted. Within some Aboriginal and Torres Strait Islander communities, however, historical dance (following Casey (2011, p. 66), I use the term 'historical' rather than 'traditional' because of assumptions that 'traditional' refers to an unchanging culture) has continued to be performed, for example, in the Yolngu nation North-east Arnhem Land in northern Australia (Burarrwanga et al. 2013). The public performance of Indigenous dance re-emerged in the 1980s as part of a "cultural renaissance in Indigenous arts and culture" (Miller 2005). Aboriginal and Torres Strait Islander peoples teach, dance and perform with young people and school groups at local events, arts and cultural festivals throughout Australia. Some contemporary Indigenous dance groups combine culture, music and stories with dance moves and expressions, collaborating with Elders and artists from different nations.

Indigenous dance companies with international profiles include the Bangarra Dance Theatre based in Sydney, NSW, formed in 1990, and Marrugeku, based in Broome, in north Western Australia, formed in 1994. Bangarra distinguishes between "contemporary (dance) that is newly created, using original movement" and "traditional (in dance) … dances that are handed down from one generation to the next, transferring story, cultural life and cultural practices" (Bangarra Dance Theatre 2014). For example, in *Terrain*, a dance referencing Lake Eyre, an inland sea, Bangarra (2014) weaves embodiments of country into contemporary choreography, exploring the strong connections between Aboriginal peoples and the land, including land rights. In *Patyegarang*, dancers tell the story of a young woman from the Eora nation who shared her knowledge and culture with an eighteenth century colonial Lieutenant, as recorded in his diaries.

The powerful role of Indigenous historical and contemporary dance in contributing to the well-being, cultural knowledge and educational engagement of Indigenous students within school education in Australia is recognised in the literature.

Incorporating Aboriginal cultural heritage, including a dance group, in a NSW primary school helped to reduce suspensions and absenteeism among Aboriginal students (Britton 2000). Jampijinpa (2008) related with passion the power of *Milpirri*, a dance performance developed in an Aboriginal community in *Warlpiri* country in northern Australia: how it reconnected young people with Elders and their culture and contributed to increased school attendance. A "rap curriculum" for young *Nunga* (Aboriginal) young men in South Australia provided the potential to perform identity and agency in a contested school education environment through critical thinking (Blanch 2009, p. 125). Thorpe (2011) explored the development of the *Watbalimba Dance Group* and a holistic method of teaching and learning culture through the language of song, story and dance as a means of embedding local Aboriginal cultural knowledge within education systems. Wannik Dance Academies for Koorie girls in three schools in the state of Victoria are a government dance programme "aligned to the regular school curriculum" (Victoria Department of Education and Early Childhood Development 2013). Aboriginal dance can be a powerful tool in teaching mathematics with Aboriginal school students (Matthews 2012). Bangarra Dance Theatre offers *Rekindling* (2014), an education workshop programme for secondary school students from regional New South Wales to research stories within their communities and develop performances. Through the NSW Department of Education and Communities, Bangarra Dance Theatre provides opportunities for secondary students to learn and perform contemporary Aboriginal dance in Aboriginal Dance Workshops, from which a small number of students is selected to join the NSW Public Schools Aboriginal Dance Company (NSW Department of Education and Communities 2014).

4 About the Research

In 2012 and 2013, I undertook doctoral qualitative research with Aboriginal and Torres Strait Islander students in six schools within the land of the Gumbaynggirr nation in the mid-north coast region of New South Wales. Through the research, Aboriginal and Torres Strait Islander students shared their experiences of learning cultural knowledges and perspectives through the curriculum, cultural events and activities held at the schools.

Respecting indigenous ethical requirements, I co-constructed the research with the local Aboriginal Educational Consultative Group (AECG), the key representative body in New South Wales, and divided the research into two phases, obtaining a separate ethics approval for each phase. Phase one was a feasibility study, where I discussed with the AECG the proposal for research with Aboriginal and Torres Strait Islander students. The AECG recommended schools, appropriate protocols and required the presence of an AECG member at each discussion group. In phase two, I employed a research methodology of group discussions with open-ended questioning (approved by the AECG) to engage in conversation with students in three primary schools and three secondary schools about their cultural learning experiences.

Thirty-nine students from Year 3 to Years 11/12 who identified as Aboriginal (38 students) and Torres Strait Islander (one student) participated in two discussion groups at each of the six schools: 26 girls (10 in three primary schools; 16 in three secondary schools) and 13 boys (6 in three primary schools; 7 in three secondary schools). Principals, Aboriginal staff and Aboriginal education co-ordinators invited the students to participate, and obtained consent for their participation from parents or caregivers and the students. I interviewed each school principal, teachers of Indigenous perspectives, and "yarned" with Aboriginal support staff about cultural learning and activities in their schools. Yarning is an indigenous methodology in which the participants and the researcher negotiate and build relationships of trust and share information (Dean 2010).

The location in which the research took place is regional, coastal and semi-urban. Through the nineteenth and twentieth century colonial government policies and practices marginalised access to land, ways of living, language and cultural practices for the people of the Gumbaynggirr nation (Somerville and Perkins 2010; Thomas 2013). Many were forced to live on reserves or church-operated missions (Arrawarra Sharing Culture n.d.). Some communities, however, maintained connections with the land, living in coastal camps, leading later to successful land rights claims (Smith and Beck 2003). Speaking language and practising culture was prohibited in schools and local knowledge and history were ignored. However, in the last two decades the establishment of a Gumbaynggirr cultural centre and a language and culture co-operative has revitalised the language and connections with culture, including dance (Muurrbay Aboriginal Language and Culture Co-operative 2008; Somerville and Perkins 2010).

In the 2011 Census (Australian Bureau of Statistics 2011), 3.2 % of the population counted in the region was Aboriginal and Torres Strait Islander. The schools participating in the research varied in population, size and their connections to culture. Aboriginal and Torres Strait Islander populations ranged from 4.9 % (five students) in one primary school to 13 % in one secondary school. Discussions with Indigenous students focused on the subject areas in which they learn Aboriginal and Torres Strait Islander perspectives and knowledges; the extent and delivery of the content; their thoughts about such learning; the cultural activities and events they participate in at school; and the involvement of local community Elders in their learning. I recorded and transcribed discussions for analysis and review with students and staff. From these discussions, Indigenous dance emerged as a significant and meaningful experience for some students. I discuss next the perspectives of these students and staff regarding Aboriginal dance emerging from the research.

5 "Aboriginal Dancin'": Student and Staff Perspectives

The New South Wales school curriculum recommends all students have opportunities to experience and appreciate Aboriginal and Torres Strait Islander historical and contemporary dance as "integral to the expression of Aboriginal cultural identity"

(Board of Studies New South Wales 2009, p. 5). For example, Creative Arts K-6 lessons include students dancing to contemporary Aboriginal music, and incorporating historical dance moves. However, such content is optional and inclusion depends on individual schools' leadership, staffing, resources, skills and connections with local communities. The learning and performance of Aboriginal and Torres Strait Islander dance discussed by students in this research is not positioned as a discrete subject, although dance was an elective for some secondary students. The student dance performances and activities were extra-curricular, a "cultural 'add-on'" (Whitinui 2010b, p. 20). Although the schools acknowledged the positive value of dance for the Aboriginal students in terms of leadership and cultural connections (Myers 2007), dance performances did not translate directly to academic credits in the educational system.

Aboriginal students active in dance performances discussed opportunities to perform, connect and engage with their culture. Students at one primary school discussed dance activity when celebrating NAIDOC (National Aboriginal and Islander Day Observance Committee) with the local community, demonstrating their active involvement with dance through the cultural centre:

> ...NAIDOC week down at [the local cultural centre] (Year 4 girl)
> ...and down there we like make food and stuff and dance, do the Aboriginal dancin'... (Year 6 boy).
> Yeah, animal dancing...kangaroo...emu (All)
> ...in NAIDOC week with [Aboriginal staff member] we ... went around in circles, stomping our feet, Aboriginal dancing... and he said you can see inside like a snake (Year 6 boy).

The students engaged enthusiastically in discussions about participating in these dance activities within the cultural event celebrating NAIDOC. For students in other primary schools, there was less dance activity. I invited students to draw and/or write about their cultural learning and their desires, and one student wrote that she would like to learn *"Aboriginal dance moves"* (Year 6 girl), suggesting a lack of opportunity at school. The school principal commented on the difficulty of teaching and obtaining funding for cultural knowledge and activities:

> ...it'd be nice if we had more Indigenous teachers or Elders or people with knowledge who'd be happy to come to our public schools for free... I don't think we should be paying for it. I have a moral issue with us having to pay to educate the whole community of Indigenous culture. (Primary Principal)

In one secondary school, a student discussed her experiences learning dance at primary school:

> Before I came here my old school used to like have Aboriginal people come in and teach us all the dances. I did that for about three years ...but they don't do it anymore. I wish they still did it ... (Year 7 girl).

In two secondary schools, students discussed their engagement with learning and performing dance. An Aboriginal boys' dance programme in one school began as a project initiated by the Aboriginal staff member and became highly successful through the dedication and commitment of the staff, students and with support from the school. Dance performance as part of ceremony was less common in the area, as one student commented (see below.) The school's Aboriginal Education Officer became aware of the positive value of connecting with culture for the Aboriginal students' well-being and engagement with learning. He related how he drew on his own experiences to introduce the dance programme for Aboriginal students in schools. He had learned to play *didjeridu* (the Aboriginal musical instrument also known as a *yidaki*), taught a friend to play, and together they developed Aboriginal dance to be accompanied by *didjeridu*. Building on their knowledge of historical dances that imitate and incorporate animal moves, they used "ochre…to decorate bodies…went into the bush to observe animals…", and recreated dances based on the observed animal behaviour. Through this process and recreating the dance the staff member connected with his culture and heritage, and recognised the power of this connection. He introduced the programme in two secondary schools for Aboriginal students, and commented that they engaged and connected strongly with learning and performing the dance, more than any departmental programme or activity. This reflects the potential of cultural dance to enable students to develop critical understanding of the worlds they live in (Cruz Banks 2009).

The Aboriginal boys in the secondary school discussed the meaning for them of participating in dance performances:

> *It's been 20 years since anything like this has happened… in Gumbaynggirr country…we thought just to bring pride and honour back into our community* (Year 11/12 boy).
>
> *…a couple of the boys got asked to go and do the dancing, that's how it all started. And we just started getting noticed from other people you know, every now and then we get a phone call or an email asking us to go and dance and perform for them …which is pretty good* (Year 11/12 boy).
>
> *…there's about 15 of us… from* [year] *7 or 8* (Year 11/12 boy).
>
> *I really hope that we keep going… (*Year 8 boy).

The Aboriginal boys' dance group is invited to perform at many events in the area. The school sought additional funding to continue the programme, and brought students from nearby primary schools to participate. The school principal spoke of the value of the boys' dance programme in engaging the students and in developing leadership skills, but acknowledged that performances took some time from study, especially the Year 12 students:

> *…something that we are really proud of. Sometimes it's an administrative nightmare because the Year 12 boys complain that they're out of class too often and I understand that completely… but it's still worthwhile… maybe when the boys or girls get into Year 12 we sort of say it's time to concentrate on your studies. I do think the Year 12 boys miss too much class…but it was good for them in terms of leadership so that was the payback.*

From the principal's perspective, the intensive dance engagement was meaningful for the school and the students' skills development. Yet the principal's comment regarding the dance performance conflicting with Year 12 class study suggests a lack of a model to incorporate the dance as valid study within the curriculum structure.

At the same school, a Year 7 girl wrote "girl dancing" in her 'wish list' developed in the discussion group, suggesting girls are also interested in learning

Aboriginal dance following the success of the boys' group, and the boys' responses. At a third secondary school, female students spoke of their participation in workshops with the Bangarra Dance Theatre, and performance with the Aboriginal Dance Ensemble at the annual NSW Schools Spectacular:

> ...we had an audition to get in and we got in, there were 4 of us... someone from Bangarra dance studio was there ...There was exactly 300 indigenous students dancing into one dance, from Sydney to Dubbo and the north coast... We had to have our hair slicked back... and have white paint...in our hair...and down our body across our chest and across our back (Year 11/12 girl).

Some students take dance electives within class study, but although the dance performance was acknowledged proudly as a major achievement in the school and community, the performance was not accredited towards study.

The students' comments indicate the value for them of Aboriginal dance and cultural performance, of pride and cultural connection, and their participation involves a substantial time commitment. Benefits of dance performance are affirmed in research literature. Aboriginal students' dance includes skill-learning "not only in telling about ontology and epistemology, they physically become one with ontology and epistemology" (Williams 2007, p. 227). In the same way, Aboriginal people express a powerful and intangible sense of belonging and well-being when they reconnect with language and culture (*Aboriginal women's heritage: Nambucca* 2003; Somerville and Perkins 2010) and when they maintain living with cultural ways (Burarrwanga et al. 2013). However, for the NSW schools discussed in this chapter, dance performance was extra-curricular and without academic accreditation. While there was some recognition of the contribution to student cultural well-being, critical understanding and overall learning, a lack of cultural measures or standards for evaluating the contributions to Indigenous students' education through dance performance (Whitinui 2010a) limits the formalisation of the educational and academic values of Indigenous dance performance. At the intersection of cultures in education, the "cultural interface" (Nakata 2011), integrating Indigenous dance into curriculum remains a challenge in Australia, and other colonised countries. Despite the accreditation of *kapa haka* in secondary education in Aotearoa, Whitinui (2010a) noted the difficulty of moving Māori dance beyond the periphery in some mainstream schools.

6 Conclusion

In this chapter, I have discussed Aboriginal students' expressions of engagement, pride and connection with their cultural heritage in response to their participation in Aboriginal dance programmes within three NSW schools. While the value of such participation is acknowledged and celebrated in the schools, academic recognition of extended or ongoing Indigenous cultural dance performance is limited. The current Australian government's challenge to the place of Aboriginal and Torres Strait Islander dance within the optional cross-curriculum perspective in the national *Australian Curriculum* complicates the position for schools and staff.

Intersecting with a dominant culture, and against a history of multigenerational systemic and structural opposition towards Aboriginal and Torres Strait Islander knowledges and languages, the equitable inclusion of Indigenous cultural learning, including dance, in mainstream education in Australia continues to be a challenge for Aboriginal and Torres Strait Islander communities and students, teachers and school principals. Because of its perceived ideological basis, the inclusion of Indigenous perspectives and practices is contested still by some teachers (Nakata 2011) and politicians. While the personal development gains for all students of dance programmes are acknowledged through curriculum, the recognition of the educational skills, pedagogies of learning, movement, performance, and contributions to "cultural and social wellbeing" (Whitinui 2010a, p. 3) of Indigenous dance would contribute towards achieving equality within a curriculum that claims to be Australian.

References

Aboriginal women's heritage: Nambucca. (2003). Retrieved from http://www.environment.nsw. gov.au/nswcultureheritage/AboriginalWomensHeritageInNambucca.htm

Arrawarra Sharing Culture. (n.d.). *Fact Sheet 1: Gumbaynggirr nation.* Retrieved from http:// www.arrawarraculture.com.au/fact_sheets/pdfs/01_Gumbaynggir_Nation.pdf

Australian Bureau of Statistics. (2011). *Census Quick Stats 2011: Coffs Harbour statistical area level 3.* Retrieved from http://www.censusdata.abs.gov.au

Australian Curriculum Assessment and Reporting Authority (ACARA). (n.d.). *The Australian Curriculum v. 3 Aboriginal and Torres Strait Islander histories and cultures.* Retrieved from http://www.australiancurriculum.edu.au/CrossCurriculumPriorities/Aboriginal-and-Torres-Strait-Islander-histories-and-cultures

Australian Curriculum Assessment and Reporting Authority (ACARA). (2013). *The arts.* Retrieved from http://www.acara.edu.au/arts.html

Bangarra Dance Theatre. (2014). *Bangarra dance theatre.* Retrieved from http://www.bangarra. com.au

Blanch, F. R. (2009). *Nunga rappin: Talkin the talk, walkin the walk: Young Nunga males and education.* Unpublished master's thesis, Flinders University, Adelaide, Australia.

Board of Studies New South Wales. (2009). *Cross-Curriculum content: Mapping of Aboriginal and Indigenous cross-curriculum content in mandatory K-10 Syllabus*: Board of Studies New South Wales. Retrieved from http://ab-ed.boardofstudies.nsw.edu.au/go/7-10/cross-curriculum-content/

Britton, P. (2000). *Improving the self-concept of Aboriginal students: A holistic approach.* Paper presented at the Aboriginal Studies Association 10th annual conference, University of Western Sydney.

Burarrwanga, L., Ganambarr, R., Ganambarr-Stubbs, M., Ganambarr, B., Maymuru, D., Wright, S., & Lloyd, K. (2013). *Welcome to my country.* Crows Nest: Allen & Unwin.

Casey, M. (2011). Performing for Aboriginal life and culture: 'Aboriginal theatre and Ngurrumilmarrmiriyu'. *Australasian Drama Studies, 59*, 53–68.

Cruz Banks, O. (2009). Critical postcolonial dance recovery and pedagogy: An international literature review. *Pedagogy, Culture & Society, 17*(3), 355–367. doi:10.1080/14681360903194368.

Dean, C. (2010). A yarning place in narrative histories. *History of Education Review, 39*(2), 6–13. doi:http://dx.doi.org/10.1108/08198691201000005.

Human Rights and Equal Opportunity Commission. (1997). *Bringing them home: Report of the national inquiry into the separation of Aboriginal and Torres Strait Islander children from their families.* Sydney: Human Rights and Equal Opportunity Commission.

Jampijinpa, P. S. (2008). Milpirri: Performance as a bridge that joins the ancient with the modern. *Ngoonjook, 33*, 53–60.

Legge, M. (2011). Te ao kori as expressive movement in Aotearoa New Zealand physical education teacher education (PETE): A narrative account. *Asia-Pacific Journal of Health, Sport and Physical Education, 2*(3), 81–95.

Mackinlay, E. (2005). Moving and dancing towards decolonisation in education: An example from an indigenous Australian performance classroom. *Australian Journal of Indigenous Education, 34*, 113–122.

Matthews, C. (2012). *Maths as storytelling: Maths is beautiful.* Port Melbourne: Cambridge University Press.

Miller, L. (2005). Creating pathways: An indigenous dance forum report. *Dance Forum, 15*(4), 12–13.

Muurrbay Aboriginal Language and Culture Co-operative. (2008). *Gumbaynggirr language revitalisation.* Retrieved from http://www.muurrbay.org.au/languages/gumbaynggirr/

Myers, T. (2007). Raising the bar: The Aboriginal education priority. *Teacher: The National Education Magazine,* Nov, 54–56.

Nakata, M. (2011). Pathways for indigenous education in the Australian curriculum framework. *The Australian Journal of Indigenous Education, 40*, 1–8. doi:10.1375/ajie.40.1.

NSW Department of Education and Communities. (2014). *Aboriginal dance workshops.* Retrieved from http://www.artsunit.nsw.edu.au/events-initiatives/aboriginal-dance-workshops

Reynolds, H. (2000). *Why weren't we told?: A personal search for the truth about our history.* Ringwood: Viking.

Smith, A., & Beck, W. (2003). The archaeology of no man's land: Indigenous camps at Corindi Beach, mid-north coast New South Wales. *Archaeology in Oceania, 38*(2), 66–77.

Somerville, M., & Perkins, T. (2010). *Singing the coast.* Canberra: Aboriginal Studies Press.

Thomas, L. (2013). *Aboriginal history of the Coffs Harbour region.* Retrieved from http://libraries.coffsharbour.nsw.gov.au/Local-Heritage/collection/Pages/Aboriginal-history-of-the-Coffs--Harbour-region.aspx

Thorpe, W. (2011). *Watbalimba: Language of song, story and dance.* Unpublished MEd thesis, Monash University.

Torres Strait Island Regional Council. (2014). *Torres Strait Island history.* Retrieved from http://www.tsirc.qld.gov.au/our-region/torres-strait/history

Victoria Department of Education and Early Childhood Development. (2013). *Wannik dance academies for Koorie girls.* Retrieved from http://www.education.vic.gov.au/about/programs/aboriginal/pages/wannikdance.aspx

Whitinui, P. (2010a). Indigenous-based inclusive pedagogy: The art of Kapa Haka to improve educational outcomes for Maori students in mainstream secondary schools in Aotearoa, New Zealand. *International Journal of Pedagogies & Learning, 6*(1), 3–22.

Whitinui, P. (2010b). Kapa haka 'voices': Exploring the educational benefits of a culturally responsive learning environment in four New Zealand mainstream secondary schools. *Learning Communities, 1*, 19–43.

Williams, S. T. (2007). *Indigenous values informing curriculum and pedagogical praxis.* Unpublished PhD thesis, Deakin University, Melbourne.

Wiltshire, K., & Donnelly, K. (2014). *Review of the Australian Curriculum: Final report.* Retrieved from http://www.studentsfirst.gov.au/strengthening-australian-curriculum

Katie Wilson PhD (SCU), GradDipVisArts (UNSW), GradDipLib (Canberra), BA (VUW). Katie's PhD explored the experiences of Aboriginal and Torres Strait Islander students in relation to Indigenous knowledges and perspectives in schools. Her research interests focus on children and young people in schooling; higher education; collaborative and indigenous research methodologies; and indigenous education policy and curriculum. Katie was born in Wellington, Aotearoa/New Zealand and is a descendent of the Te Atiawa people of Taranaki.

Part II
Culturally Responsive Pedagogies

The chapters in this section provide a range of voices, contexts and approaches to how music and dance education can be developed along lines that are culturally responsive to both learners and their wider communities. The chapters, however, also share some similarities either in their worldviews or their ideas on pedagogical development. Drawing on the voices of teachers, for readers with an interest in primary education, Liz Melchior and Linda Locke, splice together Māori and Western social and critical pedagogical models to shape learning within the context of a bicultural agenda, as appropriate for *The New Zealand Curriculum*. Based in university studies, Te Oti Rakena investigates similar notions of how indigenous Māori and Pacific values may be accounted for in a Western colonial pedagogical model. His research presents welcome student narratives and considers how culturally safe learning may be developed. The historical overview of Oceania that he provides could be helpful for international readers.

For readers who may be interested in intersections between the pedagogy of dance teaching within cultural communities and formal educational contexts, the chapters by Jane Freeman-Moulin and Janinka Greenwood make for some stimulating debate about how teaching approaches shift according to different indigenous values and identities. In both chapters, one set in Tahiti and the other New Zealand, reflective personal narratives illustrate how the transmission of cultural knowledge, as embodied in dance and music, can be risky, difficult, and vulnerable to socioeconomic and educational forces. The authors are sensitive to a range of issues including how the values and traditions of indigenous dance teachers, artists and communities can be overlooked, and how their dances can be commodified and possibly lost.

In an overview of educational complexities resulting from intersecting cultures in which current praxis of Western dance education is critically questioned, Linda Ashley's chapter makes visible many of the underpinning ideologies with which the authors in this section, and educators internationally, are wrestling. Emphasising the need for further research and radical change in the educational provision of Oceanic indigenous dances and dancer-teachers, she provides a view of culturally responsive pedagogy that shifts beyond an intercultural variation of Western pedagogy or fusion dance to problematising how diverse cultures can be included equitably in dance education in ways that foreground and respect the indigenous owners of dances.

Making Connections: Culturally Responsive Pedagogy and Dance in the Classroom

Liz Melchior

Abstract Bi-cultural perspectives and the development of culturally responsive pedagogy are increasingly acknowledged in teaching and teacher education in Aotearoa/New Zealand. In a culturally responsive classroom, effective teaching and learning occur within meaningful contexts where students' contributions are voiced and valued. This chapter explores ways that models and strategies for culturally responsive pedagogy apply to teaching and learning dance in the primary classroom. A brief overview of culturally responsive pedagogy from a Māori worldview provides a framework for the discussion. Observations and stories from classroom teachers and their students demonstrate how collaborative processes that involve critical thinking, teaching from existing strengths, and valuing students' prior knowledge and experience, develop increased connectedness between teachers and their students, students and each other, and students and dance.

Keywords Dance • Education • Culturally responsive • Pedagogy • Learning • Classroom • Culture • Curriculum • Connections

1 Introduction

Teachers in New Zealand primary schools are responsible for implementing the dance curriculum in the classroom and what they do has the potential to impact profoundly on the children they teach (Buck 2003). As a dance educator in initial teacher education, with a background in primary teaching, I believe that dance can play a vital role in developing connectedness in a culturally responsive classroom.

Bi-cultural perspectives and the development of culturally responsive pedagogies are increasingly acknowledged and valued in teaching and teacher education in Aotearoa New Zealand. Government initiatives and educational research focussing

L. Melchior (✉)
School of Education, Te Puna Akopai, Faculty of Education,
Victoria University of Wellington, PO Box 600, 6140 Wellington, New Zealand
e-mail: Liz.melchior@vuw.ac.nz

© Springer International Publishing Switzerland 2016
L. Ashley, D. Lines (eds.), *Intersecting Cultures in Music and Dance Education*, Landscapes: the Arts, Aesthetics, and Education 19,
DOI 10.1007/978-3-319-28989-2_6

on ways of improving educational outcomes for Māori students (Bishop et al. 2007; Ministry of Education 2013–2017), highlight the importance of the teacher's role in creating a culturally responsive environment for learning (Hynds et al. 2011; MacFarlane et al. 2007; Bishop and Berryman 2006). For this to happen, teachers need to be aware of and understand their personal biases, their own cultures, and more importantly, the biases and cultures of their students (Baskerville 2009). However, responding to the diverse needs and interests of students whose cultural and language backgrounds differ from their own can be challenging for teachers (Hynds et al. 2011). Acknowledging and understanding these differences encourages a classroom culture where all students feel welcomed and supported, and are provided with rich opportunities to learn (Chepyator-Thomson 1994).

Studies concerned with the impact of teacher expectation on student achievement (Bishop and Berryman 2006; Bishop and Glynn 1999; Hynds et al. 2011; Macfarlane et al. 2007) have found that student achievement is enhanced when students feel acknowledged and valued for their contributions, where, "students safely bring who they are and what they know into the learning relationship, and where what students know, and who they are, forms the foundations of interaction patterns in the classroom" (Bishop and Glynn 1999, pp. 165–166). The Te Kotahitanga Project (Bishop et al. 2007), designed to raise achievement for Māori students in New Zealand secondary schools, identified positive personal relationships as the most important indication of an effective teacher, concluding that students who have positive interactions with their teachers and peers in the classroom develop a sense of connectedness and belonging.

In this chapter I draw on current national and international research to discuss ways that dance experiences in the classroom develop connectedness. Students who are given opportunities to experience dance as participants, creators, viewers and critical inquirers, within social and cultural contexts that are relevant to their own lives, develop confidence in themselves as learners and as contributing members of a group (Melchior 2011). Narratives from three teachers and supporting comments from their students provide insights into how children make connections with their peers, with their learning, and with dance as a means of expression. To provide a framework for the discussion I give a brief overview of culturally responsive pedagogy from a Māori world-view and describe how the key concepts apply to arts education and dance in the New Zealand curriculum.

2 Background

2.1 Culturally Responsive Pedagogy

Alton-Lee's (2003) investigation into best practice in New Zealand education found that teaching in ways that are responsive to student diversity and cultural identity can have a positive impact on low and high achievers at the same time. As Macfarlane et al. (2007) noted, "All students benefit from being in a culturally inclusive classroom.

However many students from non-dominant cultures are not free to be whom and what they are when they go to school" (p. 71). Teachers who have high expectations of their students and actively engage them in learning increase student achievement. Conversely, teachers who have low expectations and engage in deficit theorising tend to blame their students for underachievement (Hynds et al. 2011). This attitude is commonly associated with negative outcomes for indigenous and other minoritised students (Castagno and Brayboy 2008; cited in Hynds et al. 2011, p. 340). Teachers who make a difference believe in their students' abilities to succeed and use a variety of teaching strategies to engage and challenge their students in learning. This requires a shift from a teacher-driven to a student-centred approach, where interactive discourse is encouraged and students have ownership of their learning (Hynds et al. 2011; Spiller 2013).

According to Darling-Hammond (2003) teacher quality and effectiveness is more consistently related to student achievement than is their subject content knowledge. Hynds et al.'s (2011) evaluation of the Kotahitanga Project highlights the importance of a positive learning environment to create a sense of belonging and whanau (family). *Whakawhanaungatanga* (the process of building relationships) is the key for improving behaviour and learning outcomes for Māori students (Bishop and Glynn 1999). A classroom with an atmosphere based on trust is a safe place to learn, where teachers listen to students and value their perspectives. Reciprocity is important when establishing trusting relationships, with teachers and students sharing their own lives and interests. Baskerville (2011) reported on a process of storytelling to activate student voice and build cross-cultural relationships and understandings in the drama classroom. As the teachers took part in the storytelling with the students all experienced the position of teacher and learner. Students' prior-knowledge and new knowledges were valued, connections between stories were made, and students' cultures were honoured. Collins and Ogier (2013) highlight the importance of the teacher's role in facilitating students' talk for learning by posing open questions that encourage and support students to form and articulate creative ideas and take risks in their learning.

2.2 Culturally Responsive Pedagogy and the Arts in Education

It is well documented that learning in the arts has the ability to make a positive difference to young people's lives by offering unique opportunities to make connections with other people's stories and experiences, and to imagine, enact and experience their world from different perspectives (Hindle et al. 2011; Baskerville 2009; Donelan 2009; Eisner 2002; Melchior 2006, 2011; Ministry of Education 2000, 2007). The *Champions of Change* (2002) report states:

> When well taught, the arts provide young people with authentic learning experiences that engage their minds, hearts and bodies. The learning experiences are real and meaningful for them" (cited in Melchior 2006, p. 12).

According to Donelan (2009), rich learning experiences in the arts promote embodied intercultural understanding, cultural knowledge and respect for differences, "enabling students to imagine, engage with, interpret and express a range of cultural experiences and perspectives – those that are familiar as well as those that are new and challenging" (p. 23). Hindle et al. (2011) concur, endorsing arts education as a vehicle for social change in the classroom through the creation of contemporary cultural knowledge that transforms the learning experience by enabling students to draw on contexts that are meaningful to them. They concluded that teachers who use culturally responsive pedagogies in the arts are more inclined to ask the kinds of open questions that engage students in higher-level thinking and co-construction of knowledge. The following statement in the New Zealand curriculum supports this notion:

> Arts education explores challenges, affirms, and celebrates unique artistic expressions of self, community and culture. It embraces toi Māori, valuing the forms and practices of customary and contemporary Māori performing, musical and visual arts (Ministry of Education 2007, p. 20).

The curriculum vision statement, which promotes the development of young people as, "…lifelong learners who are confident and creative, connected, and actively involved" (p. 4), has significance for dance and how it is taught.

2.3   Culturally Responsive Pedagogy and Dance in the Classroom

Research highlights two basic approaches to teaching dance in the classroom; a child-centred approach based on interaction and discovery, and a discipline-based approach, based on transmission of specific movement vocabularies by the 'expert' teacher (Bresler 2004, cited in Giguere 2011, p. 9). The transmission model is the way many teachers feel most comfortable teaching dance, as it is also the way they were taught (Melchior 2006). Dance education in the classroom involves much more than the mastery of steps (Buck 2003). There is a strong emphasis on socially constructed learning (Vygotsky 1962). Teaching dance as an active meaning-making process rather than a transmission activity requires an interactive approach where teachers and students co-construct learning through the relationships they develop with each other and with the curriculum. This includes choosing appropriate content or contexts for learning, and teaching in ways that actively motivate and engage all students, creating an emotional response (Zavatto and Gabbei 2008). By recognising student diversity and relating movement vocabulary to their experiences, there is a shift from *disembodied* knowing to *embodied* knowing (Shapiro 1998).

In Aotearoa New Zealand generalist classroom teachers are mostly responsible for teaching dance as they are able to make connections within and across the curriculum to find relevant and meaningful contexts for teaching and learning dance (Melchior 2006). In supporting the notion of teaching dance across the curriculum,

Bolwell (2011) promotes, "…a re-visioning that is filled with new challenges and new possibilities" (p. 13). Integrating relevant dance ideas within the context of other learning allows students to draw on rich concrete experiences and images for movement exploration (Donelan 2009). A culturally responsive learning environment for dance is fostered when movement concepts are related to students' prior knowledge and experiences within structures that encourage creativity through co-operation and collaboration, leading to a sense of achievement and success for all. Keun and Hunt (2006) reinforce the importance of the teacher's role in enabling and nurturing children's creativity, by providing an environment that stimulates students' creative ideas, encourages responses and, most importantly, makes children feel that their ideas are valued. This enables what Craft (2000, cited in Keun and Hunt 2006) defines as "Possibility thinking", which involves being "imaginative, posing questions, and play" (p.37). Students need to be introduced to a broad range of movements and activities in an interactive learning environment. Exploring movement concepts through guided improvisation, open-ended problem solving, sharing, responding and critical reflection enables students to construct their own meanings of dance (Buck 2003; Chappell 2010; Melchior 2011; Renner 2007). Teacher participation and modelling enhances student motivation and engagement and is an important component of an experiential approach to learning (Hindle et al. 2011).

2.4 Dance in the New Zealand Curriculum

The New Zealand curriculum describes dance as "expressive movement that has intent, purpose, and form" (Ministry of Education 2007, p. 20) and defines a concept of dance literacy:

> Students develop literacy in dance as they learn about, and develop skills in, performing, choreographing, and responding to a variety of genres from a range of historical and contemporary contexts (Ministry of Education 2007, p. 20).

Hong (2000) further explains dance literacy as "a process of meaning-making which opens doors to new ways of seeing, new ways of thinking and therefore new ways of knowing the world" (p. 2). Hong regards dance literacy as serving two essential and complementary purposes: the development of literacy in and about dance, and the development of learning through dance, where dance experiences can be used to enhance learning in other areas. The following statement from the curriculum supports this:

> In dance education students engage in ways that integrate thinking, moving and feeling. They explore and use dance elements, vocabularies, processes, and technologies to express personal, group and cultural identities, to convey and interpret artistic ideas, and to strengthen social interaction (Ministry of Education 2007, p. 20).

Students learn in, through and about dance through four interrelated curriculum strands (key aspects of learning): Understanding [dance] in context; Developing practical knowledge; Developing ideas; Communicating and interpreting. Students develop an awareness and understanding of dance in sociocultural contexts past and present, with particular focus on the unique forms of traditional Māori dance and multicultural dance heritages of New Zealand society. They develop practical knowledge in dance and extend their personal movement vocabularies as they explore dance elements (body, space, time, energy and relationships) and other dance genres and styles. They develop ideas in dance as they select and combine dance elements and explore choreographic processes in response to a range of stimuli. They communicate and interpret dance in a variety of informal and formal settings, as they share, perform, interpret and evaluate, responding to their own and others' dance (Ministry of Education 2000, 2007). A spiral process of action and reflection, where students continuously build on and revisit previous learning, "ensures that students' learning is in-depth, relevant and meaningful" (Ministry of Education 2007, p. 20).

Social constructivist and socio-cultural theories highlight the importance of social and cultural contexts in learning. This involves an holistic approach based on collaboration, shared responsibility and shared ownership of the classroom where there are opportunities to do things differently, to admire creativity and allow students to be true to themselves (MacFarlane et al. 2007).

3 A Case Study

3.1 Setting the Scene

In my role as dance educator in the Faculty of Education at Victoria University of Wellington, New Zealand, I spent 10 years as a dance facilitator providing professional development and support for teachers in their classroom during the implementation phase of the arts [dance] curriculum. As Hill et al. (2002) point out, teacher professional development is most effective when it is negotiated and designed to meet the needs of individual teachers and their students within the context of the classroom over a period of time:

> If teachers are to be able to improve practice they need to be able to take risks, make mistakes, and engage in honest self-reflection. This requires a culture where relationships bind them together in a supportive, enquiring community (Hill et al. 2002, p. 2).

In order to involve teachers in the process of identifying and explaining specific issues and challenges in their practice an action research approach to the teacher professional development was considered appropriate (Merriam 1998).

As a participant researcher I played a dual role in facilitating and interpreting (Stake 1995) the actions and reflections of the teachers through an experiential learning cycle, which emphasises experience, reflection, thought, and action (Kolb

1984, cited in McDonald and Melchior 2007). This involves a process of goal setting, planning, observation, modelling, team teaching, and critical reflection. Semi-structured interviews and journalling were the main data gathering tools, with baseline data emerged from classroom observations and initial interviews with the teachers. Journaling was used to reflect on the impact of teaching on student participation and engagement. Interviews with the teachers towards the end of the professional development period were recorded on digital audio to evaluate the process in relation to their identified goals. Student responses to their dance experiences were also recorded (Melchior 2011).

I decided to focus on three teachers; Alice, Kirsten and Rita (whose names have been changed to protect their identity) with whom I developed an ongoing relationship following the period of professional development. Alice was teaching dance as a performing arts specialist at an intermediate school and Kirsten and Rita were generalist classroom teachers at the same primary school. I visited Alice on a number of occasions to carry out observations and engage in critical reflection, as I wanted to find out what strategies Alice used to create a safe, supportive and stimulating environment for teaching and learning dance. I used insights gained form Alice's practice to inform my interactions with Kirsten and Rita, who were introducing dance into their programmes for the first time and claimed to have little prior knowledge or experience of dance or how to teach it. They had both identified the same goal; to teach dance in ways that would motivate and actively engage all their students in learning by making dance an integral part of their classroom programme.

A Māori world-view of culturally responsive pedagogy provided a framework for the discussion of the teachers' experiences with dance in their classrooms. Macfarlane (2004) identifies factors for culturally responsive pedagogy through five cultural concepts: *whanaungatanga* (reciprocal relationships), *rangitiriatanga* (teacher effectivess), *manaakitanga* (ethos of caring), *kotahitanga* (unity and bonding) and *pumanauratanga* (the beating heart). I have used Macfarlane's 'Educultural Wheel' as a deductive categorising lens for reporting on teaching and learning dance in Alice, Kirsten and Rita's classrooms in the following discussion (Melchior 2011).

4 Findings and Discussion

The first concept, *whanaungatanga*, evident through the reciprocal relationships that teachers develop with their students (Macfarlane 2004) is an essential element of culturally responsive pedagogy. Alice, Kirsten and Rita had already established positive learning environments through the responsive relationships they had with their students. They knew their students well, and considered their interests and learning needs as paramount when planning their teaching programmes. They acknowledged student diversity in their classrooms. As Kirsten elaborated:

> In my class I have Māori, Sāmoan, African, Korean and Pākehā (NZ European) – mostly girls – and the girls dominate. In dance everyone is involved and it equalises them. The boys love dance and they really benefit from working co-operatively in groups. They thrive on problem-solving activities with multiple solutions.

The teachers practised *Ako* (Royal-Tangaere 1997), a concept of reciprocal teaching and learning that provides opportunities for students to share their prior knowledge and participate in learning on an equal level with their teachers, building mutual respect and positive relationships. Alice noted that working in pairs or groups enabled students to contribute ideas and learn from each other, saying: "The students learn to work co-operatively as a group – they don't argue about who's in the group – they negotiate when and how they move." Kirsten and Rita were delighted at their students' willingness to participate in dance activities and contribute to the group process. Kirsten described how her students were reacting:

> There are some children with extreme behaviors in this class. They were unwilling to participate [in dance] at first as they don't like working with others, but now they all join in most of the time. They still find the work a challenge but they are making progress, and they are enjoying dance. [Child] still prefers to work by himself so I let him, because he is participating and that's an achievement.

Rita had a similar response, explaining: "The children have made huge progress with their ability to work co-operatively in a group and their willingness to share their dance with the rest of the class."

For reciprocal relationships to be fostered and developed in the classroom it is also important for students to learn something about their teacher's interests and concerns (Hynds et al. 2011). As a way of recognising and valuing Kirsten and Rita's prior knowledge and experience I encouraged them to identify their strengths and interests and to use these as starting points for teaching dance.

Rita drew on her expertise in Indian dance forms, bringing her cultural identity into the classroom for the first time; something she had never before considered appropriate or even relevant. She told her students stories about her childhood and a special dance performed to celebrate Diwali (New Year). Rita showed them the dance on video and asked them to identify movements they liked. They practised their movements and added rhythm patterns to recreate their own class dance. Rita explained, "We tried out everyone's movements to respect everyone's ideas and see which ones we would keep." The children were so proud of their dance they asked to share it with the rest of the school in assembly. Rita was genuinely surprised at the children's interest in her culture and their enthusiastic responses and she felt acknowledged and appreciated for who she was. This experience was affirming and empowering for Rita, who exclaimed, "I've become more confident to organise dance and talk about it, because I really love it and I'm so excited!"

Kirsten utilised her passion for language and literature by adapting strategies she used for teaching written language (brainstorming ideas, demonstration, individual and group work, reviewing and revising, publishing) as a model for teaching dance. She spoke enthusiastically about how this process worked for her:

I make links to literacy. We read big books [large size picture books for early readers designed for shared reading] and we find the action words. Dance action words are now in the language the children use in class. Dance is great for language development. So many descriptive words go with dancing and it's such rich language, and there's the instructional language too. It's great for ESOL kids... 'Hear it, do it, remember it.' When dancing children revisit movement ideas and vocabulary and basic words are reinforced, adding more layers and challenges each time.

The second aspect of McFarlane's Educultural Wheel, *rangatiratanga*, is evident in the teacher's assertive presence and awareness that good teaching is culturally inclusive. This includes positive behaviour management strategies, understanding and warmth, clear expectations, knowing what and how to teach and why it is important (Macfarlane 2004). Effective arts teachers set appropriate challenges in the classroom, expect students to be responsible for their own learning, as well as supporting others' learning and behavior, and use co-operative learning strategies so that students learn to work with one another (Hindle et al. 2011).

Alice explained the expectations she had for student achievement in her dance classes and also for herself as a teacher:

My job is to provide opportunities for students to excel in their learning and to share and present their dance works. It's not about me and my ideas; it's about them and their ideas. I believe that socialisation is the key to learning and social constructivism the best model to learn from.

She talked about the importance of using relevant and meaningful contexts for teaching and learning dance by making links to other learning in the classroom:

The kids [students] were doing safety and well being and making up speeches in class. They danced their speech topics (prisons, alcohol, drug abuse etc.) and they made a deeper connection with their learning in a physical and emotional way.

Kirsten described how dance opened up new possibilities and ways of learning for her students. As well as teaching language structures and maths concepts through dance she used dance as a way of reinforcing their knowledge and understandings of other learning. She described one of these contexts:

We're doing '*Me in my environment*' and bringing in a Māori perspective, using Māori movement words for the elements [the guardians of nature] and learning Māori movement patterns that the children can use to create their own dances about the environment. They have such creative ideas; they blow me away!

Kirsten and Rita both discovered the importance of providing appropriate scaffolding for learning in the dance lesson so that children are not frustrated by something that is too hard or bored by something that is too easy:

I started off by modelling [ways of moving] different body parts and responding to action words, to build up confidence...now I teach dance in a way that connects with other learning (Kirsten).

We work a lot with words; dance language, with lots of scaffolding through individual exploration and discussion. They transfer these skills into creating their own dances. At the moment we're doing water. Dance can make the abstract more real (Rita).

They often brought their classes together to share dance work or to participate in collaborative dance experiences. I was invited to come and watch their students performing a combined class dance they had made in response to their science learning about space and the planets. The children were obviously excited about their dance and were keen to tell me about their particular contributions to the creative process. I captured some of their comments below:

> Our group is showing what's in space. We've got a comet, Hubble and earth – Hubble takes pictures in space (boy, age 6).
> We were doing earth spinning round and making day and night, and astronauts bouncing (girl, age 7).
> Our dance is about grey earth and the sun flashing light on earth. The earth is spinning round (girl, age 6).
> The earth is tilted slightly – we can show it with our bodies. We do moon walking in slow motion' cause there's no gravity (boy, age 7).

Rita explained the process:

> Each child came up with a movement and taught the others in the group. They all know exactly what they're doing and which aspect they're representing…stars, comets, meteors, planets. The children have ownership – they develop confidence with something to share. They know everyone gets a turn and they are all going to learn each other's moves. I can't believe I've done it all myself or rather, they've done it!

The third concept, *manaakitanga* (the ethos of caring), is the foundation for successful and reciprocal teaching and learning experiences. Teachers provide a safe, comfortable learning environment for their students where common ground is established and the students are actively engaged in their learning (Macfarlane 2004). Students are encouraged to be role models for their peers through modelling and assuming leadership roles. This is a way of scaffolding learning by making concepts easily understandable to everyone, including students with other languages and students with special learning needs (LePage et al. 2005). Movement and dance are effective ways for these children to express and communicate their ideas and feelings.

Alice, Kirsten and Rita all talked about students in their class who had special learning needs and found it difficult to socialise with their peers. They noticed how these children developed confidence and were able to connect with others through participating in dance experiences. Rita expressed her delight at the way her students were able engage with dance, explaining the impact on her EAL (English as another language) students and an autistic child:

> Dance is wonderful for EAL students developing language – not just dance words, descriptive language. I was blown away when [child] contributed in the circle! He said 'I feel cold' and made a movement to show how he felt.
> [Child] just loves to dance – he goes from group to group joining in – the kids are really supportive.

Kirsten and Alice reported similar observations:

> [Child] has auditory processing problems; she has difficulty socialising in a group as she finds it hard to make decisions, but she loves to dance. She made up a movement so I put

her in a group and the other children copied her movement. For the first time she was like any other kid in the class (Kirsten).

[Child] is physically uncoordinated but he likes dance. He has lots of ideas and because he can choose what and how he wants to dance he succeeds (Alice).

In a culturally responsive environment teachers are encouraged to involve parents/caregivers and families in the classroom, and to engage the support of community people as resources. This creates possibilities for rich learning experiences in dance where the teacher becomes a learner alongside the students. A parent of one of Alice's students came in and taught a Sāmoan sasa to the class. The children learnt a variety of traditional movement patterns and the stories behind them before selecting and combining elements to create movements representing different occupations in their own communities. Alice described the process:

We learnt the song and the traditional sasa movements first as a class. Then in groups they made up their own actions to represent each line of the song. The children really enjoyed creating their own movements within the familiar structure of the sasa and extending the dance from sitting to standing to travelling.

The fourth concept, *kotahitanga* (unity and bonding), is evident in the teachers' inclusive teaching strategies, behaviour management and positive feed-back (Macfarlane 2004). Teachers who respect cultural differences are more likely to believe that students from non-dominant groups are capable learners (LePage et al. 2005), thus creating *kotahitanga*. Teachers in Aotearoa New Zealand are encouraged to explore and operate by the underlying principles of partnership, protection and participation as represented within the Treaty of Waitangi (Hindle et al. 2011). In Alice's dance classes these principles are evident through power sharing; reciprocal rights and responsibilities in the classroom:

I say to my children "You bring your identity and your physicality into this space. You bring who you are as a dancer – hip-hop, crumping, rugby – and we build on these experiences.

Alice described one of the many opportunities she provides for her students to explore and express their identities through dance:

We looked at the Treaty [of Waitangi] from the children's perspectives and through drama and dance interpreted experiences of early settlers coming to New Zealand. The children made artefacts and had to dance them. Their solo dance artworks were integrated into a drama performance. They showed perspectives of Māori and their gods, the missionaries and their god, traders, whalers, etc. They had to do their own research. Some children chose their ancestors…it was an amazing experience…everyone learnt so much and developed an understanding from both sides. They said things like "I didn't realise…now I know, now I understand.

In her classes there was a blending of the distinction between the teacher and the learner and a strong feeling that everyone wanted to be there. Comments from some of her students elaborate:

We're all bonded because we work together (girl, age 12).

We can tell a story through dance…we communicate well together and we co-operate with each other (boy, age 11).

People give good feedback to each other…it gives us confidence (girl, age 11).

It's more fun than in class…we're really happy when we're here…we're happy sometimes in class, but not the same sort of happy (boy, age 12).
    When I get back to the classroom it feels like a part of me just died (girl, age 12).

The central concept, *pumanauratanga* (the beating heart), extends outwards to
the four interconnected concepts in the 'Educultural wheel' (Macfarlane 2004). By
making the classroom a culturally responsive place for Māori students, all students
benefit, with increased 'connectedness' between the teacher and the students, the
students and each other, and the students and their learning. Alice, Kirsten and Rita
recognised the potential for dance as an opportunity to involve children in a creative
process, which involves working in groups, sharing ideas, feelings, and experiences
and connects them with their learning in a different way. With a focus on process
and discovery, through clearly structured learning activities and open-ended tasks,
enhanced by effective questioning, demonstrations and formative feedback, the
teachers were able to co-construct their own meanings of dance with their students.
Buck (2003) observed that teachers who see themselves as being actively involved
in a creative process feel more confident about teaching dance, and this was certainly the case for Kirsten and Rita. They each exclaimed:

I'm more confident to teach dance now that I know how much the kids love it and how well
they respond. The flow over into the classroom is really obvious (Kirsten).
    I just don't want to stop [teaching dance] now – the kids have developed so much con-
fidence and they love it – I'm going to keep doing it. I find it hard to fit it in but it's worth it
(Rita).

When reflecting on the value of dance as an embodied way of knowing Kirsten
noted that participating in dance helped them to develop confidence and increased
their ability to make connections with each other, and with their learning: "Dance
enables the children to shine who wouldn't otherwise … children who have difficulty with formal learning in class." She was convinced that making dance an integral part of her classroom programme benefitted all her students, often in ways she
did not expect. Alice, Kirsten and Rita continued to find ways to motivate and
engage their students in dance by choosing meaningful contexts for learning.
Displays of dance terminology, captioned photos and children's written responses
to dance experiences on their classroom walls, made dance visible and valued, for
all to see.

5   Conclusion

All three teachers co-constructed their own meanings of dance in the classroom
with their students through rich contexts for learning that related to the students'
lived experiences (Shapiro 1998). This aligns with Craft's (2000) research (cited in
Chappell 2010), which highlights the importance of teachers acknowledging children's contributions to the creative process by allowing then to take ownership of
the process as well as the product. Dance taught as creative problem-solving

encourages multiple solutions and promotes higher order thinking. Students who are able to express ideas and emotions during the creative process of dance making are also developing thinking and reasoning skills, as they question, analyse and evaluate (Giguere 2011).

The teachers were encouraged to utilise and value their pedagogical knowledge and use their curriculum strengths and interests to develop effective strategies for teaching dance, taking opportunities and negotiating barriers as they arose (Buck 2003). They recognised that children learn in different ways and that effective learning comes from challenge and a sense of freedom and discovery that fosters ownership (Sansom 2009). Although they had already established safe and trusting classroom environments where students were willing to participate and take risks in their learning, they each acknowledged the positive effects that dance experiences had on their students and their learning. They talked about enhanced relationships, with increased connectedness between the students, and with dance as a way of expressing their learning.

This case study adds to the body of knowledge about culturally responsive pedagogy and dance in the primary classroom and highlights possibilities for dance as an integral part of children's education and development. Research into student perceptions of how they make connections through dance learning would produce further insights. As Sansom (2009) reiterates, "Dance, as an embodied understanding of ourselves, can connect to a moral and ethical pedagogy that not only honours the life of the child but also makes possible a new way to envisage being human" (p. 161). When students are given rich learning opportunities to participate in dance in a positive and supportive environment, where they are encouraged to talk about their experiences and have choices within tasks, they are more likely to connect with dance as an important part of their learning (Renner 2007). Quality teachers are constantly searching for different ways to motivate and engage their students in learning and I hope more generalist primary teachers will be inspired to integrate dance into their students' learning.

References

Alton-Lee, A. (2003). *Quality teaching for diverse students in schooling: Best evidence in schooling: Best evidence synthesis*. Wellington: Ministry of Education.

Baskerville, D. (2009). Navigating the unfamiliar in a quest towards culturally responsive pedagogy in the classroom. *Teaching and Teacher Education, 25*, 461–467.

Baskerville, D. (2011). Developing cohesion and building positive relationships through storytelling in a culturally diverse New Zealand classroom. *Teaching and Teacher Education, 27*(1), 107–115. Elsevier.

Bishop, R., & Berryman, M. (2006). *Culture speaks: Cultural relationships and classroom learning*. Wellington: Huia Publishers.

Bishop, R., & Glynn, T. (1999). *Culture counts: Changing power relationships in education*. Palmerston North: Dunmore Press.

Bishop, R., Berryman, M., Cavanagh, T., & Teddy, L. (2007). Te Kohitanga: Phase 3 Whanaungatanga: *Establishing a culturally responsive pedagogy of relations in mainstream secondary school classrooms*. Wellington: Ministry of Education.

Bolwell, J. (2011). Embedding literacy and numeracy in the dance curriculum. *DANZ Quarterly, 25*(3), 12–13.

Buck, R. (2003). *Teachers and dance in the classroom "So, do I need my tutu?"* A thesis submitted for the degree of Doctor of Philosophy. University of Otago, New Zealand.

Castagno, A. E., & Brayboy, B. M. J. (2008). Culturally responsive schooling for indigenous youth: A review of literature. *Review of Educational Research, 78*, 941–993.

Chappell, K. (2010). Creativity in primary level dance education: Moving beyond assumption. *Research in Dance Education, 8*(1), 27–52.

Chepyator-Thomson, J. R. (1994). Multicultural Education: Culturally responsive teaching. Source: *JOPERD-The Journal of Physical Education, Recreation & Dance, 11/1/1994*. HighBeam Research. www.highbeam.com

Collins, F., & Ogier, S. (2013). *Expressing identity: The role of dialogue in teaching citizenship through art*. London: University of Roehampton. http://dx.doi.org/10.1080/03004279.2011.

Darling-Hammond, L. (2003). Keeping good teachers: Why it matters, what leaders can do. *Educational Leadership, 60*(8), 6–13.

Donelan, K. (2009). Arts education as intercultural and social dialogue. In C. Sinclair, N. Jeanneret, & J. O'Toole (Eds.), *Education in the arts: Teaching and learning in the contemporary curriculum* (pp. 22–28). Victoria: Oxford University Press.

Eisner, E. (2002). The arts and the creation of mind. In *What the arts teach and how it shows*. (pp. 70–92). Yale University Press. http://www.arteducators.org/advocacy/10-lessons-the-arts-teach#sthash.TgIU4lNS.dpuf

Giguere, M. (2011). Dancing thoughts: An examination of children's cognition and creative process in dance. *Research in Dance Education, 12*(1), 5–28. London: Routledge.

Hill, J., Hawk, K., & Taylor, K. (2002). Professional development: What makes it work? *Set: Research Information for Teachers*, 2. Wellington: NZCER.

Hindle, R., Savage, C., Meyer, L., Sleeter, C., Hynds, A., & Penetito, W. (2011). Culturally responsive pedagogies in the visual and performing arts: Exemplars, missed opportunities and challenges. *Curriculum Matters, 7*, 26–47. http://search.informit.com.au/documentSummary;dn=7 09632005792433;res=IELHSS.

Hong, T. (2000). Developing dance literacy in the post-modern: An approach to curriculum. Paper presented at *Dancing in the Millennium Conference*, Washington DC, January 30, 2013. http://www.tki.org.nz/r/arts/artpd/research/updatest_e.php

Hynds, A., Sleeter, C., Hindle, R., Savage, C., Penetito, W., & Meyer, L. (2011). Te Kotahitanga: A case study of a repositioning approach to teacher professional development for culturally responsive pedagogies. *Asia-Pacific Journal of Teacher Education, 39*(4), 339–451. Taylor & Francis Online. doi:10.1080/1359866X.2011.61468.

Lai Keun, L., & Hunt, P. (2006). Creative dance: Singapore children's creative thinking and problem-solving responses. *Research in Dance Education, 7*(01), 35–65.

LePage, P., Darling-Hammond, L., & Akar, H. (2005). Classroom management. In L. Darling-Hammond & J. Bransford (Eds.), *Preparing teachers for a changing world. What teachers should learn and be able to do* (pp. 327–357). Sponsored by the National Academy of Education. San Francisco: Jossey-Bass.

Macfarlane, A. (2004). *Kia Hiwi ra! Listen to culture – Māori Student's plea to Educators*. Wellington: New Zealand Council for Educational Research.

MacFarlane, A., Glynn, T., Cavanagh, T., & Bateman, S. (2007). Creating culturally-safe schools for Māori students. *The Australian Journal of Indigenous Education, 36*, 65–75. Australia: University of Queensland.

McDonald, L., & Melchior, E. (2007). Investing in transfer of learning: Dancing the talk. *New Zealand Annual Review of Education, 17*, 73–90.

Melchior, E. (2006). *If you can walk you can dance. How generalist primary teachers develop confidence and competence to teach dance.* A thesis submitted in partial fulfillment of the requirements for the degree of Master of Education, Victoria University of Wellington, Wellington.

Melchior, E. (2011). Culturally responsive dance pedagogy in the primary classroom. *Research in Dance Education, 12*(2), 119–135. London: Routledge.

Merriam, S. (1998). *Qualitative research and case study applications in education revised and expanded from case study research in education.* San Francisco: Jossey-Bass Publishers.

Ministry of Education. (2000). *The arts in the New Zealand Curriculum.* Wellington: Learning Media.

Ministry of Education. (2007). *The New Zealand Curriculum for English medium teaching and learning in years 1–13.* Wellington: Learning Media.

Ministry of Education. (2013–2017). *Ka Hikitia accelerating success: The Moari Education Strategy.* http://www.education.govt.nz/ministry-of-education/overall-strategies-and-policies/the-maori-education-strategy-ka-hikitia-accelerating-success-20132017/

Renner, S. (2007). Some practical considerations for teaching dance in schools. *DANZ Quarterly (8).*

Royal-Tangaere, A. (1997). Māori human development learning theory. In P. Te Whaiti, M. McCarthy, & A. Duroe (Eds.), *Mai I Rangiatea: Māori wellbeing and development* (pp. 46–59). Auckland: Auckland University Press.

Sansom, A. (2009). Mindful pedagogy in dance: Honouring the life of the child. *Research in Dance Education, 10*(3), 161–176.

Shapiro, S. (1998). Towards transformative teachers: Critical and feminist perspectives in dance education. In S. Shapiro (Ed.), *Dance, power and difference: Critical and feminist perspectives of dance education* (pp. 7–23). Champaign: Human Kinetics Publishers.

Spiller, L. (2013). *Teachers' misunderstandings that affect the learning of their Pasifika students.* URL: http://researcharchive.vuw.ac.nz/handle/10063/2248

Stake, R. (1995). *The art of case study research.* Thousand Oaks: Sage.

Vygotsky, L. (1962). *Thought and language.* Cambridge, MA: MIT Press.

Zavatto, L., & Gabbei, R. (2008). The real dance revolution: How to make dance meaningful for all students. *Strategies, 21*(5), 25–28.

Liz Melchior is dance lecturer in primary and secondary teacher education programmes at Victoria University of Wellington, New Zealand. A passionate advocate for dance in schools, her research interests focus mainly on culturally responsive dance pedagogy. Liz was a dance facilitator for the Ministry of Education during the implementation period of the arts curriculum, providing professional development and support for teachers in the classroom. She started the Wellington Dance in Education Network (Well Dance), was instrumental in setting up the Dance Subject Association of New Zealand (DSANZ) and is a member of the Dance and the Child International (daCi) Executive Committee.

Legacy and Adaptation: The Orff Approach in the New Zealand School Setting

Linda Locke

Abstract This chapter is based on recent doctoral research by the author, who undertook a critical analysis of the Orff approach in the professional lives and practices of New Zealand teachers in the Aotearoa/New Zealand state school context. In this multiple case study, findings were based on an analysis of questionnaire, observation and interview data. The chapter begins by discussing the Orff legacy, offering a view of its foundational principles and referencing some current critique. It then reports on ways in which teacher participants, drawing on their own understandings of the approach, put it into practice in their classrooms in ways that reflect New Zealand's bicultural heritage and the increasingly diverse character of New Zealand classrooms.

Keywords Orff Schulwerk • Music education • Biculturalism • Cultural diversity • Praxial music education

1 Introduction

Orff Schulwerk, the name most frequently given to the pedagogical practice inspired by the work of composer Carl Orff, and composer, dancer, musician and teacher Gunild Keetman, highlights the European origins of this approach to music and movement education. Austrians and Germans know this approach as *Elementare Musik und Tanzpaedagogik* (elemental music and dance pedagogy) which avoids the problem of solely attributing the approach to Orff and the unfortunate erasure of Keetman in the term, whose work is central to the legacy of this approach. The unfamiliarity of both the name Orff and the term 'Schulwerk' leads many Antipodean educators to a conclusion that the approach implies a mono-culturalism, that renders it irrelevant to our richly bi-cultural and in many cases multicultural Aotearoa New Zealand school settings. However, the wide dissemination of this approach

L. Locke (✉)
Doctoral Researcher, University of Waikato, Auckland, New Zealand
e-mail: milliel@vodafone.co.nz

© Springer International Publishing Switzerland 2016
L. Ashley, D. Lines (eds.), *Intersecting Cultures in Music and Dance Education*, Landscapes: the Arts, Aesthetics, and Education 19,
DOI 10.1007/978-3-319-28989-2_7

into similar seemingly unlikely contexts attests to its perceived applicability by music educators in many geographically and culturally disparate parts of the world. Every year, representatives from many countries around the world gather at The Orff Institute[1] in Salzburg to attend the 'Orff Forum', described by it's current director, Professor Barbara Haselbach, as a think-tank in which leading music teachers from a diverse range of educational contexts are able reflect on the issues involved in the application of the Orff approach in their particular settings.

This chapter draws upon my doctoral research, *The Orff approach in the professional lives and practices of teachers in the Aotearoa/New Zealand state school context* (in process), which was informed by my own Orff-influenced professional practice over two decades as a music teacher in a primary school. Drawing on questionnaire, interview and classroom observation data, this chapter will discuss some of the beliefs that inform the practice of these teachers, illustrated by some relevant examples of Orff-inspired practice in a range of New Zealand school settings (primary, intermediate and secondary) which highlight issues of adaptation in the Aotearoa New Zealand context. My research, I must emphasise, was not premised on the idea that there is one 'definitive" version of what the Orff approach is or should be. Indeed, as discussed below, there are manifestations of it in some settings which have been subject to varieties of critique.

Taken as given that quality music education has a crucial part to play in the intellectual, social and emotional development of the person, and that access to an education in music is the right of every child (Baker et al. 2012; Hoffman Davis 2008; Mills 2005) my research has been informed by a praxial philosophy of music education. According to Regelski (2002), teachers are ethically obliged to engage in a cycle of action and reflection (central to the notion of music education as praxis) in order to reassess from time to time whether the action ideals embodied in the curriculum (any curriculum) are those which ought to be regarded as ideal or good for students. My doctoral research reflects a concern with the question of what is good or ideal for students. In this research, teachers were asked to appraise, in the light of their knowledge of their students, their setting and the New Zealand curriculum, the contribution that the principles and processes of the Orff approach could make to the 'good' of music education in their particular context in Aotearoa New Zealand.

As findings relevant to the issue of legacy and adaptation are presented and discussed in this chapter, readers are invited to evaluate, in the light of their own experience and perspectives, the contribution this approach might make, not only to individual music teacher practice but also to the vitality and development of music education opportunities for *all* students within Aotearoa New Zealand school settings or indeed any state-mandated, music education curriculum.

---

[1] The Orff-Institute established in 1963 is the pedagogical centre for study, research and dissemination of Orff Schulwerk.

2 My Background

Two decades ago, after having been a primary school teacher for many years, and a keen amateur musician in my private life, a range of serendipitous circumstances led me to becoming a music specialist in an Auckland, inner-city primary school. Music specialists are not the norm in New Zealand state primary schools. Rather, the subject 'Music-Sound Arts' is usually taught (or not taught) by classroom teachers as part of their classroom programme. Although one may argue that the ideal of music as an integrated, meaningful experience in children's daily lives is highly desirable, the expertise required to teach music in the primary school classroom is not usually available in the generalist teaching population. This is due to a number of factors, including the limited opportunities many teachers have to develop either musical expertise and/or professional expertise in music education.

Although I had been a keen amateur musician since childhood, participating in a range of both solo and group musical activities, neither pre-service nor in-service opportunities in my teacher education had equipped me with the confidence or competence to teach music to children in the school setting. After a chance encounter with a book describing the principles of Orff Schulwerk (Warner 1991), I decided to attend an Orff Schulwerk workshop offered by a visiting North American teacher. The highly interactive, hands-on, creative, music-making experiences I enjoyed during this week-long workshop, ignited my interest and curiosity. Subsequently, when I returned to my teaching position and shared my new-found interest, my school principal, who rated highly the part experiences in music could play in the lives of children, persuaded me to take up a position as part-time music specialist in his school.

Thus began my engagement with the Orff approach and music education in the Aotearoa New Zealand primary school context. As I sought to develop a quality music programme for all students, which was both responsive to local context and at the same time fulfilled the requirements of the national curriculum, I drew heavily upon my understanding of the pedagogical approach manifested in the work of Carl Orff and Gunild Keetman, and contemporary interpretations of their work. The philosophy of Orff Schulwerk, in which every person is seen as having an innate capacity to identify as an 'artist', provided me with a basis upon which to a build a conceptual framework and a range of specific tools and skills that shaped and informed the educational activity in my music classroom.

3 Orff Schulwerk

Orff Schulwerk emerged in a European milieu, where a number of theorists and avant-garde artists became engaged with the idea of education, and in particular education in the arts, as being able to enhance the life of every individual, and in turn the well-being of society. Firmly grounded in humanistic notions (Johnson 2006) and therefore able to be critiqued, to some extent, as being part of the grand modernist project (Allsup 2010), the Orff approach emphasises the part that musical learning can play in the development of the whole person (Dolloff 1993; Goodkin 2004).

Orff's early theoretical writings (reprinted in Haselbach 2011) advocate an approach to music education for children, in which *play* is central. The role of play in children's learning is now highly theorised (e.g. Vygotsky 1978) but in the 1930s this notion in regard to music education was innovative. Orff developed and integrated tuned and untuned percussion instruments into a musical ensemble, which, as a result of the simplicity of their technology, enabled musical play involving exploration and improvisation (Haselbach 2011, pp. 66–68). Central to the Orff approach is the use of language and movement based on themes relevant to the world of the child, as starting places for rhythmic and melodic exploration and improvisation (Goodkin 2004; Hall 1960; Keetman 1970; Thomas 2011; Warner 1991).

In recognition of the international dissemination of the Orff approach in the 1960s, Orff was quick to point out that local adaptation was essential (Orff 1963 reprinted in Haselbach 2011). Local and cultural traditions should compel adaptation to particular contexts of elemental music-making, wherein "music forms a unity with movement, dance and speech" (p. 114). *Music for Children*, composed collaboratively by Orff and Keetman in the early 1950s and translated and adapted into English by Margaret Murray (Orff and Keetman 1959a, b, 1963, 1966a, b) was not to be regarded as a musical canon, but rather as one possible illustration of a musical outcome of the Orff Schulwerk approach (Nykrin 2011; Orff 1932).

Orff's (Orff 1963 in Haselbach 2011) oft-quoted statement, "Looking back I should like to describe the Schulwerk as a wildflower....wild flowers always prosper, where carefully planned, cultivated plants often produce disappointing results", used the wildflower metaphor to describe the way Orff pedagogy had developed from the 1920s to the 1960s, and also illustrated what he considered to be a key principle of the Orff process. "Every phase of the Schulwerk will provide stimulation for new independent growth; therefore it is never conclusive and settled, but always developing, always growing, always flowing..." (p. 134).

De Quadros' (2000) collection of examples of 20 different adaptations of the Orff approach from around the world demonstrates the breadth and diversity of interpretation. These examples include theoretical justifications for the contextualisation of the Orff approach (Drummond 2000; Dunbar-Hall 2000; Goodkin 2000); arrangements or compositions in particular cultural styles (Burton 2000; Takizawa 2000); and two examples of the application of the Orff approach which employ music created *by* children themselves (Hartmann 2000; Marsh 2000).

As mentioned in the introduction, the Orff approach should neither be seen as monolithic nor beyond critique. Dolloff's (1993) critical overview of the Orff approach and the role it can play in the cognitive, musical and artistic development of children elucidates the theoretical ancestry of the Orff approach and describes it as one which "promotes musical development through hands-on active music making...and a multiplicity of musical activities and opportunities for practising artistic behaviours" (p. 44). However, citing Orff himself, she suggests that an over-emphasis on the pentatonic, at least in North America, was a weakness as a result of misapplication.

> Time and again the question is asked whether a child must only play pentatonic, avoiding any other kind of music. This is nonsense of course, since it is both impossible and undesirable to shut a child off from all other musical influences. It is the main purpose of pentatonic training to help a child to form a musical expression of his (sic) own. (Orff 1962, p. 57)

Benedict (2009) used a Marxist lens to critique the Orff approach within the American schooling system as an example of music methodolotary[2] (Regelski 2002). Drawing attention to "the implementation of these methods in a strict and unmindful manner (which) often alienates both teacher and student from musicking" (p. 213), she drew attention to the potential in this approach (or indeed any approach) for slavish mimicry. Similarly, Abril (2013) critiqued a range of negative potentials in the approach, such as the way it can construct an infantile version of childhood or become overly prescriptive and/or formulaic in sequencing learning. When such potentials are realised, artistic development may be limited or suppressed rather than enabled.

A newcomer to the Orff approach may become overwhelmed by the proliferation of material claiming to represent the approach, which can easily be accessed via the Internet. Not only are historical accounts of the development of the Orff approach, and literature that explicate and discuss key principles and processes accessible; as well, there is an enormous and ever-growing body of documentary and YouTube material from teachers, particularly in the North American setting, who identify as Orff Schulwerk practitioners. While such material may be helpful in gaining an initial understanding of the Orff approach, the sheer volume of material and the context-specific nature of much of it may not necessarily illuminate its key principles and processes and may inadvertently contribute to a misinformed construction of a kind of Orff orthodoxy.

Typically teachers pursuing an interest in the Orff approach (as I did) have an experiential introduction to the approach as a result of attendance at a workshop led by a knowledgeable Orff practitioner, in which the adult learner is fully engaged as an ensemble participant. The Orff emphasis on successful participation for all in creative music-making characterised by a unity of movement, speech and music is experienced first hand; teachers as participants do not merely learn *about* a pedagogical process, but learn *in* and *through* that process. Embodied experiences and reflections on those experiences enable participants to come to know and understand both musically and pedagogically how the approach 'works'.

What then are the key principles of this approach? And to whose voice does legitimacy belong in relationship to the articulation of a set of principles? At the 2013 Orff Forum, Barbara Haselbach and Wolfgang Hartmann (2013) provided a

---

[2] A term coined by Regelski to signify a rigid adherence to a method which fails to take account of local conditions.

summary of the key principles of the Orff approach, which, in their view, differentiated this approach from other approaches to music education. Haselbach's status as the founding dance teacher of the Orff Institute and Hartmann's as a graduate of the Institute and a respected contemporary music educator give considerable legitimacy to the following (summarised) articulation of key principles.

- The Orff approach is not primarily specialist music or dance training but the enrichment of the whole person through means of expression with music and dance.
- The processes of learning, working and creating are primarily experienced in the group and demand and develop appropriate behaviour and attitudes.
- The Orff approach integrates a range of art forms (as in ancient Greek 'mousike')
- By providing appropriate instruments that can be experienced playfully and that do not have technical obstacles, the possibility of artistic expression with instruments can be included in the work.
- The students are creatively involved in the work as an open process and thereby also determine the direction and the result. In the Orff approach the work process and the artistic results have the same importance.
- Opportunities for the student to experience him/herself as a creator and co-creator through improvisation and composition in sound and movement are provided.
- The Orff approach sees itself as an open pedagogy that is applicable in its principles in all educational fields of work and can also be assimilated in different cultures.

The Orff New Zealand Aotearoa (ONZA) document, which guides the delivery of workshops for teachers in New Zealand, offers an expanded picture of the activities and foci that may be found in this approach to music education. The bulleted list of guiding principles which follows is compatible with the principles listed above and reflects a commitment to a flexible and locally responsive adaptation of the approach in the Aotearoa New Zealand context:

> The Orff approach approach includes singing and instrumental playing with percussion instruments, recorder playing, chant, recitation, story, poetry and body percussion. Instrumental playing is also integrated with movement, singing and speech. Theoretical aspects of music and dance are revealed through creative work, practice and performance and then, based on the learning experience, discussed, recorded and written. At the core of the approach are the teaching-learning processes of imitation, exploration, improvisation and composition, which reflect fundamental Orff approach principles:
>
> - rhythm as an important origin of speech, movement and music;
> - an emphasis on speech, movement and music as an integrated domain;
> - a sequential learning process involving imitation, exploration, improvisation and composition;
> - the centrality of creativity and musical discovery;
> - the fostering of inquiry, innovation and active participation;
> - learning progressions from simple to complex, from experience to concept, from unison to ensemble;
> - respect for individual differences – readiness, skill level and activity preference;
> - child-centredness and culturally contextualised learning;
> - a valuing of communal music-making;
> - a focus on artistry and the aesthetic.
> - (Orff New Zealand Aotearoa 2012, p. 9)

4   A Critical, Praxial Approach

Ethnomusicologist Borgo (2013) suggests the use of the plural denotation music(s) in recognition of the phenomenon of "musicking" (Small 1998) as a diverse set of socio-cultural practices. A praxial music education philosophy emphasises the appropriateness of evaluating any music in its own terms, and acknowledges the situatedness and multiplicity of practice, i.e. that musics are "multi-dimensional, fluid, polysemic, and unstable" (Bowman 2005, pp. 70–71). Burnard (2005) suggests that a praxial view offers much to the teacher of general music education:

> ...it firmly locates the musical understandings of teachers and learners within our personal autobiographies of learning, so that we find authority in our individual musical experiences. Furthermore, the praxial view of general music education affirms the complexity of children as reflective music makers and validates listening, performing, improvising, arranging and conducting as interdependent forms of creative doing. (p. 267)

Bowman argues that a praxial philosophy of music education recognises the need for "*mindful doing*", (2005, p. 69) which leads to an inevitable engagement with moral and political issues. Bowman suggests that as music teachers we need to be concerned not just with what *is* but with what *ought* to be:

> Music education is not just about music. It is about students and it is about teachers and it is about the kind of societies we hope to build together.... (Bowman 2005, p. 75)

The highly influential educational philosophy of Paulo Freire (1994, 1985, 2011; Roberts 2003) informs critical pedagogy (Abrahams 2005a, b) and challenges educators to engage with what Bowman calls the 'what ought to be' dimension of music education. Freirean dialogical praxis, the process of action and reflection with the ethical goal of humanisation, is highly relevant to a praxial music education seeking to be responsive to the multiplicity of musical practices in ways where the importance and the complexity of the context are recognised and acknowledged (Locke 2015).

A praxial approach to music education, informed by Freirean critical dialogical praxis, demands full and active involvement in learning experiences by all participants in any given socio-cultural setting. All the players in a learning ensemble must be positioned as capable of making valid choices and contributions. This requires a shift in thinking away from notions of music teaching as the identification and nurturing of special talent, towards the offering of opportunities in which all students can engage in meaningful musical behaviour. Abrahams (2005a), drawing on Freirean pedagogy, suggests that critical pedagogues need to ask four questions when planning music instruction: "Who am I? Who are my students? What might they become? What might we become together?" (p. 63). These questions offer a starting point for both procedure and content.

Clearly a critical praxial pedagogy in its concern with particularities of context and informed by a process of action and reflection is not compatible with the imposition of 'once and for all' solutions for programmes, which involve the adoption of a fixed or formulaic method. Reflective music educators with a concern to develop relevant, contemporary, contextualised, critical practice should regard all 'methods' with a healthy degree of suspicion, as they have a dangerous potential to become a set of formulaic prescriptions that oppress and hinder authentic and ethical musical development.

Advocates of the Orff approach have consistently resisted the description of Orff Schulwerk as a method, preferring to describe the Schulwerk as an artistic approach (Frazee 2012; Haselbach et al. 2008) indicating both an emphasis on artistry and an intended flexibility of application. Orff and Keetman consistently insisted that their substantial body of compositional work, *Music for Children*, (Orff and Keetman 1959a, b, 1963, 1966a, b) be viewed as models to inspire others to create. Frazee (1987) describes the approach as "a pedagogy of suggestion" with "tremendous liberating possibilities" for teachers and students previously confined by the conventional role of music education, which, at its worst, is characterised by mechanical instruction (p. 12). Orff Schulwerk as a pedagogy of suggestion would actively resist prescriptiveness and/or a one-size fits all approach. A pedagogy of suggestion asks both teachers and students to find their own solutions and, at its best, embraces the critical reflection that is at the heart of a praxial approach.

In Shamrock's (1995) view, Orff pedagogy can be thought of as an "idea" (p. 32) based upon "interaction with musical elements through spoken language, singing, movement and playing instruments" (p. 38). Shamrock identified as basic operational principles of the Orff approach:

- Active participation for all learners in a group setting with any intellectualising to emerge as reflection upon experience;
- Opportunities for improvisation and invention of original material included at every level. (p. 38)

On the basis of her research, these principles lend themselves to application within both Western and non-Western cultural contexts, although factors such as the rhythmic and intonation patterns of the mother tongue, dominant pedagogical ideologies and socio-cultural practices of indigenous musics will and should impact upon an adaptation of the approach to any given setting (pp. 32–42).

5   The New Zealand Context

My doctoral project investigated the lived experience of music teachers who had chosen to undertake extensive, New Zealand-based professional development in the Orff approach, as they sought to apply Orff principles and processes deemed relevant in their respective settings. Of the nine participants in the study, six were primary-school music teachers (four specialist music teachers, one classroom-based teacher and one performing arts teacher), one was a performing arts teacher in an intermediate school, one was head of music at a secondary school and one was a music education consultant with extensive previous experience in school settings. In what follows I will discuss findings from my study, in which the application of Orff principles and processes to the Aotearoa New Zealand school setting can be seen as consistent with a critical praxial approach to music education.

6   The Orff Approach and the New Zealand Curriculum

In the New Zealand Curriculum (Ministry of Education 2007), 'The Arts' is one of eight specified learning areas, within which Music, as one of four arts disciplines, is designated 'Music-Sound Arts'. The following broad categories of achievement objectives form an umbrella for all arts disciplines at each of eight levels:

- Understanding music (or dance) in context;
- Developing practical knowledge;
- Developing ideas;
- Communicating and interpreting.

The New Zealand Curriculum incorporates values,[3] defined as "deeply held beliefs" (p. 10) which should be "encouraged, modelled and explored" and "part of the everyday curriculum", and "key competencies",[4] the development of which is both "an end (goal) in itself and the means by which other ends are achieved" (pp. 12–13). The document was seen to signal an opportunity for teachers and schools to work in new ways (Bull 2009). According to Bull, both a strength and weakness of the curriculum is the way in which the document functions to set the direction for learning and to provide guidance to schools on designing their *own* curriculum. This, she argues, lends itself equally to being interpreted as reinforcement of the status quo or as giving permission for developing something transformatively different. The non-prescriptive nature of the curriculum allowed the teachers in my study to instigate and develop their own music programmes. In addition, the Orff approach was justified in terms of enabling teachers to address the broad objectives of the curriculum contained within the 'values' and 'key competencies' section.

Most participants in my study viewed the curriculum as broadly based and open-ended with several describing it as "not too prescriptive" and therefore allowing for considerable freedom of choice of focus and material. Karen,[5] a music specialist in a primary school, viewed the New Zealand Curriculum as written in such a way that "just about anything could fit", saying she loved the fact that it was not "too prescriptive". She described herself as having a pragmatic approach in which she aimed to have the students purposefully engage in music-making, which she believed she could both broadly connect with, and justify in terms of, the curriculum.

---

[3] Excellence, innovation, inquiry and curiosity, diversity, equity, community and participation, ecological sustainability and integrity.

[4] Thinking, using language symbols and texts, managing self, relating to others, and participating and contributing.

[5] All names are pseudonyms.

On the other hand, Alex, a music specialist in a primary school, said "I could make any unit of work fit", expressing a frustration with the vagueness of the New Zealand Curriculum, which for her meant that the document lacked sufficient detail to enable the effective planning of a music and/or movement programme.

For many participants, the Orff approach offered frameworks and content that they believed enabled them to perfectly satisfactorily meet the requirements of the New Zealand Curriculum. Belle, a music specialist in a primary school, reported that when planning her music programme, she began with her chosen area of interest and then "made the curriculum fit around this", adding:

> You can cover most aspects of the curriculum through the Orff approach. The Orff approach is wide and varied and you can cover a lot of basic things in a creative way.

Several participants identified distinct connections between the New Zealand Curriculum and the Orff approach. Gladys viewed the Orff approach, as she understood it, as a "comfortable fit" with the curriculum: "It [the Orff approach] is made for it [the curriculum] really, I believe". Rosie, a teacher of teachers with an in-depth knowledge of the Orff approach and a contributing writer to the music curriculum in New Zealand spoke with conviction about the "match" of an Orff-based programme with the requirements or "expected outcomes" of the New Zealand Curriculum:

> There is not anything more potentially powerful than the Orff approach for music and movement education in addressing the principles, values and key competencies that are the expectations of our curriculum document.

Describing the Orff approach as artistic and participatory, Rosie specifically made connections between the music strands and related achievement objectives (AOs) and the Orff approach as follows:

The New Zealand Curriculum: The Arts: Music	Rosie's description of how the Orff approach addresses each AO
Developing practical knowledge in music	The Orff approach emphasises 'practical skills and introduces students to the elements of music through practical experiences.'
Developing ideas in music	The Orff approach 'provides opportunities for creativity, composition and improvisation.'
Communicating and interpreting in music	The Orff approach enables the 'doing of wonderful things to put a performance together.'
Understanding music in context	The Orff approach emphasises 'tapping into the cultural and imaginative world of the child'

Alex expressed her view about the relationship between the New Zealand Curriculum and the Orff approach as follows:

> I don't think if you are teaching in an Orff way you are neglecting the curriculum at all. In fact, I think you are doing a service to the New Zealand Curriculum by teaching in the Orff mode!

Now "aligned" (NZQA 2011, p. 10) with the National Curriculum, the NCEA (high school qualifications system) has become a kind of de facto curriculum in the senior secondary school. Henry, head of music in a secondary school, described his programme as tailored to the requirements of the NCEA. At the time of my study, he was engaged in an ongoing project in which he was developing through trial and subsequent reflection, a sequential programme in composition for students at Years 9, 10 and 11 which, "borrowing very heavily from the Orff approach", enabled active engagement with composition. He was anticipating a high rate of success with *Achievement Standard 91092* ('Compose two original pieces of music').[6]

7 The Orff Approach and New Zealand as a Bi-cultural Nation

The Treaty of Waitangi is the founding document of Aotearoa New Zealand. The New Zealand Curriculum includes the Treaty as one of the guiding principles under-pinning planning of programmes in schools. Honouring of the Treaty involves a commitment from teachers to embrace bi-culturalism. New Zealand teachers are made aware, through pre-service and in-service education, of their professional obligation to honour the Treaty and to fully acknowledge the bi-cultural character of our nation. The document 'Tātaiako Cultural Competencies for Teachers of Māori Learners' (Ministry of Education 2011) challenges teachers to know their students' history, tikanga[7] and world view, and to reflect this in the classroom curriculum and environment (p. 3). As we have already seen, a principle of the Schulwerk is its challenge to teachers to adapt it to their own cultural context. As a person-centred pedagogy, Orff Schulwerk is clearly compatible with the competencies for teachers of Māori students as identified in Tātaiako.

As well, the Orff principle of unity of speech, movement and music resonates with the following description of Māori Music:

> Just as the Māori view the world holistically, so too the music. Māori music is first and foremost an expression of and accompaniment to everyday life and then it is a performing art…It is song-poetry and dance…In the western world and other world cultures, it is rela-tively simple to identify song, poetry and dance as three separate art forms; but not so in the Māori world – they are all one. (Papesch 1998, p. 12)

In the school-based situation, teachers will encounter kapa haka, in which a community-designated leader works with students, teaches Māori song, dance, chant and haka. Whitinui's (2004) explanation of the significance of kapa haka from a Māori perspective similarly captures the holistic nature of this art form:

> Kapa haka allows Maori to reveal the potential of self-culture and identity through the art of performing. It also possesses the ability to link the performance to appreciating individ-ual uniqueness (difference) while helping students to come to know the value of human potential (Hindle 2002). Kapa haka instils levels of creativity through the expression of

---

[6] "Henry" subsequently completed a Masters thesis, which showed that, in stark contrast to previ-ous cohorts, these students all achieved the standard, a number with "Excellence". See http://www.nzqa.govt.nz/ncea/assessment/view-detailed.do?standardNumber=91092

[7] Behavioural guidelines for daily life and interaction in Māori culture.

body movements and actions, the expression of words, the connection between the living and those who have passed, principles reflecting life and knowing, as well as, how Maori live today. (Whitinui 2004, p. 92)

None of the participants in this study were directly involved in kapa haka. However, some participants reported on the strength of the kapa haka programmes in their schools. For example Gladys said: "In our school parents come in and run the kapa haka programme and it is fantastic; the children love it and they perform really well." Francis, a music specialist in a primary school, saw the approach taken in kapa haka as "not Orff-like at all", describing it as a "very prescriptive approach in which the instructor trains the students in singing and movement routines". Kate, a classroom teacher in a primary school, saw kapa haka as "a complete form, a complete system on its own, in which specific movements mean specific things". As a "pākehā person", she hesitated to become involved because, as she said, "I have limited knowledge of kapa haka and the protocols associated with it."

Gladys also saw kapa haka as a "whole different style to Orff", and said that she "really valued the kapa haka programme and would do anything she could to support it". She added that "kapa haka really developed the students' musical abilities, particularly their ability to sing harmonies", commenting that it "ignited the (musical) process" which was what her programme aimed to do as well. She often noticed that the students who were active in kapa haka were the ones drawn to the musical opportunities offered in her programme. She said that she liked to collaborate whenever she could with the kapa haka group to stage musical performances, where her music groups and the kapa haka group performed alongside each other. Gladys expressed the view that "the challenge is to work with the Māori community in a way that is effective and empowering".

In my own experience of school-based kapa haka, a notable feature that resonates with the Orff principle of successful participation for all students in music and movement education, is the inclusion of all students regardless of background or perceived talent. I recall several kapa haka performances in which the diversity of children participating, including students who faced considerable challenges to their learning in other areas of the schooling context, added a special and memorable dimension.

All participants indicated either through the questionnaire, interview responses or teaching practice, an engagement with New Zealand as a bicultural nation in terms of a desire and/or commitment to integrating Māori material in their Orff-based or Orff-inspired classroom programmes. Several participants reported that access to YouTube had greatly enhanced their ability to open up a much wider range of listening and viewing experiences for their students, mentioning, in particular, examples of traditional Māori musical instruments, recordings of action songs, and retellings of Māori myth. Māori material (action songs, stories, rhymes in te reo[8]) was used in five of the eight classes I observed.

---

[8] The Māori language.

However, despite the fact that all participants viewed Māori material of unquestioned relevance, some spoke of anxiety about their ability to appropriately handle it and indicated a desire for up-skilling in this area. Alex said that it was incumbent on "all teachers and all music teachers" to be committed to growing their knowledge of Māoritanga in the first instance, by actively finding out "what we don't know". In her view all aspects of the music programme should take account of Māori culture and, in particular, she supported the use of Te Reo in the music programme, adding that there was plenty of suitable Māori material available in schools. Furthermore she said 'the emphasis on rhythm and the use of body percussion' in the Orff approach suggested there was a lot of scope for the Orff approach to:

> really fuse with New Zealand culture and Māori culture in particular. We have a rich heritage of Māori music – It's mind, body and soul....Māori music is always expressed very physically, isn't it?

Her lesson was notable for its integration of Māori material: titi-torea[9] and action song and the use of a story with soundtrack, 'Ihenga' (Aunty Bea 2011) for composition. She justified the use of this story by referring to "the way the traditional Māori instruments and contemporary instruments had been fused together to give a very New Zealand feel".

Kate endorsed the use of Māori myths and legends as a basis for improvisation or composition. This, she said, recognised our indigenous culture, gave students the opportunity to both deepen their understanding of narrative and at the same time gave students an experience of collaborative creativity through the Orff approach to music and movement improvisation and composition/choreography. Kate was concerned about the appropriateness of adapting Māori music for use with Orff instruments, specifically mentioning a possible problem with 'different scale and tuning systems' and issues around the suitability of adding a tuned percussion accompaniment to a traditional melody saying: "I think it would actually detract from it to add a bass line and ostinati." In Francis's view, a commitment to bi-culturalism involved becoming cognisant of indigenous musical 'elements', such as common intervallic patterns and preferred instrumentation, and finding ways to integrate them into classroom music-making.

Phoebe, a performing arts teacher in a primary school, for whom English was a second language and who grew up in the Northern Hemisphere, spoke of the challenges of integrating Māori material, saying:

> As a foreigner I need to have the song explained to understand the meaning and the context. But to teach this material I also need to have a teacher who can guide me through an aesthetic experience of discovering this material.

Despite her self-perceived need for guidance in the use of Māori material, Phoebe's lesson, which I observed, used as a starting point for composition a series of images retelling the Māori legend of Maui fishing up Te Ika a Māui.[10]

---

[9] Games and songs using short double sticks.

[10] Translated as 'the fish of Maui', Te Ika-a-Māui is the Māori name for the North Island of New Zealand.

Gladys, a performing arts teacher at an intermediate school, who had grown up in rural New Zealand, recalled that as a child she had wished she were Māori because, as she recalled, "a lot of Māori kids I knew at school were so musical that it seemed like the happiest day in their life when they sang, did titi-torea and did the poi.[11]" Māori songs and games were always included in her programme, whether there were Māori students in her class or not. She was aware of lots and lots of Māori students who come into her school who have not had much previous exposure to a school-based music programme but indicate their keenness to learn, with statements such as, "Hey, Miss, I don't know how to play the bass but I really want to." Gladys's approach, she said, was to say, "Okay! Well, you're the bass player then. Here's a chart. Now work it out!" "And," she said, "they just do." This indicates Gladys's belief in her students, her willingness to support risk-taking behaviour for the purposes of new learning and her provision of a flexible structure (providing charts as starting point for the bass player) to support learning.

Given the bi-cultural ideal woven through all curriculum and curriculum-related materials, the application of Orff to material specific to the Aotearoa New Zealand context such as Māori myths and contemporary, well-known traditional Māori songs and dance was an inevitable and natural outcome of the application of the principles and processes of the Orff approach for these teachers. As well, the Orff approach with its emphasis on integration with other art forms was perceived to be a comfortable fit with the participants' overall understanding of Māori Performing arts.

Having said that, participants also expressed some reticence and anxiety regarding an indiscriminate application of so-called Orff musical devices, such as the use of typically Orff intervallic patterns or the Orff instrumentation, to indigenous music, whose "delineated meanings" (Green 2005, p. 80) may not be readily accessible to a person from outside the culture. In other words, there was a recognition of the need to be sensitive to and observe the boundaries set by tāngata whenua[12] in regard to their cultural taonga.[13]

8   Diversity and the Orff approach

Aotearoa New Zealand is home to over 200 different ethnic groups. In recent years, New Zealand's Māori, Asian and Pacific populations have been growing faster that the 'European or other' population. The table below shows the cultural diversity of the school rolls for the eight participants in my study who were classroom teachers (Table 1).

---

[11] Balls on strings uses in song and dance routines.

[12] Literally 'people of the land', the Māori term for the indigenous people of Aotearoa New Zealand.

[13] Literally a 'treasure'. Something considered to be of value.

Table 1 Approximate percentages of the ethnic make-up of student populations (Locke 2016, p. 186)

	Māori	New Zealand European	Pasifika	Asian	Other Indian, Middle-Eastern, African
Karen	12 %	18 %	38 %	8 %	24 %
Alex	17 %	59 %	10 %	8 %	6 %
Phoebe	1 %	60 %	1 %	38 %	
Belle	5 %	60 %	5 %	30 %	1 %
Francis	10 %	71 %	3 %	16 %	
Kate	1 %	1 %	94 %	2 %	2 %
Gladys	8 %	48 %	5 %	36 %	3 %
Henry	40 %	22 %	35 %	2 %	1 %

The Principles of the New Zealand Curriculum acknowledge Aotearoa New Zealand as a multicultural society and reference the obligation to acknowledge and value the histories and traditions that stem from the culturally diverse nature of the student population (Ministry of Education 2007, p. 9). Not only is there considerable diversity within the classroom but, as well, advanced technologies enable communication with distant places and the accessing of knowledge and material artefacts from all over the world. Not only has this impacted upon the sense of the *exotic* and *far away*; it has enabled teachers in all parts of New Zealand to find ways of acknowledging and celebrating the diversity of the particular communities within which they work.

The music education community has readily acknowledged the potential richness that a multi-cultural society offers in terms of access to and opportunity for celebration of diverse musical practices (Sheehan Campbell 1997). However, theories of dynamic multi-culturalism (Elliott 1990) and more recently, critical multi-culturalism (Benedict 2009; May and Sleeter 2010; Morton 2010) urge us think beyond simple categories of cultural difference. Rather, we need to take account of many kinds of difference: differing musical tastes, differing practices, differing forms, purposes and sources of legitimation of musicking, and so forth (Davis 2005; Jorgensen 1998; Lamb 2010). In line with a vision of arts education as potentially transformative, Morton urges music educators to provide spaces for inter-cultural understanding, critical dialogue and/or socio-political action. In order to achieve this, music education must open itself up to variety, be inclusive and in particular avoid the "fixities" (Greene 1995, p. 163) of a Eurocentric aesthetic sensibility or an essentialising or static view of culture (May 1999).

Belle described the Orff approach as "very open to world music…it looks out the whole time and easily adapts to different world music". Francis spoke of his inclusion of African traditional music repertoire because of the way it integrated music, movement and the opportunity for improvisation – processes which are themselves at the heart of the Orff approach. He also endorsed the idea of "including anything that is going on in culture", including contemporary New Zealand music.

Most participants in this study expressed the view and/or illustrated in their Orffinfluenced pedagogical practice a concern to respond to the *cultural* diversity of

their classroom demographic. However, this orientation sat within the Orff emphasis on the use of pedagogical material and practices that resonate with the lived
world of the child (or student). Mary Shamrock (1995) summed this up in stating
that "the implication surrounding the speech examples in (*Music for Children*) was
that teacher and students in any given situation would develop comparable mini
compositions based on text material meaningful and appropriate to the group"
(p. 11).

Gladys was aware of criticism of the Orff approach as an out-moded Eurocentric
approach, but indicated that this was, in her view, a reflection of a failure to understand that the Orff process was "transplantable in any culture that needs music education like we do". She described the Orff approach as "organic" and as "developing
a life of its own as it responded to the particular context". The Orff approach, she
said, "enables music to be accessible to everybody and that's good for children, I
think – for all learners actually."

Notable in Gladys's lesson, which I observed, was the successful participation of
Alice, a child with learning difficulties as a result of cognitive processing impair-
ment. The nature of the classroom ensemble experience was helpful to Alice in the
way many repetitions of a piece, as layers were built up and added, enabled her
multiple opportunities to attempt a correct reproduction of one particular melodic
pattern on her barred instrument. As she was quite well coordinated, and her difficulty seemed to be with pitch rather than with rhythmic patterning, the forgiving
nature of the sound of the marimba and the strong scaffold provided by others
around her meant inaccuracies did not detract from the informal performance she
was part of. The repetitive style of the material allowed her to continually focus on
a simple part, while others progressed to more complex parts. Gradually, her
approximations grew more accurate, while at the same time her active participation
in the musical ensemble was yielding many benefits. She was acting as a musician,
listening to others, coordinating eye and ear as she played, and her engaged
expression and relaxed demeanour suggested she was fully engaged in a satisfying
musical learning experience.

Teachers in the study repeatedly stressed an increased sense of capacity in
enabling successful learning experiences for *all* children as a significant impact of
their engagement with the Orff approach. For many this involved a significant
change in the way they viewed musical literacy. While acknowledging conventional
music literacy as *part* of musicianship, it was no longer seen as a pre-requisite for
musical participation. Classroom practice reflected this shift to a focus on "aural
sensibilities" (Morton 2010, p. 207), which played a central role in activities typically integrated within the Orff approach such as playing instruments, singing,
dancing, and story-telling, described by Morton as dimensions of music-making
reflective of world-wide traditions which foster inclusivity.

Karen found herself interrogating how the Orff approach functioned and might
function in engaging with cultural diversity:

> Orff isn't all about the instrumentarium is it? It's also about recognising and honouring
> music from other cultures. I've got all these culture-bearers in my class – children who
> bring with them the music of their culture.

In response to the large group of Pasifika students in her classes, Karen put a strong emphasis on the ukulele in her classroom work. Not only did the ukulele have an appeal for its familiarity; she found it an easy instrument to include in ensemble work as an accompaniment instrument. As well, its C G E A tuning lent itself to melodic exploration of the pentatonic.

Karen experienced the first-hand thrill of working with a "culture bearer" in an interesting process of exchange that resulted from her introducing a Swahili song, *Si Mama Kaa*, to her year 2 class. When a Tanzanian student from this class sang the song to his mother at home, she immediately recognised the song from her childhood days in Tanzania. With much delight she visited the classroom the next day, sang her version of the song and spoke of her memories from childhood related to it. This process not only supported the learning of the song but provided a meaningful and genuine living context, therefore reducing the sense of song as something fixed and static uprooted from another world. The relational process also embodied respect, sincerity and openness, values referred to in Tātaiako, which support learning for Māori (but indeed for others as well) through the development of relationships between school and community.

For Kate, responsiveness to cultural identity involved the affirmation and inclusion of student-led ideas, which expressed their cultural heritage, i.e. Pasifika-influenced gestural movement in choreographed liturgical dance sequences. For Gladys, it was the provision of an opportunity for student-initiated performances, which highlighted particular cultural performance styles or strengths. During the class I observed, she enabled a spontaneous drumming performance, when she became aware of the talent of two West-African boys in her class.

9   Conclusion

Teachers in this study rated most highly, as a key principle of the Orff approach, successful participation for all students. This principle, a cornerstone of the approach, can be seen, however, as the modus operandi for an ethical teacher in any setting, but particularly for a teacher in a New Zealand school setting in which an underlying value of the curriculum is inclusivity (Bolstad et al. 2012, p. 3). Similar to my own experience the Orff approach had offered teachers in this study a range of specific processes and strategies, that enabled this professional ideal of 'success for all' to become a practical reality.

The principled call for the adaptation of the Orff approach to local context involves, on the one hand, adaptation to the New Zealand setting in contrast to the European one (and other countries in which the ideas have also taken root, e.g. Canada, USA and Australia), and on the other hand, adaptation to the context at the local level, i.e. the cultural and socio-economic conditions of a particular school community. This adaptation must also be an ongoing process, informed by other influences, such as advances/developments in musical performance and composition and current thinking/practices of local and international music education communities.

New Zealand music educators, who engage with the ideas of the Orff approach, *may* discover that they can employ content, strategies and resources based on these ideas within a critical pedagogical approach to music education, where they create a rich and varied music programme and encourage learning experiences that are multiple and liberating. Sequences of learning, model lessons or units may inspire or even scaffold planning, but the relevance and vitality of a music programme depends upon a reflexive exercise of freedom in which a cycle of activity and reflection on activity are finely balanced.

Applications of the Orff approach in some New Zealand primary, intermediate and secondary context contexts have resulted in opportunities for students to participate equitably in musical ensembles comprised of authentic (as opposed to 'toy') instruments that do not require highly developed technical or music reading skills (Locke and Locke 2011). Critical dialogical praxis in sound could be said to exist when students are enabled to engage in holistic music-making, i.e. music-making that involves listening, playing, moving, improvising, conducting and so on, which draws on the "autobiographies of learning" (Burnard 2005, p. 267) that the students bring to the classroom.

In conclusion then I ask invite readers to evaluate in the light of their own experience and perspectives, the contribution the Orff approach might make to music teacher practice and to the overall vitality of music education for *all* students, not just within Aotearoa New Zealand school settings but also within any state-mandated, music education curriculum. In the Aotearoa New Zealand context the on-going adaptation of the Orff approach demands of teachers a critical awareness of social and cultural practices, as played out in the communities within which we live and teach. It also demands a sensitivity to the various ways in which identity is expressed through all forms of artistic endeavour – contemporary and historical, mainstream and fringe, traditional, popular and 'high' culture. New Zealand identity and culture are a changing and dynamic reality. Furthermore, it needs to be acknowledged that identity is not a simple or fixed matter but rather, it is argued, individuals are constituted by multiple identities, and simple definitions and delineations can no longer be applied (Mansfield 2005).

References

Abrahams, F. (2005a). The application of critical pedagogy to music teaching and learning. *Visions of Research in Music Education, 6*. Retrieved from http://www-usr.rider.edu/~vrme/v6n1/visions/Abrahams%20The%20Application%20of%20Critical%20Pedagogy.pdf

Abrahams, F. (2005b). Transforming classroom music instruction with ideas from critical pedagogy. *Music Educators Journal, 92*(1), 62–67. doi:10.2307/3400229.

Abril, C. R. (2013). Critical issues in Orff Schulwerk. In C. Wang (Ed.), *Orff Schulwerk: Reflections and direction* (pp. 11–25). Chicago: GIA Press.

Allsup, R. (2010). Philosophical perspectives of music education. In *Critical issues in music education* (pp. 39–60). New York: Oxford University Press.

Baker, B., Hamilton, A., & Roy, D. (2012). *Teaching the arts: Early childhood and primary education*. Sydney: Cambridge University Press.

Bea, A. (2011). *Ihenga*. Rotorua: Aunty Bea Publications.

Benedict, C. (2009). Processes of alienation: Marx, Orff and Kodaly. *British Journal of Music Education, 26*(2), 213–224.

Bolstad, R., Gilbert, J., McDowall, S., Bull, A., Boyd, S., & Hipkins, R. (2012). *Supporting future-oriented learning and teaching: A New Zealand perspective*. Wellington: Ministry of Education.

Borgo, D. (2013). *What does it mean to be musical?* San Diego: UCTV. Retrieved from http://www.youtube.com/watch?feature=player_embedded&v=wVP8tWg7SQY.

Bowman, W. (2005). The limits and grounds of musical praxialism. In D. J. Elliott (Ed.), *Praxial music education. Reflections & dialogues* (pp. 52–78). Oxford: Oxford University Press.

Bull, A. (2009). *Thinking together to become 21st century teachers: Teachers' work.* (Working Paper #1). NZCER. Retrieved from www.nzcer.orgnz/pdfs/21st-century-teachers-200906.pdf

Burnard, P. (2005). What matters in general music? In *Praxial music education. Reflections & dialogues* (pp. 267–280). Oxford: Oxford University Press.

Burton, B. (2000). Voices of Turtle Island: Native American music and dance. In *Many seeds, different flowers. The music education legacy of Carl Orff* (pp. 28–39). Perth: CIRCME.

Davis, R. A. (2005). Music education and cultural identity. In D. K. Lines (Ed.), *Music education for the new millennium: Theory and practice futures for music teaching and learning* (pp. 47–64). Malden: Blackwell.

De Quadros, A. (Ed.). (2000). *Many seeds, different flowers, the music education legacy of Carl Orff*. Perth: CIRCME.

Dolloff, L. A. (1993). Das Schulwerk: A foundation for the cognitive musical and artistic development of children. In *Research perspectives in music education* (pp. 1–57). Toronto: Canadian Music Education Research Centre.

Drummond, J. (2000). A voice for all to hear: The Orff legacy and the "new" music education. In *Many seeds, different flowers. The music education legacy of Carl Orff* (pp. 50–57). Perth: CIRCME.

Dunbar-Hall, P. (2000). World music, creativity and Orff pedagogy. In *Many seeds, different flowers. The music education legacy of Carl Orff* (pp. 58–66). Perth: CIRCME.

Elliott, D. J. (1990). Music as culture: Toward a multicultural concept of arts education. *Journal of Aesthetic Education, 24*(1), 147–166.

Frazee, J. (1987). *Discovering Orff: A curriculum for music teachers*. New York: Schott.

Frazee, J. (2012). *Artful-playful-mindful: A new Orff-Schulwerk curriculum for music making and music thinking*. New York: Schott Music Corporation.

Freire, P. (1985). *The politics of education*. London: Macmillan.

Freire, P. (1994). *Pedagogy of hope: Reliving pedagogy of the oppressed* (R. R. Barr, Trans.). New York: Continuum.

Freire, P. (2011). *Pedagogy of the oppressed* (New rev. 30th-Anniversary ed.). New York: Continuum.

Goodkin, D. (2000). Orff-Schulwerk in the new mythology. In *Many seeds, different flowers. The music education legacy of Carl Orff* (pp. 79–93). Perth: CIRCME.

Goodkin, D. (2004). *Play, sing, dance*. Mainz: Schott.

Green, L. (2005). Musical meaning and social reproduction: A case for retrieving autonomy. *Educational Philosophy and Theory, 37*(1), 77–91.

Greene, M. (1995). *Releasing the imagination*. San Francisco: Jossey-Bass.

Hall, D. (1960). *Orff-Schulwerk for children. Music for children. Teacher's manual*. Mainz: Schott.

Hartmann, W. (2000). Creative playgrounds—music by children. In *Many seeds, different flowers. The music education legacy of Carl Orff*. Perth: CIRCME.

Haselbach, B. (Ed.). (2011). *Basic texts on theory and practice of Orff Schulwek* (Vol. 1). Mainz: Schott.

Haselbach, B., & Hartmann, W. (2013). *Summary of the key principles of the Orff Schulwerk approach*. Symposium discussion document presented at the Orff Forum, Salzburg, Austria.

Haselbach, B., Solomon, M. H., & Maubach, C. (2008, July 6). *University of Waikato*. International panel discussion of Orff educators.

Hindle, R. F. (2002). *The Māori arts in education*. Paper presented at the UNESCO regional meeting of experts on art education in the Pacific, Nadi, Fiji.

Hoffman Davis, J. (2008). *Why our schools need the arts*. New York: Teachers College Press.

Johnson, D. C. (2006). Carl Orff: Musical humanist. *International Journal of Humanities, 3*(8), 1–6.

Jorgensen, E. (1998). Musical multi-culturalism revisited. *Journal of Aesthetic Education, 32*(2), 77–88.

Keetman, G. (1970). *Elementaria* (M. Murray, Trans.). London: Schott.

Lamb, R. (2010). Music as a socio-cultural phenomenon: Interactions with music education. In H. F. Abeles & L. A. Custodero (Eds.), *Critical issues in music education* (pp. 23–38). New York: Oxford University Press.

Locke, L. (2015). Music education as a "practice of freedom". In M. Peters & T. Besley (Eds.), *Paulo Freire: The global legacy* (pp. 503–516). New York: Peter Lang.

Locke, L. (2016). *The Orff approach in the professional lives and practices of teachers in the Aotearoa/New Zealand school context*. Unpublished doctoral thesis. University of Waikato, Hamilton, New Zealand.

Locke, L., & Locke, T. (2011). Sounds of Waitakere: Using practitioner research to explore how Year 6 recorder players compose responses to visual representations of a natural environment. *British Journal of Music Education, 28*(3), 263–284.

Mansfield, J. E. (2005). The global musical subject, curriculum and Heidegger's questioning concerning technology. In *Music education for the new millennium* (pp. 131–146). Malden: Blackwell.

Marsh, K. (2000). *Creative processes in Australian children's playground singing games: beyond the ostinato* (pp. 144–164). Perth: CIRCME.

May, S. (1999). Critical multi-culturalism and cultural difference: Avoiding essentialism. In S. May (Ed.), *Critical multiculturalism: Rethinking multi-cultural and anti-racist education* (pp. 11–34). London: Falmer Press.

May, S., & Sleeter, C. (Eds.). (2010). *Critical multiculturalism: Theory and praxis*. New York: Routledge.

Mills, J. (2005). *Music in the school*. Oxford: Oxford University Press.

Ministry of Education. (2007). *The New Zealand curriculum*. Wellington: Learning Media Ltd.

Ministry of Education. (2011). *Tātaiako. Cultural competencies for teachers of Māori learners*. Wellington: Ministry of Education.

Morton, C. (2010). Breaking through the "crusts of convention" to realise music education's potential contribution to critical multi-culturalism. In *Critical multiculturalism: Theory and praxis* (pp. 203–213). New York: Routledge.

Nykrin, R. (2011). 50 years "Music for children – Orff-Schulwerk" Thoughts about the present status of a music educational classic (2000/2010). In B. Haselbach (Ed.), *Texts on theory and practice of Orff Schulwerk* (pp. 274–317). Mainz: Schott.

NZQA. (2011). *New Zealand Qualifications Authority annual report 2010–2011*.

Orff, C. (1932/2011). Music out of movement. In B. Haselbach (Ed.), *Texts on theory and practice of Orff Schulwerk: Basic texts for the years 1932–2010* (pp. 94–103). Mainz: Schott.

Orff, C. (1962/1977). Demonstration with recordings. Lecture at the University of Toronto. In I. McNeill-Carley (Ed.), *Orff re-echoes Book 1 – Selections from the Orff Echo & the supplements* (pp. 53–59). Cleveland: American Orff-Schulwerk Association.

Orff, C., & Keetman, G. (1959a). *Orff-Schulwerk. Music for children* (M. Murray, Trans., Vols. 1–1, Vol. Pentatonic). London: Schott.

Orff, C., & Keetman, G. (1959b). *Orff-Schulwerk. Music for children* (M. Murray, Trans., Vols. 1–2, Vol. Major: Drone bass triads). London: Schott.

Orff, C., & Keetman, G. (1963). *Orff-Schulwerk. Music for children* (M. Murray, Trans., Vols. 1–3, Vol. Major. Dominant and subdominant triads). London: Schott.

Orff, C., & Keetman, G. (1966a). *Orff-Schulwerk. Music for children* (Margaret Murray, Trans., Vols. 1–5, Vol. Minor: Drone bass triads). London: Schott.

Orff, C., & Keetman, G. (1966b). *Orff Schulwerk. Music for children* (M. Murray, Trans., Vols. 1–V, Vol. Minor: Dominant and subdominant triads). London: Schott.

Orff New Zealand Aotearoa. (2012). *Orff Schulwerk levels workshop guidelines.* Orff New Zealand Aotearoa.

Papesch, T. (1998). Te puoro reo o kui mā, o koro mā, waiaata tawhito- traditional Māori music. *Sound Ideas, 2*(1), 12–21.

Regelski, T. (2002). On "methodolatry" and music teaching as critical and reflexive praxis. *Philosophy of Music Education Review, 10*(2), 102–123.

Roberts, P. (2003). Knowledge, dialogue and humanization: Exploring Freire's philosophy. In *Critical theory and the human condition: Founders and praxis* (pp. 169–183). New York: Peter Lang.

Shamrock, M. (1995). *Orff Schulwerk: Brief history, description and issues in global dispersal.* Cleveland: American Orff-Schulwerk Association.

Sheehan Campbell, P. (1997). Music, the universal language: Fact or fallacy. *International Journal of Music Education, 29*(2), 32–39.

Small, C. (1998). *Musicking.* Hanover: University Press of New England.

Takizawa, T. (2000). Orff seeds in Japanese culture. In *Many seeds, different flowers. The music education legacy of Carl Orff* (pp. 205–211). Perth: CIRCME.

Thomas, W. (2011). "In the beginning was the word..." on the significance of the spoken word in Orff-Schulwerk. In *Texts on theory and practice of Orff-Schulwerk* (Vol. 1). Mainz: Schott.

Vygotsky, L. (1978). *Mind in society: The development of higher mental processes.* Cambridge, MA: Harvard University Press.

Warner, B. (1991). *Orff-Schulwerk: Applications for the classroom.* Englewood Cliffs: Prentice Hall.

Whitinui, P. (2004). The indigenous factor: The role of kapa haka as a culturally responsive learning intervention. *Waikato Journal of Education, 10,* 85–97.

Linda Locke is an Auckland-based music educator who has worked for many years as a primary school music specialist. Her doctoral research investigated applications of the Orff approach in the Aotearoa/New Zealand context, and was entitled: *The Orff approach in the professional lives and practices of teachers in the Aotearoa/New Zealand school context. A critical analysis for the Orff Schulwerk approach in the New Zealand school system.*

Forging Genuine Partnerships in the Music Studio Context: Reviving the Master-Apprentice Model for Post-colonial Times

Te Oti Rakena

Abstract This chapter discusses the relationship between the music teacher and the music learner in the vocal and instrumental studio context. The discussion is specific to Aotearoa/New Zealand and is framed within a narrative that describes the creation and implementation of a postgraduate studio pedagogy course. Creating a culturally safe and psychologically safe studio context is increasingly complicated in this post-colonial context. The course was designed to support performance students planning to teach in the community by enhancing their knowledge of studio teaching practices with contemporary studio based research relevant to the South Pacific context. The aim of the course was to produce future teachers who think both as music instructors and as critical cultural workers and in this way mitigate the possibilities of mis-learning and resistance in future studio teaching and learning partnerships.

Keywords Māori • Pacific Island • Music instruction • Studio pedagogy • Community teaching • Community music

1 Forging Genuine Partnerships in the Music Studio Context: Reviving the Master-Apprentice Model for Post-Colonial Times

In this chapter I pay homage to those "others", my *Pākehā*[1] research colleagues with whom I have personally forged partnerships in the hope of making meaningful change in education. These colleagues are descendants of European settlers but think and act in a manner free of the colonial shackles that shaped our country, and in particular the New Zealand education system. Through these partnerships they

T.O. Rakena (✉)
School of Music, National Institute of Creative Arts and Industries, University of Auckland, 6 Symonds Street, Auckland, New Zealand
e-mail: t.rakena@auckland.ac.nz

© Springer International Publishing Switzerland 2016
L. Ashley, D. Lines (eds.), *Intersecting Cultures in Music and Dance Education*, Landscapes: the Arts, Aesthetics, and Education 19,
DOI 10.1007/978-3-319-28989-2_8

119

have displayed a commitment to *Te Tiriti o Waitangi*[2], our founding document, attempting to restore value and respect to the indigenous *Māori* culture and developing nation-building practices that have addressed some of the past colonial violations in a significant and sustainable way. In this more emancipatory milieu, distanced from motherland Europe across space and time, these researchers find inspiration in the practices of the "other". They recognise the significance of their location in the South Pacific, and understand the importance of shifting between cultural paradigms in order to forge genuine partnerships with students from all cultures and across all educational contexts. The intersection of these peoples' cultures and worldviews with those of a transformed colonial body has created a culturally-safe site, that provides innovative educators the opportunity to explore current and past educational practices and to create a reservoir of diverse knowledge with which to contemporise an inherited curriculum.

2 Genuine Partnerships in Post-Colonial Contexts

The title of this chapter is deliberatively provocative. Two important concepts are introduced: the nature of partnership, and the intersection of legitimate and expert power[3] in the post-colonial music studio teaching and learning context. In these terms lie important issues that have impacted education and performance practice in the South Pacific. The term 'partnership' has special nuance in post-colonial New Zealand. The founding document Te Tiriti o Waitangi, the Treaty of Waitangi, explicitly outlines a bi-cultural partnership between the indigenous people, Māori, and the British Crown. The complexities associated with respecting this document historically and in contemporary society are evident across all aspects of the community (Mutu 2011; Walker 2004; Nairn and McCreanor 1991). Respecting the core message of the treaty is seen by some as key to nation building and has been incentive for the Ministry of Education to support research projects that explore the impact of teaching practices on Māori and work in partnership with Māori educators, students and their families to increase participation, achievement and academic success (Ministry of Education 2008; Gorinski and Abernethy 2007).

Success for Māori partly involves overcoming the impact of past government initiatives in Māori education that deliberately disadvantaged them within the state's education system. Legislative action such as the Education Ordinance of 1847, which provided funding for mission schools, and the Native Schools Act of 1867 were schemes that used schooling of Māori as a means of social control, assimilation, and the establishment of British law. The amount and type of knowledge made available to Māori through these schemes was a deliberate attempt to create a labouring class by limiting intellectual development and prioritising manual instruction (Simon 1998, p. 73). Current discourse on educational underachievement by

Māori often cite these initiatives as the historic origins of institutional practices that have lead to the under-representation of the indigenous in the statistics by which educational success is usually measured, and contributed to current sociological trends and educational outcomes (Bishop and Glynn 2003; Pihama et al. 2002; Smith 1999; Simon 1998). Studying music at an advanced level is thus a conflicted location for Māori as it is both a position of higher learning, from which Māori were deliberately excluded for many generations, and a performance discipline connected with the tourist and entertainment industry, a stereotypical positioning of the native by the colonial body and Māori themselves (Spiller 2010; Condevaux 2009). The question for us in this chapter is how do we ensure that future one-to-one studio instructors are aware of this legacy and have the cultural sensitivity and tools to begin to repair this schism?

In the second decade of the twenty-first century, the situation is further complicated as the nation becomes more ethnically diverse. In the 2010 Social Report released by the Ministry of Social Development, statisticians expect this cultural diversity to increase with Asian, immigrant Pacific Island minorities and Māori ethnic groups growing the fastest. While demographics may be changing, the creation of special interest groups such as New Zealand Asian Leaders, a group that is attempting to address the significant disparity between Europeans and Asians in top-level management jobs in New Zealand businesses, indicates that many of those in positions of power are still descended from the colonising majority. The work of groups like this help dispel the myth of an egalitarian New Zealand, and test the notion of power sharing in postcolonial nations. In this chapter we investigate how this power differential interacts with the received master-apprentice tradition of teaching in the music studio.

Educating a performing musician with a musical identity grown in the South Pacific has become progressively complicated in this post-colonial context. The transmission of tastes, values, practices, skills or knowledge of the colonial body privileges the hegemonic social strata and can reinforce the superiority of the colonial hierarchy (Kok 2011). This makes university Schools of Music especially problematic as their core business is to preach the elevated values of the Western European art aesthetic in an environment that is striving to empower local artists and celebrate regional knowledge and cultures. Green refers to this trend as the "push and pull effect of globalization versus localization" (Green 2011, p. 13). Acknowledging that the learning outcomes expected from a music studio environment are universally defined by traditions and conventions founded in the profession's needs (Shulman 2005), the training of a performing musician remains within the conventions of the master-apprentice model and within the studio context. In our increasingly diverse community, student cohorts (apprentices) are becoming more culturally, historically, socio-economically, and educationally removed from performance teachers (masters).

3   The Music Studio Teaching and Learning Partnership

This chapter discusses the relationship between the music teacher and the music learner in the performance studio. The discussion is specific to *Aotearoa*[4]/New Zealand and is framed within a narrative that describes the creation and implementation of a postgraduate studio pedagogy course. The course was designed to support performance students planning to teach in the community by enhancing their knowledge of studio teaching practices with contemporary research relevant to the South Pacific context. The aim of the course was to produce future instrumental and singing teachers who think both as music instructors, and what Freire (1998) described as critical cultural workers. In order to achieve this, the conventional course content was supplemented with readings and reflective activities. The coordinators located literature that critically engaged with the power differentials that emerge in the Eurocentric studio model. They also explored local research that integrated Pacific-based knowledge and creative values into studio teaching and learning, and introduced students to studio based research projects that promoted intercultural activities. For the purposes of this article, I will focus on one example used in the course, *Success for All*[5], a local research project that was funded by the *Teaching, Learning, Research Initiative* a New Zealand government-funded scheme for collaborative research.

A core component of the course involved guiding students to reflect on and discuss their individual stories and experiences in the New Zealand studio context. Through this process students examined past studio relationships. They assessed teaching practices that lead to strong performance outcomes, and analysed undemocratic teaching practices (McLaren 1998) that created tensions in the teacher-student dyad. By processing those memories we predict that students will avoid the same scenarios in their future studio teaching. Using local research projects as examples of non-traditional approaches to studio teaching, and with mutually agreed processes in place, course coordinators and students were able to co-construct a comprehensive and relevant university course with and for performance students embarking on a career in studio teaching in the community.

4   The State of the Literature

The body of literature that addresses the one-to-one music studio teaching and learning context is increasing but still limited, a problem music educationalist Ryan Daniel suggests is in part due to the isolation of people working in the field, and perhaps due to the notion that success in the field is due to aptitude (as cited in McPhail 2010, p. 34). Much of the recent literature examines performance training in higher education (Carey et al. 2013; Perkins 2013; Burwell 2013; Zhukov 2012; Gaunt 2010; Nerland 2007). For a performance student preparing to work in the community as an instrumental or voice teacher, a limited body of research exists on interpersonal studio relationships in pre-tertiary contexts and little literature on encounters between the studio teacher and student with different cultural world-views. For those working in post-colonial contexts, the literature that considers the position of the indigenous learner and how this may be expressed in the one-to-one teaching arena is even more restricted. In addition, studio teachers in New Zealand have rarely received any type of training unless they are attached to a specific methodology, or have pursued advanced degrees in the universities of the privileged west. This means gaining experience in different cultural settings or mentor teaching is seldom an option.

We find the opposite in music education and in the wider education arena where pre-service training is rigorous (Phelan 2001). Most of the relevant literature is focused on pre-service training for non-studio teachers and strategies for producing culturally responsive teachers for the classroom (Adler 2011; Ullman and Hecsh 2011; Barnes 2006; Wiggins and Follo 1999; Grant 1994). While there is a strong body of work relating to cultural diversity as demonstrated in the area of multicultural education in the United States of America, the literature that addresses post-colonial situations with an indigenous power imbalance is still narrow. Ladson-Billings (1995) points us towards several studies that aimed to improve achievement for indigenous Hawaiian, and Native American children. She observed that success was little more than fitting minority students into the current social structures of the schools, a hierarchical structure she defined as meritocracy. The educational concepts that were implemented to help these target populations seemed to do little but reproduce the existing inequities (p. 467).

In classroom contexts it has long been recognised that "understanding concepts of diversity and their implications is difficult for beginning teachers" (Boyer 1996 cited in Wiggins and Follo 1999). If this is true of the classroom context, then it is more relevant in the one-to-one studio partnership where teaching activities can pass unregulated. Carey et al. (2013) note that pedagogical activities evaded scrutiny for many years because of the "intimacy and inaccessibility of the space in which it was conducted" (p. 149). The studio pedagogy course under discussion in this article was developed to help emerging studio teachers move safely into the community and to have the skills to create culturally safe and "psychologically safe" (Adler 2011, p. 610) music studio teaching and learning sites.

5   The Music Studio

It could be said that viewing the music studio context through a cultural lens is unnecessary when the skills and traditions learned are those of the western European classical music concert platform. In a sense the learner commits to a mutually agreed third space when they enter the studio and are entrusted with the skills that ensure the successful propagation of the performance conventions associated with that tradition. The learner also commits to an intimate relationship with an expert teacher. The term most often used in the instrumental teaching and learning literature is "master" and "apprentice" (Burwell 2013, p. 276). Burwell notes that the roots of instrumental teaching and learning clearly lie within this apprenticeship model, where skills are acquired through a process of doing and knowing (p. 279). She also notes that the terms "master" and "apprentice" are "rarely systematically defined" (p. 277) in the literature but gives evidence that the "master" dominant authority can be a critical component of the teacher-learner interaction (p. 283). What is apparent from the wider education literature is that power differentials play an important role in all learning environments. According to Illeris "all learning requires the integration of two very different processes, an external interaction process between the learner and his or her social, cultural or material environment and an internal psychological process of elaboration and acquisition" (Illeris 2009, p. 8). He goes on to suggest that the acquisition of knowledge is not only a cognitive matter but involves the students' attitudes to the intended learning, their interests and mobilisation of mental energy, which he terms the incentive dimension. He states, "The value and durability of the learning result is closely related to the incentive dimensions of the learning process" (Illeris 2009, p. 12). The nature of the relationship between the "master" and "apprentice" is therefore crucial to the success of the one-to-one teaching learning environment, a context that quickly exposes teachers unfamiliar with cultural norms other than their own. This can impact motivation and undermine trust, key elements in the learning process (Zhukov 2012; Gaunt 2010). It is essential in this context, for future teachers to have a deeper awareness of the historical discourses that have contributed to current education practices (Adler 2011; Phelan 2001) and in this way increase their awareness and sensitivity to the cultural dimension of the individual student. In New Zealand, this sensitivity begins the process of decolonising the music studio and reviving the master apprentice model for a cultural framework that encompasses diversity and its more complex strand indigeneity.

6 The Course

Abrahams (2005) recognised that studio teachers, who work within the pedagogy model of master-apprentice, develop specific rituals and establish strong power dynamics within their teaching space that can make it difficult for them to critically self-reflect and therefore reluctant to open themselves to new realities (p. 5). This difficulty can cause professional development interventions to be ineffective or at least limited in their power to make meaningful change. One of the objectives of this particular course was to plant the seeds for organisational and professional changes in the new generation of community studio teachers. Entitled *Studio Pedagogy and Research* the course aimed to provide students with the necessary skills to locate and implement research-based information in the music studio context by exploring the theoretical principles that underlie learning and teaching pupils of all ages and at all levels. To accommodate the community focus the course developers included as a learning outcome the following objective: To understand

and empathise with the complexities of teaching and learning in Aotearoa/New Zealand and the Pacific context.

For this course we drew on a historical definition of culture as offered by Aronowitz and Giroux (1991): "A set of activities by which different groups produce collective memories, knowledge, social relationships, and values within historically controlled relations of power" (p. 50). The coordinators were aware that ideally, culturally nuanced education "must be infused throughout the total programme rather than addressed through an add-on workshop approach" (Grant 1994, p. 13), and so the students were directed to scrutinise all course readings and lecture offerings through a cultural lens. This meant assessing the effectiveness of the research design and methodology from their own cultural perspective, identifying the worldview of researcher(s) and the research participants, and evaluating who would benefit from the outcome of the research. In this way the students begin to regulate the usefulness of the research data by being aware of the cultural and power position(s) of the researcher(s). The students then applied the same framework to their educational experience. They reflected on the position of the teacher in their studio context and their experience as students. They created narratives, which they shared with the class. To prepare for this task a local research project was used as a model and demonstrated how these narratives might be used to inform their future teaching practices.

7   Success for All

Success for All was a research project based in Aotearoa/New Zealand that explored the educational experiences and expectations of Māori and indigenous Pacific Island populations by gathering narratives from several different teaching and learning contexts across a large university. In these narratives students identified key studio practices that contributed to building strong teacher/learner partnerships. In the music studio context, the strength of this partnership was key to successful performance outcomes. The research project was designed to optimise students' bicultural perspectives, which produced robust data for discussion and analysis.

The value of the bicultural student point of view has been discussed by a variety of researchers across different disciplines and cultures. Walker (2004) refers to the relationship between Māori and Pākehā as having a certain asymmetry as Māori have been impelled to learn and to function in two cultures in order to survive the political economy (p. 389). Donaldo Macedo (in Freire 2000) describes his memories of a colonised existence in Cape Verde as being "culturally schizophrenic, being present but not visible, being visible but not present" (p. 11). Susan Adler (2011) suggests that bicultural students can provide narratives that will inform the hegemonic teaching strata, as "students from cultures that are different from the mainstream might be more informed and insightful because they had to be bicultural to survive" (p. 613). What is key in Adler's rationale is that these students have had to adapt to the dominant culture's social system in order to survive. This is a powerful statement that contextualises other academic discussions that propose citizens of a multicultural society can change cultural frames depending on the situation and as Spring notes, that to some extent all people learn to function in different cultural contexts (Spring, cited in Wren 2012, p. 78).

The participants in the *Success for All* project, have been forced to engage daily with a social system that has excised control over their land, resources and education possibilities. It presupposes therefore that these students through this experience have developed a particular epistemological perspective (Adler 2011). Adler (2011) uses W.E.B. Du Bois' term *double consciousness* to describe this type of bicultural sensitivity (p. 613) and acknowledges that there are multiple ways of developing this epistemological perspective. The *Success for All* research project, involved a multi-cultural, trans-disciplinary research team made up largely of researchers equipped with this bicultural sensitivity. The team agreed on several protocols that would ensure culturally safe research practices and power sharing partnerships. The team used non-western research methodologies as a framework for the project and included a "give way rule". This rule permitted all researchers to critically analyse the research data with an understanding that the group would allow a member of the team with specific cultural knowledge, parallel with that of the research participant, to decide on the final interpretation of the related data.

Within this project, the research aimed to improve performance outcomes for Māori students and Pacific Island students through enhanced teaching. Two research questions framed this discussion. (1) What teaching practices in the music studio context help or hinder Māori and Pacific Island success? (2) How can this information guide teaching and university practices in order to best support Māori and Pacific Island success in preparing for or completing a music degree? The team used the Critical Incident Technique[6] to analyse the students' stories. The Critical Incident Technique asks participants to provide descriptive accounts of events that facilitated or hindered a particular aim. As conceptualised originally, a critical incident is one that makes a significant contribution to an activity or phenomenon (Flanagan 1954). The stories that resulted from the students' interviews were collaboratively grouped by similarity into categories and sub-categories that reflected the quality of the incident and which, in this instance would inform the training and practices of future studio teachers.

To ensure that research processes were delivered in a culturally appropriate manner, the project design integrated *Kaupapa Māori Research* and *Pacific Island Research* methodologies. Kaupapa Māori Research is a well-established academic discipline and research methodology (Smith 1999) that locates Māori at the centre of research enquiry. It requires researchers to have an understanding of the social, economic, and political influences on Māori outcomes and can use a diverse range of research tools. Pacific Island research methodology ensures that the researchers design a study that prioritises the wellbeing and empowerment of Pacific Island peoples within New Zealand (Anae et al. 2001; Health Research Council 2005). Ethnic-specific differences within the grouping Pacific Island are respected, along with the central importance of principled relationships to all for ethical research practice (Airini et al. 2015).

What was apparent in the *Success for All* project, is that the apprentice's identity in this relationship was often dependent on the master's assumptions of the role, rather than the apprentice's needs. Respondents stated that to have an effective master-apprentice partnership, dialogue must be established; the teacher must be willing to move beyond historical precedents and meet the apprentice within their epistemology, and authoritarian language needs to be limited. What is also clear from the respondents' narratives is that apprentices seek out expert practitioners, and are willing to accommodate an imbalance of power if the master is truly an expert in their field.

The narratives indicated that, within the Aotearoa/New Zealand context, there continues to be a struggle for some educators to relinquish assumptions based in their own worldview and shift the cultural paradigm to the worldview of the student. The findings revealed that without this change it is difficult to understand the Māori and Pacific Island students' educational needs, and will result in the core component of studio learning and assessment—critique—becoming a dehumanising process. The narratives supported the notion that learner-centred teaching that displaces issues of culture and power—in this case an approach that disconnects the student from his or her relationship with the colonial power base and/or ignorance of subjugated knowledge—creates an abstract relationship void of trust and potent with resistance (Edwards and Usher 2007). Teaching approaches that had the potential to transcend a Eurocentric view of culture and identity were trusted and respected. An example that demonstrates this shift in cultural paradigm was the acceptance by a tutor that learning is not understood by these students to be an individual process but a social phenomenon that references the family and community rather than the self. Tutors who approached teaching and learning as a shared process, which includes a community beyond the teacher, learner and institution, were seen as more capable of creating a studio learning culture that was commensurate with the Māori and Pacific Island worldview.

8   Double-Consciousness

By introducing students in the studio pedagogy course to the data provided by the *Success for All*, students were then able to bring this discussion into the music studio context. Through critical engagement with this information we were able to raise the students' cultural awareness in the following ways: They were able to observe non-western research methodological processes in action; they experienced through the student voice the impact a collision of cultures has on student learning, and they witnessed the teachers struggle to connect with students because they were unaware of differences in epistemologies. From this transformed position we were able to lead students through a deeper analysis of their worldviews, and critically perceive the cultural conditions that shaped their studio experiences.

To begin this reflective process the first assessment in the studio pedagogy course mirrored the two research questions outlined in the *Success for All* research project.

Assessed as an oral presentation, it used as a reference the Māori concept of *mihi*, a component of the formal welcoming ritual in Māori contexts. In brief, one identifies oneself to the gathered community by citing genealogical connections and interests, and revealing any connections the speaker may have to the location and the people present at the ritual. The concept when transferred to the studio context is an opportunity for the student to identify themselves within the musical dimension as a performer, studio participant and future teacher. Called *Me the Learner*, the students prepared a short presentation that outlined their individual learning experiences and described their journey through music education. They were asked to critically reflect on the teaching practices that helped or hindered their musical development and draw on pedagogical themes discussed in class and in selected readings. This process was then analysed, as in the *Success for All* project, using the critical incident method, and the categories presented to the students the following week.

While *Success for All* provided the opportunity to uncover the stories of indigenous Māori and Pacific Island students, fourth year performance students of Pākehā heritage and Asian heritage, including Indian, Korean and Chinese, provided the narratives in this course. The students engaged fully in this process, appreciating the time and space to reflect on their own studio experiences. The categories largely intersected with those of the *Success for All* project with a reframing of some of the broader categories, and the deduction of the ethnic specific. Recurring themes from students' narratives and key concepts extracted from the literature shaped the following set of music studio competencies students saw as key in past relationships with tutors, and crucial to developing a genuine partnership with future students. The students saw a good relationship as central to a genuine partnership in the studio and identified the practices within the teaching-learning context as successful if they retained the *joy of musicking*[7] throughout the training period. Inspiring and motivating students to autonomous learning occurred when an effective teacher allowed space for questions and encouraged active learning. The class defined a genuine partnership as a transparent relationship, free from authority or cultural dominance balanced with appropriate "instructivist" (McPhail 2010, p. 34) moments that ensured the transmission of expert knowledge.

In order to create a safe studio context and mitigate the possibilities of mislearning and resistance, the future teachers quickly developed strategies that centred on establishing and supporting dialogical relationships with students. Freire and Macedo (1995) state that critical pedagogues need to move beyond a simplistic understanding of dialogue as a technique and see it as a process that establishes an epistemological relationship. In this way it is "an indispensable part of the process of learning and knowing" (p. 379). A series of questions were created to help students assess the nature of the studio dialogue, and to ensure it contributed to future learning.

1. How inclusive is the studio language and is it contributing to establishing or increasing a strong sense of efficacy?
2. What external influences are impacting the studio dialogue?

3. Is there a language code[8] at work here that excludes less privileged students or minority students?
4. Are we self-regulating our non-verbal behaviours?
5. Are we are monitoring the student's non-verbal language?

Students were aware that in their musical development both formal and informal music learning contributed to motivation and incentive for continuing to learn. These included group learning activities, structured ensemble music making, and free jamming. All these activities facilitated social connections, joyful musicking, learning from peers, multiple feedback possibilities and real life utilisation of skills. This is a music studio example of what Illeris (2009) describes in his constructivist model of learning as the *interaction* dimension. As briefly introduced earlier in this chapter, within his model he positions two areas of learning as equal and mutually beneficial; (1) *content*, which he describes as what is learned, knowledge and skills and opinions; and (2) *incentive*, which provides the mental energy that is necessary for the learning process to take place including feelings, emotions, motivation, and volition. These two dimensions are always initiated by impulses from the third area, the *interaction* process, which builds up the sociality of the learner. Traditionally the industry standard for music studio teaching has been to focus on what Illeris describes as content. Increasingly, the focus on content is shifting to a more balanced view of music studio teaching and learning where the impact of the incentive dimension on the acquisition of skills is explored. In this new construct teachers are encouraged to consider a variety of processes within the interactive dimension that best balance the other two dimensions and provide stronger outcomes for the student. This is supported by recent research studies such as Zhukov (2012), Green (2012), Creech and Hallam (2011) and Gaunt (2010), who seek more holistic solutions to studio teaching and learning issues.

Using the *Success for All* research frameworks the students from the pedagogy course were able to develop a list of 10 praxes that integrated personal experience with research data that had been distilled through an academic filter shaped by a newly awakened cultural sensitivity. This framework will help them transition more confidently into their roles as a community teachers. These practices are:

1. Be in constant dialogue with student,
2. Create flexible but structured lessons,
3. Constantly assess developing self-efficacy, self awareness and autonomy,
4. Watch for unhealthy performing practices,
5. Track progress,
6. Make space for self-reflection,
7. Make sure the studio environment fosters students' passion for music,
8. Ensure music learning is fun by creating a safe studio space for students to explore,
9. Create a culturally safe environment, where culture extends beyond the ethnic to encompass gender, gender identity, religion, sexual orientation, and disabilities; and

10. Ensure the teaching-learning context has relevance to the students' lived experience.

Practices that emerged from narratives with indigenous students were utilised by sighted student teachers working with blind students, students working in gender-specific contexts, students dealing with issues related to sexual orientation and students working in intergenerational contexts.

9 Moving Beyond the Binary

Within the course, discussions around the narrative findings offered an opportunity for the pedagogy students to critically analyse performance learning within a socio-cultural construct that liberated students from the power model of the master-apprentice tradition. The reflective activities and group discussions allowed space for individual students to articulate their ways of knowing the studio experience. This process put into practice Tanaka's (2003) theory of *intersubjectivity*, an intercultural educational framework he suggests as an alternative to the traditional discourses around culture and power. The focus moves to the individual as a "subject", having a personal history and agency rooted in time and place, with multiple shifting subjectivities, meanings that have evolved from an individual's social location, ethnicity, gender, religion, sexual orientation etc. In this framework no one culture dominates and the subject is able to relate stories with relationship to their subjectivities, and does so without turning the individual's present into an object, or "other" (Tanaka 2003, p. 16). In Tanaka's (2003) analysis of several attempts by universities in the United States to increase diversity and cultural awareness, de-centring white majorities without finding a place in the overall framing of multicultural perspectives was seen as a recurring issue underlying racial discontent within these universities. Giving all the students in this course the opportunity to speak equally and be in dialogue with their peers and tutors allowed our course to move away from a "dominant-minority or binary view of teaching-learning and instead focus on the mutual process of change that occurs when multiple cultures, and associated subcultures come into contact with each other" (Tanaka 2003, p. 46).

In this chapter I have discussed partnerships and power in the post-colonial context in Aotearoa/New Zealand and I have outlined some of the educational discourses that have shaped current teaching and learning practices in these Islands. I translated these terms and conversations into a language commensurate with the one-to-one music studio, and I have tried to describe the hidden learning that can be present within a post-colonial master-apprentice music partnership. In describing this hidden learning I referred to a research project that illustrated what it is like to be an indigenous minority student in the music studio. I then demonstrated how this could change future teachers perspectives of effective studio teaching when embedded in the curriculum of a postgraduate studio pedagogy course.

Phelan (2001) states that teacher education maintains existing educational and social structures by teaching prospective teachers to assimilate and accommodate to existing ways of thinking and acting dominant discourses that are prevalent within a given context during a particular period in time (p. 584). I believe that in this course we have provided the option for a different pathway to our students. I would hope that our students, like my research colleagues, recognise the significance of their location in the South Pacific and understand the importance of being able to shift between cultural paradigms in order to forge genuine partnerships with all students from all cultures and across all educational contexts. I hope that they have been transformed and appreciate peoples' cultures and worldviews. But mostly my aspiration is that we have given them the courage to create teaching and learning sites that allow their students the opportunity to explore the reservoir of diverse knowledge offered to them by our young but increasingly multicultural society. As Tanaka (2003) says: "You have to be in it for yourself in the sense you have to risk something personally when you learn about others cultures; you have to be willing to change yourself" (p. 40).

Notes

1. Peter Shand in his article *Scenes from the Colonial Catwalk: Cultural Appropriation, Intellectual Property Rights, and Fashion*, (2002) defines the term as a specific identifying nomenclature given by Māori to people who are of nominally European, predominantly British descent.
2. The Treaty of Waitangi is a series of documents signed in 1840 through which New Zealand become British Crown colonies.
3. This references French and Raven's 1959 original study that divides power into five separate forms (a revision in 1965 included a sixth) of which legitimate power refers to the agent's right to make a request based on their position in this case as a member of the colonial body and expert power refers to the idea that the agent has expertise and knowledge desired by the student, as in the master-apprentice tradition.
4. The most widely accepted Māori term for New Zealand.
5. See http://www.tlri.org.nz/tlri-research/research-completed/post-school-sector/success-all-improving-maori-and-pasifika-student for a full description of this project.
6. See http://www.apa.org/pubs/databases/psycinfo/critical.aspx for a 301-page bibliography covering more than 50 years of research on the development and use of the Critical Incident Technique.
7. This refers to Christopher Small's term from his book of the same name.
8. This refers to Bernstein's Code Theory, which argues that different positions within society have different language use patterns, which shape the assumptions of the group, and about the group and influence the ability of these groups to succeed in education.

References

Abrahams, F. (2005). The application of critical pedagogy to music teaching and learning. *Visions of Research in Music Education, 6*(1), 2–16.

Adler, S. M. (2011). Teacher epistemology and collective narratives: Interrogating teaching and diversity. *Teaching and Teacher Education, 27*(3), 609–618.

Airini., Brown, D., & Rakena, T. (2015). Success for all: Eroding the culture of power in the one to one teaching and learning context. *International Journal of Music Education* 0255761415590365

Anae, M., Coxon, E., Mara, D., Wendt-Samu, T., & Finau, C. (2001). *Pacific Island education research guidelines.* Wellington: Ministry of Education.

Aronowitz, S., & Giroux, H. A. (1991). *Postmodern education: Politics, culture, and social criticism.* Minneapolis: University of Minnesota Press.

Barnes, C. J. (2006). Preparing preservice teachers to teach in a culturally responsive way. *Negro Educational Review, 57*(1/2), 85.

Bishop, R., & Glynn, T. (2003). *Culture counts: Changing power relations in education.* Palmerston North: Dunmore.

Burwell, K. (2013). Apprenticeship in music: A contextual study for instrumental teaching and learning. *International Journal of Music Education, 31*(3), 276–291.

Carey, G., Grant, C., McWilliam, E., & Taylor, P. (2013). One-to-one pedagogy: Developing a protocol for illuminating the nature of teaching in the conservatoire. *International Journal of Music Education, 31*(2), 148–159.

Condevaux, A. (2009). Māori culture on stage: Authenticity and identity in tourist interactions. *Anthropological Forum, 19*(92), 143–161.

Creech, A., & Hallam, S. (2011). Learning a musical instrument: The influence of interpersonal interaction on outcomes for school-aged pupils. *Psychology of Music, 39*(1), 102–122.

Edwards, R., & Usher, R. (2007). *Globalisation & pedagogy: Space, place and identity.* London: Routledge.

Flanagan, J. C. (1954). The critical incident technique. *Psychological Bulletin, 51*(4), 327.

Freire, P. (1998). *Teachers as cultural workers: Letters to those who dare to teach* (D. Macedo, D. Koike, & A. Oliveira, Trans.). Boulder: Westview Press.

Freire, P. (2000). *Pedagogy of the oppressed.* New York: Continuum International Publishing Group.

Freire, P., & Macedo, D. P. (1995). A dialogue: Culture, language, and race. *Harvard Educational Review, 65*(3), 377–403.

Gaunt, H. (2010). One-to-one tuition in a conservatoire: The perceptions of instrumental and vocal students. *Psychology of Music, 38*(2), 178–208.

Gorinski, R., & Abernethy, G. (2007). Maori student retention and success: Curriculum, pedagogy and relationships. In T. Townsend & R. Bates (Eds.), *Handbook of teacher education* (pp. 229–240). Dordrecht: Springer.

Grant, C. A. (1994). Best practices in teacher preparation for urban schools: Lessons from the multicultural teacher education literature. *Action in Teacher Education, 16*(3), 1–18.

Green, L. (2011). *Learning, teaching, and musical identity: Voices across cultures.* Bloomington: Indiana University Press.

Green, L. (2012). Musical "learning styles" and "learning strategies" in the instrumental lesson: Some emergent findings from a pilot study. *Psychology of Music, 40*(1), 42–65.

Health Research Council. (2005). *Guidelines on Pacific health research.* Wellington: Health Research Council of New Zealand.

Illeris, K. (2009). *Contemporary theories of learning: Learning theorists – In their own words* (1st ed.). London/New York: Routledge.

Kok, R.-M. (2011). Music for a postcolonial child: Theorizing Malaysian memories. In L. Green (Ed.), *Learning, teaching, and musical identity: Voices across cultures* (pp. 73–90). Bloomington: Indiana University Press.

Ladson-Billings, G. (1995). Toward a theory of culturally relevant pedagogy. *American Educational Research Journal, 32*(3), 465–491.

McLaren, P. (1998). *Life in schools.* White Plains: Longman.

McPhail, G. J. (2010). Crossing boundaries: Sharing concepts of music teaching from classroom to studio. *Music Education Research, 12*(1), 33–45.

Ministry of Education. (2008). *Ka Hikitia – Managing for success: The Māori education strategy 2008–2012.* Retrieved from http://www.minedu.govt.nz/theMinistry/PolicyAndStrategy/KaHikitia.aspx

Ministry of Social Development. (2010). *2010 the social report: Te purongo oranga tangata.* Retrieved from http://www.msd.govt.nz/about-msd-and-our-work/publications-resources/publications-index-2010.html

Mutu, M. (2011). *The state of Māori rights.* Wellington: Huia Publishers.

Nairn, R. G., & McCreanor, T. N. (1991). Race talk and common sense: Patterns in Pākehā discourse on Māori/Pākehā relations in New Zealand. *Journal of Language and Social Psychology, 10*(4), 245–262.

Nerland, M. (2007). One-to-one teaching as cultural practice: Two case studies from an academy of music. *Music Education Research, 9*(3), 399–416.

Perkins, R. (2013). Hierarchies and learning in the conservatoire: Exploring what students learn through the lens of Bourdieu. *Research Studies in Music Education, 35*(2), 197–212.

Phelan, A. M. (2001). Power and place in teaching and teacher education. *Teaching and Teacher Education, 17*(5), 583–597.

Pihama, L., Cram, F., & Walker, S. (2002). Creating methodological space: A literature review of Kaupapa Māori research. *Canadian Journal of Native Education, 26*(1), 30–43.

Shulman, L. (2005, Summer). Signature pedagogies in the professions. *Daedalus,* 52–59.

Simon, J. A. (1998). Anthropology, 'native schooling' and Maori: The politics of 'cultural adaptation policies'. *Oceania,* 61–78.

Smith, L. T. (1999). *Decolonizing methodologies: Research and indigenous peoples.* Dunedin/London: University of Otago Press/Zed Books.

Spiller, C. M. (2010). *How Maori cultural tourism businesses create authentic and sustainable well-being.* Doctoral dissertation, ResearchSpace@ Auckland.

Tanaka, G. K. (2003). *The intercultural campus: transcending culture & power in American higher education.* New York: P. Lang.

Ullman, C., & Hecsh, J. (2011). These American lives: Becoming a culturally responsive teacher and the 'risks of empathy'. *Race Ethnicity and Education, 14*(5), 603–629.

Walker, R. (2004). *Ka whawhai tonu mātou: Struggle without end* (Revth ed.). Auckland: Penguin.

Wiggins, R. A., & Follo, E. J. (1999). Development of knowledge, attitudes, and commitment to teach diverse student populations. *Journal of Teacher Education, 50*(2), 94–105.

Wren, T. E. (2012). *Conceptions of culture: What multicultural educators need to know.* Lanham: Rowman & Littlefield.

Zhukov, K. (2012). Interpersonal interactions in instrumental lessons: Teacher/student verbal and non-verbal behaviours. *Psychology of Music, 41*(4), 466–483.

Te Oti Rakena (DMA) trained in the United States at New England Conservatory in Boston and received his Doctorate from the University of Texas at Austin. Currently he is the Associate Dean Māori and Pacific Island at the National Institute for Creative Arts and Industries, University of Auckland. An established performer in the Opera and Music Theatre genres he is a published researcher in the areas of vocal function, non-western vocal performance and studio pedagogy. He has won two University of Auckland Excellence in Equity awards for his work with indigenous and minority students and received a University of Auckland Excellence in Teaching award for the implementation of innovative teaching practices in the area of vocal studies.

Changing Pedagogical Approaches in *'Ori Tahiti*: "Traditional" Dance for a Non-traditional Generation

Jane Freeman Moulin

Abstract In the twenty-first century, dance education on the island of Tahiti is intricately tied to new ideas about movement, technical virtuosity, and access to dance training combined with the view of contemporary Tahitians that the classroom offers a superior venue for transmitting the traditional art of *'ori tahiti* (Tahitian-style dancing). This physical and conceptual transformation reflects a period of social and artistic change that began in the 1980s and 1990s, one that moved Tahitian society from the practice of learning traditional dance as an informal participatory group activity for a specific community event to the transformed notion of dance education as a product of teacher-based learning intended to fulfill individual goals. This chapter discusses a brief history of this transformation and contrasts traditional informal *'ite* (watch; know) learning with classroom training acquired through *ha'api'i* (formal education). Discussion then turns to private dance school instruction as one example of contemporary artistic training and considers Tahiti's response to the challenges posed by this pedagogical shift.

Keywords Pacific • Polynesia • Tahiti • Traditional dance • Artistic transmission • Dance schools • Conservatory • Dance education • *'ori tahiti*

1 Introduction

In mid-twentieth century French Polynesia, the purposeful linking of classroom pedagogy and Tahitian dance would have been a rather curious misfit. The Tahitian view of *'ori tahiti* (Tahitian style dancing)[1] was that it was a community affair—not the purview of specialised teachers and students. Instead, when a specific gathering called for dance, the community came together (whether as an ongoing dance troupe

---

[1] Dancing in a "Tahitian style" refers to characteristic leg and lower torso movements that are the foundation of traditional dance. See Moulin (1979, p. 28–33) for a complete description.

J.F. Moulin (✉)
University of Hawai'i at Manoa, 2411 Dole St., Honolulu, HI 96822, USA
e-mail: moulin@hawaii.edu

© Springer International Publishing Switzerland 2016   135
L. Ashley, D. Lines (eds.), *Intersecting Cultures in Music and Dance Education*, Landscapes: the Arts, Aesthetics, and Education 19,
DOI 10.1007/978-3-319-28989-2_9

or an ad-hoc amateur village or district group) to rehearse a set of dances and songs that would animate the event and demonstrate the dynamism, competence, and vitality of the troupe and its performers. The focus was on the group's ability to relate a story through dance and the songs it accompanied, the coordination and ensemble of the troupe, choreography, and beauty of the presentation—not on the skill of the individual dancer.

Tahitians of this time assumed that *anyone* could dance. A person needed only to be where people were dancing and use ears and eyes to absorb the song texts, drum patterns, song melodies, and movements. Following what others were doing did not require any formalised pedagogical approach. A dancer would become as good as his/her observational skills allowed, and the main thing was to *do*, not to sit around talking about it abstractly or theorizing how best to transmit it.

Dance education on Tahiti today, however, is a vastly different story. In an intricate choreography of artistic transformation, new movements call for demanding techniques, increased stamina, and a focused, intensive study—all of which have multiple ramifications for traditional dance. Not surprisingly, this artistic development is intimately linked to concurrent social modifications in Tahitian society, the whole combining to create and sustain an ever-growing cadre of highly trained, virtuosic dancers who have an international presence as performers and teachers.

This chapter reviews a brief history of this transformation, stretching from the 1960s to a period of widespread change in the 1980s and 1990s. It delineates a binary approach to artistic pedagogy that developed as Tahitians moved from a view of learning traditional dance as an informal participatory group activity for a specific community event to the transformed notion of dance education as a product of teacher-based learning intended to fulfill individual goals. I use the term 'traditional dance' to refer to *'ori tahiti*, a style of dancing that Tahitians feel is their heritage. Importantly, Tahitians do not view this as an inflexible and unchanged link to the past, but rather a dance that may be updated and reconfigured to suit modern life and aesthetics.

Discussion then turns to the private dance school as one example of contemporary pedagogy in action and follows contemporary Tahitian usage by employing the term 'school' throughout to refer to the physical training studio, rather than an artistic movement or stylistic practice. Finally, it considers Tahiti's response to both the initial and the subsequent challenges posed by this pedagogical shift. I argue that the emergent pattern echoes developments in other parts of the Pacific (especially Hawai'i); that the change involves dancers, dancing, and the dance itself as well as associated social values; and that the phenomenon of formalised classroom instruction and the concurrent internationalisation of Tahitian dance raise issues regarding the commodification of culture and the spectre of potential challenges to cultural ownership and control.

2   Background: A Society in Transition

In the 1960s Tahiti was a culture in transition. The opening of the international airport in 1960 created a direct link to an outside world and offered the prospect of an
expanded tourism industry. This focus on tourism also veiled the projected but
unannounced French plans to turn French Polynesia into a site for nuclear experimentation. Eventual commencement of nuclear testing in 1966 brought both an
influx of French military personnel and the need for an infrastructure to support the
testing and its personnel, thereby creating numerous government and service-
oriented jobs in a society in which many people were not that many years away from
a reliance on subsistence and barter for basic needs. All combined to usher Tahiti
swiftly into a new world of increased cultural interactions, global politics, urbanisation, and a growing wage economy.

The years of the 1970s arrived as Tahitians happily basked in the glow of an
expanding economy in a time before notions of cultural identity began to resonate
in the worlds and works of Tahiti's poets, choreographers, musicians and dancers.
While ideas of a nostalgic past had existed long before this,[2] Tahitians in the 1970s
did not spend a lot of time worrying about tradition or widespread disruption to their
society. Caught up in an expanding economy that promised the newness and material comforts of modernity, many Tahitians readily embraced the changes.[3] As part
of a newfound global access and the nascent tourism industry, opportunities for
dancers to travel abroad and to entertain at home on a regular basis became well-
established. In terms of the fundamental dance movements and choreography, however, Tahiti was only starting to gaze across the waters.

As a dancer in Tahiti's professional troupes during the mid 1970s,[4] I was fortunate to experience a Tahiti still attached to early- and mid-century practices and was

---

[2] Already as early as 1892, the official July celebrations (now known as Heiva) took on an aura of
historic otherness when a competition was launched for "ancient costumes" (*Journal Officiel*. No.
29, 21 juillet 1892.)

[3] Despite the benefits of an expanded economy, challenging social issues also accompanied the
rapid shift, including: a burgeoning immigrant population as job seekers moved from the outer
islands to Tahiti, growing urbanisation and the appearance of slums in the capital, a population
explosion that contributed to young male unemployment, and emerging fears over radiation-asso-
ciated illness.

[4] I performed with the troupe TeMaeva (1973–1974) at Tahiti's hotels and danced with this award-
winning group for the annual Tiurai competitions (now called Heiva i Tahiti) in 1974 and 1976. I
also was a regular member of the professional troupe Tahiti Nui (1974–1976; billed abroad as The
Royal Tahitian Dancers), with whom I went on tour to South America, participated in the 1975
Tiurai, and performed several times weekly at Tahiti's tourist hotels. My ongoing engagement with
Tahitian music and dance has continued over the years, with return field trips in 1985, 1989, 1995,
1998, 2000, 2006, 2009, and 2012.

able later to contrast those with the artistic values of the following generation. One of the most significant contrasts revolved around transmission in the traditional arts, especially as late twentieth century alterations in pedagogical models prompted widespread transformations on many levels. Earlier education in dance and music was based on the principles of participatory learning. Those interested in acquiring a skill, whether canoe building or dancing, went to where people engaged in that activity; they observed, eventually joined in, and learned through actual embodied experience. In contrast, formal dance instruction, usually as private lessons given by well-known dancers in their homes, was for tourists and French residents who did not have access to the personal and community networks that facilitated participation in dance. Simply put, this was not a *Tahitian* way of learning dance.

3   Change in Pedagogical Models

A confluence of forces during the 1980s and 1990s brought modifications in the transmission model for music and dance (Moulin 2001). For dance, the change was early and especially dramatic, drawing particular stimulus from two fundamental sources. One was the global fitness craze of the mid-1980s, when Tahiti's fitness centres began to offer dance classes as physical activity for an increasingly sedentary population, something for which Tahiti's wage earners were prepared to pay. A second, highly significant phenomenon of this same period was the opening and subsequent growth of the Conservatoire Artistique, with its confirmation of Tahitian dance and music as worthy of intensive and systematic classroom instruction. By 1985, Conservatory dance instruction had evolved from travelling teachers who visited the public schools to classes housed in the new Conservatory buildings near the capitol, where staff began in earnest the process of developing a sequenced, multi-year curriculum. This physical move also expanded Conservatory classes beyond school-age children to include both adult learners and the very young.

The Conservatory is proud of its role in "democratising" the arts and making them available to all. Their website states: "The decision to teach 'Ori Tahiti' at the Artistic Conservatory of French Polynesia (Conservatoire Artistique de Polynésie Française) gives full recognition to this art form that is no longer considered to be 'reserved to a frivolous elite'" (CAPF website). Indeed, in 2014 CAPF enrolled approximately 1700 students regardless of ethnicity, age, physical appearance, previous experience or personal connections; over 600 were students in "traditional dance" (ibid.). Nevertheless, some Tahitians counter by complaining that spaces are limited and require a financial outlay not possible for many families, meaning that those who cannot afford the instructional fee, albeit very reasonable, are still marginalised (R. Peretia, personal communication, 28 July 2012).[5] The website's

---

[5]Yearly fees in 2014 were 36,000 CFP for children and 43,200 CFP for adults, roughly equivalent to US $382 and $457, respectively.

retrospective view of dance as the privilege of "a frivolous elite" undoubtedly refers to the selective professional groups, many of whom hand-picked dancers based on body type, height, weight, and physical attractiveness as well as dance skill.

The move to the CAFP (Conservatoire Artistique de Polynésie Française) validated the indigenous culture and placed Tahitian performative arts on the same level as those of the Western conservatory, deeming them worthy of focused study and granting government-recognised diplomas equivalent to those awarded in France. The changes that accompanied this seemingly simple establishment of sequential classroom learning, however, turned out to be profound. The dance taught at CAFP spurred radical change. Its classroom setting and practice of codifying dance steps and breaking down movement sequences to teach isolated, individual movements required new dance terminology for teachers who now needed a vocabulary for talking about dance. Its teachers created (in the view of some) or researched and revived (in the view of CAFP personnel) movements unknown to those involved in post-1950s Tahitian dance, as the classroom promoted a shift in instruction from what I have proposed as an informal 'ite (watch; know) model to one that focuses on artistic knowledge acquired through ha'api'i (formal education) (Moulin 2001, p. 234–37). Classroom setting, standardised movements, verbalisation, and "research" into older ways of dancing all demand not only changes in pedagogy, but fundamental shifts in how people *think* about dance and conceptualise their understanding of it. The following chart summarises the contrasts between these two ways of transmitting dance knowledge (Fig. 1):

	INFORMAL, PARTICIPATORY DANCE GROUP LEARNING ('ITE)	FORMAL, CLASSROOM LEARNING (HA'API'I)
Orientation:	Group	Individual
Primary purpose:	Perform in public	Acquire technique & repertory
Leader:	Dance director, who conducts rehearsals of whole compositions	Teacher, who works on isolated movements & whole compositions
Dancers:	Usually teenagers & young adults	All ages
Methodology:	Observation & imitation	Explanation, demonstration, correction; movement drills
Amount of Verbalisation:	Low	High
Location:	Outdoor public places	Government institutions, Private dance schools
Financial outlay:	None	Yearly (CAPF) or monthly tuition

Fig. 1 Contrasting transmission models for Tahitian dance (Adapted from Moulin 2001, p. 235)

The effects of this change were relatively rapid, with 1990–1995 as a crucial period, and the resultant modifications reverberated throughout the dance community to create challenges for cultural officials, dance directors, and elders. The main actors encompassed three groups: CAPF dance teachers, headed by Louise Kimitete; directors of Tahiti's traditional dance groups (both professional and amateur), many of whom were dancers of the pre-1985 period; and dancers themselves, predominantly those in their teens and early twenties. Traditionally it was the dance directors who made the decisions about choreography, using the stage of the national competitions in July to present their grandest creations to the Tahitian public. These dance competitions, which date back to 1894 (*Journal Officiel*. No. 33, 181, 16 août 1894) and remain the highlight of the dance year, are now known as Heiva i Tahiti.[6] The Conservatory, however, did not participate in the Heiva competitions and, consequently, was neither subservient to nor controlled by the regulations and decisions of the artistic community of Heiva judges, cultural officials, and dance directors.[7] The youth wanted what was new and exciting, and the CAPF offered that. Importantly, because it functioned *outside* the realm of traditional cultural and artistic authority, this ended up temporarily relocating the nexus of dance power by moving the undeniable drive for change out of the hands of the directors and into the Conservatory with its young dancers.

By 1995, the dance community was experiencing a momentary but definite rupture as youth demanded the new movements taught by CAPF and as dancers of the previous generation, who were not trained in the new techniques, suddenly felt estranged from their own culture when criticised for only "doing the old things" (T. Robinson, personal communication, 24 July 1995; M. Lai, personal communication, 20 July 1995). Importantly, not only did movements of the dance change, but so did fundamental ideas about access to dance and who can participate in it. No longer restricted to the traditional age group between adolescence and marriage, the dance suddenly sparked issues of propriety. Elders found it shocking to see 3 and 4 year olds performing highly sexualised movements; moreover, a society that formerly viewed older dancers as humorous was now forced to accept that dancers of any age, including seniors, had a right to learn and perform. Indeed, the very locus of traditional authority and the power structures surrounding dance were in flux. The centre was now youth-driven, new, and creative rather than residing in the older knowledge of the elders and acknowledged dance troupe directors. There was also a conceptual shift in notions about the function of dance and the best way to learn it that defied earlier ideas of performance. As scores of highly trained dancers, with a virtuosity honed by years of dedicated and extended CAPF study, moved into the premier dance troupes during the latter half of the 1990s, the very look of the dance also changed, prompting some choreographers to start to explore the wide range of

---

[6] The Tahitian delight in *heiva*, meaning 'dance festival; entertainment', was noted by early European explorers. President Gaston Flosse applied the term to the July festivities in 1986 in an effort to resituate the event—moving the focus away from the July 14th celebration of the French *Fête Nationale* (Bastille Day) to a more Tahitian-centred celebration of tradition.

[7] CAPF, with its institutional structure, government support, publicly-funded salaries for teachers and accompanying musicians, permanent facility, and new curriculum also enjoys enviable benefits that set it apart from the typical dance group, fitness centre, or private dance school.

creative possibilities offered by the new movements and the highly trained youth who had been perfecting them for many years. This was a period when definitions of "tradition" were challenged repeatedly by these new productions, with Heiva judges finding it impossible to judge the "apples and oranges" of old and new approaches to performance. Temporarily dividing the competition into "traditional" and "creative" categories in 1998 proved awkward and unhelpful.

In the years following the turn of the century, the situation stabilised and calmed when dance directors began to embrace and become comfortable with the new styles represented by CAPF teaching and, importantly, gained a deeper appreciation for both the Conservatory-trained dancers and the work done by the CAPF staff. Although CAPF had played a *major* role in the changes that transpired, it was no longer the creative pulse of the community as dance directors eventually reclaimed their roles in guiding the choreography and dance presentations. In a typical path of innovation for any culture, yesterday's shockingly "new" became today's standard, and by 2012 many Tahitians viewed the CAPF as the "*berceau*" (cradle) of traditional dance rather than a vehicle of unbridled change. The classroom teaching it embraces, and which specifically necessitated some of the earlier departures from older approaches, is now firmly embedded in Tahitian society and accepted as the most effective way to learn. By 2014, CAPF enrolled 842 students in the traditional arts (dance for children, dance for adults, ukulele and guitar, percussion, and choral singing), and 623 of these were in dance (CAPF website). Emblematic of its earlier willingness to push boundaries and redefine traditions, however, CAPF still proclaims a stance of favouring creativity over replication:

> Traditional dance is above all "interpretation". It is undoubtedly linked to a certain period of time but it is also the reflection of a constantly evolving culture. Meeting the technical requirements based on the codification of dance steps and gestures, traditional dance also calls on the personality that it helps to reveal. It encourages creative movement and non-verbal communication. (ibid.)

The mention of personality, with its association of the individual is notable here, because one of the most fundamental transformations in the rising popularity of the classroom model was the confirmed move from dance as a collective art driven by community need to an individualistic one reliant on personal goals. Rather than focusing on learning complete dances as embodied practice, dance in the classroom favoured the abstraction of both practice and the ways in which the material is broken down and taught. Importantly, it also normalised the concept of acquiring dance technique and repertoire for individual purposes in a society where, earlier, group performance and cohesion had held the highest value.

4   Private Dance Schools

Dance is widely popular in twenty-first century Tahiti. In addition to the publicly-funded Conservatory, there are also private dance schools that focus specifically on *'ori tahiti* and play a major role in training. Some of these are operated by an older generation of former dancers in Tahiti's professional groups, and others now are headed by young CAPF graduates. Although the latter receive formal diplomas and certifications, no umbrella organisation in French Polynesia certifies the schools or their teachers; in addition, there is no formal association that tracks the number of private schools or their enrollments. Notably, students at both CAPF and the private schools are overwhelmingly female; in fact, many of the private schools teach only female students.

Besides the stamp of authority granted by the French government and the official diploma desired by a new generation of students, there are some other differences between the two types of school. One is that the government-sponsored, non-commercially-based CAPF only accepts new students at the beginning of the school year. Also, attendance is mandatory. Student learning is impacted by non-attendance, but the class is also affected if the teacher is forced repeatedly to review material for newcomers. Conservatory teacher Louise Kimitete points to this enrollment and attendance policy as one of the main differences between the CAPF program and the private schools (L. Kimitete, personal communication, 24 July 1995).

CAPF embraces a set curriculum and spells out a 4-year dance sequence on its website. The first year stresses the development of listening skills and technical basics. The following years focus on expanding the set of dance steps with variations, endurance training, and deepening dance knowledge while broadening the dancer's understanding of oratory, music, and culture in general. An emphasis on originality permeates the curriculum and culminates in the final year with knowledge of thematic development and a choreographic creation that demonstrates both traditional and modern elements (CAPF website). In discussions, Kimitete (1995) stressed that each student must compose an *'ori tahiti* dance segment and perform this at the year-end juried exams. In her view, this sequenced, carefully-prepared curriculum with formal examinations is a distinguishing feature of CAPF training (ibid.).

In contrast, private dance schools neither offer a multi-year curriculum nor provide students a set, written plan of study with formal exams. This is, however, appropriate given the niche market they serve—the student not seeking intensive, extended study but looking for a certain amount of flexibility (to change schools, to attend all classes or not, to discontinue study for a month or two if need be, to start anytime throughout the school year). Importantly, however, the lack of a written curriculum does not imply that the teacher has no set goals or overall curricular plan for the classes.

There are multiple reasons for students to select the alternative of private dance school instruction. Those who cannot find a space at CAPF, who prefer a less rigorous approach to instruction, who have schedules that do not fit the CAPF courses, who require some flexibility in attendance, who do not desire an extended program or a formal certification, or who prefer the convenience of not going into town are all able to turn to one of the many private dance schools that have blossomed on the island. The differences between the two, public and private, reflect to a large extent the student's reasons for study. Those who truly seek to pursue professional careers in traditional dance overwhelmingly migrate to CAPF classes (although that is certainly not the only entry ticket). Others find a choice of possibilities in the private sector; it is mainly a question of selecting a good "fit" on both practical and aesthetic grounds. Because some disposable income is necessary, most dance students are from middle or upper income families—families that also tend to embrace formal education. The private schools service a range of these students by offering classes that vary widely in their cost, intent, and purpose. The important point here, however, is that the consecutive development of the two types of formal education underscores the success of a pedagogical *model*, confirming that conceptual changes about arts pedagogy are now firmly engrained in the minds and practices of a new generation. The reasons for some of these conceptual transformations are detailed elsewhere (Moulin 2001, p. 239–40); my focus here is on the private dance school as a vehicle for delivering dance education.

In their modern classroom form, private dance schools have existed on Tahiti since the late-1980s, emerging at roughly the same time as CAPF was starting to expand its school programs. Makau Foster appears to have been the first to branch out of the fitness centres in 1988 and to establish her own private dance school, one that has been extremely successful throughout the last quarter century. Over the years, other well-known dancers, including Jeannine Maru, Coco Hotahota, Tumata Robinson, Moeata Laughlin, and Tiare Trompette have also started schools that grew into thriving training centres and commercial ventures. The evidence for the establishment of the dance school as a superior place to learn is now further underscored by the appearance of private schools on other islands of French Polynesia. On one hand this is expected, given Tahiti's role as the focal point of dance in French Polynesia and the consequent tendency for other islands to copy what Tahiti does. On the other hand, these outer islands represent the remaining bastions of traditional dance practice and life ways. Seen in this light, the change is monumental.

I first started examining classroom teaching for *'ori tahiti* in 1995 with a follow-up research trip in 1998 that included dance classes with Makau Foster. Then, in 2006 I studied in the district of Puna'auia for 5 months (mid-March until mid-August) at Heiragi, a school founded in 2003 by former CAPF student Véro (Véronique) Clément.[8] Return fieldwork and continued study with Véro for 3 months in 2012 (mid-May until mid-August) provided many hours of classroom video that allowed me to document instruction more fully, chart the developments in that school over time, and track the dance school phenomenon in general.

---

[8] The conservatory was not a possible site for participatory fieldwork as it does not allow "casual" participants (less than one full academic year) or provide classes during the months of school holidays (mid-June through August). After observing instruction at different schools, several factors influenced my choice of École de Danse Heiragi in 2006: with 280 students, it was a large size school and thus a vibrant dance community; three levels of adult classes, in addition to five levels for children, afforded opportunities to observe a range of instruction; Heiragi offered both morning and evening classes that allowed me to dance four hours a day; tuition was reasonable; it was convenient to my home in Puna'auia; the teacher's dance style suited both me and my dance background; and—most importantly—I view her pedagogical approach as both representative and effective.

Horaires danse Tahitienne 2015-2016.
A partir du 17 aout 2015

	Lundi	Mardi	Mercredi	Jeudi	Vendredi	Samedi
08h30 09h30	Débutantes	Débutantes		Débutantes		
09h30 10h30	Intermédiaires Confirmées	Intermédiaires Confirmées		Intermédiaires Confirmées		
13h15 14h15			Filles 5-6 ans		Filles 5-6 ans	
14h15 15h15			Filles 7-10 ans		Filles 7-10 ans	
15h15 16h00			Filles 3-4 ans		Filles 3-4 ans	
16h30 17h30	Débutantes	Débutantes	Ados 1	Débutantes	Ados 1	
17h30 18h30	Intermédiaires Confirmées	Intermédiaires Confirmées	Ados 2	Intermédiaires Confirmées	Ados 2	
18h30 19h30	Débutantes	Débutantes		Débutantes		

Fig. 2 Dance class schedule at Heiragi, 2015–2016. (École de Danse Heiragi 2015)

Heiragi maintains a year-round schedule. Many students sign up for classes in late August and continue through the normal Tahitian school year, which ends in June; others join as schedules allow. After June, many people in Tahiti leave for extended vacations in France and elsewhere. Since this travelling population aligns with those who can afford private dance instruction, the dance schools are all affected. Many close down for 2 months, but classes for adult women continue at Heiragi throughout the vacation months.

The dancers at Heiragi represent the long-term residents of a multi-cultural Tahiti (islanders from throughout French Polynesia,[9] Chinese, and French) as well as temporary residents, generally from France and the French colonies (particularly the Caribbean), and short-term visitors of different origins. During my periods of research there were occasional students from South America, New Zealand, Hawai'i and, in 2012, Japan. This last group is an especially interesting one that I will return to shortly. Given Heiragi's location across the road from a conclave of French military residences, it is not surprising that there are several military personnel and military wives in these classes. There is also, apparently, a turnover in students; in 2012 I did not find one adult student who was in the class in 2006.

Heiragi offers classes for both children and adult women. Although enrollments in 2014 reflected a drop due to the economic crisis in Tahiti, there were around 160 students in late 2014 (75 young children, 45 adolescents, and 40 adults) (V. Clément, personal communication, 22 November 2014). The schedule from 2015 to 2016 (Fig. 2) demonstrates a range of options, a feature typical of the larger dance schools.

---

[9]The five archipelagos of French Polynesia are the Society Islands (which includes Tahiti), Tuamotu Islands, Marquesas Islands, Gambier or Mangareva Islands, and Austral Islands.

In this particular school, paying for a class allows an adult student to attend all classes offered at that level, and many students opt to attend class two times per day. Others enjoy the flexibility of being able to choose class time based on their daily schedules, catching up with material during the evening class if the morning was busy with other commitments; still others sign up for more than one level in order to increase their practice time, and several students avail themselves of this added training. In 2015, classes cost 8000 CPF per month for each level (approximately US $72), which is a fairly standard fee.

Terminology for dance movements is a hallmark of the development in Tahitian dance pedagogy. In the early days of CAPF, a small group of Tahiti's top dance leaders (including Paulina Morgan, Coco Hotahota, Louise Kimitete and one other unknown person) gathered together to codify the known dance movements for both men and women (P. Gueret, personal communication, 12 July 1995). Whereas movements in the mid-1970s did not have specialised terms for the female lower torso movements critical to *'ori tahiti* and only limited vocabulary for the male leg movements (Moulin 1979, p. 21–31), new movements and their associated terminology were added in the early 1990s (M. Lai, personal communication, 20 July 1995), resulting in an official list of 19 movements for women and 23 movements for men (Maison de la Culture, 1998, annexe 2).

Despite the effort to standardise vocabulary, variations still exist, in the terms used as well as their interpretation in movement. The terminology used by Véro Clément reflects both her CAPF training and her personal Tuamotuan roots. As with other schools I have observed, it only partially aligns with the official list from the Heiva office.[10] These steps and their terminology are important signals of change in that they represent both the move to more verbalisation about dance movements and the classroom pattern of practicing isolated movements and techniques in class, hence the need for vocabulary to reference them. This is in strong contrast to earlier ways of learning dance by doing complete dances, without any attempt to remove movements from their choreographic context. The dance class, however, has the tendency to isolate, repeat, and perfect movements outside of that larger context.

The timing of my two study periods at Heiragi coincided with a special event held for the dance schools on Tahiti. Given the growing popularity of the dance schools and the desire to provide a venue for them to perform—whether a small or large group and with dancers of any age—the cultural office Te Fare Tauhiti Nui launched a non-competitive Heiva for the dance schools in 1994, at which time it featured three dance schools: CAPF, Makau Foster's dance school, and that of Moeata Laughlin (Maison de la Culture 2014, p. 16–17). Now held yearly in June to mark the end of the instructional year, this Heiva des Écoles de Danse allows participants, like dance students around the world, to present the results of their study. In one sense, it also functions to restore the traditional focus on event,

---

[10] The list distributed by Véro, unchanged from 2006 to 2012, includes the following:

āfata, amaha, 'ami, fa'arapu, hura, otamu, patia, rere, rere mahuta, tā'iri tāmau, tāmau, tāmau fa'atere, tāmau tahito, teki, tokarega, toro, tua ne'e, tui, ueue, and *varu.* Some of these are for hip movements; others are foot, torso, or locomotor movements.

ensuring that dance remains a performance art and not only a rehearsal art, and it does this in the very traditional Tahitian way of bringing multiple groups together. In 2014, the event featured over 2000 dancers from 35 dance schools, including six from the outer islands, and had expanded to seven nights of performances plus one full evening for the CAPF classes,[11] a gala that by itself features 600 or more students (*Tahiti Info* 2014). The immense popularity of the dance school Heiva and its continued growth over time stand as visible testament to both the development of the dance school as an institution for artistic training and the entrenchment of formalised learning in Tahitian society.[12]

A look at a typical Heiragi class during the month of July 2012 is revealing. In one sense, this post-Heiva time means the pressure of the Heiva is off and less class time is absorbed by the details of overall programming, formation changes, costumes, and logistics. Also, this year Véro combined her intermediate and advanced classes to offer a 2-h session twice a day (morning and evening). Morning and evening classes are not exact replicates, so there is variety for those who want to do both sessions. The following is a first person account that draws on my field notes of the morning class held on July 24, 2012.

A Typical Lesson: École de Danse Heiragi

I arrived at class early today in order to snag nearby parking…a big issue…and then chatted quietly with the other women as we waited for class to start. We all wear the requisite pareu *dance skirt, but length, color and way of tying it are left to personal preference. There are approximately 20 women at class today—the typical mix of ethnicities and ages. About half are in their late teens and twenties and half in their thirties and forties; there are only a couple of older dancers. A couple of young women from Martinique are new to the class today.*

We line up in lengthwise rows in a studio that can accommodate probably up to three rows of nine to ten dancers each,[13] and we face the mirror that covers one full wall. Class starts with stretching exercises; many are the same ones I know from fitness classes in the United States. Then Véro performs various foot movements associated with 'aparima (story-telling) dances, and we dance along with her. Occasionally she announces the sequence of steps beforehand; at other times, we simply follow her visual example. Today, she pays special attention to the step "hura" but incorporates other steps as well, eventually adding hand gestures to the foot and hip movements and varying the basic step in different ways.

Class then turns to the specific, isolated movements of 'ori tahiti, and we devote about half of the two-hour class to an intense focus on these. It is clear that Véro is trying to build not only technique, but also stamina, encouraging students to push themselves in response to her shouts of "Allez les filles!" (Go girls!). Given Tahiti's tropical climate, we are soaked with sweat in the crowded, non-air conditioned space; bringing a towel to class is de rigeur. We stop for occasional water breaks.

---

[11] Fourteen schools presented more than 100 dancers, while 21 schools had smaller groups of less than 100 (*Tahiti Info* 2014).

[12] Those who cannot afford classroom instruction, still have possibilities to learn dance—mainly through participation in district or amateur groups or through school performances. In a climate of increasing dance virtuosity, however, such informal options provide less opportunity than the classes (either public or private) to practice and to "perfect" the dance.

[13] Heiragi reports that the studio can accommodate up thirty to forty dancers (V. Clément, personal communication, 22 November 2014).

Exercises move to the walls as Véro focuses on hip movements; she has us place one or both hands on the wall to ensure that all are maintaining an erect posture with shoulders absolutely still, an essential of 'ori tahiti. *Exercises move out onto the floor when Véro wants to work on traveling steps, with successive rows of dancers moving down the length of the room. She gives sporadic corrections as we dance to recorded music from a variety of sources—from Tahitian recordings to the pan-Polynesian fusion of Te Vaka to a banghra-inspired song and even a hiphop selection—knowing that each exercise will last at least 3:00-4:00 minutes.*

Véro then plays some recordings of short drumming selections and selects one. Although only about thirty seconds long, it is a complete musical composition. Going phrase by phrase, she encourages us to suggest a series of movements to dance to this pehe *(rhythmic pattern). Up until this point, this is the first time we are actually working on a "real" dance rather than exercises. The assignment is unique in that it is not the presentation of her own choreography; students seem to appreciate the departure from the norm and eagerly throw out names of movements to incorporate. I feel like I learned so much from watching her masterful shaping of each suggestion into a choreographed sequence.*

We then begin to practice the 'aparima *(story-telling dance) we started working on a couple of weeks ago. Since attendance by some is erratic, we have to spend time reviewing gestures already presented last week as Véro tries to contain the chaos and bring everyone on board. She presents the dance carefully, phrase by phase, going over the covered material several times and occasionally rotating the lines of dancers so that different students are in front. We neither receive copies of the associated song text nor spend time practicing the song itself. Some dancers sing along softly, but there is no requirement to participate vocally. Song no longer appears to be part of the training of the dancer.*

The four Japanese students who arrived a couple of weeks ago are still here. Well-trained and serious, almost driven, in their approach to dance study, they have come to spend one month (the limited time of their tourist visa) in Tahiti, taking dance classes and attending the Heiva i Tahiti competitions. A few weeks ago, I was surprised to see a well-known Japanese hula teacher appear at the door. I cannot help but think of Hawai'i and the unrelenting hula fad in Japan.

After a brief announcement, class ends rather abruptly and on time, without any cool down exercises. We pick up our things and, after quick good-bye kisses, head for our cars. We will be back in the studio in a few hours.

Some important points emerge from this account, specifically evidence of the ongoing processes of democratisation, individualism, commercialisation, pedagogical change, and internationalisation. Since these are emblematic of larger community-wide practices that lie well beyond Heiragi, they merit some exploration and analysis.

The value of increased access is evident in the wide age and ethnic range as well as the country origins of students. Access is, moreover, facilitated by allowing new students to join at any time of the year and any day they please. On one level, it may not be optimum for the teacher, but I am amazed at how women thrown into a class with little or no previous experience are able to pick up very quickly.

The highly individualistic approach to learning that is part of the classroom model shows clearly in the emphasis placed on developing individual skills rather than the coordination of group effort. Moreover—and in contrast to both earlier ways of learning and the rehearsals of professional and amateur dance troupes—the dance studio allows and even relies on the use of the mirror as a learning aid. At the outdoor rehearsals of Tahiti's dance troupes, dancers focus on what others are doing and try to carefully coordinate their movements. The studio mirror, however, permits a student to watch closely what *she* is doing and this subtly shapes the dancer's perspective. For example, a reliance on the mirror changes the dancer's relationship with the dance, moving it to a visual, "outside" the body experience rather than knowing it foremost as a physical and embodied one. The use of the mirror also reinforces dance as *individual* actions to be critically observed and perfected rather than requiring a dancer to think of his/her place in the group and learn to judge and time movements accordingly.

The dance class is a paid activity—it is a cultural commodity packaged and shared for a fee by a teacher who, simultaneously, is a businessperson who needs to ensure a profit. Venue and parking become linked to profits for many schools that struggle with a shortage of available and suitable spaces, the high cost of location rental and utilities (the latter leading to non-air conditioned spaces), and a scarcity of parking to accommodate their clients. Whereas earlier communities did not mind the few hours of loud music that accompanied evening dance practices held in the open air 2 or 3 days a week, today's residents complain about dance rehearsals in their neighborhoods, leaving dancers to practice in gyms, on the wharfs or in abandoned lots and forcing dance classes out of residential areas into store fronts and other business spaces. In 2006, well-known dance director Coco Hotahota pushed to come up with a solution and implored district officials to create or designate special practice facilities for dance. To date, that has not happened. An underlying reason might be that so much of dance activity today is no longer communal, but commercial.

The revised pedagogical model first espoused by CAPF is apparent in Véro's teaching. She incorporates some exercises where students watch and copy, but she also has "listen and do" activities intended to build both a vocabulary for talking about dance and the ability to conceptualise movement from verbal cues. There are named steps, and movements are isolated, demonstrated, rehearsed, and corrected. Foot and lower torso movements may be separated from hand movements for learning purposes, and there is some effort to engage students in exploring the creativity of choreographing a sequence, at least on a group level. All of these are in strong contrast to pre-Conservatory ways of learning dance as complete compositions from beginning to end. The work on isolated movements brings to mind the practice in Hawaiian hula of commencing class with repetitions of named steps (e.g. *kāholo, 'uwehe, 'ami, hela,* etc.), and I recall that Louise Kimitete, the guiding force behind CAPF efforts to standardise movements, lived in Hawai'i for many years of her adult life and was good friends with *hula* legend 'Iolani Luahine.[14] But this work session is considerably more sustained than the typical *hula* warm-up. Instead, teaching approaches the feeling of a ballet class.

---

[14] This connection undoubtedly also explains the presence of some shared terminology between Hawaiian *hula* vocabulary and the conservatory list of movements.

Other influences emanate from outside CAPF. The first year I saw warm up stretching exercises in the Tahitian dance classroom was in 2012. This appears to be something Véro has adopted from her own experiences in taking fitness classes, one that signals the physical training and even athleticism of contemporary dancers. The dance class has become an incredibly intense workout session; there are times when people simply must stop momentarily in the middle of an exercise to catch their breath and restore their courage to continue. I do not recall this level of intensity when dancing with the professional troupes of the 1970s, although such endurance training is certainly both a requisite of contemporary choreography and evident in the technical abilities of today's dancers.

The influence of technology on dancers is evident. Traditionally dancers were expected to sing—and to sing enthusiastically. Their voices contributed to the overall performance, and anything less than a 100 % effort would produce admonishing yells from the musicians. The norm for the private dance schools is to use recorded music, which removes any reliance on the dancers as singers.[15] Consequently, most dance teachers focus class time on the movements and give scant attention to the song text and its harmonisation. Even if live music is used for the Heiva des Écoles, the huge performing space of To'ata requires heavy amplification, placing the primary responsibility for vocal performance on the mic'ed musicians, not the dancers. Not surprisingly, many dancers do not even sing—a noticeable shift from older patterns of presentation and, importantly, basic notions of performance in most Polynesian islands.[16]

CAPF claims "more than 6000 foreign groups practice a form of Ori Tahiti" (CAPF website). Indeed, the internationalisation of Tahitian dance is now firmly established, with performing groups around the world and the largest concentrations in Hawai'i, Japan Mexico, and the west coast of the United States. The unexpected arrival of four Japanese students to the class, however, underscores something not part of the dance school in 2006. News of Heiragi has obviously hit Japan! These visiting students represent a new form of internationalisation. Whereas students far from Tahiti's shores—together with the festivals, competitions, and invited Tahitian teachers or judges—are numerous, imagining and promoting French Polynesia as a site for dance learning is a relatively recent phenomenon.

---

[15] At the 2013 Heiva des Écoles, several schools had live musical accompaniment, a definite departure from 2012 and earlier. Heiragi reports that Véro called on the musicians of Heikura Nui to accompany her performance in 2013 and 2014; Véro was able to do this in exchange for her choreographic help with Heikura Nui's dancers (V. Clément, personal communication, 22 November 2014). Both this and an increase in attention to, and money spent on, costumes signal a tendency of the dance schools to emulate performances of the regular Heiva i Tahiti troupes. Although not a competition in terms of prizes or judged honors, the dance schools at the Heiva des Écoles still vie to outdo the others, and teachers are well aware of the connection between a beautiful performance and class enrollments the following August.

[16] Hawai'i, where one or more non-dancers deliver the song text, is a notable exception to this larger Polynesian practice of viewing the dancer as a singer.

5   Responses to the Challenges of Pedagogical Change

When I did initial research on the dance schools in the 1990s, the most crucial issues surrounding artistic transmission were the redefinition of artistic teaching as salaried labour reliant on capitalistic relationships, the centralisation of dance authority in the Conservatory, a non-traditional separation of music and dance, and the privileging of individual goals above group effort (Moulin 2001, p. 243–44). The question of age appropriateness in movements and costuming[17] was also a concern.

By 2012, these issues were resolved for the most part. The commodification of dance training is accepted, with dance schools blossoming across Tahiti and beyond. The radically different ideas of dance transmitted in CAPF training are now normalised. As graduates established themselves as dancers and teachers across Tahiti and beyond, a corresponding shift in authority has returned the creative spotlight to the dance directors and teachers who embraced the changes. Dance education itself has become decentralised, moving away from CAPF to include numerous private dance schools in the community that now assume a major role in artistic transmission. Tahitians have opted for modernity, choosing the technology of the microphone and loudspeaker over the sound of dancers' voices and accepting that individual goals are an appropriate reason for dance study. Dancers and teachers no longer fret about age appropriateness, because they have figured out movements and costumes that are suitable for different groups of dancers.

In short, a multitude of changes have occurred, changes that initially encountered a reluctant society but eventually were adopted by it. Many of these required Tahitians to reconsider fundamental questions, such as the role of tradition in culture, what the dance should look like and who should perform it, and whether dance is an arena where individualistic goals trump communal needs. If the 1990s was a period when Tahitians tangled with these ideas, the early twenty-first century confirms their acceptance of the new values that surround the forces of modernity, democratisation, and individualism.

There are, however, lingering social concerns that beg resolution, namely the growing virtuosity demanded of dancers and the internationalisation of dance knowledge and practice, particularly as this relates to cultural commodification. Since these issues certainly are not restricted to Tahitian dance, they offer a peek into forces that have the potential to reshape the future of dance and dance instruction—in Tahiti as well as across the Pacific.

---

[17] Older women, whose performance would have called forth disparaging remarks in earlier years, are now deaf to any challenges regarding their claim to a place on the stage; young dancers are no longer overly sexualised, with some teachers sensitive to this and avoiding certain rhythmic patterns that some view as provocative. Before, dance was the realm of teenagers and young adults and cultural preferences favoured a display of their youthful bodies. Today costumes have expanded considerably beyond the traditional *more* ("grass" skirt) and *pāreu* (wrap-around cloth) to include long dresses as a convenient way to cover aging dancers or opulent bodies. In general, there is a much wider range of attire for dance—from simple island dresses in cotton fabrics to dressy fabrics and styles that emulate evening gowns.

When students start at 4 years old and dance several days a week for 12, 15, or more years they acquire not only proficiency in dance, but a virtuosity in movement that is not possible with less intensive training. The website for the Conservatory is clear about its role in developing this:

> Furthermore, the dance class...aims to train professional dancers. It links the acquisition of knowledge to the mastering of techniques and the individual practice to the collective practice. (CAPF website)

Clearly, CAPF has the goal of educating professional, not casual, dancers. On the economic level, this opens a welcomed market for the private dance schools; on a societal level, virtuosity creates a specialised class of performer—the professional. Despite any claims to democratisation, CAPF's very purpose is to train an elite corps of performers who will somehow take their highly specialised training back to the collectivity of community practice. In essence, one might ask what has happened to the folk in this former folk art. What role do those without professional aspirations or CAPF certificates play in the future of dance? It is also worth asking if the professional groups can absorb an ongoing, seemingly endless stream of new graduates. Some will use their CAPF diplomas to open their own dance studios, but even that option has a defined limit. Others, however, have no intention of assuming professional careers in dance. One acquaintance, a young lawyer with a well-paid government job, enrolled in CAPF classes merely because she thought she should have a paper to authenticate all the time invested in pursuing her passion for dance. This is modern Tahiti, with its increasingly well-educated youth who value the classroom as a place to learn, even when not for career purposes. Although Tahiti has long been proud of its tendency to resist outsider definitions of itself or its Polynesian roots, this mode of classroom learning and its resultant virtuosity are a strong contrast to other Pacific Islands. Tahiti stands out among its Polynesian neighbors as remarkable for its large, active corps of "professionals" in what is normally billed as traditional dance.[18]

If the dawn of tourism and the opportunity to tour abroad in the 1970s and early 1980s represented the beginning commercialisation of Tahitian dance, the schools mark the true commodification of dance knowledge, with information available to those who can pay and students who are able to "purchase" multiple sources of material simultaneously rather than relying on trusted personal connections. Since an established dance school can have 100–300 students, a serious teacher who can overcome the hurdles of venue and marketing has the opportunity to earn a substantial income (Moulin 2001, p. 238). There is, however, a significantly larger commodification of culture materialising on the horizon that revolves around the internationalisation of dance.

---

[18] Hawai'i, with its developed infrastructure for tourism and over eight million visitors per year (Hawai'i Tourism Authority 2014), has more opportunities for professional dancers to perform in the tourist hotels and at commercial *lu'au*s, but these performing groups do not rival the size of professional troupes in Tahiti. Often Hawaiian commercial performances utilise as few as one or two *hula* dancers and a trio of musicians.

Since Japan represents the most recent, and in many ways the most potent example of what this internationalisation might involve, I focus here on that population of dancers. What is important to realise is that my aforementioned comment of the appearance of Japanese dancers at Heiragi is not a unique event. It represents a new explosion of interest on the part of young Japanese females in learning Tahitian dance. Much of this traces to the 2006 release of the Japanese film *Hula Girls*, the real-life story of a small Japanese town that remade itself as a Polynesian centre in an effort to draw tourists to rescue its failing economy. Much of the dance featured in the film, however, was not Hawaiian *hula*, but rather a Japanese take-off on the iconic *'ori tahiti*. This film opened eyes to a style of Polynesian dance that was different from the Hawaiian hula that has become so prevalent in Japan since the 1980s. A momentary look at the issues surrounding Hawaiian dance in Japan helps in comprehending the vast intricacies and potential of this interest.[19]

> There's really no way to exaggerate the popularity of hula in Japan. These days there are halau [hula schools] from Beijing to Boston and everywhere in between, but Japan has embraced Hawai'i's indigenous dance traditions like nowhere else. ... Lisette Marie Flanary, a Brooklyn-based filmmaker who is working on a documentary titled *Tokyo Hula*, estimates the number of hula dancers in Japan at 600,000.... (Boehm 2011, p. 2)

This phenomenon is not without its struggles, however. It has raised numerous challenges along the way for *hula* practitioners, including thorny questions surrounding cultural authority and who can teach, cultural control over who has the right to "sell" cultural knowledge or gain from the rich mine of associated profits, and the place of Japanese dancers in the homeland of *hula*.

Hula in Japan is a major business, and the question of who can and will profit from the immense cash potential is far from an inconsequential one. Many Hawaiian performers and teachers have moved to Japan, where they reap immense rewards and take on rock star popularity, but performance is not the only realm subject to commercial exploitation. There are also side markets of hula consumption in which predominantly Japanese entrepreneurs have profited, such as: workshops, festivals and competitions; the spin-off sales of *hula* skirts, implements, ornaments, and other accessories; or the profits reaped from organised cultural tourism tours to visit Hawai'i and fulfill the sought-after dream of dancing there. In addition, there are concerns about who profits from the *kumu hula*'s (*hula* master's) years of study and expertise in the culture. Is it the *kumu*, or primarily the Japanese dance teachers who align themselves in sister relationships with known Hawaiian masters?

---

[19] *Hula* has a long history in Japan, largely due to the popularity of Hawaiian music and dance for a pre-World War II generation combined with interest fuelled by rising tourism to Hawai'i in the 1980s and 1990s, an insatiable *hula* boom in the Land of the Rising Sun that started in the 1980s and still continues today, and a now established pattern of young Japanese females coming to the islands to learn hula and returning home to teach it. In an amazing replication of the Japanese *iemoto* system of training in the traditional arts, Japanese dancers applied a hierarchical network of teachers and assistants to create *hula* studios all over Japan (Kurokawa 2004, p. 126–163).

Aside from the financial aspects, there are significant implications for culture in general when dancers from other countries want to participate in Hawai'i's own hula festivals. At what point do people in Hawai'i feel displaced by outsiders who claim their dance, are driven to excel in it, and would, apparently, be quite content to engulf it with little regard for cultural sensitivity or their role in all of this? Some performers in Hawai'i view those teaching abroad as selling—and selling out—their culture, prompting reflection on whether this is all just a tremendous capitalistic free-for-all where everyone should grab while the grabbing is good. That this issue is so strongly centered in East Asia has much to do with market size, patterns of East Asian consumerism, the extreme nature of the "difference" between Asian and Pacific cultures (the attraction of the Other), and the lure the South Seas dance promises to those who feel this allows them to transcend or enrich their everyday lives.

These same issues now loom on the Tahitian cultural horizon. Like their *hula* counterparts, some of the Japanese girls who arrived at Heiragi bore Polynesian names—this time, Tahitian ones. More than a schoolgirl desire to embrace a new culture, these names carry additional meaning in Japan. Part of the training in traditional Japanese arts involves the formal bestowing of a professional name to mark an important stage of learning—complete with a hefty fee to the teacher who confers it. The practice, now firmly entrenched in Japanese *hula* schools, may be spilling over to the realm of *'ori tahiti*. An overt form of dance commodification, earning a Polynesian name in Japan can cost a student hundreds of dollars, not to mention the fees invested in years of lessons.

In a premonition of the throngs of Japanese dancers who now attend the Merrie Monarch Hula Festival in Hilo, Hawai'i, the 2012 Heiva i Tahiti competitions were dotted with Japanese tourists and dancers. With Japanese tourists now commanding large blocks of the limited seats for the annual Merrie Monarch festival in Hawai'i, it is notoriously difficult for local people to secure places. It is not hard to envision a similar potential for the Heiva i Tahiti, although the factors of added distance from Japan, the high cost of visiting French Polynesia, and French language presently keep many dance tourists away.

It is obvious that some of the intensity of this very real invasion of culture can be managed in ways that do minimal damage to the culture bearers themselves rather than allowing excessive and uncontrolled exploitation or relinquishing control to outside interests. In a 2006 meeting with Heiva Nui officials Julien Mai and Tiare Trompette, they asked what I thought about developing an international dance festival in Tahiti where different groups would attend and present their own dances. I suggested, instead, a festival wherein Tahitian dancers and dance schools from around the world could attend and present their work. Besides the normal benefits of cultural tourism for the hotel, restaurant, and tourism industries, this would offer opportunities for local musicians, dance instructors, instrument makers, and costume suppliers to make contacts with these schools and establish direct working relationships with them. In 2007, Tahiti offered its first international Farereira'a, which is now an event that draws hundreds of participants from the international *'ori tahiti* world, offering them the opportunity to dance in Tahiti without infringing on established Tahitian dance structures and dance events.[20]

The private dance schools have now begun to witness some of the external craving for dance instruction, and CAPF offers 1-week sessions that allow international students to study with CAPF personnel. When a Japanese tour operator pushed hard to have CAPF distribute diplomas at the end of the week (another requisite feature of Japanese instructional consumerism), CAPF officials refused, replying that "There is only one diploma offered and that is the result of many years of study" (H. Maamaatuiahutapu, personal communication, 23 March 2010). Instead, students receive a paper stating that they have completed the 1-week course. All students must start at Level 1; as of the end of 2012, 136 students had completed courses and passed one of the six levels of training (CAPF website). Of these, 87 (roughly 64 %) were Japanese. Even so, this number is insignificant considering the Japanese market for Polynesian dance. Despite a growing trend of inviting outstanding Tahitian dancers to give workshops in Japan, many Japanese teachers of *'ori tahiti* continue to learn—and teach—with little or no direct access to the dance tradition or Tahitian cultural practitioners (R. Perreira, personal communication, 29 May, 2015).

6 Conclusions

The move to formal education has involved an evolution of social and artistic thought that touches on new ways of conceptualising the functions and roles of dance in society, the foundational movements of the dance, access to dance knowledge, and the overall look of the presentation. It is a move that reflects the ideas and values of a new generation of Tahitians with increased income, education, and adoption of Western values. A relatively rapid late twentieth century development, it had its roots in pedagogical modifications, such as: the codification of dance movements, the increased verbalisation of dance instruction, and the notion of a sequenced curriculum. On one level, it represents a rupture with the previously embraced past, but it also represents an increased professionalism that is part of an older, ongoing story of dance and its transformation from the village celebration to the national and international stage.

Democracy in the arts is important to society if local troupes and large numbers of local dancers are to participate. Looking at the art as a whole, however, the actual dance of pre-Conservatory years was in many ways more inclusive than the virtuosic traditions coming out of CAPF today. Yes, the CAFP entrance point is democratic, but the final artistic product is far from that due to its formalised curricula,

---

[20]Tahitians are actively trying to protect their own performing spaces. The Heiva i Tahiti officials, for example, decided to limit the number of non-resident performers competing after finding that some groups recruited extensively in California to fill their ranks (H. Maamaatuiahutapu, personal communication, 22 May 2012).

dedicated terminology, virtuosic movements, specialised teachers, and required years of study. As Tahiti moves toward a global presence in dance education and performance, it copes with a nexus of reformed ideas concerning what excellence in dance entails, the value/role of formal education, views of the purpose/function of dance, and dance as a commodity of international importance. In short, changes in the pedagogical model impact dancers, the process of dancing, and the dance itself as well as the values of the people who produce it.

What is important in all of this is that Tahitians, who maintain an ethnic majority in their highly colonised space, have demonstrated that they will actively use Western paradigms of education to fulfill Islander needs. There are current moves to restore Tahitian ways of doing/seeing/being—in everything from birthing practices to religion—however, Tahitian youth, their parents, dance leaders, and cultural officials have clearly voiced their preference for this new model of dance learning along with the artistic results and the expanded economic opportunities it produces. The spread of dance schools to rural areas of Tahiti and other islands in French Polynesia signals both a maturity in the development of this model of dance education and its acceptance as a standard by which artistic transmission is delivered and judged throughout this island nation. The interest of *'ori tahiti* to a global world of dance is further evidence of that maturity, making the classroom not only a passive venue for transcending international boundaries but an actual facilitator of that step across oceans.

Tahitians have a long history of cultural preference for change over retention (Moulin 2007; Moulin 1996). Unfazed by insinuations, criticisms and even evidence that they are distancing themselves from their Pacific cousins and Polynesian roots, thousands of young French Polynesians enthusiastically embrace the new and delight in the expanded opportunities it affords those impassioned by the dance. From all appearances, there is little public discussion about notions of cultural ownership, the commodification of dance for personal or transnational corporate gain, or a possible need to protect the culture from exploitation. The unanswered question at this point is how Tahiti will deal with that potential and whether, especially in a phase of growing commercialism and tourism across Oceania, the dance classroom represents a uniquely Tahitian-Hawaiian form of modernisation or if it is a model that will be adopted, developed, and embraced by other Pacific cultures in the years to come.

Acknowledgements Fieldwork in Tahiti in 1995 and a follow-up research trip in 1998 were funded by grants from the NEH Endowment Fund and the Research Relations Fund of the University of Hawai'i at Mānoa. I am grateful for this funding support as well as the insights and thoughts shared by several of Tahiti's outstanding dancers and teachers. My sincere thanks goes to Véronique Clément for kindly allowing me to attend her classes and for providing me with valuable research material. I would also like to acknowledge several leaders in the dance field—especially Coco Hotahota, Marguerite Lai, Tumata Robinson, and Louise Kimitete—for assistance during the early stages of the research and for their input during discussions over the years. Heremoana Maamaatuiahutapu, former Director of Te Fare Tauhiti Nui (Maison de la Culture) and the Heiva Nui organisation, was instrumental in granting permission to document Heiva performances; his ongoing friendship and help with various projects is much appreciated. In my 2006 and 2012 research trips I met wonderful women at Heiragi who have enriched my life in many ways; I thank them for their smiles, encouragement, kindness, and friendship. My thanks as well to Aya Kimura and Allison Henward, fellow professors at the University of Hawai'i, who offered important suggestions during the preparation of the manuscript. To all, *māuruuru 'e māuruuru roa.*

References

Boehm, D. (2011, October/November). E makaukau! *Hana Hou!, 14*, 1–6.
Conservatoire Artistique de la Polynésie Française (CAPF). [n.d.]. *Official website.* Retrieved from http://www.conservatoire.pf/index.php?option=com_content&view=frontpage&Itemid=1
École de Danse Heiragi. (2006). *List of 'ori tahiti dance movements.* Photocopy.
École de Danse Heiragi. (2015). *Horaires danse Tahitienne 2015–2016.* Photocopy.
Hawai'i Tourism Authority. (2014, September). *Visitor highlights: Monthly visitor statistics.* Retrieved from http://www.hawaiitourismauthority.org/research/research/visitor-highlights/
Journal Officiel des Établissements Français de l'Océanie. (1892). Fête nationale du 14 juillet. No. 29, 21 juillet 1892.
Journal Officiel des Établissements Français de l'Océanie. (1894). Prix distribués à l'occasion de la Fête Nationale. No. 33, 16 août 1894, p. 181.
Kurokawa, Y. (2004). *Yearning for a distant music: Consumption of Hawaiian music and dance in Japan* (Unpublished doctoral dissertation). University of Hawaii at Mānoa, Honolulu.
Maison de la Culture/Te Fare Tauhiti Nui. (1998). *Réglement général du concours de chants et danses de Polynésie Française.* Photocopy.
Maison de la Culture/Te Fare Tauhiti Nui. (2014). Heiva des écoles: l'appel grandissant de la scène Heiva des écoles: l'appel grandissant de la scène. *Hiro'a: Journal d'informations culturelles,* 80 (mai), 13–19.
Moulin, J. (1979). *The dance of Tahiti.* Pape'ete: Christian Gleizal/Les Éditions du Pacifique.
Moulin, J. (1996). What's mine is yours? Cultural borrowing in a Pacific context. *Contemporary Pacific, 1*, 128–153.
Moulin, J. (2001). From Quinn's to the conservatory: Redefining the traditions of Tahitian dance. In H. Lawrence & D. Niles (Eds.), *Traditionalism and modernity in the music and dance of Oceania* (Oceania Monographs 52, pp. 233–250). Sydney: University of Sydney/Oceania Publications.
Moulin, J. (2007). Untying the knots in the 'aha tau, the sacred cord of time. In R. Moyle (Ed.), *Oceanic music encounters: The print resource and the human resource* (pp. 79–94). Auckland: University of Auckland.
Tahiti Info. (2014). *20ème Heiva des écoles de danse: un grand cru.* Retrieved from http://www.tahiti-infos.com/agenda/20eme-Heiva-des-ecoles-de-danse-un-grand-cru_ae297339.html

Interviews

Clément, Véronique. Phone communication, 22 November 2014
Gueret, Patrice. Pape'ete, 12 July 1995.
Kimitete, Louise. Pape'ete, 24 July 1995.
Lai, Marguerite. Pape'ete, 20 July 1995
Maamaatuiahutapu, Heremoana. Honolulu, 23 March 2010; Pape'ete, 22 May 2012.
Peretia, Robert. Puna'auia, 28 July 2012.

Perreira, Rose. Honolulu, 29 May 2015.
Robinson, Tumata. Pape'ete, 24 July 1995.

Jane Freeman Moulin (PhD, Ethnomusicology, University of California at Santa Barbara, M.A., Ethnomusicology, U.C.L.A., B.A., Music Literature *(cum laude)*, UHM) is Professor of Ethnomusicology and Chair of Undergraduate Studies in Music at the University of Hawai'i. Dr. Moulin is the author of *The Dance of Tahiti*, *Music of the Southern Marquesas Islands*, and *Music in Pacific Islands Cultures* (co-authored) as well as numerous journal articles and encyclopedia entries (including the *New Grove's Dictionary of Music and Musicians* and the *Garland Encyclopedia of World Music*) dealing with the music and dance of French Polynesia.

Dancing into the Third Space: The Role of Dance and Drama in Discovering Who We Are

Janinka Greenwood

Abstract This article argues that because identity and culture are experienced physically, emotionally and kinaesthetically as well as constructed cerebrally, there is value in exploring their flow, their complexity and their intersection through aesthetic and embodied means. It explores how the use of dance and drama within broad educational contexts offer opportunity for such exploration.

It reports three cases. The first is a historic one: the work of Arnold Wilson's *Te Mauri Pakeaka programme*, 1975–1988. Here the focus is on the way physicality and exploration of form allowed participants to venture into new spaces and find embodied meanings. The second is from a more recent project, Mariao Hohaia's *Taitamariki Ngapuhitanga Kauapapa* in 2006. Here the focus is on devising a performance that allowed participants from widely different cultural backgrounds and experiences to find space to develop their own understandings, contribute and collaborate. The third is from a recent workshop at the 2014 Drama NZ Conference. Here the focus is on how engagement with dance and the dancer provoked and allowed teachers to move out of their comfort zone as knowers and directors, and discover different worlds.

Keywords Identity • Culture • Aesthetic • Dance and drama • Embodied meaning • Exploration of form

1 Scene 1: A Community Centre in the 1980s

A group of students are exploring the story of Reitū and Reipae – the mythical ancestresses of Whangarei and the northern Hokianga – in dance and music. Reipae has been abandoned on the sands of Onerahi while her sister flies away on the magical bird summoned by Oneone. The student taking the role of Reipae lowers her body to the floor in anguish, her legs split like a ballerina, while around her the

J. Greenwood (✉)
University of Canterbury, Christchurch, New Zealand
e-mail: janinka.greenwood@canterbury.ac.nz

© Springer International Publishing Switzerland 2016
L. Ashley, D. Lines (eds.), *Intersecting Cultures in Music and Dance Education*, Landscapes: the Arts, Aesthetics, and Education 19,
DOI 10.1007/978-3-319-28989-2_10

swing of poi evokes the departing bird's beating wings. The mythic history is Māori. The actors are both Māori and Pākehā. The programme in which they are participants is one that has been developed to allow schools, that at this time are still predominantly monocultural, the opportunity to explore the Māori values and ways of seeing the world. Art making based on local histories is the catalyst.

2   Scene 2: A Northland Beach in 2005

At the edge of the ocean a circle of children are exploring in dance the movement of their ancestral canoe as it voyaged from the East Coast of New Zealand to its final settlement at Takou Bay. Summer waves break over their feet and the water lifts in frothing foam. It is school holiday time and the participants have been drawn together by a local project that brings children to their tribal home ground to work with their elders recovering elements of tribal knowledge they would have gained in an earlier time through intergenerational teaching but that have now been lost in mainstream schooling. Parents sit on the sand dune watching.

3   Scene 3: A Conference Workshop in 2014

A woman in a rich red sari has just finished dancing and now sits on a classroom chair. Some 30 or so primary school teachers ask her questions about, first, her costume and the meaning of her dance and, then, her life. They are participating in a drama conference workshop probing ways teachers might explore the diverse cultures of their localities. The workshop's premise reconnoitred the ways a book based exploration of neighbourhood cultures might shift its energy when the auntie of one of the children is seen dancing in a cultural festival and is invited to bring her dance into the classroom.

The moments captured in each of these scenes exemplify the way dance, and performance making more generally, can be used as a tool for exploring the complexities of cultural diversity. They are drawn from three case studies that will be used to examine particular aspects of the relationship between art making, pedagogy and cultural diversity.

When art making processes, such as the ones referred to above, are completed and the work is performed, the finished product may look streamlined and easy. However, the apparent simplicity is deceptive. The processes involve the deliberative and strategic use of art as a means of learning about cultures and the spaces where cultures meet, overlap or clash. When they occur as part of education programmes they involve navigation of the complexities of intercultural spaces and of the relationship of schooling to culture.

4   Focus of This Chapter

An exploration of arts in education – and particularly as a means for exploring cultural diversity within New Zealand – involves recognition and some scrutiny of three dynamic, multi-faceted, intersecting and protean fields: schooling, art-making, and cultural identity. The discussion that follows strategically selects and addresses some features of each of these fields in order to expose the complexity of the arena in which teachers of the arts operate. These features highlight how teaching in and through the arts may allow teachers to be agentic in provoking new awarenesses of the cultural diversity of the society in which their students live. They also show where there may be opportunity for rich exploration of identity and relationships within the complexity of cultural diversity. It then draws on three case studies, crystallised in the scenes above, to give practical illustration to the concepts that are being teased out. Each of the three cases examines a different cultural intersection and different ways in which arts, particularly dance and drama, were used to make meaning within that intersection. It begins with a brief overview of the way New Zealand public and educational discourses tend to present New Zealand's cultural identity.

5   Public and Educational Rhetoric About Cultural Diversity

Our curriculum (New Zealand Ministry of Education 2007), our initial teacher education programmes (for example, University of Canterbury 2014), and a succession of ministerial directives (for example New Zealand Ministry of Education 2013a, b) emphasise the importance of culture and identity, prompting schools and their teachers to shape programmes of learning that recognise the importance of culture in their students' lives and in the development of a fair and equitable society. And so as teachers, and the author counts herself as one, we are concerned with culture and identity, not only in terms of honouring the students within our specific classrooms but also because we recognise that education is one of the forces that shape the country we live in.

But what kind of a country do we in fact live in? Public discourses about culture and identity in New Zealand are contradictory and sometimes polarised. Our country projects itself as bicultural in terms of its commitment to the Treaty of Waitangi.[1] It also projects itself as multicultural in terms of its awareness of the multiplicity of immigrants to whom it is home. However, it also tends to present itself as western, Anglo-centric, and a player in the monetarist monoculture of the global power-centre. The contradictions are perhaps to be expected because of our history and the shifts of values and power. New Zealand is country that was once totally Māori and

---

[1] The Treaty of Waitangi, 1840, established New Zealand as a British colony at the same time as it guaranteed Māori rights to land, chiefly sovereignty and other existing possessions.

interconnected by migration and metaphysical frameworks to Oceania. It became a British colony. It then reconfigured itself as an independent state, that despite its indigenous population and the numbers of worker migrants, predominantly Chinese, Dalmatian and Pasifika, who serviced its industries and agricultural production, saw itself as proto-Anglo and as a player in western economics, cultural production and political alliance. Māori assertion of the last decades has led to social and some constitutional recognition of the Treaty of Waitangi, declarations of biculturalism and contestations of sovereignty. Increased immigration has further challenged prevailing national concepts of Euro-western identity and provoked statements of multiculturalism, and the shifting centres of global economic and political power have turned New Zealand's face to the military deployments of the United States and to the markets of Asia. New global discourses introduce concepts of transnationalism (Vertovec 2009), of the mobility of talent (Solimano 2008) and migrant identities (Silvey and Lawson 1999).

In the political domain competing visions that grow from these discourses are played out as rhetoric and as attempts to seize and hold dominance. In the daily lives of some of our people they are ignored, while in those of others they are fiercely contested, sometimes verbally, sometimes physically. In education and social services they are agendas for exploration, but often are sublimated into expressions of political correctness.

This article argues that because identity and culture are experienced physically, emotionally and kinaesthetically as well as constructed cerebrally, there is value in exploring their flow, their complexity and their intersection through aesthetic and embodied means. It explores how the use of dance and other arts within broad educational contexts offer opportunity for such exploration.

6 Arts, Schooling and National Cultural Identity: Roles, Complexities and Intersections

The relationship between arts and culture is almost axiomatic. Cultures throughout history and around the world have evolved arts that express their understandings of the meaning of life and relations, and have developed and refined art forms that express the particular semiotics and aesthetics that are meaningful to those that share the discourses and aesthetic histories of that culture. Other chapters in this book examine specifics of that relationship. In this way arts act as carriers of significant elements of cultural identity. In the making of art, makers can use, adapt or even break the culturally derived semiotics held in form in order to express their own understandings of how they relate to their cultural identity or to that of others. Art may take the role of cultural treasure (Bourdieu 1993) or of homely means to explore meaning (Halprin 2000). In our classrooms art, at various times and in various ways, is expected to serve both those roles. We teach the canons of our art forms, we teach the skills for technical proficiency within the canons, we teach processes for improvisation, devising and composition, we encourage play within the art, and we use art as a well-honed and strategic tool for learning. Parental, and student, expectations may put pressure on schools and their teachers to attend more particularly to some of these functions than to others, and create competing curriculum pressures.

That there should be such competing expectations is embedded in the roles schooling plays in our society. At one level school is the caregiver that allows parents to participate actively in society by working. At such it is expected to work on behalf of and in collaboration with parents to transmit the knowledge systems valued by parents, in unison with their society. The extent to which such unison occurs depends in large part of course on the degree to which the school's society is homogenous and convergent in its values and aspirations. At another level schooling is a means of social construction. Schools adapt students to serve the needs of their society and that involves inculcating the civic attitudes that are required by the society and developing the skills needed. Gee (2012), taking the subject of literacy education for example, argues that when a state requires and funds school programmes that develop literacy, it does with expectations that: most graduating students will acquire the literacy skills needed for informed consumption and capable participation in the work force; a smaller proportion will develop literacy skills needed to evolve new enterprises (predominantly, in Gee's account, computer and other technological literacies); and an elite group are encouraged to develop the rich critical and creative literacies that will allow them to become shapers of the course of society. Gee's critique is one particularly targeted at contemporary neo-liberal America but the model of social construction might equally apply in a wide range of societies, those of traditional indigenous cultures included. It might be legitimately argued that such kinds of social construction are productive of social harmony and national progress. From another perspective schooling is a potential tool for personal and social liberation (Freire 1972; Giroux 1988). In this view schooling allows a space for critical examination, comparison of differences, strategic deconstruction of received ideas, and creative exploration of how things might be different. It might be argued that New Zealand's curriculum constructs its statement of vision and key learning areas in terms of a model of education as a tool for liberation, and it has developed its reporting systems and student assessments in terms of a model of social construction. Teachers, individually and through their various professional communities, try to find their space between.

As discussed earlier, cultural identity in contemporary New Zealand is by no means homogenous. Populations are diverse, and interactions within and between cultural groups are multi-faceted and constantly evolving. Individual themselves may have multiple concepts of cultural identity – in some case contextually layered but compatible, and in other cases conflicting or even dysfunctional. Therefore, concepts of cultural identity are complex and to an extent fluid. Teaching in this area is inevitably also complex and involves much more than transmissional instruction. Among the areas that teachers might themselves need to explore and navigate, and enable their students to navigate are: appreciation the integrity of those with different values and histories; finding the freedom to express their own values; developing

Fig. 1 Alternative strategies that might shape pedagogy in the intersecting fields

the ability to relate to others; understanding the political dynamics that promote various constructions of cultural and intercultural identity; and developing strategies to move, with respect and honesty, between cultural spaces.

Figure 1 above encapsulates alternative strategies that might shape pedagogy in the intersecting fields.

Thus the spaces where the fields intersect are fluid and complex and teaching within those spaces requires a degree of improvisation as well as careful unpacking of assertions and opinions. The pages that follow explore three case studies of how work in dance and drama was used to explore the potential of these complex and intersecting spaces. The first two cases come from now historic projects of which the proceedings and results have been documented in detail elsewhere (including Greenwood and Wilson 2006; Greenwood 2010). The third case is drawn from a recent and quite short conference workshop.

7   Case 1: Te Mauri Pakeka Project 1978–1989

Arnold Wilson's *Te Mauri Pakeaka* project was developed as a way to gently confront and change the monocultural orientation of New Zealand schooling. His work was one of a number of initiatives in the 1970s that sought to challenge the prevailing ideology of assimilation and the marking of difference as deficit. Other initiatives included the introduction of Māori language as a normal school curriculum subject, the accelerated training of native speakers of Māori language as teachers, the development of social studies units loosely labelled as *taha Māori*,[2] marae[3]-based professional development programmes for principals and departmental administrators, as well as direct action initiatives such as the Land March,[4] the occupation of Bastion Point[5] and the attack by Tama Toa on the Engineering students' haka.[6]

What *Pakeaka* offered that was different, and proved over time to be very effective, was a lived experience of living in a Māori space, working with Māori communities and elders to explore local stories of place. The project used art-making as a catalyst for cultural exploration. Each school group, usually consisting of about 20 students and three or more teachers, would develop an art work based on a local history. To research the history and the traditional forms of Māori art they needed to consult with those who held the knowledge, the elders of the community and the artists who had been invited into the project as resource people. Living on the marae served a number of purposes: it took the work out of the normal running of school life and school cultural biases; it made the need for consultation self-evident and practicable; it changed the rhythms of learning to those that characterised communal interaction on the marae; it allowed people to directly experience Māori values rather than just hear them talked about; and it allowed sustained time and space to play with and make art. In the first years, because Arnold Wilson himself was a sculptor, the visual arts predominated, but in the early 80s work in dance and drama became equally important project goals. At this stage I became involved in the project, working sometimes with my own students and at other times as a resources person for other groups. I draw on my own experience as well as the reports of other participants in the observations that follow.

At this time experimentation with theatre and dance forms that drew both on traditional Māori performative styles and intentions and Western traditions was a fairly new development (although it had a number of historic antecedents, such as Pei Te Hurinui Jones' translation of *The Merchant of Venice* into classical and poetic Māori language and Te Puea's development of the touring kapa haka[7] as means of

---

[2] *Taha Māori* might be translated as *the Māori side*. The term was used to denote studies about Māori protocols and values.

[3] A marae is a communal Māori space, belonging to a particular tribe, sub-tribe or extended family. It normally has an open outside area, a meeting house, a dining hall and perhaps other buildings.

[4] The historic Māori Land March from the Far North to parliament in Wellington took place in 1975 and protested the continuing alienation of Māori land.

[5] Bastion Point was Māori land that was being taken to build a high cost subdivision. Ngati Whatua occupied the land for 506 days.

[6] For many years Engineering students in Auckland had performed a travesty of the haka as part of the capping parade that accompanied graduation. Tama Toa, a group of Māori student activists, responded to the mock haka with a real physical challenge. Arrests and court cases followed.

[7] A group who rehearses and performs the haka. While the haka itself is a dance of challenge or affirmation that is embedded on traditional Māori culture, the kapa haka is a relatively modern development.

fundraising for tribal development projects). The lack of antecedents was challenging for participants because there were no given models to follow, and at the same time it allowed space for those who were willing to explore possibilities of meaning and form. While devising in the Pakeaka context offered freedom, it also involved a continuing process of critical reflection – about the interplay of traditional and new meanings, about the aesthetic impact of layering elements from different cultures, about the way various groups of audience might react to the work and to those performing it.

The course of devising was often marked by hesitation and even temporary withdrawal. Māori students were sometimes uncomfortable with the sort of improvisations that Pākehā teachers has developed as part of their teaching repertoire and Pākehā students often felt exposed by their awkwardness in performing the haka. Teachers were also walking into territory that was entirely new to them. Participants' art making experiences formed visible parallels to the ways they might be experiencing entry into each other's worlds. Somehow, however, the challenge of a final night performance to a massed audience and the growing camaraderie of living together created impetus for the work to continue and gather energy. The physical experience of success in the first stages of making provided incentive for further experimentation, the taking of new risks. The sustaining tension of group commitment, the visceral sensation of doing things in the body, the reward of breaking through a frustrating impasse and achieving a new promising possibility kept the work on fire.

The dance of Reipae, described in Scene 1 above, illustrates some of the pedagogical, artistic and cultural negotiations that took place through this project. In as much as schools act in loco parentis, taking some of the responsibilities of parents and also carrying some of their aspirations, schooling was seen to be failing Māori families[8] in that it neither achieved the academic success parents would want nor was it allowing the development of Māori values. The social construction that was taking place entailed understandings of history, arts, language, social values and relationships and even human value in terms that were firmly eurocentric. The Pakeaka project was seeking to disrupt this production. It allowed schools to step out of their normality and step into a different space that operated on the basis of different values and that referenced different histories, different arts and language and different ways of relating to people and land. In doing so it created the opportunity for a dialogic space and the possibility of engaging in deconstructive and liberationist pedagogy. The making of the dance of Reipae stimulated inquiry into a significant Northland story that highlighted ancestral ties between tribal groups and held the key to the meaning of local place names that at time retained their Māori root but had been anglicised. It further opened the door to exploring Māori language (the place names themselves, the words for lyrics and dialogue) and Māori ways of seeing the world (the importance of whakapapa – ancestral relationships; the significance of land and our relationships to it). Because the work took place in a Māori

---

[8]The 1986 *Report of the Waitangi Tribunal on the Te Reo Māori Claim* concluded that Māori children were not being properly educated because of prolonged systemic failure.

setting the makers lived their day immersed in the flow of a Māori way of living, sometimes consciously noting differences, often intuitively opening themselves up to different ways of relating.

The making of the dance also provoked a different relationship with art. The most obvious manifestation was the exploration of new forms and of ways that forms from Māori and Western cultures might be brought together and how they might (or might not) fit aesthetically. However, as well as being allowed to access new forms, the makers were introduced to the roles art played in the Māori world: the way social encounters were punctuated by music and dance that wove relationships between people, and the way that the carvings, weavings and painted rafters of the marae expressed ancestry and relation to the land. Further, the *Pakeaka* project actively invited experimentation; art making was presented as opportunity to explore, a means to investigate, play with, and express meaning.

The focus of the *Pakeaka* project was predominantly on the way Māori culture would be recognised within education and become a living framework for teaching and learning. The existence and value of other cultures was acknowledged, and throughout the programme other cultural groups were encouraged to bring their arts into the work. Photographic records show girls in Dalmatian costumes playing balalaikas, sinuous Pasifika forms in carved murals, swinging skirts of white pandanus, Indian saris. Māori space was presented as a space where others could enter, bringing their own culture with them. What was being contested, nationally as well as in this project, was the role of Māori culture in defining New Zealand identity. Biculturalism was the catchword of the time.

The significant audiences to the work developed in the project were also defined in terms of biculturalism. Over the 9 years in which I was involved in the *Pakeaka* project, there were many changes in the ways audiences, both those involved in the project and those who watched the final work in theatres and on marae, reacted. In the earlier years the crossing between Māori and Pākehā worlds was for many a novel experience. For Pākehā, like myself, the art forms, the language and the protocols of behaviour were strange – sometimes alienating, often exhilarating. My Māori teaching colleagues already had experience in working in another culture's language and behavioural codes, but the conventions of process drama, contemporary dance movement and devising were unfamiliar and even prohibiting. Those who attempted the crossing were usually welcomed from the other side and felt invigorated by the adventure. The middle of the decade brought new kinds of polarisations. Some Pākehā became defensive when they found themselves accused of compliance in racism when they had seen themselves as colour blind. Some Māori resented Pākehā intrusion into the culture that, while it was their birth right, they had been barred from through the assimilationist tendencies of the preceding era. Criticism of the art work, accusations of appropriation or inauthenticity became more vocal, and there was increasing tendency to slide into political correctness. Sometimes there were tears. Work on the story of Reitū and Reipae had been warmly encouraged, but on the evening of the performance one member of the audience was vehement in her criticism: the posture of the dancer playing Reipae, she said, was not appropriate for portraying Māori. The issue was debated and overall the arguments affirmed the work. Nevertheless, for a long time it was the criticism that echoed in the minds of the performers. The enterprise of crossing between cultures is a vulnerable one and while work in the arts offered an accessible way to enter and explore the cross-cultural space, it did not offer immunity from the tensions that attend the interplay of cultures in society. Perhaps nothing in devising or in liberationist pedagogy, as in navigating cultural complexity, is really safe.

8   Case 2: Taitamariki Ngapuhitanga Kauapapa Project 2006

The second case took place outside the frame of formal schooling. It was part of a project developed by Mariao Hohaia to bring young Māori back to their home marae in order to learn tribal history and values from their elders. The project took place in the summer holiday break in a number of marae across Northland. I was involved in the group at Takou Bay and there the elders had selected the story of the ancestral canoe, Mātaatua, and its journey to their home. We were to devise a performance that would be shared first with the local community and then in the annual tribal festival. The project's goals could be described in terms of restorative justice. Schooling at this time did acknowledge many aspects of Māori culture. The schools near Takou Bay did teach Māori language, they had active kapa haka groups, and school professional development addressed ways that the needs of Māori students should be met. However, the traditional processes of intergenerational teaching which had been ruptured by colonisation were not part of schooling. A primary aim of the project was to restore the pedagogical relationship. This involved bringing not only the elders but as many of the wider family as possible into the project. It also involved working on the tribal land so that the histories would become understood not as something remote out of books but as a located and real part of what determined identity and belonging, So the first days of the workshop began on the beach were the Mātaatua canoe had come ashore and had brought the children's ancestors to establish their homeland.

I was invited into the project because the director had been a student of mine and knew of my previous work in intercultural spaces. Initially I had been paired with a Māori actor as co-facilitator. A few weeks before the workshop began two facilitators on other marae sites had to pull out and so the director asked if I would ask my son (a primary school teacher) and daughter-in-law (a teacher of dance) to come in with me on my site so that he could re-shuffle the teams. We were the only three Pākehā in a Māori project. Working in art allowed us a space where we could contribute.

At the outset of the workshop the elders decided that the work would not be entirely in Māori language nor would it be traditional. The children and their families were not fluent speakers of Māori and they wanted them to be able to own the work. They wanted the children to find their own ways into the work, they said. They would tell the story, stay and support the development, offer language or advice if it was asked for, but they did not want to constrain the development of the work. The important thing was for the children to explore their heritage in the presence of their families and they wanted that to be fun and meaningful for them.

We worked on the beach for the first day because most of the families, who lived and worked in various cities, came back home to camp over Christmas. We wanted the exploration of ancestral history to be densely connected to the pleasure of summer at home. Extended families joined the children in the improvisations along the shore line. Then Maran, the dance teacher, took the children into the edge of the water to devise the voyage of the canoe along the North Island coast. She is an American New Zealander who is diffident using the Māori words she has been learning, very conscious of the way the sounds of her first language intrude on the Māori. When she moves into dance, however, there is little diffidence: the movement wells out of some compressed energy with her body and she allows it to flow. Dance allows her a space where she can express meaning without shyness about the limitations of her language learning and without fear that she might impose her understandings on those of the group.

Later in the week a torrential summer storm came, families packed up their tents and the work had to squeeze into a neighbourhood double garage. As the rain poured down outside the energy gained on the beach somehow remained in the room with group. They brainstormed ideas and phrases for songs and new haka, they created soundscapes that recaptured the splashes of the sea and the shriek of flying gulls, and they squeezed out every inch of the crowded space as they wove the dance they had made into the narrative of voyage and settlement.

The relationship between art and culture in this case was one where the local culture, the elders and their extended community, gave freedom for the art work to emerge in ways that were meaningful for the children and they actively supported the facilitators from outside the culture because they saw them as productive enablers of the process.

Implications for the relationship with schooling are more complex. From one point of view it might seem that the facilitators became intermediaries in the transmission of cultural knowledge and that they might have been interrupting the intergenerational pedagogical relationship in the same ways as many schools were. However, there were important differences. The learning took place on the community's own land. The community took part. Even when the storm prevented families from continuing to join in the active devising, various ones would drop in at some time to watch the work. Sometimes after watching they would come back with a contribution. For example, after watching the group devise a movement sequence and chant describing the chiefly leadership of the brothers who captained the canoe on its initial voyage from across the Pacific, a mother came back with a pair of giant masks she had made that she thought would complement the children's work. At another point a group of fathers took the boys away to practice the haka they had written and devised so that it would have the proud stance the fathers considered it needed. In these ways the families were not just audience to the final performed aspects of the work they were audience to the whole of the learning process: an audience that could step in and participate in ways that felt organic to the work in progress.

9   Case 3: New Zealand Drama Conference Workshop 2014

While the previous two cases were drawn from significant projects, this last case arises from a very short experience during a conference workshop. It is reported, albeit briefly, because it brings other elements to the discussion.

Whereas the first two cases were concerned with the bicultural foundations of New Zealand's cultural make-up, this case considers the increasingly multicultural mix. It also acknowledges that the challenges of contemporary multiculturalism are not only complex but in a constant state of shift. Detailed analysis of the issues of immigration, transnational migration, asylum seeking, and international capital development is well outside the scope of this chapter, as is analysis of the various interests that arise, blend or clash as a result of this increasing global movement. What is significant is the fact that our schools now serve very varied multicultural populations and that it is a challenge for teachers to know what is important in each child's cultural background and how the differences can be best managed in order to create effective learning (academic and life) for all students. This case reflects on one way art experience might open the door to grounded inquiry.

The workshop in this case was targeted at primary teachers and was entitled: 'Cultures in our community: A cross-curricula unit involving arts, literacy and social studies'. Its aim was to shift the concept of culture from something abstracted and generic to a lived encounter. It arose out of an identified professional development need and found its specific form as a result of discussions with a group of my international doctoral students who had been engaged in an intercultural dance festival.

The workshop began with a question to the participants, asking if they preferred to walk away with a detailed resource they could use in their own classrooms or undertake an open-ended learning adventure. The ensuing conversation suggested that both were desired goals. Consequently it was agreed to try to achieve both.

It opened with a shared reading, as in a classroom, of Patricia Grace's *Watercress Tuna and the Children of Champion Street* (1984). In Grace's story a magical eel brings each of the children of Champion Street a gift that special to their culture and that they can use to dance. Printed copies of a detailed unit of work based on the story (Greenwood 2005) were then tabled, but instead of working through the unit the scene cut to a cultural festival where the auntie of one of the children in the class was dancing. Abanti, a doctoral student from Bangladesh, had offered to play the auntie and she now entered the workshop richly costumed and her hands began to shape the mudras as she moved into a dance in the Manipuri tradition. The group watched the dance, reacting to it with admiration, but clearly seeing it as something exotic. Then the next phase was introduced: what if this auntie was willing to come into the classroom, what kinds of questions might we ask her? How could we involve her in developing a unit of study that would fulfil our curriculum intentions? At first the questions were fairly formal: about the dress, the country of origin, the occasion of the dance. Then when Abanti explained that it was a dance that a bride might traditionally dance for her new husband, more personal questions were asked about relationships between men and women, courtship, and the practice of arranged marriage. There was real curiosity when Abanti explained that an arranged marriage was by no means a forced marriage and talked about the role family and friends take in helping to select a good partner. Then the talk turned to religion and when the group learned that Abanti was Muslim she was asked if she was expected to wear a veil, and what she felt about people of other religions. Over the next hour the discussion flowed over a wide range of topics. Members of the group had heard that Bangladesh was a very poor country, that it flooded dangerously. They were surprised to learn about the land's fertility, and about the value of the arts. What about schooling? What was a classroom like? What were the country's politics? Was it not part of India? What about the language? Would Abanti not prefer to stay in New Zealand instead of returning to Bangladesh? And so on. The teachers became increasingly absorbed in the discussion and probing in their questions. When Abanti offered to teach the group part of her dance at the end of the session, the offer was taken up with enthusiasm rather than politeness. And as they walked out the door the participants also picked up copies of the original unit plan.

In this case dance had been the stimulus to curiosity. The live presence of the dancer created a human link to the culture that the dance came from. The improvisation that occurred in this case was not in the dance itself: Abanti had presented a traditional cultural treasure. The improvisation was in putting aside the planned (and probably fairly useful) unit, in opening the door to a member of the multicultural community and in collaboratively exploring what they could gather that could be the basis for rich cross-cultural teaching. The dance itself opened up the space where the dialogue could take place.

10   Third Space

The concept of the third space is one that has been used in a variety of ways. Bhabha (1990) presents the third space as a way of describing what occurs in the processes of postcolonial migrations when previously different cultures meet, impact on each other and to a greater or lesser extent fuse. The third space, he proposes, is syncretic but also evolving. It represents something new that grows out of the cultures that existed before but is no longer compliant with the old or even recognisable in terms of the old. In earlier writing I have used the term in a similar way (Greenwood 1999, 2005), and later applied it to describe the possible shifts to learning that might arise when schools open their doors to their communities (Greenwood 2015). Here I play with the concept again and consider it more broadly as the space where change can be envisaged and indeed occur when schools, arts and diverse cultures meet and generate inquiry. In this way it is not a space to arrive at; rather it is a space where possibilities are created.

The three cases explored above illustrate some of the dynamics that give the third space energy. Figure 2 below suggests how the third space arises from an exploratory and dynamic interplay of schooling, art and cultural diversity.

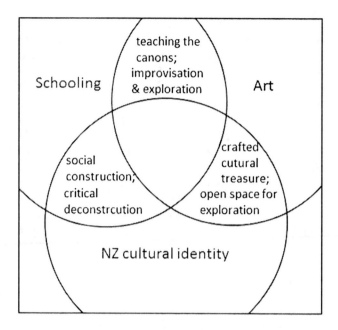

Fig. 2 Suggestions that how the third space arises from an exploratory and dynamic interplay of schooling, art and cultural diversity

In these three cases art making, specifically dance in the examples, was the catalyst that allowed participants to step into another culture and explore meaning. Because culture is something experienced emotionally and even viscerally as well as conceptually, the physicality of movement and visual imagery allows a potent point of entry, one moreover that can bypass the fixed positions that often manifest verbally. The process of exploring and embodying meaning through form offers a platform for response and dialogue. So two important energising dynamics are the courage to enter, and the courage to present something that will elicit further dialogue.

In each of the three illustrative cases art making offered a medium for learning and teaching. It showed how learning can be supported and even accelerated when it is interactive and when learners are encouraged to experiment and seek meaning. Collaboration and inquiry are further elements.

In the three cases the walls of the classroom were in some way dissolved. In the first two, learners were purposefully brought into a different cultural space and into dialogic engagement with community. In the third the melting was metaphorical. A planned unit was put aside because a possibility arose that offered the possibility of more grounded learning. A member of the community was invited in and recognised not merely as someone from an exotic and different culture but as a holder of knowledge who had something meaningful to share. Engagement and power sharing with community is another powerful dynamic in the third space.

Although each of these cases reports a successful initiative (otherwise they would not be cited here), the ventures were not without risk. The third space is not necessarily a safe space. But it is one that has open possibility and potential for change and growth. Not entering the space also carries risk. In the 1970s and 1980s the risk of ignoring Māori needs in education was emphatically proclaimed, in academic discourse (for example Walker 1996) and in concerted public action, such as the threat in 1984 to withdraw Māori children from the School Certificate examination.[9] Today the danger of ignoring ways to create possibility for cultural dialogue is demonstrated globally by conflict and deprivation. The changes that need to occur in our pedagogical understandings and approaches will serve not only the needs of those we might consider as the 'other', those marked by cultural difference from what has come to be seen as normal, but also the needs of all New Zealand children who deserve to see beyond the limitations of blinkered vision. So safety is not always an element of the third space.

But because the space opens possibilities for greater justice and collaboration, it is worth dancing into.

References

Bhabha, H. (1990). The third space. In J. Rutherford (Ed.), *Identity: Community, culture, difference* (pp. 207–221). London: Lawrence and Wishart.

Bourdieu, P. (1993). *The field of cultural production*. New York: Columbia University Press.

Freire, P. (1972). *Pedagogy of the oppressed*. Harmondsworth: Penguin.

Gee, J. P. (2012). *Social linguistics and literacies: Ideology in discourse*. New York: Routledge.

Giroux, H. (1988). *Teachers as intellectuals: Towards a critical pedagogy of learning*. Granby: Bergin & Garvey.

Grace, P. (1984). *Watercress tuna and the children of Champion Street*. Auckland: Penguin.

Greenwood, J. (1999). *Journeys into a third space: A study of how theatre enables us to interpret the emergent space between cultures*. PhD thesis, Griffith University, Brisbane. http://library-catalogue.griffith.edu.au/record=b1403509

Greenwood, J. (2005). Journeying into the third space: A study of how theatre can be used to interpret the space between cultures. *Youth Theatre Journal, 19*, 1–16.

Greenwood, J. (2010). Tracing the voyage of an ancestral canoe: Working in drama cross-culturally. In J. Shu, P. Chan, L. McCammmon, A. Owens, & J. Greenwood (Eds.), *Planting trees of drama with global vision in local knowledge: IDEA 2007 dialogues*. Hong Kong: IDEA Publications.

Greenwood, J. (2015). When a ngarara bit the taniwha's tail: Education, the arts and the third space. *Dance Research Aotearo, 2*(1), 42–57. http://dx.doi.org/10.15663%2Fdra.v3i1.36.

Greenwood, J., & Wilson, A. M. (2006). *Te Mauri Pakeaka: A journey in to the third space*. Auckland: Auckland University Press.

---

[9] At that time the marks in School Certificate, a national examination, were generated by a bell curve distribution. Māori typical fell into the lower portions of the curve. Withdrawal of Māori candidates would have shifted the achievement of the rest of the population. The threat to withdraw Māori children was made in protest against the fact that marks in Māori language were benchmarked against the candidates' marks in English.

Halprin, A. (2000). *Dance as a healing art: Returning to health through movement and imagery.* Mendocino: LifeRhythm.

New Zealand Ministry of Education. (2007). *The New Zealand curriculum.* Wellington: Learning Media Limited.

New Zealand Ministry of Education. (2013a). *Ka hikitia: Enhancing success 2013–2017.* http:// www.minedu.govt.nz/~/media/MinEdu/Files/TheMinistry/KaHikitia/ KaHikitiaAcceleratingSuccessEnglish.pdf

New Zealand Ministry of Education. (2013b). *Pasifika education plan 2013–2017.* http://www. minedu.govt.nz/NZEducation/EducationPolicies/PasifikaEducation/ PasifikaEducationPlan2013.aspx

Silvey, R., & Lawson, V. (1999). Placing the migrant. *Annals of the Association of American Geographers, 89*(1), 121–132.

Solimano, A. (2008). *The international mobility of talent: Types, causes, and development impact.* Oxford: Oxford University Press.

University of Canterbury. (2014). *Master of teaching and learning.* http://www.education.canterbury.ac.nz/documents/brochures_2015/MTchgLn.pdf

Vertovec, S. (2009). *Transnationalism.* Oxford: Routledge.

Walker, R. (1996). *Ngā pepa a Ranginui: The Walker papers.* Auckland: Penguin.

Janinka Greenwood   (PhD) Professor of Education in the University of Canterbury, sees herself as a lifelong explorer and inquirer. The arts have given her tools to explore cultures and the complex ways people make sense of their lives and work for the well-being of their families and wider society. She writes for theatre, and community arts. Her doctoral research looked into the role of drama in defining and interpreting the space where cultures meet. Recent publications include: *Research and Educational Change in Bangladesh* (Co-editor with Everatt, Kabir & Alam, Dhaka University Press, 2013); Strategic artistry: Using drama processes to develop critical literacy and democratic citizenship. *Asia Pacific Journal for Arts Education*, 2012 *11*(5); *Te Mauri Pakeaka: A Journey in to the Third Space* (Co-author with Wilson, A. & Wilson, A.M., Auckland University Press, 2006).

Untangling Intersections of Diverse Indigenous Heritages in Dance Education: Echoes, Whispers and Erosion in the Creases

Linda Ashley

Abstract In *Untangling intersections of diverse indigenous heritages in dance education: Echoes, whispers and erosion in the creases,* Linda Ashley examines the intersections that arise when Western dance education engages with dances from diverse indigenous heritages. Ideologically, this pedagogy embraces a sense of altruism where the individual learner's well-being, creativity, ownership and the 'whispers' of future growth are valued. Highlighting culturally different understandings of key pedagogical concepts, this chapter is also relevant for dance educators who are charged with fostering learning in 21st century diverse classrooms globally. In untangling how the heritage and ideology underpinning dance education creases with Oceanic and other indigenous heritages, the possible effects on and potential for erosion of indigenous dances are explored. The chapter considers how dance education could grow its current praxis in order to accommodate contrasting pedagogical beliefs. Emerging from the untangling, a suggestion for a teaching strategy based on examples of Māori contemporary dance is provided.

Keywords Culturally responsive pedagogy • Cultural difference • Creative dance • Cultural authenticity • Indigenous dance • Super-diversity

In this chapter I attempt to untangle the intersections that arise when dance education engages with dances from diverse indigenous heritages. In untangling how the heritage and ideology underpinning dance education intersects with that of Oceanic and other indigenous heritages, I explore how dance education creases with the cultural richness of the Pacific Island people and other cultures. The notion of intercultural creasing (Schechner 1988) offers ways of discussing the nuances of the intersections and how Oceanic dances and ways of life can become vulnerable to erosion.

Present in echoes from ancient, colonial and post-colonial eras, Oceania is rich in indigenously authentic dances and dancers. In New Zealand, a cultural mosaic of

L. Ashley (✉)
Independent Researcher, 74 Koutunui Rd., RD 1, Auckland 3177, New Zealand
e-mail: d.lines@auckland.ac.nz

© Springer International Publishing Switzerland 2016
L. Ashley, D. Lines (eds.), *Intersecting Cultures in Music and Dance Education*, Landscapes: the Arts, Aesthetics, and Education 19,
DOI 10.1007/978-3-319-28989-2_11

dance knowledge is embodied in schools, whilst elsewhere in Oceania more homogenous populations reside. Highlighting the cultural diversity that echoes across Oceania, and the dances that are or have potential to be studied in education, this chapter is also relevant for dance educators who are charged with fostering learning in 21stC diverse or "super-diverse" (Vertovec 2007, p. 1024) classrooms globally.

As part of a Western cultural heritage from countries such as England and the USA, early 20th century dance education is underpinned by a late modern, liberal, progressive ideology in which learning experiences are characterised by individual creativity in making dances. Such learning was and still is valued because it can nurture benefits for the learner such as a sense of ownership of and improving interest in learning. Ideologically, this pedagogy has an underlying sense of altruism on behalf of the teacher wherein authenticity relates directly to demonstration of individual well-being, creativity and whispers of future growth.

Illustrating how dance education could grow its current praxis and accommodate contrasting notions of ownership, authenticity and altruism that arise when studying dances from Oceania, I annotate the chapter with snapshots from my own research (Ashley 2010) and other relevant literature from New Zealand and offshore. United Nations documentation and relevant literature are woven throughout the paper establishing international intersections for consideration. Taking an holistic overview of the complex situation I draw on a range of literature that highlights how intersecting ideologies crumple together historical, theoretical, educational, sociological, political, cultural and economic issues. I feel that to ignore this 'spaghetti junction' of issues, although it could present readers with a density of ideas, could be to underplay the level of complexity that educators face.

The chapter begins at Sect. 1 with a brief personal narrative in which my position on this topic is contextualized. Section 2 follows in which some general background to issues of diversity, authenticity, creasing and cultural erosion in Oceania and overseas is presented. Ideological foundations that echo in current dance education are analysed in Sect. 3. Exploration of different ideological echoes that can occur when culturally diverse dances are taught comprises Sect. 4. Section 5 turns to what can occur in the creases between culturally different echoes in dance education. Emerging from the untangling, I provide a teaching strategy based on examples of Māori contemporary dance that some teachers may find useful.

1 My Journey in the Intersections

This chapter represents a fraction of my ongoing research since 2004 in which I endeavour to explore how to better understand why and how dance educators can build respect for the people whose dances and cultures are studied in dance education, as well as treat the dances ethically and contribute to their conservation rather than their erosion. The resulting multiple layers of considerations make the exploration of connected ideologies, theory and practice in this chapter an essential part of understanding what we, as dance educators, are doing, why we are doing it and how we may best provide culturally democratic dance education. Consequently, my musings on the culturally complex and diverse experiences that have potential to surface in dance education aim to broaden appreciation of the challenges and ideological mismatches that could arise in the intercultural creases.

As I described in the introduction to this book, my work in dance and dance education involved making meaningful dance as art in which the emphasis lay on the importance of the individual. On arriving in Aotearoa, New Zealand in 1997 and finding well-established dance education practice I felt somewhat at home. Lingering doubts about teaching culturally diverse dances and their place in schools, however, were reinforced as I took on the bi-cultural agenda of the country, encountering Māori kaupapa (knowledge, values and practices (Smith 1999) in the form of kapa haka and also experienced the rich performing arts of Auckland's Pacific Island diaspora. Interrogating the intersections between Western dance education, as I know it, and dances from other cultures became increasingly important to me as I continued to practice, enjoy and see the benefits of dance education but also detected its shortcomings. My curiosity finally found an outlet on commencing doctorate studies (Ashley 2010), setting me on a journey that is still ongoing today.

As an experienced dance educator from a reflexive perspective, I interrogated a journey of 40 years in dance and dance education. I still endeavour to follow reflective theoretical practice in my work, and subsequently have expanded my awareness of how what I see and do, and don't do and see, rests on understanding the values that are operational from moment to moment. In applying reflexive and reflective lenses on this state of affairs the questions which I faced included: How might pedagogical practices in dance education, set within Western modern ideology, embrace values brought by Oceania's culturally diverse population? How did we get to be this way, and what could/should we do about it? These questions remain as critical at this time as they were when dance first became part of New Zealand's national curriculum framework in 2000.

2 Background – Diversity, Authenticity, Creases and Erosion

2.1 Diversity in Oceania – Pluralist People, Echoes of Authenticity

Spread across 3.3 million square miles (8.5 million square kilometres) on the world's largest ocean, Oceania includes over 20 nation states located in Aotearoa, Australia, the USA and the myriad of islands in Polynesia, Melanesia and Micronesia. Mervyn McLean's, *Weavers of Song* (1999) provides comprehensive coverage of the breadth of Oceanic peoples' cultural worldviews and practices.

As Paul Heelas et al. (1996) observes, however, island people, having been aware of 'others' through interisland trade and war over many centuries, act out pluralistic awareness. The distinct differences and similarities across Pacific Island peoples and cultures produce a pluralist terrain of a special kind because of migration that occurred between 3000 and 4000 years ago. Leading world authority on human evolution, Bryan Sykes (2001) has produced convincing evidence from extensive studies of mitochondrial DNA that the peoples of Oceania from Papua New Guinea to Hawai'i share an ancestry from either coastal Taiwan or China. Archeological finds of pottery of the South East Asian, Lapita people across the Pacific Islands reinforce Sykes' theory.

From a perspective of dance research:

> The Lapita culture is the cultural heritage of almost all Pacific Islanders today, and thus provides a powerful evidence base for shared values and connections and, I would add, the exchange of ideas, forms, patterns, rhythms and choreographies. (Teaiawa 2014, p. 15)

Katerina Teaiwa describes the inter-island sharing of Lapita cultural heritage and its diverse variations as a process of 'remix'. Echoes can be noticed, for instance, in the authentic dances of the Polynesian people of Sāmoa and Tonga today. Tongan dancer Niulala Helu explained:

> To introduce a new movement into Tongan dance I usually look for a Sāmoan movement and I take that. In Tonga there's only four basic motifs in our dance, and that four have created so many more. And we've borrowed movements from Fiji and I've noticed when I was learning from the masters, how they borrowed it. So for example (demonstrates with hand gesture), this is a Tongan motif, now if you want to borrow something you have to make sure that it is a motif. Rather than it looks borrowed. Don't just use it and make it look contemporary. (Ashley 2012, p. 141)

Helu also described the "cultural motion" in Oceania, "like what we've been touching on is the borrowing of movement. There is this big, big motion within Polynesian society" (Ashley 2012, p. 142). It is within this context of an ocean of motion, the echoing and pluralist creasing of authentic heritages dancing across the waves of the Southern Pacific, that Western dance education pedagogy is located.

2.2   Oceania – Creases and Erosion

In present day Oceania, remixing also includes dances that do not have local roots such as hip hop and Western contemporary dance. In examining the remixing of authentic echoes of Oceanic past commonalities with local and global cultural differences, creases (Schechner 1988) is useful imagery to describe the irregular folds in which the worlds of dominant and other cultures intersect. Creasing is as active in dance education as it is in theatre and community dance.

Past erosion of Oceania's cultures that resulted from creasing with colonial missionary culture is well-documented. In the present day, accelerated and increased erosion of Oceanic indigenous, authentic dance heritages is possible from globalisation, impacting within the creases between environmental change, immigration, jet-travel, media, neo-liberal economics, hyperspace and education. Without some positive intervention to protect dance heritages, the current diversity of Oceanic dance traditions could become fading echoes across the ocean waves.

Protecting Oceanic indigenous, authentic dance heritages is set against a backdrop of the United Declaration on the Rights of Indigenous Peoples (UNDRIP) article 31, as adopted by UN General Assembly Resolution 61/295 on 13 September 2007:

> Indigenous peoples have the right to maintain, control, protect and develop their cultural heritage, traditional knowledge and traditional cultural expressions, as well as the manifestations of their sciences, technologies and cultures, including human and genetic resources, seeds, medicines, knowledge of the properties of fauna and flora, oral traditions, literatures, designs, sports and traditional games and visual and performing arts.

Acknowledging the same threat of erosion, UNESCO's Article 2.3 of the 2003 Convention for the Safeguarding of the Intangible Cultural Heritage encourages nation states to establish systems of Living Human Treasures[1] in order to safeguard the bearers of traditional heritages and the transmission of knowledge and skills to younger generations.

A living example of why such safeguards are important can be found in Micronesian, central equatorial Pacific. 33 low lying atoll islands of Kiribati are threatened to be wiped out by rising sea levels before the end of the century, or sooner. Teburoro Tito, President of Kiribati in 2001, described their dances "...as brightening the struggle of life on a tough sun scorched atoll...[drawing people together] to appreciate each other and to share in the joy of what our forefathers referred to as the secret and unique gifts of the spiritual world to the Tungaru people" (as cited in Whincup and Whincup 2001, p. 12). Kiribati dances provide an example of how "dancers embody centuries of history in the minutiae of their movements and the words of the ancient songs" (Whincup and Whincup p. 14). Arm, head and eye movements follow the musical rhythms and illustrate the lyrics, maintaining cultural legacies and histories. Kiribati is a particularly striking example for Oceania if we consider populations who could be forcibly displaced from their homelands not by war, but by the increasing threat of global warming. 103,000 citizens of Kiribati will become refugees and where they may live is currently unknown. Kiribati dances are a part of a rich heritage and sustaining these living treasures via traditional inter-generational transmission may well be threatened if the population is displaced. The Kiribati people are rightfully anxious about maintaining their heritage and their plight could be described as acute in terms of UNDRIP and UNESCO articles. The population of the low lying atolls that make up Tuvalu are similarly threatened. Mindful of UNDRIP's and UNESCO's advice, issues arising from intersections between different indigenous and culturally diverse influences in Oceanic dance education deserve scrutiny.

---

[1] http://www.unesco.org/culture/ich/?pg=00061

2.3   Super-Diversity in the Creases

Oceania also contains nation states, such as Aotearoa, New Zealand and Australia, that host more widely diverse populations than can be found on some of the region's islands. This diversity raises additional issues that may resonate with dance educators in many parts of the world. By way of contrast to more homogenous island populations, immigration in present day cosmopolitan New Zealand rose approximately 20 %, from 57,302 in 2008/9 to 295,903 in 2013/14. The 2013/14 figures included 160 different nationalities.[2] From these figures it would seem that migration is increasing cultural diversity in Aoteaora. Aotearoa's earlier migrant profile, being more likely to predominantly feature Pacific Island and British ethnicities, has shifted to include a more diverse cocktail amongst which economic migrants and refugee quotas from all over the globe are incorporated.

The United Nations High Commissioner for Refugees (UNHCR) identified the forced displacement of 51.2 million people in 2013 (an increase of 6 million people on 2012) as a global crisis. The UNHCR report also showed that 50 % of the refugee population were under 18 years of age and that this was the highest figure in a decade.[3] Such vicissitudes are global and contribute to the vastly increased pluralist populations that characterise many present day nation states.

In Great Britain, Steven Vertovec (2007) labelled this increased range of diversity and immigration "super-diversity" (p. 1024). He argued that Britain's previous immigration profile, consisting of citizens that mainly orginated from Commonwealth countries or previous colonial territories such as the Carribean and South Asia, contrasts with the current "level and kind of complexity surpassing anything the country has previously experienced" (p. 1024). His explanation of the complexities deserves detailed reading. In outlining the implications of super-diversity he observes that:

> The growing size and complexity of the immigrant population carries with it a range of significant public service implications. Executives in local authorities around Britain have voiced concerns about the ability of transport systems, schools and health services to manage new needs... Such concerns flag up a substantial shift in strategies across a range of service sectors concerning the assessment of needs, planning, budgeting, commissioning of services, identification of partners for collaboration and gaining a broader appreciation of diverse experiences in order generally to inform debate. (p. 1048)

In selecting schools as a site where new strategies are needed in order to respond to a complex interplay of different languages, cultural values, racial tension and religions, Vertovec depicts how this complexity, going beyond ethnicity, requires the re-evaluation of "policies for community cohesion, integration, managed migration and managed settlement" (p. 1047).

Accepting that: "Diversity in Britain is not what it used to be" (Vertovec, p. 2007: 1024), present day dance education in the UK is set within Vertovec's notion of

---

[2] http://www.immigration.govt.nz

[3] http://www.unhcr.org/5399a14f9.html

'super-diversity' in which the dominant culture/s and diverse others crease. Super-diversity, however, is by no means a solely British problem. It is widespread internationally and becoming more prevalent in Oceania. With this in mind it would be helpful to firstly scrutinise a Western dance education legacy, as found in its historical origins, because of its ubiquity in the intercultural creases of some parts of Oceania and overseas.

3   A Late Modern Legacy – Ideological Echoes in Dance Education

In this section I describe the underpinning beliefs, originating from a Western late modern ideology that echo through dance educators' current practice. Ideology, by its nature, comprises cultural histories, socio-political perspectives, values and pedagogy. In the second half of this section I explore the ways in which this ideology echoes within dance education as three embodied teaching strategies, authenticity, altruism and ownership.

3.1   Ideological Late Modern Echoes in Whispers of the 'Future-New'

For some social-theorists modernity is far from over as the postmodern is relegated to a hyper-technological version of late modernity.[4] Late modernity, driven by a global market economy, is differentiated from preceding eras because it "lives in the future, rather than the past" (Giddens 1998, p. 94). Characterised by a dynamic interplay between individual innovation and future growth, ideologically it privileges future-based change over that derived from past traditions.[5] With a preference for listening to whispers of what can be, late modernity is, therefore, informed by its own traditional ideology of the 'future-new'. An icon of late modernity is the "spatial metaphor of the avant-garde...that explores hitherto unknown territory" (Habermas 2001, p. 39). The innovative avant-garde is a driver of dominant political, cultural, economic and educational policies.

However, this is not a binary of 'old world' tradition versus innovative modernity in which a romantic or naïve view of tradition becomes "unarguable truths, symbols of containment, or intellectual weapons..." (Hagood 2006, p. 33). So-called traditional cultures invest in innovation but possibly within more restricted frames of

---

[4] Marshall Berman (1982) and Anthony Giddens (1998).

[5] Zygmunt Bauman's (1996) observation is pertinent. "It is the novelty that conjures up tradition as its other, as something it is not, something that it is up against, or something it lacks and misses" (Heelas et al. 1996, p. 49).

who is innovating, how and why, and they may not be so reliant on late modern's prioritisation of the 'future-new'.

The issue here is that once dominant ideologies become personal experience certain people's interests are privileged. Those with greater proximity to resources could be, directly or indirectly, more empowered to act. In privileging the interests of individual innovation over that of the group, Western pedagogical models and teaching are no exception. Arguably, many people live at this ideological intersection where whispers of a future-new involve tuning into echoes from a relatively recent past. A deeper understanding of these echoes, I feel, could better inform our comprehension of the diverse demands being made on 21st century dance educators in relation to whose values are dominant and the effects of creasing on dance and dancers from diverse cultural heritages.

3.2   Late Modern Echoes in Dance Education

In this section I trace how echoes of a late modern ideology are embodied in the praxis of present day dance education. Many teachers may recognise such echoes in their own teaching, and this section could be informative for those wishing to enhance their understanding by disentangling the cultural values that they practice in their work. Although there is undoubted educational value to be gained from Western late modern dance education, developing critical awareness of ideological foundations could further inform how to implement culturally democratic teaching for diverse and super-diverse settings.

Dance education's ideological foundations are sometimes overlooked. Relatively lesser studied, even though one could easily argue the case for it being relevant to dance studies, dance education is frequently conceptually set apart from its close cousin modern/contemporary dance. This oversight is illustrated by Rebecca Enghauser's (2008) otherwise insightful conceptual approach to developing a broader awareness and deeper understanding of modern theatre dance for dance educators. The five features by which Enghauser characterises modern dance, however, also underpin dance education and I now tease out how a late modern ideology of the 'future-new' drives child-centred pedagogy and individual discovery learning, to result in culturally specific understandings of authenticity, altruism, and ownership, as practiced by dance educators.

3.3   Authenticity

In Enghauser's description of the feature of "invention/revolution" (p. 37) she draws attention to modern dance as an avant-garde rebellion against established models and traditions such as classical ballet. Offering "a timely manifestation of a more individualistic and varied form of expression" (p. 36), this could also be describing dance education. Enghauser describes the feature of "individuality" (p. 39) in modern dance as characterised by the unique qualities and liberal rights underpinning each individual's personal, authentic dance work. Both modern dance and dance education externalise "personal, authentic experience" (Cohen 1966, p. 4).

Inclusion of individual learners in movement experimentation is deemed to benefit them by facilitating enjoyment of and motivation to learn, alongside improvements in well-being and confidence. Such Western late modern ideology has predominated in dance education texts and teaching crossing many decades (Green Gilbert 1992; Kassing and Jay 2003; Preston 1966; Shapiro 2008; Smith-Autard 2002). Similarly, the characteristic "experimentation/process" (p. 40) also underpins the pedagogical legacy of dance education, as featured in the teaching of individual-centred, creative learning experiences. The title of North American pioneer of dance education Margaret H'Doubler's 1974 book, *Dance: A Creative Art Experience*, captures the modern zeitgeist.

In my investigation, teachers talked about creative dance as offering opportunities to learn in a "free, expressive manner unfettered by a prescriptive dance form, for example, square dance" (2010, p. 107).[6] Dance as featured in *The New Zealand Curriculum* (New Zealand Ministry of Education 2000, 2007) results from a long history of dance education in schools and at tertiary level. The lineage emphasises fostering innovation and risk-taking, encouraging "students to break free from the 'rules' of learning to really think on their feet and find new methods of expression".[7] New Zealand is not alone in this. As a recent article reveals, creativity is a key factor in the ideologies of dance education in many countries across the globe including, amongst others, the UK, USA, Singapore, Finland and Canada (Snook and Buck 2014).

Authenticity in dance education is also traceable in echoes of terminologies and processes used in creative dance. Emerging from early 20th century pioneer, European Rudolf Laban, these terms bring a sense of technical authenticity, echoing in such remarks as: "It is important for the dance educator to author assessment tools so language remains authentic and relevant to dance education" (Kranicke and Pruitt 2012, p. 117). Although not a codified technique such as Martha Graham's, the terms embody cultural authenticity. In 'Modern Educational Dance', as it was first named in England by early 20th century physical educators (Best 1999; Preston 1966) creative dance could be a highly abstract affair, concerned predominantly with individual movement experimentation exploring themes and improvising with what are commonly now known as the 'Dance Elements', namely: body; space; time; weight/dynamics; and relationships. The Dance Elements, as well as other

---

[6] Arguably however, a teacher's construction of creative process and choice of theme are culturally prescribed and prior authentic experience can advantage some learners over others; equity becomes a malleable concept.

[7] http://seniorsecondary.tki.org.nz/The-arts/Who-are-the-arts-for/The-arts-disciplines/What-is-dance-about

Western dance terminologies, frequent the dance component of the 2007 *New Zealand Curriculum,* however the legacy is not overtly referenced.

3.4 Altruism

In Enghauser's characteristic of modern dance as "community/collaboration" (p. 40) a modernist understanding of altruism echoes throughout. Prioritising individual satisfaction as a default setting for dance education, a 'learning community of individuals' positions learners as being set to better themselves in a culture of the future-new. Longstanding dance educator Susan Stinson advocates that teachers' liberal sense of caring for individual learners is contingent with the "virtue" of "justice". A pedagogical foundation of altruism echoes as Stinson argues that

> …all educators, including those in dance, have a responsibility to help students discover and develop them[selves] – not because of their intimate connection to our own disciplines, but because they matter to us as humans and to our future as a civilisation. (2005, p. 87)

Similar altruistic intentions also drove the teachers in my study. One teacher valued how: "[The teaching] extended children's movements. Each group member performed their movement sequence in a safe environment, where all children felt included" (Ashley 2010, p. 103). Such altruism is testament to the longstanding evidence in dance education research of the educational values that accrue for learners when learning when learning in, through and about creative dance.

3.5 Ownership

Altruism and authenticity are often correlated with providing the learner with a sense of ownership of both the learning and the dances that the learners make. Revolving around the question of "Who am I?" Enghauser's category "personal/ cultural inquiry" (p. 41) emphasises personal values and beliefs and/or identities with an individual's cultural lineage.

When investigating teachers working in New Zealand schools, as they faced a new challenge to teach about culturally diverse dances presented in the 2002 *Arts in the New Zealand Curriculum,* I found that ownership was a key value that underpinned their praxis. Teachers commented about the correlation between successful teaching and ownership of learning by the learners in such remarks as: "The lesson was very successful. Children have ownership of the little actions they made which lead to the final product" (Ashley 2010, p. 103).

Stinson (2005) highlights ownership, discovery and creation as key for success of the learning process. Individual ownership, an echo of early 20th century European and North American modern dance education, has roots in progressive, liberal education ideology as marked by publications such as John Dewey's (1916), *Democracy and Education.* Later key texts by educators such as Lev Vygotsky

(1962) and Jerome Bruner (1986) endorse similar pedagogical roots and favour logically constructed learning experiences that encourage individual creativity and problem-solving.

This category interests me because it has potential to set individual ownership at the centre of pedagogy from within a future driven ideology, rather than an ideology in which ownership is communal and listens to echoes from an indigenously different past.

I locate the wholly laudable ideological underpinnings, as embodied in dance education, of individual ownership and altruistic pedagogy alongside authenticity of individual creativity and technical terms as echoes of a late modern Western European and North American legacy. Educational justice becomes confluent with authentic, individual, creative expression, as provided by an educationally altruistic community. With considerable justification in terms of its proven educational benefits for the learner, the pervasive 'future-new' ideology remains key in dance education. I endorse such educational values but I am concerned about the effect on other indigenous dance heritages as they overlap in the intercultural creases. Importantly, as the ideology of the future-new intersects with indigenously different echoes in dance education, comparing and contrasting them could foster greater understanding of how teachers, facing diverse cultures in their work, could better implement culturally responsive dance education.

4   Different Echoes: Altruism, Authenticity and Ownership

In this section I consider how ownership, altruism and authenticity echo conceptually and differently in cultures other than the Western, late modern, liberal, progressive one from which dance education emerges.

4.1   Altruism

In my study (Ashley 2010) participants Valance Smith, Niulala Helu and Keneti Muaiava, as teachers who teach their own indigenous dances in schools and tertiary institutions, described a need to possess high levels of skill in specific dances and knowledge about the practices of previous generations before embarking on teaching their dances to others. These specialists meet the 2007 UN's profile of Indigenous Peoples (as cited in Iokepa-Guerrero et al. 2011) that includes tendencies to:

- be accepted by the community as one of their members;
- self identify with their community of birth;
- demonstrate strong and historical links with their territories and surrounding natural world;
- know their historical continuity with pre-colonial and/or pre-settler societies.

I find that positioning these specialists as indigenous alongside the opinions that they expressed in my research reveals ideological echoes from their heritages.

In relation to altruistic teaching, such pedagogy may hold relevant cultural values integral to studying some dance genres, as described here by Sāmoan dance specialist Muaiava:

> … in Sāmoan culture you SSHH! You're not allowed to … like it's disrespectful. In saying that, they weren't trying to keep the knowledge away, they weren't trying to be mean. It was just the way that you show respect by shutting up. (Ashley 2012, p. 150)

Another Sāmoan source, however, identifies such "cultural silence" as a way of protecting cultural knowledge and property (Tamasese 2005, p. 62). Such indigenous educational ideologies conceptualise altruistic teaching as copying or rote learning of embodied knowledge, encouraging respect for others as experts and emphasising a sense of conformity.

Research has shown that cultural preferences for pedagogy exists. Teaching styles that reproduce knowledge (rote/mimetic learning) are preferred in countries such as Korea and China because the cultural emphasis is on standardising student performance (Cothran et al. 2005). In explaining pedagogy based on Taoist philosophy and its implications for dance training in Taiwan, Wen-Chi Wu (2013) identifies the acquisition of technique as essential to releasing creativity. She highlights that even though this can take a long time to achieve, it "should not be hastened merely by importing European concepts of creativity or American methods of choreography" (p. 221).

Some Western dance educators claim that emphasising technical proficiency would be more in tune with current times, as exemplified by the success of such popular television hits such as *Dancing with the Stars* (LaPointe-Crump 2006, 2007). Envisaged as a means to redress prioritising "personal creativity and expressiveness over dance as a shared cultural form" (LaPointe-Crump, 2006, p. 3), this rationale values the shared community that results from precision ensemble work, and possibly more contentiously that: "One step away from being evaluated in a class is auditioning for a company or show" (LaPointe-Crump, 2007, p. 4). This could surprise many dance educators striving to teach inclusively to classes with diverse interests and physical needs. Juju Masunah (2001), for instance, identified behaviourist learning in traditional Indonesian dance as educationally inappropriate because it required substantial time to reach an acceptable elitist standard, and also that the accompanying religious beliefs were unsuitable for the majority of learners in schools.

In culturally diverse classrooms, religion and spirituality can carry significant hurdles for indigenous dance teachers. An example of the compromises required that lurk in the creases of pedagogical ideologies can be found in the teaching of *Bharatha Natyam* by Madam Jeyanthi in Singapore schools (Lum and Gonda 2014). Responding to cultural diversity, school policies, and time constraints, she was charged with balancing and preserving her own traditions whilst also promoting intercultural understanding and embracing the cultural identities of others such as Muslim and Chinese children. When parents refused to allow their children to participate because it was perceived as bowing to a different god, Madam Jeyanthi compromised her spiritual beliefs, the *guru–shishya* relationship of teacher and student and the dance vocabulary. Madam Jeyanthi describes how she simplified the Indian dance for these learners but also relates how,

> ... we don't mention it as Bharatha Natyam when we teach in schools. So we mention it as Indian dance. So when you mention Indian dance, we introduce ... classical steps, folk dance, we bring in hip-hop steps, (and) we bring in fusion steps, contemporary movements... (Lum and Gonda 2014, p. 115)

The compromise here seems to tilt the pedagogical balance towards Western ideology. I wonder how traditional forms can be made relevant and interesting for learners whilst retaining different altruistic values of how dance is taught. By its own liberal standards Western education has some obligation to respect not only the dances of other cultures but also the pedagogical ideals that the dance teachers bring with them. Such a nexus[8] of ideology, praxis and content demonstrates how in education, "social justice is an active and malleable concept that can and should transform depending on circumstance and context" (Johnson et al. 2011, p. 309).

4.2   Authenticity

Pedagogical differences could be especially marked if we remind ourselves that late modern society is distinguished by a tendency to live in the future rather than the past. In my research, the dance specialists often referred to the need to seek advice from community elders when making new dances in order to honour traditional values, movement vocabulary, and also to achieve acceptance as being authentic from their community, as viewers and shared owners. A tertiary dance educator's comment in my research: "Māori dancers like to honour the past of their cultural ancestry before they go forward–research own family heritage of dance over 100 years" (Ashley 2012, p. 207) also reverberates in this echo:

> Elders are the knowledge keepers and knowledge teachers of Indigenous societies. The perspectives, skills, knowledge, stories, and teachings of Elders must have its place in Western academy and higher education. (Iokepa-Guerrero et al. 2011, p. 15)

In discussing how Hawaiian *kupuna* (elders) play important roles at the University of Hawai'i, Noelan Iokepa-Guerrero points out that *kupuna* are envisaged as perpetuating indigenous cultural wisdom and excellence by straddling the traditional and the modern. In the same echo, however, the specialists in my study pointed out that elders were not against new ideas but that innovation needed to be within culturally authenticated traditional parameters. This sense of authenticity is evident in Māori leader Sir Peter Buck's (1987) explanation of how some conventions in kapa haka that guide what is acceptable innovation arise from historical precedent but others are more spontaneous. In recognising kapa haka as an art form that like others combines heritage with innovation, he depicts a certain complexity as to the

---

[8] Nexus is a term that I explore in greater depth in Ashley 2012.

process of creativity being more tied to a living continuous sense of a non-Western past. Through consultation with elders, authenticity tends towards communal consensus, rather than determined by autonomous individuals iconoclastically breaking 'rules' and acquiring sole possession.

In some Oceanic communities, however, the obligation to listen to echoes from the past can go even deeper than respecting living elders as protectors or guardians of a culture. Epeli Hau'ofa (2004) envisages the compression of time and space into precious vessels such dances, songs and visual art works that act as vectors reconnecting lost relatives from the past with the present; a Janus connection through time. Poignantly evoking images of trading culturally formed concepts of time and space, cultural treasures cross the Pacific linking spatial and temporal locations through the trade of artefacts as containers of traditional actions, beliefs and practices. In Melanesian Vanuatu, rather than subscribing to the concept of individual innovation, Tannese people traditionally prefer to attribute creative forces to anonymous spirits and ancestors.

A better understanding of this echo of authenticity can be found in Karen Hubbard's (2008) analysis of traditional jazz dance being "great-grandparents' jazz" (p. 110). Hubbard differentiates authentic jazz dance technically in terms of posture, dynamics, improvisation and cool attitude, from that in which mainstream Eurocentric influences have resulted in such forms as lyrical jazz, Broadway jazz and funk and the associated "pasted-on smile and being propelled by the music while performing manic manouevres and manipulations" (p. 112). Giving Afro-American jazz dance as an example of validating a sense of belonging to African heritage draws attention to the intersections that are current in Oceania being transferable for dance education in other countries. It also reinforces the idea that those who own certain dances may be best employed to teach them in the interests of cultural authenticity and avoidance of erosion by supporting the owners' rights to financial reward for passing on their legacies.

4.3   Ownership

The dance specialists in my study expressed various opinions on ownership including who might best teach certain dances, how the dances should be taught and why, as well as certain conditions surrounding how dances are created. Smith, a Māori, kapa haka specialist, felt that in order to qualify to teach about Māori culture and its dance traditions, individuals would require 5000 h of study. A major topic of conversation amongst the dance specialists was providing appropriate fiscal remuneration for teaching their indigenous dances.

In Oceanic cultures there are differing cultural values towards ownership of dances and songs, some of which involve fiscal transactions or goods exchanged for dances. Mervyn McLean (1999) points out that ownership of dances as property that can be bought and sold is more of a Melanesian rather than Polynesian cultural concept. He draws on the work of Margaret Mead in Melanesian, New Guinea to document established trade routes of song, dances and fashions from communities living on the coast to more inland villagers who would pay for the latest trends with feathers, pigs, shell rings and tobacco. In turn, when the inland villagers tired of the latest fashion they would trade them to those living even deeper in the interior and use their profits to buy the next 'best thing'. Jun'ichiro Suwa (2001) also describes how, in the coastal district of Madang, Papua New Guinea some dances that were seen as collectively owned were traded between villages as commodities for goods. Despite no actual money being involved, such consumerism may sound familiar to many readers. Kirk Huffman (1996) records a common traditional copyright system used across the islands of Vanuatu dictating that only those who possess the rights can give public renditions of songs, stories, carving designs, rhythms or dances, and if permission has not been granted compensation may be demanded by magic, fines or even death. In Aotearoa, iwi (tribes) own dances and songs and control performance rights. Hence, when haka are borrowed without permission tensions can run high. Importantly, international copyright law does not protect art that is sourced from spiritual forces.

In Polynesia there is documentation of transactions bestowing public recognition on villages or families who own the artefacts via gifts of baskets of flowers. The cultural owners, according to McLean (1999), see trading of art as demeaning and are gratified solely if others adopt their dances. Transactions are more connected with honouring status and fostering inter-island social harmony. In the Cook Islands, touring groups of adults and children, *tere*, were recorded as visiting other islands in the late 1800s (McLean 1999). Gifts could be exchanged but some visits were used to raise funds for community purposes. When I visited the Cook Islands in 2009 I watched a performance that was a feature of the weekly local market. The group was raising funds for a tour of Australia. One immediate conclusion could have been that this was for the tourists but previous longstanding practices indicate connectedness to past economic practices.

A symbiotic consequence of their owners' ability to adapt dances and make money in businesses such as tourism could be that artists, as Living Human Treasures, may be supported to maintain their traditional dance practices, and pass on their cultural knowledge to the next generation. It could well be that adapting some dances for commercial gain also sustains the livelihoods of the owners and could help avoid erosion of the more traditional forms. Education could, some may say should, provide another enclave where threatened dances and dancers might be better protected from erosion. However, indigenous artists would require a substantial presence in the timetable, appropriate reimbursement, some reshaping of infrastructural policy and support to work with Western pedagogical ideology.

Having identified some of the diverse cultural values associated with ownership, authenticity and altruism, next I consider the intercultural creases between different ideologies as they intersect in dance education.

5   Untangling Echoes in the Creases – A New Dynamic

As culturally different echoes intersect in richly diverse educational settings, different understandings of three key ideological concepts ownership, altruism and
authenticity become entangled. The possible effects of creasing on transmission of
different cultures are captured in this statement from UNESCO[9]:

> Universal education provides important tools for human development. But it may also inad-
> vertently erode cultural diversity and disorient youth by obstructing the transmission of
> indigenous language and knowledge.

In pondering the erosion of indigenous knowledge as it intersects with what is
labelled 'universal' education, UNESCO identifies a need to establish new dynamics between teachers, students and community knowledge-holders. If 'universal' is
read as implying a Western educational ideology, the new dynamic would need to
balance notions of tradition as echoes of 'past-significant' with a late modern man-
tra of individual whispers about the 'future-new'. UNESCO indicates a need to
identify spaces and processes that allow less-recognised knowledge systems to be
represented equitably.

UNESCO provides guidelines for arts education in its Seoul Agenda (2010).[10] Of
the Agenda's three goals, Goal 3 focuses on "resolving the social and cultural challenges facing today's world" (p. 8). The four practical strategies for arts education
associated with this goal aim broadly at developing:

1. Innovation in society
2. Socio-cultural well-being
3. Social cohesion, cultural diversity and intercultural dialogue
4. Responses to major global challenges, from peace to sustainability

These strategies and their corresponding actions reverberate with the tenor of this
chapter. Arguably, the ideological positioning of innovation at the top of the list of
practical strategies could be read as prioritising the 'future-new'. Nevertheless, the
actions that UNESCO associate with Goal 3 include valuing: the traditional and the
contemporary; conservation of identity, diversity and heritage; and adaptation to the
local relevancy of learners including minorities and migrants. These guidelines are
helpful for dance educators when considering creating a new dynamic in their work.

In the following sections, I explore what a new dynamic for dance education
might entail. I look beyond extant praxis and the social privileges that it can confer
as to how dances are taught, who teaches them, how they are made, and the associated financial rewards. Giving practical examples from Oceania and elsewhere, I
attempt to identify some challenges that can impact on balancing an emphasis on
mainly the individual with one that considers communal needs and values when a
diverse range of cultures intersect in dance education. I consider possibilities and

---

[9] http://www.unesco.org/bpi/pdf/memobpi48_tradknowledge_en.pdf

[10] http://www.unesco.org/new/fileadmin/MULTIMEDIA/HQ/CLT/CLT/pdf/Seoul_Agenda_EN.
pdf

hurdles that dance educators may need to negotiate, and strategies that could support implementation of socially just praxis for dance education. I include examples where efforts have been made to establish new dynamics between teachers, learners and the cultural community. A main sticking point, however, could be pedagogical differences and it is to this issue that I now turn.

5.1 Altruistic Creases – Socially Just Pedagogy for Dance Education

As dance educators reach out to increasingly diverse learners, the creasing could involve balancing different pedagogical echoes arising from how altruism is understood culturally. As driven by culturally diverse preferences for passing on cultural taonga (treasures), a challenge faced by dance education is informed by being mindful of how "traditional dance forms are passed from generation to generation without reference to national or international standards" (Adshead-Lansdale and Layson 1999, p. 22). Potential for pedagogical mismatches in how dance is taught raises questions about if or how the knowledge of respected elders and specialists from communities could be represented in dance education that may be driven by inclusive pedagogy, curriculum expectations and national standards. Nyama McCarthy-Brown's (2009) solution is to re-evaluate national standards in order that different indigenous dance traditions and learners may be treated equitably.

If UNESCO's 'universal' pedagogy is underpinned by Western progressive ideology, rote learning and teaching methods that are appropriate in the village may not translate into schools because they could be interpreted, wrongly in my opinion, as a backward step educationally. Finding strategies that could balance what has been labelled a pedagogical model of an "authoritarian father" (Stinson 1998, p. 27) with 'universal' education is a longstanding contention. A hurdle commonly cited is that of guest teachers struggling to teach inclusively. Teachers in my research commented that sometimes "traditional Island teachers, they teach as they have been taught, and that method doesn't go along with the way that we teach anything in NZ" (Ashley 2012, p. 58). A tertiary dance educator explained:

> The only factor with a traditional style of teaching children the same steps, even in contemporary style of dance, is when you've taught them a sequence the children tend to look at each other and compare themselves to others. They can tend to lose a bit of confidence there. (Ashley 2012, p. 27)

Displacing rote learning of steps by emphasising creative dance was one of the founding strategies of dance education. Despite dance educators' suspicion of technical skill, there was some infiltration of North American dance techniques—such as Martha Graham's into the UK in the 1960s and 70s. The resulting acrimony between the two factions is well-documented (Preston-Dunlop and Espana 2005). Dance educators took exception to giving up the recognised sense of inclusion of a wide range of learners that accrued in creative dance, along with the associated benefits to the learner of increasing confidence and interest to learn. I suggest that vestiges of this battle can linger in current praxis.

The implications of UNDRIP's article 31 give rise to a need to establish a socially just sense of altruism that includes, respects and rewards knowledge holders from a variety of different cultural heritages via institutional change in educational and political settings. Efforts to reinforce socially just treatment of different indigenous heritages could transform dance education according to local contexts.

An Oceanic example of the folds of pedagogical altruism in dance education can be found in Sāmoa's *Performing Arts Curriculum* (Sāmoan Ministry of Education, Sports and Culture 2004). Written for dance and drama in secondary schools with funding from a New Zealand Aid programme, it has similarities with its Aotearoa equivalent. There are also marked differences, such as the compulsory teaching of named Sāmoan dances reflecting Sāmoa's more homogenous population. As an, "integral part of the Sāmoan culture and the society in which we live our everyday lives" (p. 17), the preservation of indigenous Sāmoan traditional dances such as *mā'ulu'ulu* and *fa'ataupati* is noticeable, and, unlike New Zealand's curriculum, pedagogy of rote learning, imitating and performing are emphasised throughout. Similarly the contextual study in the document focuses predominantly on Sāmoan and Pacific Island dances. Ballet, creative dance, hip hop and other genres are included throughout the document but in lesser amounts to locally indigenous dances. Some research into how the implementation of this curriculum is progressing could be most exciting.

In the New Zealand curriculum, a policy designed to meet the challenges of providing culturally equitable education is culturally responsive, pluralist pedagogy. New Zealand's *Educational Review Office* (2012, (ERO)) identified that acknowledging, celebrating and promoting learners' diverse cultural and ethnic identities is key in fostering engagement with learning, particularly for lowest performing students. In my research (Ashley 2012) some teachers associated cultural relevance with the learners' well-being. For example one teacher noted: "This opportunity also gave many students a chance to shine if they were familiar with the culture or indeed from that ethnic group. It made them feel special" (p. 62). Key words such as confidence, self-esteem and motivation were common in teachers' responses. Interestingly, these words are those that are often attached to the altruistic ideology of Western dance education. One could argue, therefore, that inclusion of pedagogy from diverse cultures is altruistic because it benefits the learner via: "Teaching that invites the students' lived experiences links to issues of social justice" (Sansom 2011, p. 49). Such pedagogy focuses on establishing cultural diversity in everyday teaching practice and classroom ethos. A different dynamic of altruism might emerge from within these creases in which the pedagogies of diverse cultures may be, somehow, included.

5.2 Authenticity – Untangling Ethical Creases

In this section I explore intersections between different worldviews that are embodied when making dances comes under the spotlight in dance education. In the intercultural creases of teaching dance to diverse groups of learners, echoes of Western key cultural concepts regarding innovation become entangled with values from different indigenous sources. Mindful of various guidelines for respecting the rights of indigenous people to maintain, control, protect and develop their cultural heritages, ethically untangling making dances in dance education could produce a more socially just dynamic awareness of how authentic culturally diverse dances are created.

Teaching how to create dances from a relatively greater range of freedom and choice of movements, dance structures and individual poetic license of a Western palette presents teachers with different challenges from making dance that involves technical levels of skill, knowledge of cultural protocols and a more restricted range of movement choices. For instance, adding creative dance as a default to a learning experience about a non-Western dance, a common strategy used by teachers in my research, is possibly not culturally appropriate from some indigenous dance specialists' worldviews. Such pedagogical appropriation of creative process is, I feel, a keystone in the authentication debate because it calls on the very shortcomings that most concerned the teachers in my investigation, namely their lack of physical skills and contextual knowledge.

Although traditions of cultures generally feature innovation and creativity, there seems to be a delicate balance in which individual authenticity could be valued over a sense of collectively negotiated innovation. In acknowledging change as a constant, everything could be perceived as authentic. However, my concern lies more in how dance education is ethically "dancing out the colliding still unassimilated elements of contemporary life" (Siegel 1998, p. 97), with an emphasis on avoiding further erosion of the authentically visible differences as found in the dominant recognisable movement features, theatrical conventions and creative processes.

As recognised in UNESCO's Seoul Agenda, encouraging arts educators to cooperate with local communities, dance artists, parents and family is key to building sustainable arts education. Elders could be welcomed into schools under a Living Human Treasures national policy, and this strategy could meet the needs of responding to indigenous minorities in super-diverse school populations. Equally in more homogenous isolated populations, it could assist dance artists to sustain their own heritages and foster intergenerational transmission of traditional arts, safeguarding intangible cultural knowledge of dance from erosion. Another solution is to facilitate teachers in schools to teach their own cultural heritages inclusively (Ashley 2014a). Finding ways of providing teachers with means to ethically include a wide variety of cultures is an area that could benefit from greater research.

At this point I pose a question. If, working within a Western, late modern tradition in which individuality and child-centredness are prioritised, what are dance educators if they are not respected elders? I am using elders in a Western sense here because as teachers their cultural paradigm could well be underpinned by pedagogically valuing and even prioritising the view of the individual learner/creator over their own. As provocateur, I position this question as pivotal to 21st century dance education because of its potential to make a dynamic shift in how dances are made and justifying who is remunerated to teach what.

Thinking in terms of the intersections found within creases is a helpful image when considering how creative dance could promote opportunities for learners to consume, borrow or 'own' the dances of others via the making of what is sometimes known as fusion dance. Intercultural fusion dance, whether in education or theatre, can give the individual ethical license to procure the dances of others under a cloak of creativity in the folds of which respect, ethics, tradition, authenticity, innovation, ownership and social justice jostle (Ashley 2013b, c). 20th century and 21st century Western dance theatre is rife with choreographers borrowing from other people's cultures undercover of a "Western license to thrill" (Ashley 2014b). In discussing the topic of intercultural dance theatre, Sansan Kwan (2014) unravels the inevitability of the continuation of such borrowings, concluding that an "ethics of interculturalism" (p. 197) might be described as simply the obligation to continue pursuing the impossibility of communion in intercultural encounters. I present a counterpoint to Kwan's view by thinking of traditional dances as endangered species, and that standalone innovation of echoes from authenticated indigenous pasts warrants greater attention ethically in present day dance education. When authenticity as defined by Western ideology, predominates in fusion dance, attempts to domesticate the exotic can leave the domestic as the most recognisable characteristic.

Importantly, cultural values can drive culturally different creative processes. Making culturally specific traditional dances the most noticeable feature could foster greater awareness of which authentic cultural memories are informing dance education and theatre. The avoidance of fusion or hybridity is a struggle worth pursuing if dance education is to retain its relevance in a super-diverse world. A world in which fusion dance, as we know it, is not necessarily wrong but it may not be right for everyone. As some indigenous dance traditions are eroded by what is commonly recognised as the modernist 'tradition of the new', intercultural fusion raises the possibility of disintegration of cultural identities through the ways in which innovation is implemented in 'universal' education.

5.3   Ownership: Echoes from Pasts and Whispers of Futures

Mindful of 'universal education' as a site where some indigenous dances and dancers could be set apart from the normative transformative events of the owner's living culture, in this section possibilities surrounding who could teach what and why are untangled in search of a new dynamic in employment.

In my investigation the dance specialists' teaching provided culturally complete learning experiences in which cultural literacy and dancing co-existed; they 'owned it'. Echoes of an indigenous traditional dance past were evident in the way that they taught. In my work on a university Bachelor of Dance programme I observed them teach with a seamless combination of dancing with contextual background alongside opportunities for creative thinking, albeit with a relatively restricted movement palette. Their teaching strategies included the learners' diverse physical and cultural needs along with indigenously authentic knowledge and dancing, informing what I feel is an oversight that has ramifications for who teaches what and why in diverse dance education.

As echoes from different pasts intersect with whispers of possible futures, dance educators could be depicted as untangling a notion of tradition that could appear to be difficult. In my investigation, a perspective shared by teachers is captured in this teacher's remark: "I'm not qualified to say what is traditional. I mean that's a whole other argument. What is traditional dance?" (Ashley 2012, p. 154) Although some teachers in my study were teaching about some culturally different dances, they pointed out that they lacked the practical skills and cultural literacies, referring to such teaching as being too theoretical, and requiring too much preparation, time, resources and money. Recognising the immediate educational value and success when teaching creative dance, the teachers predominantly did so. For these teachers, their own tradition seemed tuned into the future-new and was not so attuned to echoes from the unfamiliar indigenous traditions of other cultures. One tradition that dance educators could teach about and 'own', however, is that of dance education itself. Not teaching about its contextual significance reinforces a hegemonic position of 'ease' for teachers who can teach creative dance without the need for extra preparation, money, resources and, in its fullest sense, Western dance literacy (Ashley 2013a).

Provision of explicit policy, funding and infrastructure for dance specialists to make their heritages available in ways with which they feel culturally comfortable could develop a new educational dynamic that supports indigenous people's rights to maintain, control, protect and develop their cultural heritages. If a new dynamic between teachers and community is to be established, a system somewhat similar to peripatetic music instrumental specialists could provide helpful guidelines. Such a scheme could provide a number of advantages such as developing: regular school visits rather than one-offs; suitable educational support and advice for dance specialists; a system of payment for guests comparable with other curriculum areas; and closer relationships between teachers, learners and local communities.

The problem of how many different dances schools can realistically include when facing issues of budget and time is unavoidable. Nevertheless, if there was a properly funded pool of indigenous dance teacher/owners then this could be a positive start. This idea could work for both primary and secondary schools although their reasons for working with chosen experts could differ. Different needs, according to age, are clearly outlined in the dance component of *The New Zealand Curriculum*. Mandated by government in 2003, the curriculum framework encompasses a policy whereby younger children benefit from engagement with their cultures of origin whilst older students are better served by widening their cultural dance experiences into the less familiar. It provides a platform from which teachers can invest in cultural difference as a response to their own culturally diverse school populations.

New Zealand's Ministry of Education's online register of dance specialists, Artists in Education,[11] helps to create awareness of dance specialists who are interested in working in schools. However, such schemes are not without their problems such as the responsibility of payment of guest specialists remains with individual schools. Untangling the finance thread is, it seems, key to providing socially just treatment in recognising the ownership and cultural intellectual copyright of culturally diverse dance teachers. Such shifts are by no means straightforward because of cultural differences that can arise in the creases between emphasising communal ownership and culturally different understandings of pedagogy and authenticity in Western dance education.

6   A Practical Strategy for a New Dynamic

In an attempt to at least partially unravel this Gordion Knot of ownership, altruism and authenticity, perhaps some untangling of ethical teaching strategies may be achieved by imagining a spectrum of ownership. Being able to disentangle indigenous dances in the creases of a spectrum, as a teaching strategy, could further inform current dance education by better articulating which cultural terrains are being danced on when watching, interpreting, performing, studying and making dance.

In order to annotate how the spectrum could work I compare and contrast three examples of Māori contemporary dance, and also indicate analogies with creative dance in education. The spectrum can, therefore, be applied by teachers to not only contextual analysis and interpretation of dance but to how they are teaching dance-making in terms of which lineage they may be working within ideologically. At one end of the spectrum the individual is more important than the community, whilst at the other the individual is a representative of the well-being of a collective culture. Importantly, the recognisable movement features of the dances would look noticeably different at each end. I draw attention to how both ends of the spectrum are informed by different traditions, including cultural parameters associated with innovation.

Tracing Māori theology, Stephen Bradshaw's[12] choreography *Mauri* (2003, Atamira Dance Company)[13] fuses traditional Māori haka and waiata-ā-ringa (action song), with Western contemporary dance. I place it near the middle of the spectrum as being authentically Māori but bearing mainly recognisable Western movement imprints. Nourished by Māori spiritual beliefs and its own past, Bradshaw identifies a continuum for 'new' Māori dance. This continuum is similar to my spectrum inso-

---

[11] http://artsonline2.tki.org.nz/artistsined/considerations.php

[12] Readers may wish to read more from Māori contemporary dance practitioner Stephen Bradshaw at: http://contemporarymaoridance.com/2014/02/07/what-is-maori-contemporary-dance/

[13] The Ministry of Education DVD resource for schools, *Contemporary Dance Aotearoa* (2004) features *Mauri*, and learning materials are on the Ministry TKI site giving free access to all teachers www.tki.org.nz/r/arts/dance/contemporary/mauri/curric_links_e.php

far as it acknowledges how gradual the transition between fewer or greater Western influences can be. In my spectrum, however, I distinguish how the dances at each end look noticeably different from each other in terms of more or less, in this instance, recognisably authentic Māori movement. The look of movement vocabulary as well as the themes, costumes, staging, accompaniment and creative process discerns one end from the other. Also, a continuum ideologically prioritises *progress* to a future-new, whereas a spectrum respects approaches to innovation as simply culturally different.

Towards the future-new end of the spectrum, full-length works *Mana Wahine* (Okareka Dance Company 2014)[14] and *Moko*[15] (Atamira Dance Company 2014), albeit underpinned with Māori myth, values, beliefs, practices (such a moko, tattoos), te reo language, visual art, movement from kapa haka and culturally appropriate processes, bear a predominantly authentic Western contemporary dance appearance. I perceive in these works an approach that has some equivalent in dance education, as found in a description of making dance based on Māori kowhaiwhai (visual artwork) given by one of the teachers in my investigation:

> 'Worked on kowhaiwhai patterns and looked at how we can work Māori dance movement in with those…. Kowhaiwhai because I wanted to make sure there was a New Zealand element… So the focus for the kowhaiwhai is of course haka, but what you're trying to teach them is how to use the space and how to make pathways. But you've given them that as a sort of context and allowed them to pull those other things in. (Ashley 2012, p. 147)

The teacher identified this as a contemporary dance unit of learning that borrows Māori movements (learnt from a sheet) and some spiritual symbolic significances in combination with Laban based creative dance from a stimulus of Māori visual art.

Moving towards the past echoes end of the spectrum, Māori *Hawaiki Tu* is described as "Haka Theatre", a term that directors Kura Te Ua and Beez Ngarino Watt explain in their programme notes was used over 100 years ago by Princess Te Puea Herangi. Haka Theatre infuses myth, language, music, dramatic dialogue and a Māori ethic of creative process. The "Māori movement" that Te Ua and Watt describe in their work is one element of Haka Theatre. Sometimes their dancers come from a wide variety of cultural backgrounds and ethnicities, however, the movement, an infusion of distinctly Māori strident kapa haka, lightning speed wero (spear), poi and trademark arm gestures of waiata-ā-ringa (action songs) is not predominantly Western in its appearance. Even the more Eurocentric 'creative dance' featured in *Rongo*,[16] based on harvesting, is redolently Māori in its forceful dynamic, recognisably Māori ringa (arm and hand gestures) and group relationships (Armstrong 1964; Matthews 2004; Shennan 1984). Western styled vocabulary and group relationships are less in evidence. The roots of this kind of indigenous contemporary dance run deep with Māori Ora (culture), not to say that other Māori

---

[14] Cultural adviser Tui Matira Ranapiri Ransfield talks about the production on http://www.okareka.com/mana-wahine/follow

[15] http://vimeo.com/99221711

[16] A section of the full-length work *Te Manawa* (the heart), Performed by Kura Te Ua, Karena Koria, Sophie Williams and Beez Ngarino Watt. http://youtu.be/r7jV_S98Igg

contemporary dance does not, but in this work it is somehow more tangibly embodied in the kinaesthetic echoes of a predominantly older world movement palette.[17] Facilitating choreographers such as Te Ua and Watt, as well as local elders and experts who may work in even tighter traditional ways, to become influential players in educational discourse and practices provides a new world vision of old world echoes in dance education.

7   By Way of a Conclusion

Developing socially just senses of ownership, authenticity and altruism with regard to the pedagogical values of others seems to bring Western dance education to the brink of a sea-change in terms of not only which dances are taught and who teaches them but in terms of ethical boundaries, educational priorities and infrastructural policies that support the teaching of the dances of others in ways that are acceptable to and respectful of the owners of the dances. Amongst the intersections of culturally diverse ideologies, dance vocabularies and meanings, the guidelines of UNDRIP and UNESCO carry important implications for how dance educators could act to help minority cultures avoid erosion. Listening through the Oceanic icon of the conch shell each of us chooses what to pay attention to – past echoes carried on Pacific Ocean waves, or whispers from inside the creases of a super diverse future, or both.

This conclusion marks a springboard rather than a determined endpoint because I feel strongly that this is an under-researched topic. Researching learners as they interact with guest dance specialists and research by indigenous dance specialists themselves are just two examples of the many initiatives that could produce much needed insights into how current dance education could be more culturally responsive, malleable and equitable in assisting the survival of indigenous dance heritages and the dancers who own them.

References

Adshead-Lansdale, J., & Layson, J. (Eds.). (1999). *Dance history: An introduction* (2nd ed.). London: Routledge.

Armstrong, A. (1964). *Maori games and hakas*. Wellington: Reed.

Ashley, L. (2010). *Teaching dance from contextual perspectives in the New Zealand Curriculum: Concerns, dilemmas and opportunities in theory and practice*. Unpublished doctoral thesis, University of Auckland, New Zealand.

Ashley, L. (2012). *Dancing with difference: Culturally diverse dances in education*. Rotterdam: Sense Publishers.

---

[17] For further exploration see Ashley (2015a, b).

Ashley, L. (2013a). Dancing with cultural difference: Challenges, transformation and reflexivity in culturally pluralist dance education. *Dance Research Aotearoa, 1*(1), 5–23. http://www.dra. ac.nz/index.php/DRA/article/view/12.

Ashley, L. (2013b). Culturally different dances in the New Zealand arts curriculum: Understanding about fusion, tradition and making dances in context. In T. Gray, M. Gray, J. Stevenson, L. Ashley, P. Moon, & P. Cleave (Eds.), *Kowhiti dance: Special collection* (pp. 101–143). Palmerston North: Go Press.

Ashley, L. (2013c). Diversity is celebrated here. *DANZ Quarterly, 32*, 16–17.

Ashley, L. (2014a). Encountering challenges in teacher education: Developing culturally pluralist pedagogy when teaching dance from contextual perspectives in New Zealand. *Research in Dance Education, 15*(3), 254–270. http://doi.org/10.1080/14647893.2014.910186.

Ashley, L. (2014b). Fusion dance. *DANZ Quarterly, 35*, 6–8.

Ashley, L. (2015a). Dancing in different tongues: A surplus of meaning in indigenous terrains of contemporary dance. *Dance Research Aotearoa, 3*(1), 58–75. http://www.dra.ac.nz.

Ashley, L. (2015b). Illuminating cultural terrains in dance: A symbiotic approach to analysis and interpretation. *Te Kaharoa, 8*(1), 128–157. http://www.tekaharoa.com/index.php/tekaharoa/article/view/199.

Berman, M. (1982). All that is solid melts into the air: The experience of modernity. In M. Drolet (Ed.), *The postmodernism reader: Foundational texts* (pp. 53–66). New York: Routledge.

Best, D. (1999). Dance before you think. In G. McFee (Ed.), *Dance education and philosophy* (pp. 101–121). Oxford: Meyer and Meyer Sport.

Bruner, J. S. (1986). *Actual minds, possible worlds.* Cambridge, MA: Harvard University Press.

Buck, P. S. (1987). *The coming of the Māori.* Wellington: Māori Purposes Fund Board.

Cohen, S. J. (1966). *The modern dance: Seven statements of belief.* Middletown: Wesleyan University Press.

Cothran, D. J., Kulinna, P. H., Banville, D., Choi, E., Amade-Escot, C., MacPhail, A., Macdonald, D., Richard, J.-F., Sarmento, P., & Kirk, D. (2005). A cross-cultural investigation of the use of teaching styles. *Research Quarterly for Exercise and Sport, 76*(2), 193–201.

Education Review Office; Te Tari Arotake Matauranga. (2012). *Evaluation at a glance: Priority learners in New Zealand Schools.* Wellington: Ministry of Education. http://www.ero.govt.nz/National-Reports/Evaluation-at-a-Glance-Priority-Learners-in-New-Zealand-Schools-June-2012/Findings/Issue-Two-Knowledgeably-implementing-a-responsive-and-rich-curriculum

Enghauser, R. E. (2008). Teaching modern dance: A conceptual approach. *Journal of Physical Education, Recreation and Dance, 79*(8), 36–42.

Giddens, A. (1998). *Conversations with Anthony Giddens: Making sense of modernity.* Stanford: Stanford University Press.

Green Gilbert, A. (1992). *Creative dance for all ages: A conceptual approach.* Reston: The American Alliance for Health, Physical Education, Recreation and Dance.

H'Doubler, M. N. (1974). *Dance: A creative art experience.* Madison: University of Wisconsin Press.

Habermas, J. (2001). Modernity: An unfinished project. In S. Malpas (Ed.), *Postmodern debates* (pp. 37–520). New York: Palgrave.

Hagood, T. K. (2006). Values and voice in dance education: The merit of fostering tradition, experiment, diversity, and change in our pedagogy. *Arts Education Policy Review, 108*(2), 33–37.

Hau'ofa, E. (2004). Opening keynote Foluga (The journey through time), at the *Culture moves* conference. Wellington, NZ.

Heelas, P., Lash, S., & Morris, P. (Eds.). (1996). *Detraditionalization: Critical reflections on authority and identity.* Cambridge: Blackwell.

Hubbard, K. W. (2008). Valuing cultural context and style: Strategies for teaching traditional jazz dance from the inside out. *Journal of Dance Education, 8*(4), 110–116.

Huffman, K. (1996). Trading, cultural exchange and copyright: Important aspects of Vanuatu arts. In J. Bonnemaison, K. Huffman, C. Kaufman, & D. Tyron (Eds.), *The arts of Vanuatu* (pp. 182–190). Honolulu: University of Hawai'i Press.

Iokepa-Guerrero, N., Carlson, B., Railton, L., Pettigrew, D., Locust, E., & Mia, T. (2011). The need for elders in education: Five indigenous perspectives from around the world. In V. Arbon (Ed.), *WINHEC journal: Indigenous research: Elders and knowledgeable others in higher education* (pp. 15–26). Geelong: Deakin University.

Johnson, E., Oppenheim, R., & Younjung, S. (2011). "Would that be social justice?" A conceptual constellation of social justice curriculum in action. *The New Educator, 5*(4), 293–310. org/10.1080/1547688X.2009.10399581.

Kassing, G., & Jay, D. M. (2003). *Dance teaching methods and curriculum design.* Champaign: Human Kinetics.

Kranicke, M., & Pruitt, L. (2012). Are they getting it? Creating dance assessments that honour the creative process. *Journal of Dance Education, 12*(3), 113–117. org/10.1080/15290824.2012.7 01171.

Kwan, S. (2014). Even as we keep trying: An ethics of interculturalism in Jérôme Bel's *Pichet Klunchun and Myself. Theatre Survey, 55*(2), 185–201. doi:10.1017/S0040557414000064.

LaPointe-Crump, J. (2006). Dance movement and spirit: Issues in the dance education curriculum. *Journal of Physical Education, Recreation and Dance, 77*(5), 3–12.

LaPointe-Crump, J. (2007). Competition and dance education. *Journal of Physical Education, Recreation and Dance, 78*(2), 4–5, 9.

Lum, C. H., & Gonda, D. E. (2014). Considerations of dance transmission processes: Adapting Bharata Natyam in a Singapore primary school. *Research in Dance Education, 15*(2), 107–119. doi:10.1080/14647893.2014.890583.

Masunah, J. (2001). Traditional dance in formal school education. In S. Burridge (Ed.), *Asia pacific dance bridge, Singapore papers* (pp. 102–114). Singapore: World Dance Alliance.

Matthews, N. (2004). The physicality of Mäori message transmission – Ko te tinana, he waka tuku Korero. *Junctures. Journal of Thematic Dialogue, 3*, 9–18.

McCarthy-Brown, N. (2009). The need for culturally relevant dance education. *Journal of Dance Education, 9*(4), 120–125. doi:10.1080/14647893.2014.890583.

McLean, M. (1999). *Weavers of song: Polynesian music and dance.* Auckland: University of Auckland Press.

New Zealand Ministry of Education. (2000). *The arts in the New Zealand curriculum (12711).* Wellington: Learning Media.

New Zealand Ministry of Education. (2007). *The New Zealand curriculum (32646).* Wellington: Learning Media.

Preston, V. (1966). *A handbook for modern educational dance.* London: Macdonald and Evans.

Preston-Dunlop, V., & Espana, L. (2005). *The American invasion 1962–1972.* London: Laban Centre.

Sämoan Ministry of Education, Sports and Culture. (2004). *Performing arts: Sämoa secondary school curriculum.* Auckland: Auckland Uni Services.

Sansom, A. (2011). *Movement and dance in young children's lives: Crossing the divide.* New York: Peter Lang.

Schechner, R. (1988). *Performance theory.* New York: Routledge.

Shapiro, S. B. (Ed.). (2008). *Dance in a world of change.* Champaign: Human Kinetics.

Shennan, J. (1984). *The Maori action song.* Wellington: New Zealand Council for Educational Research.

Siegel, M. B. (1998). Bridging the critical distance. In A. Carter (Ed.), *The Routledge dance studies reader* (pp. 91–97). London: Routledge.

Smith, T. L. (1999). *Decolonizing methodologies: Research and indigenous peoples.* London: Zed Books.

Smith-Autard, J. (2002). *The art of dance in education.* London: A & C Black.

Snook, B. H., & Buck, R. (2014). Policy and practice within arts education: Rhetoric and reality. *Research in Dance Education, 15*(3), 219–238.

Stinson, S. (1998). Seeking a feminist pedagogy for children's dance. In S. B. Shapiro (Ed.), *Dance, power and difference* (pp. 23–48). Champaign, IL: Human Kinetics.

Stinson, S. (2005). Why are we doing this? *Journal of Dance Education, 5*(3), 82–89.

Suwa, J. (2001). Ownership and authenticity of indigenous and modern music in Papua New Guinea. In H. Reeves (Ed.), *Traditionalism and modernity in the music and dance of Oceania: Essays in honour of Barbara B. Smith* (pp. 91–102). Sydney: University of Sydney.

Sykes, B. (2001). *The seven daughters of Eve: The science that reveals our genetic ancestry.* London: Bantam Press.

Tamasese, T. E. (2005). Clutter in indigenous knowledge, research and history: A Sāmoan perspective. *Social Policy Journal of New Zealand, 25*, 61–69.

Teaiawa, K. M. (2014). Culture moves? The festival of pacific arts and dance remix in Oceania. *Dance Research Aotearoa, 2*, 2–19. http://www.dra.ac.nz/index.php/DRA/article/view/27.

Vertovec, S. (2007). Super-diversity and its implications. *Ethic & Racial Studies, 30*(6), 1024–1054.

Vygotsky, L. (1962). *Thought and language.* Cambridge, MA: MIT Press.

Whincup, T., & Whincup, J. (2001). *Akekeia! Traditional dance in Kiribati.* Wellington: Massey University Press.

Wu, W.-C. (2013). Cultivation from within: An exploration of the attainment of creativity. *Taiwan Dance Research Journal, 8*, 166–225.

Linda Ashley   (PhD University of Auckland; MA University of London; B.Ed. (Hons), University of Liverpool) is an independent dance researcher/educator with extensive academic, choreographic and performing experience, retired as Senior Dance Lecturer and Research Leader at AUT University, Auckland, New Zealand in 2011. She is an Honorary Research Fellow at the National Institute of Creative Arts Industries, University of Auckland, 2015. As well as numerous journal articles, publications include: *Dancing with Difference: Culturally Diverse Dances in Education* (Sense Publishers, 2012), *Essential Guide to Dance* (3rd ed., Hodder & Stoughton, 2008); *Dance Theory & Practice for Teachers: Physical and Performing skills*, (Essential Resources, 2005). Linda is a member of Dance Aotearoa New Zealand (DANZ); Independent Dance Writers and Researchers Aotearoa; and Tertiary Dance Educators Network New Zealand Aotearoa.

Part III
Sharing and Constructing Identities, Meanings and Values

A third theme emerging from the authors' contributions is that of how cultural identities, meanings and values are shared and constructed in projects that have set out to encourage participation and awareness of culturally diverse arts experiences. This section examines some innovative pedagogical responses to intersecting cultures in music and dance in Oceania. Author narratives, descriptions and theories provide readers with a sense of how, in each chapter, music and dance knowledge is constructed, affirmed and valued in a postcolonial environment.

In *Songs Stories Tell and Intersecting Cultures*, Harold Anderson describes a creative, ethnographic approach he developed in the process of his research through and with his intersection with Māori in Aotearoa/New Zealand. Bringing together "the songs and the stories", he assembles elements of sound, music, image, place and participants' stories to find and share new forms of cultural expression. More generally his work shows how cultural meanings are constructed and created in conversations and intersections and his work serves as a tool to show how performance and composition can be developed in that role.

In *Being Heard: A Māori Community Narrative* composer and popular music educator Stephen Ralph Matthews outlines the process of cultural and creative negotiation he undertook in composing a bicultural music work in English and Te Reo Māori for spoken word and orchestra. The work sought to address and express the injustice of colonialisation where sacred land was taken from the local Māori community at Parihaka in the nineteenth century.

Working in tertiary education, Olivia Taouma's personal story describes how she developed a pedagogy in which her Polynesian identity was incorporated. Taouma's upbringing mirrors that of her students, as Pacific Islanders in a Western country and she taps into it as a basis for her teaching. In *Cross-Cultural Education in Dance and Song in Aotearoa and Sāmoa*, Taouma describes how she went about building a culture of learning and teaching that included Pacific values such as the importance of family, co-operation, loyalty, generosity, sharing and humility.

Trevor Thwaites discusses his theory of musicultural identity in the next chapter drawing from his experience of musical cultures of Māori, Pacific and European cultures in New Zealand schools. In *Musicultural Identity and Intersecting Geographic Contexts in Oceania* he explores the geographic spaces of music through the idea of 'musiculture' where the potential lies for diverse subcultural and intersecting perspectives to emerge from the broad palettes of music education.

In *Tama Wātea: Integrating Māori Perspectives into Dance Education: A Tertiary Example*, Ojeya Cruz-Banks considers a dance pedagogy project carried out at the University of Otago, New Zealand, with three male physical education students, a Māori dance artist, local Māori elders and their community. The project explores issues of masculinity and dance from a Māori framework through personal reflections and students' perspectives.

In the final chapter *The Ocean Swim: Rethinking Community in an Early Childhood Education Performing Arts Research Initiative* David Lines describes the creative methodology and underpinnings employed in an early childhood performing arts project where community artists worked with young children and teachers in three early childhood centres in Auckland, Aotearoa/New Zealand. The project called MAPS (Move, Act, Play, Sing) sought to develop a concept of teaching and learning in music, dance and drama that was sensitive and responsive to the intersecting cultures within each centre community. The work led to some interesting expressions of community music and dance that was enhanced by particular 'open' styles of pedagogy and artist-children-teacher-parent interaction.

Songs Stories Tell and Intersecting Cultures

Harold Anderson

Abstract This chapter synthesizes a personal narrative and an analysis of a project begun in early 2013. Although "Songs Stories Tell: Music at the Intersection of Life and Ethnography" as a music composition project began to take form during my 3-month term as the University of Otago Wallace Resident at the Pah Homestead in Auckland, the project has roots in research I did for my 2008 Ph.D. Dissertation, "A Confluence of Streams: Music and Identity in Aotearoa/New Zealand." For my dissertation I used socio-historic and ethnographic methods to build a picture of diverse elements of New Zealand culture as witnessed in the musical life of the nation. For the *Songs Stories Tell* project, I build on the ethnographic materials I collected and the methods I originally used in my dissertation to continue to gather and assemble elements of sound, music, image and place and associated stories of participants, but now as source material for music composition and performance. These materials were sourced in (and of) New Zealand among various people including Māori and Pacific Island peoples as well as people of European descent, who may be said to be, or to have become "indigenous" in the sense that they "belong" to the place. More to the point, these folk are instrumental in making our place and its future. Indeed it is my thesis that the sharing and exchange of music and cultural meanings is constructive of new, local meanings and it is my purpose with this project to participate in the process. Through sharing of sounds, stories and music, all of the participants in this project are engaged in a musical conversation that is mutually and reflexively constructive of our identities as New Zealanders.

Keywords Auto-ethnography • Music and narrative indigeneity • Ethnomusicological community • Symbolic interaction • Syncretic music • Music and identity

H. Anderson (✉)
45-J Ridge Rd, Greenbelt, MD 20770, USA
e-mail: 3339ha@gmail.com

© Springer International Publishing Switzerland 2016   205
L. Ashley, D. Lines (eds.), *Intersecting Cultures in Music and Dance Education*, Landscapes: the Arts, Aesthetics, and Education 19,
DOI 10.1007/978-3-319-28989-2_12

1   Prelude—Sensations of "Home"

When I think of the feeling of "home," three moments come to mind. The first is the sense of loss I felt when I revisited the site of my childhood home in Cleveland Ohio in the 1980s after decades away and found that you couldn't even tell that my house, the site of so many dear memories, had ever been there. The second was when I first came to the shore of the Chesapeake Bay at a place called Carr's Beach, just south of Annapolis Maryland, and I looked out on the water and surrounding greenery and felt as if I could imagine the place centuries removed and that I had somehow returned to some special destiny. That beach has long since been redeveloped as condominiums and no longer has public access. The third is the only one that is still repeatable, is touching down at Auckland airport in the wee hours when the international flights from the USA arrive. And as you step out into the pre-dawn, the air is thick and humid and has the smell of the Manukau Harbour and the soft breeze of the Pacific night, and it breathes you in as you breathe it, and you are home.

2   Intersecting Cultures

My life in New Zealand is at an intersection of cultures. When I migrated to New Zealand in 1984 as a self-identified African American musician looking to retain my sense of self even as I sought to find a niche in a new country, I came to realize that my musical identity was based on a set of signposts which referenced a particular cultural, geographic and historical landscape, and that, in order to find and establish an identity consistent with my past in a new place, my musical identity would have to be translated, transformed and re-negotiated locally, through the construction of common landmarks and new points of reference—at my point of intersection with New Zealand and its culture(s).

I had expected that notions of what would be considered "pop" music and sentimental song would be necessarily subject to local tastes and circumstances, but what I didn't expect was that local understanding of (presumably "universal") genres like "jazz" and blues would be so much at variance with my sense of these musics, not only as indigenous vernacular or cultural expressions but also (and even) as regards musical vocabularies and terminology, canons and repertoires, skill sets and notions of basic esthetics.

In order to establish and orient myself as musician, I had to learn a new set of meanings so that I could begin to "translate" between cultural and idiomatic landscapes and expressions in order to establish continuity with my origins and my past and also to make a way forward.

After more than 30 years of study, playing and teaching music and learning local and national vernacular expressions in New Zealand. I am now looking to construct new meanings. Through sharing these experiences and providing some actual accounts of the process I want to demonstrate a method for how intercultural understandings may be reached and new meanings grown.

3 Songs Stories Tell

After years of listening and observing how people responded to music and participated in music making, I began to ask people to share songs that were particularly meaningful to them with the understanding that I would respond in kind with my take on their song, in an effort to make it my song, too. My initial responses would be meaningful to me—I am invested in the work, and I work hard in the hope that I might do justice to what they have shared. But I'm not always sure that my response will work for the donor—that it will add to the original meaning—but I am committed to working with them, in dialogue, until we have come to a shared understanding.

At its philosophic and conceptual core, this project, "Songs Stories Tell," is about receiving and making meanings. And "meaning," in this musical context, is about value, worth, investment and caring. Musical meanings can run a gamut from sentimentality and nostalgia to hierarchical, professional, or hegemonic. It seems that a good place to start in order to parse musical meaning is to ask "Why do you care?" Indeed the idea of "caring" implies notions of value and investment. These meanings have a connotative dimension that often relies on how people are culturally embedded.

Musical meanings may also be found in more denotative, quasi-linguistic syntactical and morphological structures where abstract forms and genre-specific conventions are primary features—landmarks—on the cultural landscape. As an expressive medium, music is unique in the opportunities it affords for blurring lines, for reflexively intertwining, juxtaposing and conflating connotative and denotative meanings.

For me, *Songs Stories Tell* is about my relationships: with people and the places and spaces that we occupy together and separately. These places are both literal and metaphoric: they are places "in the heart and mind" as well as professional and social spaces and hierarchies. And, in my interactions with my sources and with the musicians who play the music (and in the process become new sources), I begin to locate and orient myself to an emergent historical and situational landscape.

For the purposes of this chapter, I will limit my discussion to a few examples that serve to outline the shape and some of the content of my method.

[insert graphic—Songs Stories Tell steps/process
Basic process
Step-wise, the Songs Stories Tell method follows a basic process:
[Inward process]

- Personal cultural geography: personal introspection in a cultural frame

[Outward processes]

- Solicit/collect/assemble source materials based on observation, personal introspection and interaction with others
- Parse into meaningful (environmental, linguistic, cultural, and musical) "phonemic" elements
- Map meaningful elements onto an (potentially) appropriate compositional framework
- Solicit participant musicians to evaluate and perform the initial "seed" composition
- Encourage musical feedback/conversation in the form of improvised comment on seed themes and material
- Report back to original sources for comment
- Collect musical responses and extract material for further composition
- [Repeat with added meanings/value]

4 Introspection and "Inward" Process

The beginning of the journey is about getting one's bearings: coming to an accommodation if not an understanding of my inner state as it relates to my interface with the external world. This involves identifying my "normal" or preferred milieu or genre and understanding its functionality for me in terms of personal value, worth and meanings.

5 Ancestral Memory, Gospel and the Blues

Musical forms, genres and sub-genres trace an historical and genealogical arc, a musical career that springs from the distant past and proceeds to the present. Thus the career of the "Sorrow Songs" began as murky African retentions—fluttering dreams of lost languages and culture as embodied musical utterance—that Frederick Douglass described in *The Singing of Slaves, an Explanation*, flowing through like a river to their transformation and presentation as European art song by the Fisk Jubilee singers, and on to their re-emergence as rural, and then urban blues, largely through the creative impulse and religious redemption of Thomas A. "Georgia Tom" Dorsey, and re-imagining as jazz. The career of this music, these musics, spans centuries and was accompanied all the while by a concomitant merging of European language, technology and musical technique with ancient ancestral retentions of African ways being, speaking and singing.

6 Parsing the Personal and the Cultural—Exploring Genre and Ways of Making Value

So genres have a cultural history—of origins and embeddedness—and a "career" that flows from dynamic changes in the functionality of genres in relation to communities and the resulting changes through time in their meaning for originating cultures as well as overlapping communities that share and borrow and render them into a shared symbol set.

Genres are modes of expression—structures that evolve as particular ways of making and performing music and art that may be said to be unilinear or narrowly targeted in that they are generally associated with particular groups of individuals or specific segments of humanity and their ways of being and making value. As such genres are often emblematic of some kind of group identity and have evolved in order to meet people's needs—physical and spiritual.

For example, Black Music forms in the New World may be said to have originally been dictated by slavery and bondage and the condition of a people in its aftermath: songs that have been told have been shaped by need and have functioned to fill a void of agency, and a structural deficit of human dignity and lack of recognition of cultural and personal human value,—"I've been buked and I've been scorned..." And the career of the music may be said to have evolved from those origins and shaped by that initial structural condition and subsequent changes.

Individuals may be born into or choose or gravitate towards a particular genre as a vehicle for personal expression and self-fulfilment. Individuals are not constrained to any single genre, but rather tend to choose a range of expressive genre in order to suit a variety of moods, purposes and situations. This is a variety of "code switching" whereby a person develops a stylistic repertoire that is a reflection of their multiple identities—an admixture of who they are and who they become as they deploy different modes of expression in changing social circumstances. And those genres are performed as means to make or preserve meaning in away that is consistent with core identities or objectives in changing cultural contexts.

The choice of specific genre is driven by an individual's orientation and how they are embedded within a cultural milieu at any given moment. What they do with the genre is a function of how they are able to make value with it, either working within its confines, or by innovating, deconstructing, or building upon its elements using the genre itself—its grammars and conventions—as a starting point. "Value" in this context can take different forms—audience makeup and appreciation, fandom, financial reward, peer acceptance, self-satisfaction or gratification (either internal or externally generated), etc. Indeed the choice of the genre is largely driven by individual needs or desires and disposition relative to who they are and where they find themselves.

7 "Jazz" as Vernacular, Fine Art and Dialogic Medium

For me, the improvisational art form with deep African American roots that some people call "jazz" is my genre of choice, my native tongue.

As a young person (and as an aspiring musician) I was exposed to a variety of musical genres and "cultural" musics. I was weaned on expressive forms like spirituals (the "Sorrow Songs"), gospel, soul, pop, and rhythm and blues (and later, rock), interspersed with Western "fine art" traditions, choral and symphonic. All of these forms became part of my personal "toolbox"—the vocabulary for my self expression. But for me the ultimate expression, the pinnacle of accomplishment and my aspirations was Jazz music, which seemed to embrace all of the possibilities of the other genres.

I became aware very early that the primary virtue of Jazz was honesty of self-expression coupled with the courage and technical ability to make one's self manifest in sound. Translated to a cultural value, this meant prioritizing self-worth, strength, independence and courage of one's convictions in word and deed—qualities entirely commensurate with and reinforced by my family values. For me the music was an expression of cultural confidence and the sure knowledge that we stand on the shoulders of giants and that great art was our heritage. Most importantly, the music was about agency—freedom—a way to assert oneself in the world, to rise and fly high on an updraft of one's own making through self-possessed innovation.

But these essential musical attributes are also inclusive by definition, and although I was firmly rooted in the African American musical and intellectual traditions, my heroes were diverse, from Sarah Vaughan, John Coltrane, Thelonious Monk, Duke Ellington and Count Basie, to Benny Goodman, Paul Desmond, Bill Evans and Stan Getz. The point here is that, as a music, jazz has traditionally welcomed all comers as long as they brought a willingness to invest their true selves with them.

More importantly for this project is that jazz is at its core a dialogic medium—it is based on patterns of call and response whereby musicians "speak" and respond to one another and build new meanings, in the form of improvisations on a shared theme. It is important to note that this process goes beyond the notion of antiphony as it is sometimes presented in standard music theory—it is not a simple alternation between groups, but rather involves a true conversation in the sense that new meanings are made based on interactive listening and responding. These new meanings are dialectical in the sense that, while they reflect initial inputs, original meanings may change and grow in subsequent iterations. To the extent that the music is representative of the "true selves" of the participants, this means that individuals come to the musical meeting place with a willingness to be changed as the result of musical interaction.

So, after initially "receiving" a shared musical moment, I set an idea (that has now become my comment on the original) as a composition in an improvisational frame. This enables me to not only share the idea (or at least my interpretation of it) more widely, but also to seed feedback from the musicians that take up the theme, that further comments on the seed material.

8   Looking Outward—Listening, Hearing, Observing

The journey begins with introspection and then continues with a taking stock of "external circumstances"—other people and the environment. The beginning of this outward process has been the assembly of a repertoire that can serve as a lexicon and as a "map" or outline that sets out some significant cultural "landmarks" that set a stage for establishing and navigating my own social and cultural geography relative to the new place. The next step is an analytic process: an attempt to understand and relate to sounds, stories, songs and musical material, as a kind of "loving deconstruction" of source material. Subsequently the composition process continues as a reflexive dialogic process of mutual construction of new meanings.

Taking linguistic anthropology and descriptive linguistics as a starting point for deciphering relationships between people and the places and spaces that we occupy, a person cast ashore in a place where people speak an unknown language, bombarded by an incomprehensible chaotic jumble of sound, would seek first to discern which sounds were meaningful, to separate the signal from the noise. The first step would be to separate out meaningful sounds, words and phrases. Now able to discern the borders of meaningful utterances, they would seek to understand the deeper meanings.

As an outsider, unfamiliar with the lived history of a place, discrete and potentially meaningful units of sound are initially only an undifferentiated blur. And the first order of business is to discern a difference between background noise and global chatter—the enervating sameness produced by an outpouring of indiscriminate noise, primarily from commercialized film, television and radio—and sounds, music and speech, that actually have local context and meaning.

9   Repertoires—Soundworlds and Relationships

My grasp of New Zealand musical culture begins with discovering and getting a feel for what I call "community repertoires," sets of songs that might stand in as a representation, perhaps a rationalization, of an otherwise chaotic soundworld. I see these repertoires not as passively given or received, but rather populated by songs and utterances that people actively embrace and choose to sing. These songs, this music is to be distinguished from globalized media clutter consisting of pre-packaged music and played only in the background, but rather is music that has come to have special local significance. (Oddly enough the process is greatly simplified by learning to listen and to correlate embodied sounds to a living source—by watching people's lips move.)

I began with some musical material in mind—pieces of music and melodic, timbral and rhythmic elements and motives that I had encountered in the environment and that resonated for me as having a specifically New Zealand or Pacific character—pieces like Englebert Humperdinck's "Ten Guitars," a song that had immense popularity in the Pacific but was known elsewhere only as the B side of the more popular "Please Release Me," and "Ma Wai Ra," a traditional Māori "tangi" (literally "to cry out") or funeral song.

Widely known (and performed), songs like these have an environmental quality to them—they form a background in the sense that they become so much a part of the cultural landscape that they are almost taken for granted. And while the act of gathering them is in some ways more passive than directly soliciting a response from an individual, there is a compositional challenge in the analysis, to try to extract and refine a sense of what it was about the music that carries meaning and to distill and reuse that essence. Looking ahead to the composition process, the idea is to actively assemble a repertoire that frames a perspective on the culture and who I might be in relation to it. Indeed my goal is not just to passively understand the local musical "language," but to actively produce it—to compose and perform it in a meaningful way so as to extend it and to merge my fortunes with it. The goal is to master the musical language(s) of the place in a way that would enable me to express myself and my origins—where I have been and what I bring with me—and also to go beyond to make music that is relevant to myself and others in a new set of circumstances. In other words, to make music that is expressive of my cultural intersections. Ultimately the songs I choose as source material form a kernel for my version of a New Zealand "community repertoire."

10   "Ten Guitars"

In the early 1990s when, as I was conducting a workshops on music composition and improvisation, I suggested to the assemblage that a strong starting point for composition and learning the art of improvisation was to confront an "ear worm" or other melodic figure that had an insistent or persistent (possibly irritating) quality and then to reconstruct it as something more satisfying.

One member of the group said, "You mean like Ten Guitars?" I had no idea what he was talking about and several years went by before I began to understand the significance of the song. The B side of Englebert Humperdinck's "Please Release Me," "Ten Guitars" was a massive hit in New Zealand and other areas of the Pacific beginning in the late 1960s, but hardly anywhere else. According to Dalvanius Prime, "It was just schlock that was adopted by an entire generation of kiwis..."[1]

The song was received through media but was taken up—sung at parties and get togethers and repeated and reproduced in so many live circumstances that, more

---

[1] Cawthorn, Geoffrey. "Ten Guitars." 47 min. New Zealand: Messenger Films Ltd., 1996. Accessed online 14/11/2014, http://geoffreycawthorn.com/ten-guitars/

than 20 years after its introduction, it had been indelibly written into the fabric of the culture. The song stumped me in a way because it didn't easily lend itself to deconstruction to be recast into a more "satisfying" composition, the terms of the exercise. This was a seminal moment for me, because it was the beginning of my understanding that musical satisfaction was not only a matter of rhythm, harmony and melody, but also something deeper.

Dalvanius's characterisation of "Ten Guitars" as "schlock" was pretty much spot on—it is, in fact, a simple song, and it certainly qualifies as an ear worm. But even in its simplicity it has deep hooks into cultural ways of being, and taken as an exercise in meaningful dialogic composition it is non-trivial.

Some of the cultural elements of the song that elevate it to anthematic status and that would entail a loving and non-destructive deconstruction and musical remapping include: a lyric with a simple story line but with strong textual referents to social groups and functions (e.g., men playing guitars, camaraderie, etc.); self-effacing humor; an infectious melody, easily sung and with a simple 3 chord harmony; a harmonic rhythm viscerally reminiscent of and complementary to familiar motions and activities (i.e., worksongs for shearing sheep or repetitive motions in abattoirs and freezing works, etc.). And the song has what might be deemed a recursive quality—the lyrics refer to a loose band of fellows in a social situation, entertaining each other. And that is exactly how the song was performed at many a party where alcohol and conversation flowed, and people had a wonderful time!

Ultimately to honor this song (and people's affective engagement with it) would require a serious effort to retain the songs playful affect, relaxed (and non-judgmental) delivery, and general frivolity. This is a theme well worthy of Olivier Messiaen's exhortation to embrace "the charm of impossibility!"

One way to render a deconstructed "jazz" version of this piece (especially given my origins and musical language and conservative of some of these "cultural" characteristics) would be to score it as a playful cross between calypso (a la Sonny Rollins's "St. Thomas") and Ornette Coleman's "Blues Connotation." The question of whether these characteristics might have something to do with an "island" character presents itself...

11 "Ma Wai Ra"

In 2006 I attended the annual birthday celebration for T.W. Ratana at Ratana Pa in North Island New Zealand. During the series of powhiri where dignitaries from the government, political parties, and tribal groups were welcomed onto the marae, I heard the song, "Ma Wai Ra" performed in support of a speaker. It is a common practice among Māori, and by extension all New Zealanders, to sing as a response to or in support of individual speakers at formal social gatherings, particularly those that involve meetings between different tribal groups, public sector officials, and/or cultural/ethnic groups.

"Ma Wai Ra" is a particularly appropriate song and is frequently sung at such gatherings. The title of the song might be translated as "Who will take responsibility for the future?" The song is a tangi, a funeral song, that was traditionally sung on the occasion of the passing of a person who was a vital presence in a community whose loss would be deeply felt. And the implication of singing the song at a gathering of diverse groups is that everyone present has a stake in the future of the community. It is also an acknowledgment of the appropriateness, the desirability of adopting a Māori kaupapa (method and rational of action) for matters related to belonging to the land, the construction of what I call "narrative indigeneity."

The song has a somber tone and rhythm and employs a very simple motive of consecutive falling thirds followed by a funereal pedaling on the tonic. It has a small range and is very easy to sing in a group. And while singers may embellish the melody, it retains its power even in its simplest form. It is a classic example of how people can come together around a simple theme to make common purpose.

From a compositional perspective "Ten Guitars" and "Ma Wai Ra" may be taken as the seed of a "community repertoire," and the motivic content of the two songs is easily cast in a complementary fashion ("Ten Guitars" may be rendered as consecutive rising thirds). More importantly, the juxtaposition of local cultural content—situated and highly specific variety humor vs. gravity and community concern for a cherished place—is a seed for epic composition.

12 Environmental, Personal and Cultural Interaction and Intersections as Musical Meeting Places

Ultimately music may function as a kind of meeting place, where songs are a manifestation of individual's stories told (or sung) round a metaphorical campfire and rendered as duets, trios and ensembles. And composition is the rendering of the notes of the meeting as a musical conversation that takes place at the intersection of various life experiences and ways of being, hearing and understanding.

My approach initially entails musically parsing my own "story"—what is meaningful to me and how I am generally situated in the world and specifically in the moment—at the beginning of a dialogic process. The initial compositions are a set of tentative musical sketches, usually in a single voice, that are an expression of what I "hear" and what I believe I understand—in other words, how I imagine myself relative to other people, beginning with my primary "sources," and moving on to other musicians and ultimately to audiences. Based on the initial sketches, subsequent choices of genre and instrumentation begin to locate the stories relative to larger social and cultural contexts but always with reference back to the primaries.

So I begin to sing my version of their stories and I use the composition process as a way to interrogate my relationships—to the landscape and other people as well as social and cultural institutions—by re-presenting and performing analogous, overlapping or contrasting meanings and ways of being, and sending them back for comment. In this way music making and composition becomes the construction of a repertoire of a set of received, discovered and exposed meanings rendered as musical expression and interaction.

13 Musically Mapping Atmosphere, Affect and Environment

Sometimes we occupy overlapping spaces, and perhaps share a feeling or a disposition in relation to a place, a space or a moment in time. Music has tools for expressing or even reliving those feelings or those moments.

"Touching down at Auckland airport in the wee hours when the international flights from the USA arrive, as I step out into the pre-dawn, the air is thick and humid and has the smell of the Manukau Harbour and the soft breeze of the Pacific night, and it breathes me in as I breathe it—home."

This feeling, this image literally resonated for me as I began this project. All of the elements of the dream, this recollection of a place and the grounded feeling I have in relation to it, had a palpable musical component in my imagination. The deep, dark Pacific sky, long before sunset had a timbre like the chalumeau register of a bass clarinet, the poignant sweetness of the soft air summed in the interval of a major sixth, and clean soft breeze, a major second. All wrapped in a meditative mood and a cantabile-like smoothness.

I met Taupule Tania Wilson, a New Zealand born Samoan, in the early 1990s when I first moved to Auckland from Dunedin on the South Island. I met her and many other people at that time who were eager to experience and learn about African American musical genres and I was happy to share. She was a member of Auckland's Heaven Bent Choir during my brief tenure as conductor of the group. I spent as much time trying to coax Pacific musical materials from the group as I did teaching traditional African American songs and repertoires.

For this project, Tania shared a song she learned from her mother, "Moe i le moega i le po." The song text describes all of the elements of my dream of soft Pacific air and darkness and deep affection, and its poignancy was reinforced by the nature of the gift and the fact that Tania's mum had passed less than year prior to her singing the song for me.

Tania's song and mine came together on an elemental level—all of the timbral, intervallic, affective and dispositional elements were met in the resulting composition and I was able to alternately foreground Tania's and my melodies so that one served as the accompaniment for the other and vice versa.

14 Morphology: Musical Genres, Grammars and Expressive Techniques in Microcosm

Music lends itself well to symbolic rendition of appositions, contradictions and juxtapositions (e.g., through line and counterpoint) that can be said to exist between our individual understandings, situations and dispositions (e.g., through tone, tempo, rhythm, instrumentation and timbre) in relation to our place in the world and how we live and how make our way in that place—how we dance and how we sing, and who we dance and sing with and for, what (and who) we love and what we shun, what we embrace and what embraces us, and where our emphasis is.

Similarly social structures and hierarchies may be mirrored in the makeup and structure of performance groups, and the range of expressive and esthetic possibilities and hierarchies are manifest in repertoires that resemble bibliographies.

So music has a "linguistic" dimension—it functions as a way of symbolically making and transmitting meanings. But all of this begs the question of how might conventional language and the spoken word contribute to the idea of music as an interactive meeting place?

15 Parsing Musical, Linguistic and Phonemic Elements

I am conscious of the significance of language, not only as regards its rhetorical and lexical dimensions—how people use word choices and grammatical constructions and shapes to convey meanings, perhaps in order to persuade or convince—but also the musical dimensions of language itself, particularly language as it is spoken or sung, with particular attention to the use of tonal inflections and rhythms to impart meanings and emphasis, and to performances of individual and group identities as ways to make or assert value in the world.

These aural elements have what might be termed phonemical attributes—they are sounds that embody and carry immediate and personal meanings—they are the "smallest meaningful units of sound." But these "musical phonemes" also have contextual and cultural referents and meanings that flow from how, where, when and by whom they are assembled and performed, and from the "rules" that govern how musical sound is received and judged by different groups and under different circumstances. These morphological, syntactical and grammatical considerations are deeply implicated according to genre and audience, but also, and perhaps just as importantly, according to the orientation of the musicians who perform the music.

16 Spoken Word Becomes Lyric

In the Western imagination, the "literal" dimension of words, at least in "normal," prosodic English usage, tends to be hard edged and specific—indeed this is the "virtue" of the Western word, it is prized for its denotative precision. Yet in human interactions, spoken words rely heavily on a connotative dimension to achieve their end—they derive meaning from context or association as well as from tone, inflection and delivery—"it's not what you say, but how you say it." In this sense music bears a strong, and potentially synergistic, relationship to the spoken word but with an emphasis on virtues like quality and nuance.

Pacific languages in general, and especially, te reo Māori, Māori language—its rhythms and tones and accompanying gestures, its ways of making meaning, its performance conventions and ways of making value—is a central feature of the soundworld of Aotearoa as a place where peoples dwell. As such it is potentially a platform, a stage for a meeting place for intersecting cultures where we might construct new, mutual meanings.

17 No te hohonutanga

On a late summer day in the graveyard of St. Agnes Catholic church in Kaihu where many of his ancestors are buried, Bernard Makoare chanted Psalm 129–130, De Profundis, the "Psalm of the Dead," No te hohonutanga in Māori, as his contribution to Songs Stories Tell. The psalm is part of a Māori Catholic liturgical experience that is a central feature of Bernard's history and way of being in his ancestral homeplace in northern New Zealand. For Bernard, who chanted the psalm for me in the presence of his ancestors, this chant is about family history and relationships between the place, Catholicism and Māoritanga.

Using Bernard's chant as a starting point for composition entails understanding some separate and mutual "investments," his and my own, in the source material, and exploring the possibilities for rendering those meanings into music. The process is about musically exploring commonalities while respecting allowing for differences and gaps in understanding and making spaces for conversations to address those gaps and lapses in communication.

Catholicism itself is an important point of tangency for Bernard and I—we share an overlapping set of symbols based on and derived from growing up in the Catholic faith. I was raised Catholic and I attended a Catholic elementary school and was an altar boy as a young child.

Culturally my family was "split" on Catholicism—my father, had Protestant roots and a skeptical disposition, whereas my mother and especially her mother, my grandmother, were deeply devout people with a mystical bent. (These attributes seem gender related in retrospect—my sister and I are dispositionally split along similar lines).

Even as a child I was something of a skeptic and stood apart from total acceptance of religious experience, I felt almost like a kind of a commentator or neutral
observer (I distinctly remember questioning aspects of the dogma as early as age
seven), but I still gloried in the rituals and the sounds even as I danced around the
dogma. And I was respectful of the serious nature of the subject matter—morality,
good and evil, death and resurrection, human suffering and the desire to do good—
and I was ever mindful that people's feelings and beliefs were important.

Although I have not been an active participant in Catholic ritual for many years,
my childhood experience forms an important part of my social and musical development. I loved singing the responses to the Latin mass and some characteristics
of those chants—the monody, the solemnity of the tone, the measured pacing of
the delivery, the small compass cadences, etc.—stand out for me and form a part
of my musical and emotional vocabulary. I have internalized much of the music
and ritual.

I maintain a distance to the ideology, borne of time and personal and intellectual
disposition, as well as family history, even as I cherish the experience of the music
and its symbolic, linguistic and sonic efficacy. Bernard on the other hand is devout—
as we sat in the graveyard, he pointed out the headstones of multiple generations of
his family, all buried in that sacred place—and his Catholic faith has deep roots in
his family and cultural history.

18 The "Puzzle"

So the question is how to musically represent these different perspectives and dispositions in an appropriate manner—how might the differences be reconciled and
what might the characteristics of the finished piece be?

Parsing this story as a set of general musical elements: the basic mood of the
piece would be sombre or serious, but it should allow room for a contrasting perspective, a contrapuntal element that "dances" around a serious subject matter.

Several elements of the composition may be more or less directly derived from
Bernard's solo performance. And his chanting displayed many characteristics that
match my remembered experience of Catholic liturgical style: monody, solemnity
of the tone, measured pacing of the delivery, and the small compass cadences.

With regard to genre, Bernard's description of how the psalm is performed with
a congregation—a song leader reinforced by the congregation joining in at will—
has implications for the makeup of the ensemble and the style and manner of the
performance. People chant the words together in imperfect unison—they might not
breathe together and the enunciation of the words is not perfectly synchronized.
And, just as in a jazz ensemble, the commonality of the destination and the understanding and acceptance of a common goal is what binds the group and fuels the

action of the performance. Structurally (and for content) the words and their import are paramount—They should set the tone of the piece, and the rhythmic quality of the words and phrases are key to mapping the motivic structure of the piece.

19 Initially (Keeping in Mind That There Will Be Multiple Draft "Solutions" to the Problem)

I scored the piece for a jazz orchestra with brass and winds "chanting" the psalm in a heterophonic rendition of the monodic line—the heterophony is accentuated by "spontaneous" harmonies and call and response refrains, and is punctuated by improvisations on the basic lines. I used the Māori language text of the chant as the main structural element to give form to the phrasing of the melody and to the periodicity of recurring phrases. I rendered the confidence and steadfastness of faith—as a recurring 3/2 rhythmic figure overlaid with a trenchant 4 (dotted quarter notes) against three feeling in the bass and alternated with sections in 6/4. The 6/4 sections are characterized by an angular bass line cross rhythmically set off against a steady eighth note pattern in the upper voices that is limned out by the (for the most part) Māori language text. The angularity of the bass line represents my character's dance around and through the weighty material, but also in support of the serious import of the psalm.

20 Dialogues

So far we have provided examples and discussed the inward/introspective processes of mapping one's personal "cultural geography" as a method of discovery and personal introspection within a cultural frame. Next we tackled "outward processes" that involved solicitng or collecting and assembling source materials based on observation and interaction with others; parse these materials into meaningful (environmental, linguistic, cultural, and musical) "phonemic" elements; and mapping meaningful elements onto an (potentially) appropriate (i.e., morphemic) compositional framework.

In the dialogic phase of the method, we begin to test the validity of our observations and analysis by first soliciting participant musicians to evaluate and perform the initial "seed" composition and then encouraging them to provide musical and critical feedback in the form of conversation and improvised comment on seed themes and material and finally by reporting back to original sources for comment. Ideally we would like to have our sources see themselves in what we have made with their input—does the music I have written invite the originators to join in? Is my rendition of a chant in Māori singable? Does it make sense and does it resonate for listeners? How might I adjust the composition to enable and encourage ongoing participation for people as performers or audiences? We would also want the musicians who play the music to invest their talents and skills to deeply engage with the material, so we ask them, "does this music work for you—do you want to play it?" And, "how can this be written to bring you closer to the material?" These are all questions to be asked and meditated upon.

To complete an iteration of the process, we would gather our various musical and critical responses and extract material for another round of the process and further composition. The goal is to bring the participants—originators, musicians, audience— together in a cultural frame to make common or shared/overlapping purpose. And the process begins again with introspection in a cultural frame.

21 Conclusion

I have always been captivated by Mozart comic operas like the Magic Flute because they achieve the seemingly impossible task of making multiple melodies and narratives simultaneously comprehensible—they encompass worlds of sound and melody and multiple perspectives on stories all in an instant. Indeed one of the most magical things about music is its capacity to render multiple voices on the same field, at the same time in a manner that allows all of them to be heard and understood. And in the context of a pluralistic society, music can provide a model for hearing and honoring diverse voices.

An explicit focus on what people care about and how that might translate into music is at the heart of the approach I have modeled here. From a pedagogical perspective, relating music to stories of cultural embeddedness and caring mated with processes of personal discovery and self expression, invites student engagement. And explicit focus on what people care about reflexively cultivates respect and empathy. The *Songs Stories Tell* approach draws students into all the possibilities of multiple worlds of music and ways of being. It not only allows them to "like what they like," but also encourages them to delve into the why and the how of their own musical expression as a starting point to go further to explore how their personal "meanings" might play out in other performance traditions. It frames acquisition of skill sets and technique as a means to this end and in so doing, it provided an engine for them to learn with purpose. And it encourages students to hear the world in multi-vocal perspective and to learn to express themselves, not just for themselves, but so that others might hear.

Through the Songs Stories Tell, I've learned to use music as a way to listen, really listen, to my own voice and to begin to hear the diverse voices of the peoples of a Pacific nation, and to begin to sing with and to them in turn.

Harold Anderson (PhD), is an ethnographer, folklorist, photographer, filmmaker and musician. He holds an MMus in Composition from Otago University (where he was the 1999 Mozart Fellow) and a PhD in Ethnomusicology from the University of Maryland. His dissertation: *A Confluence of Streams: Music and Identity in Aotearoa/New Zealand*, and subsequent work focuses on translating and transforming historical and cultural studies into a set of living narratives and musical performances. His compositions celebrate the diversity of New Zealand music communities and feature the intersections of musical expressive vernaculars that define New Zealand's musical identity.

Being Heard: A Māori Community Narrative

Stephen Ralph Matthews

Abstract This is the story of a yearlong journey with the people at Parihaka, a small rural Māori community near thewestern cape of Te Ika-a-Māui, the North Island of Aotearoa New Zealand. It is a depiction of their generous acts of reciprocity, their commitment to manaakitanga (hospitality) and their passionate advocacy of the tikanga (values, principles) of their forebears. It is a narration of our work together to create Witnessing Parihaka, a semistaged musical work. It is a portrayal of consultation, collectivism and collaboration between a community, a composer, a poet and the performers and musicians, both Māori and Pākehā. This led to tamariki (children) and pahake (learned elders) travelling from Parihaka to Tāmaki-makau-rau (Auckland)—New Zealand's largest city—to perform on stage with the Auckland Philharmonia Orchestra.

Keywords Parihaka • Indigenous community project • Māori community narrative • Passive resistance • Collaborative practices • Indigenous knowledge • Cross-cultural exchange

Tēnā e te iti, tēnā e te rahi.
Kia areare te taringa, kia areare te ngākau.
Ki tēnei kohinga mahara ōku mō te tū a Parihaka,
ki te hāpai o te poi, ki te puaki i ngā waiata,
ki te pupuri i ngā tikanga tuku iho i runga i ngā whakatupuranga.
Ahakoa he kohinga nāku, ehara i te mea nōku,
nō Parihaka kāinga, nō Parihaka tangata me ōna manu e rua.
Nau mai, titiro mai, pānui atu, whakarongo.

To all who give this their attention.
For the ear to be open, so too does the heart.
This is a collection of experiences and thoughts on Parihaka,
the performance of poi, the expression of song,
and the transference of principles and legacies across generations.

S.R. Matthews (✉)
School of Music, Faculty of Creative Arts and Industries, University of Auckland (Te Whare Wananga o Tāmaki Makaurau), Auckland, New Zealand
e-mail: tipene.ralph@gmail.com; http://stephenralphmatthews.com

© Springer International Publishing Switzerland 2016
L. Ashley, D. Lines (eds.), *Intersecting Cultures in Music and Dance Education*, Landscapes: the Arts, Aesthetics, and Education 19,
DOI 10.1007/978-3-319-28989-2_13

Although I have written these considerations, they do not belong to me,
they belong to the village of Parihaka, to the people of Parihaka,
to their leaders from the past.
Welcome, look, read and listen.

+ + + + + + + + + +

This is the story of a year-long journey with the people at Parihaka, a small rural Māori community near the western cape of Te Ika-a-Māui, the North Island of Aotearoa New Zealand. It is a depiction of their generous acts of reciprocity, their commitment to manaakitanga (hospitality) and their passionate advocacy of the tikanga (values, principles) of their forebears. It is a narration of our work together to create *Witnessing Parihaka*, a semi-staged musical work. It is a portrayal of consultation, collectivism and collaboration between a community, a composer, a poet and the performers and musicians, both Māori and Pākehā. This led to tamariki (children) and pahake (learned elders) travelling from Parihaka to Tāmaki-makau-rau[1]—Aotearoa's largest city—to perform with the Auckland Philharmonia Orchestra.

It is my hope that this account will highlight considerations for those intending to work on similar projects and contribute to a wider discussion on collaborative indigenous creative projects. Interspersed within the main text are 12 short chronological narratives beginning with descriptions of my return to Parihaka and ending with my final thoughts and reflections on this cathartic year-long journey.

1 *Witnessing Parihaka*

Witnessing Parihaka depicts the events surrounding the invasion of Parihaka in November 1881 by a heavily armed Government militia; this was despite the people of Parihaka's use of non-violent resistance to protest against the Government taking their ancestral land. The opening lines of the text—written by the poet Robert Sullivan—evoke two powerful and pervasive Taranaki and Parihaka symbols, the maunga (mountain) Taranaki,[2] and the raukura (feather, plume, treasure).[3]

First Feather
touching hair
E tu feather

---

[1] Tāmaki-makau-rau—Auckland City.

[2] Maunga Taranaki—a 2518-metre-high dormant stratovolcano visible across the whole Taranaki region.

[3] "Te Raukura represents spiritual, physical, and communal harmony and unity. It is an acknowledgement of a higher spiritual power, which transcends itself upon earth. It is a symbol of faith, hope, and compassion for all of mankind and the environment that we live in." Port Nicholson Block Settlement Trust (2015). *Feather*. Retrieved 2015, September 21 from http://www.pnbst.maori.nz/who-we-are/feather/

Tu tonu
  Stand on
    feather

Good Thought Mountains
Rongo is peace

  Maunga is a mountain

Maungaarongo
Mountain of peace
E tu Taranaki[4]

Four Parihaka girls—Rangiawhina, Jameco, Courtney and Tatijana—performed in *Witnessing Parihaka*. At the time they attended the local kura kaupapa (Māori language and cultural immersion school) called Te Kura Kaupapa Māori o Tamarongo and they lived on the papa kāinga (village) of Parihaka. Their kaiako (teacher), Whaea Ngapera Moeahu and Parihaka pahake (learned elders) from all three marae performed with them on stage. The central section of the piece is a series of short soliloquies, spoken by eyewitnesses to the invasion and sacking of Parihaka. These characters are minor protagonists who bear witness to the village's peaceful stand. They are a Pākehā field press reporter, two Parihaka children, a Parihaka villager, a Pākehā soldier and the militia's six pounder Armstrong Gun. Two professional actors, Te Kohe Tuhaka and Stuart Devenie, performed these spoken parts. Interwoven into the musical score is the Parihaka waiata poi *E rere rā*,[5] as well as other musical references to Parihaka's musical tradition,[6] including the traditional performance by Kui Whero Te Rangi Bailey of the ceremonial drum Te Puapua, its symbolic function and musical role unique to Taranaki and the tribal group Te Ati Awa iwi. *Witnessing Parihaka* was first performed at the Auckland Writers and Readers Festival in May 2011 and then again in 2013, at a UNESCO sponsored schools concert at the Auckland Town Hall.

+ + + + + + + + + +

One: May 16, 2010: Taranaki coastline

As my partner Kiri Eriwata and I drive along the scenic northern coastal road, in the distance we catch glimpses of snow on the maunga (mountain). Winter is arriving in Taranaki. We are embarking on a journey of return and renewal; for me to a place that holds powerful memories, links to youthful ideals and aspirations, and for Kiri, to the home of her Taranaki tūpuna (ancestors), a pilgrimage to reconnect with her Taranaki whānau (extended family).

---

[4] The opening lines of *Witnessing Parihaka*, text by Robert Sullivan.

[5] *E rere rā* was composed by the people of Muaupoko and Horowhenua and speaks in support of the Parihaka leader Tohu Kākahi. This waiata poi dates back to the earlier days of Parihaka's establishment.

[6] For example, at several points in the score the orchestral music incorporates elements of the original rangi (melody) of two Parihaka mōteatea, *Piukara* and *Ko Aotea Taku Waka*.

We have been planning this trip for two months, communicating with people from Parihaka, including my partner's kuia, Whero Te Rangi Bailey and the director of the Parihaka Peace Festival, Te Miringa Hohaia.

Earlier in the year the Auckland Philharmonia Orchestra had asked if I was interested in composing a new dramatised orchestral work. I quickly realised that this was the opportunity I had been waiting for—a chance to return and be with the people at Parihaka again—an opportunity to see if we might work on a creative project together. It had been thirty years since my last visit to Parihaka. I had stayed there several times in my teens and I had become very close to four Parihaka kuia, in particular Matarena Rau-Kupa, or Aunty Marj as she was known by most people. To this day I can still vividly remember the time I spent with her, her strength of character and her tenacious determination to foster and communicate Parihaka's living legacy. These experiences created a strong and lasting impression on me; I had wanted to return for many years.

Now, as Kiri and I near the Parihaka turnoff, my mind is full of questions; will I be able to reconnect with the community, will they accept me after an absence of so many years, and will they be interested in collaborating with me? As we draw into the main entrance, night has fallen. The moon floats high in the sky, its light shining on the waharoa (entrance/gateway) and wharenui (meeting house) of Parihaka. Kua tae mai tāua—we have arrived.

+ + + + + + + + + +

2   Parihaka—A Place of Historical Significance

The settlement of Parihaka stands halfway between the foot of maunga Taranaki and the rugged west coast of Te Ika-a-Māui.[7] By the late 1860s it had grown to become a thriving village as Māori from across the region and country travelled there to seek refuge from the strife generated by the land wars that had started to engulf the country. Its two leaders, Tohu Kākahi and Te Whiti o Rongomai, led a spiritual and political movement that employed the use of passive resistance to oppose the New Zealand government from coercively taking ancestral Māori land. With the arrival of Government surveyors and land agents, to assert the continuity of iwi ownership rights, teams of Parihaka workers were formed to remove survey pegs, reconstruct dismantled garden fences and plough up their tribal lands at a range of sites across the Taranaki region. In response to this, in November 1881, 1500 militia and heavily armed constabulary surrounded, plundered and occupied Parihaka. A number of Parihaka men and their leaders were arrested and incarcerated without trial after which the occupying soldiers ransacked and looted houses, intimidating and threatening the remaining families—this included instances of rape. Further peaceful Parihaka protests and illegal arrests took place through till the middle of the 1890s—over several decades, millions of acres of Māori land was seized and taken by the New Zealand Government.[8]

---

[7] Te Ika-a-Māui—the North Island of Aotearoa New Zealand.

[8] What happened at Parihaka is a complex story. As there are inaccurate versions in the public domain the author recommends research undertaken by Taranaki based Māori researchers, for

3   Māori Community Narratives

Across Aotearoa, marae based rural communities have retained unique cultural narratives passed down from one generation to the next. As in the case of Parihaka, a significant number of these stories are saturated with the traumatic scars of colonisation, in particular the pain caused by ancestral land being taken forcibly. The disturbing effects of these events continue to be felt by the descendants and have yet to be reconciled or healed. To this day, not many people in mainstream Pākehā society have heard the descendants of the original protagonists tell these highly personal and vivid narratives.

Since returning to Parihaka in 2010 I witnessed several creative artists as well as senior representatives of arts and media organisations publicly approach the community during formal gatherings; they wanted to tell the Parihaka story to the outside world. Unfortunately a few of them did not seem to comprehend the degree of misrepresentation that has taken place in the past, the effect this has had on the community and just how intensely the community feels the mamae (pain) from the past. These feelings are real and powerful. Those making such requests would do well to first devote time getting to know the community, and to patiently observe and listen so that they might understand the prevalent issues and appreciate the needs of the people.

++++++++++

Two: August 20, 2010: Parihaka papa kāinga: Taranaki

A group of us stand huddled against the bitterly cold wind and rain outside the wharenui (meeting house), Te Niho o Te Ati Awa. It is the middle of winter. We have travelled from around the country to acknowledge the life of the kaikōrero (orator) Te Miringa Hohaia—to tautoko (support) his whānau (extended family). Soon everyone is ready. We climb the path towards the marae ātea[9] of Takitūtū, past the monument placed over the tomb of Te Whiti. As we sing and walk in step, Kui Whero Te Rangi Bailey raises the beater in time and strikes Te Puapua. Boom … boom … boom. Ka rangona atu te patukituki i te pahū i ngā takiwa o te papa kāinga—the sound of the drum resonates across the village.

Our feet touch the whenua, the same ground crossed by the Parihaka villagers and the constabulary soldiers in 1881. We remember the children who sang to these men as they surrounded and invaded their village. We arrive—the marae ātea of Takitūtū lies before us. One-by-one we enter the wharenui, Te Paepae o te Raukura. We hold the whānau in a loving embrace and shed our tears of loss. Speakers stand to acknowledge Te Miringa. "Haere, haere, haere ki tua o te arai tūturu o tō tātou tūpuna (go forth, go on, beyond the ancient veil of our ancestors)". While each of them speak in turn, Kui Whero stands bowed over Te Puapua gently accompanying each utterance, each prayer, each breath.

++++++++++

example (a) http://www.parihaka.com, and (b) Hohaia et al. (2001). *Parihaka: the art of passive resistance*, Wellington, New Zealand: City Gallery Wellington/Victoria University Press/Parihaka Pā Trustees.

[9] Marae ātea—courtyard, the open area in front of the *wharenui*, where formal greetings and discussions take place.

4 Who Should Tell These Stories?

Who has the right to tell an indigenous story and what or who are the most credible sources of information and knowledge? These are important questions for the arts and education communities to consider and reflect upon. There is no doubt that in the past "indigenous languages, knowledges and cultures have been silenced or misrepresented" (Smith 1999, p. 20) and that indigenous communities are still being adversely affected by Western attitudes, methodologies and prejudices. When creative artists (and others) choose to tell indigenous stories and rely heavily upon Pākehā written records—as opposed to indigenous oral accounts—they disassociate and disempower the communities to whom the original narrative belongs.

> If we look at written Pacific history we find that most of it is the work of papalagi[10]/outsiders, and that most of it is based on records written and kept by papalagi explorers/missionaries/clerks/etc. So we can say that that history is a papalagi history of themselves and their activities in our region; it is an embodiment of their memories/perceptions/and interpretations of the Pacific (Wendt 1987, pp. 86–87).

The narrator of the story—no matter who they are—has a genuine responsibility to consider whether they have the right to be using or referencing indigenous knowledge in an artistic work, and if so, who has given them this right and what are their obligations to the legitimate owners. Even if the outline of the narrative is publicly well known, the responsibilities remain the same.

5 Building Relationships of Trust

In the months following our first trip, Kiri and I returned and stayed at Parihaka many times. While we were there we spoke with many people, exploring if and how the project might proceed. We helped in the kitchen, washed dishes, prepared food and had many inspiring conversations with the locals and the visitors. Out of these encounters friendships grew—people got to know us and gradually confidence and trust developed between us.

+ + + + + + + + + +

Three: September 18, 2010: Te Wharenui o Te Niho o Te Ati Awa, Parihaka: Taranaki

Kui Maata Wharehoka, Whaea Ngapera Moeahu and I sit down at one of the long wooden tables in the dining room of the wharenui. Maata is the kaitiaki (guardian) of the marae and Ngapera the kaiako (teacher) at the local kura kaupapa (Māori language and cultural immersion school). It is a soft warm afternoon. We share a pot of tea and talk, joke and laugh—time passes quickly. Maata is curious to hear what my compositions sound like and so I retrieve

---

[10]Papalagi—a word in the Sāmoan language describing foreigners, usually European Westerners or Caucasians. This term or similar is also used in a number of other Western Pacific countries for example pākehā (te reo Māori) and palangi (Tongan).

my bag from the car and we listen—one at a time—through a set of headphones. An animated conversation follows. We discuss how the papa kāinga children—also students at the kura kaupapa—could be part of the new piece. Later that night in the wharenui, Kiri and I sit in the soft dusk light enchanted as the children move poi through the air and sing Parihaka waiata, recounting the stories of their ancestors. Many portraits of their tūpuna hang on the walls of the wharenui—they look on approvingly.

+ + + + + + + + + +

6   Ngā Tamariki o Parihaka

After this meeting, Maata, Ngapera, Kiri and I collaboratively worked together to develop the role of the tamariki (children). We discussed what waiata (song) they would perform, what they would do and wear on stage, and how best to prepare them to work and perform with a professional orchestra. Maata and Ngapera gave generously of their time and shared their knowledge and insights with us throughout the project. Our relationship developed through discussion, listening and sharing over many months and years and it continues to this day. At its core is the common desire to support the tikanga (values, principles) and the people of Parihaka.

Early on we decided to feature the children of Parihaka in our piece because of their prominent role at the Pāhua—the invasion and sacking of Parihaka. On November 5, 1881, early in the morning, groups of children and women gathered inside the papa kāinga. As the armed constabulary and mounted soldiers entered the village, the children greeted them, singing waiata and playing games, their peaceful response ensuring Parihaka's non-violent objectives were clear for all to see. Many of the children that welcomed the soldiers that day are tūpuna of the people who reside at Parihaka today and this is one of the reasons why the spiritual and emotional connection felt by the community towards these events is so real and palpable.

After much consultation with the Parihaka community, the poet Robert Sullivan and I met in Tāmaki-makau-rau to consider ways to portray the Pāhua in musical and dramatic terms. We began by discussing the text about the children as Robert had already written about them in a set of previous poems that acknowledges Parihaka, *Poems from Another Century, for Parihaka*.[11] Reading these poems had inspired me to ask Robert to collaborate on the project. In the following stanzas *Little Voice*, one of the Parihaka children, recounts the arrival of the soldiers on the morning of the Pāhua.

Little Voice

We can feel them coming. The horses' feet,
and the guns on wheels, make the ground rumble.
We keep skipping and singing.
The soldiers get close enough to touch us.

---

[11] Sullivan, R. (2005). *Voice carried my family*. Auckland, Auckland University Press, p. 63.

But we keep skipping and singing.
The soldiers aren't very friendly.

They yell at us.
One picks me up and drops me on the roadside.
His friends laugh at me. Say I'm fat.
Then the rumbling starts again.
My friend gets stood on by a horse.
I feel very scared.[12]

Robert and I decided early on not to quote or make a direct reference to the two Parihaka leaders, Tohu Kākahi and Te Whiti o Rongomai. This was motivated by a desire to avoid misrepresenting the tikanga, teachings, and personal appearance and opinions of these two revered leaders. During the next few trips to Taranaki I read Robert's proposed new text to Parihaka pahake for their consideration and feedback. Once they were happy I began composing the orchestral music.

+ + + + + + + + + +

Four: December 10, 2010: Māori Land Court sitting, Te Ikaroa-a-Māui, Owae Marae, Waitara: Taranaki

As Sarah Reeves stood and spoke, the words flew from her mouth, cascading, bouncing over the heads of the people in the wharenui; stories and then names — the names of men my father knew well, names from the past, names I had not heard for decades. As I sat at the rear of the whare, Aunty Marj on my left and Kui Whero on my right, the words twirled around me, encircling me. I could not hold them back. The tears flowed — unrelenting, forgiving tears.

It had been thirty years since my father's tangihanga (funeral); his tangi had been held on the other side of island Te Ika-a-Māui, at Kohupatiki marae just out of Heretaunga.[13] Further south from there, I had grown up in the town of Waipukurau. Hearing the names of the men my father — and Sarah's father — knew so well transported me back in time, their names evoking memories, stories and connections between my whānau and the kaumātua (learned elders) we knew.

As I recover I recall the wero (challenge) issued by a kuia to me at my father's tangihanga — was I going to carry on his work, supporting and helping the people? He aha ngā mea nui o te ao? He tangata, he tangata, he tangata! — what is the most important thing in the world? The people, the people, the people! Now, decades later, I ponder — have I taken up the challenge, and if so, am I up to the task?

+ + + + + + + + + +

---

[12] Excerpt from *Poems from Another Century, for Parihaka*. This section of the poem Big Voice/Little Voice was also used in *Witnessing Parihaka*.

[13] Heretaunga — Hastings, Hawkes Bay, on the east coast of Te Ika-a-Māui.

7 Connecting to the Past

Working on this project provided me the opportunity and impetus to contemplate the significance of the past and how it intersects and impacts on our daily lives. Instances such as the above visit to Owae Marae reinforced my desire to consider a number of questions; were there specific triggers that brought the past into the present, why did my sense of connection intensify when it involved people I knew— family, friends or others I felt close to, and was knowing the historic narrative essential or was simply being present at a specific place enough to prompt me or others to feel and experience the events that had taken place there?

Some people are reluctant to discuss and engage with the past particularly when this has the potential to highlight contentious issues or unresolved conflict. This unwillingness is even more noticeable when the incidents in question link people to those they know or are related to. For those living on the Parihaka papa kāinga, the past is ever present and it is frequently acknowledged, discussed and debated. Living with the past like this can be a deeply cathartic as well as a traumatic experience. Recollection and open dialogue have the capacity to spawn feelings of optimism and respect for one's tūpuna as well as the potential to uncover and heal deep-seated mamae (pain) and taimahatanga (burdens/heaviness/depression).

8 Replenishing the Pātaka of Knowledge

In the nineteenth century, Māori developed strategies to cope with and survive the introduction of foreign diseases and Western ideas and attitudes. From the 1840s onwards, the overwhelming influx of Pākehā immigrants meant land was highly sort after and to acquire vast areas of Māori land the government employed a range of coercive strategies and policies. This loss forced many Māori to move away from their homes and their whānau in search of work and a way to survive. In the case of Parihaka, the invasion and destruction of the papa kāinga and the illegal arrest and detention of hundreds of protestors also took its toll on the community. These events and a decline in the numbers of inhabitants during the first half of the twentieth century adversely affected the continuity and exchange of local knowledge and traditions. Fortunately, in recent decades more and more descendants have returned to live at Parihaka, contributing to a gradual rebuild of the papa kāinga, marae and community. Regular wananga (educational forums) are held at Parihaka to support the revitalization of Parihaka's traditions. For the community—and those who closely associate with Parihaka—the many waiata that form the core of their musical tradition function as treasured time capsules, expressive vehicles through which they can look back in time and consider and study the thoughts and feelings of the people who composed and performed them. Gradually the pātaka (storehouse) of knowledge is being replenished and restored.

+ + + + + + + + + +

Five: December 2010: Te Paepae o te Raukura, Parihaka: Taranaki

Koro Te Huirangi Waikerepuru sings; his vibrant voice fills the wharenui. "Poua ki runga, poua ki raro ... kei whea te pou e tu ana. HEI ANEI! (Drive in the pole, upwards, downwards ... where is the pole standing? HERE IT IS!)." Te Huirangi is a Parihaka pahake and an internationally respected orator. He explains the meaning of the kupu (words) he has just sung, the last verse of *Pērā Hoki*, a Parihaka waiata tawhito. He describes how pou (poles) act as powerful symbolic objects, demarcating land boundaries and communicating political ideas and principles.[14] We have been sitting together for over half-an-hour discussing the new orchestral piece. He has offered suggestions of waiata to use, explaining the origins and meaning of each. As we sit embraced by the four walls of the wharenui—a place that has witnessed so much—I ponder his many gifts as an orator and his enduring role to advocate for te reo Māori (the Māori language), and Taranaki and Parihaka tikanga. All of these are living taonga (treasures)—they are priceless and timeless.

+ + + + + + + + + +

9 Mechanisms of Survival

The loss of Māori ancestral land had a devastating effect on a people for whom the whenua (land) embodied everything essential—identity, nourishment, and the physical and spiritual space within which to exist. During the 1860s and 1870s Parihaka became a haven for many. Thousands came to live at Parihaka seeking mutual support, leadership, hope and inspiration.

I te Rā o Maehe
I te rā o maehe ka iri kei te torona
Ka mau taku ringa ki te parau
E hau nei te whenua
Ka toro taku ringa ki te atua
E tu nei ko whakatohe
Ka puta te hae a te Kāwana
E tango nei te whenua
E kore au te taea

On a Day in March: The Ploughman's Song
On a day in March I was suspended by the throne of God
With my hand to the plough
Swept across the land
My hand is extended to God
Standing resolute
The ill-feelings of the Government emerges
In the taking away of the land
It will not deter me[15]

---

[14]Carved pou are also used to represent significant tūpuna (ancestors) although Parihaka leaders did not allow this practice to be used on the papa kāinga.

[15]This waiata was composed by Tonga Awhikau, an imprisoned Parihaka ploughman who returned to Taranaki to lead the land struggle in the 20th Century. The English translation was written by Te Miringa Hohaia (Hohaia et al. 2001, p. 48).

All of the three main wharenui at Parihaka display historic photographs and portraits of their tūpuna. Upon entering Te Niho o Te Ati Awa, visitors are greeted by whakaahua—large historic photographs, portraits, paintings and other artworks depicting Parihaka's past. Many of the historic photographs capture scenes of Parihaka in the nineteenth century such as women performing Parihaka waiata poi and the welcoming home of the Parihaka prisoners. Just as these whakaahua and other objects live on, so do the memories and traditions they represent. They testify to a legacy of passive resistance and signify the community's work towards the reclamation of authority over their land and cultural inheritance.

+++++++++

10 Collaborative Practices

Working on community collaborative projects such as *Witnessing Parihaka* have significantly illuminated, invigorated and transformed my work as a composer, artist and educator. Collaboration provides opportunities for a free flowing exchange of ideas, each participant unconditionally offering his or her own perspective, skills and knowledge. These qualities, when fully engaged, provoke a multifaceted open dialogue, where new creative and imaginative ideas emerge, frequently ideas that would not have been conceived by just one member of the group working alone. This exchange can be significantly enhanced when all the participants are motivated by a mutual goal and they work together guided by a set of agreed principles. In the case of *Witnessing Parihaka* all of the participants were united by the common desire to collectively work towards the betterment of the community, in particular the children—and the flow of ideas and dialogue was highly stimulating, enriching and rewarding.

As an educator of composers and songwriters I find myself asking what more can I do to encourage my students to adopt creative work models that utilise collective and collaborative techniques. Many Western based education and arts institutions still continue to elevate the archetype of the individual—the creative artist who in essence works independently from his or her fellow artists. This model continues to be promoted as an ideal despite the acknowledged benefits of collaborative work practices.

+++++++++

Six: December 2010: Ngāmotu—New Plymouth: Taranaki

Koro Rangikōtuku Rukuwai listens intently, his eyes closed, deep in thought. For several minutes he is somewhere else. Rangikōtuku is a direct descendant of the Parihaka leader, Te Whiti o Rongomai and he is the kaitiaki (guardian) of Toroanui one of the marae at Parihaka. He was raised here as a child. The music stops; he takes off the headphones and turns to me, "Yes, I like that. I think it will work." He has been listening to some explorative drafts of instrumental music I had composed for the new piece. I wanted to know if he thought the music captured the right sort of mood. We are sitting in the lounge of Rangikōtuku's family home in Ngāmotu.[16] Kui Maata has come with me to offer support. We finish talking—the room is full of thoughts. Rangikōtuku's wife, Ngaraiti, brings out a freshly baked fruitcake and hot tea. Koinei a manaakitanga—this is hospitality!

+ + + + + + + + + +

11   Questions to Consider Before Beginning a Community Project

Before initiating or agreeing to participate in a Māori community project there are some important questions that creative artists should ask themselves, no matter what their skill set or background. Firstly, does the community think the project is directly relevant to their needs? Secondly, what is my personal motivation for doing this work and do I wish the project to ultimately benefit the community group before myself? Thirdly, am I ready and capable of fully accommodating the needs of the community including significantly changing or stopping the project if it looks like it will no longer benefit them? And, finally, who is the best person to work on such a project? Is it the person who grew up in the community or can someone from the outside offer something beneficial, for example, specialist skills? When I asked kaumātua (learned elders) this question their responses have consistently reinforced the notion that first and foremost the creative artist needs to be asked and have the support of the community, whether the artist be from within or outside the group.

  To summarise, for community collaboration to be successful, the needs of the community, that is the collective whole, need to be foremost in the creative artist's mind. Rather than being restrictive, this approach is empowering. In the case of *Witnessing Parihaka*, Kiri and I waited for confirmation that the community wanted the project to proceed. As we approached the premiere and faced the challenges of mounting and performing such an powerful and emotionally charged real-life narrative, all of us—the creators and performers—were sustained by the knowledge that we had the support and backing of the Parihaka community.

+ + + + + + + + + +

Seven: December 2010: Parihaka: Taranaki

It is the morning of the rā tapu (sacred day) at Parihaka. The respected kaikōrero (orator) and educator Ruakere Hond and I stand outside under the gaze of the burning sun. Earlier, while we sat eating breakfast, I asked him which waiata he thought would be good for the girls to perform in the new piece. Now as we talk again he suggests several options—all waiata the girls know well. Ruakere thinks the Parihaka poi manu *E rere rā* is a good

---

[16] Ngāmotu—New Plymouth.

choice. I ask if there any tikanga I need to be aware of—for example, could one verse be performed by itself? As we stand discussing these things, the final words of *E rere rā* begin to speak to us. "Ko te hau ka wheru whakamomotu e whiuwhiu ana kei te uru e kei te tonga ka hari mai ki roto ka ko harihari, hei hei hei (a destructive wind beats us down, it tears us to shreds, it is the westerly and the southerly, it penetrates, a deep internal pain, the sound of soldiers presenting arms, hei, hei, hei!)".

+ + + + + + + + + +

12   Ownership of Space

In Aotearoa New Zealand progress is gradually being made in the field of bicultural composition—practices that bring together Māori and Pākehā traditions and artists. This is occurring as acceptance and support grows for the creation of new bicultural works, cultural understanding and awareness deepens, and imaginative minds pro- ductively respond to the opportunities and demands available. One of the challenges faced during our project was how to successfully present a distinctively Māori nar- rative and Māori perspective in a performance environment that was dominated by Western performance traditions and a physical space defined by Western notions of spatial organization—a symphony orchestra performing in a large proscenium arch theatre.

> For the indigenous world, Western conceptions of space, of arrangements and display, of the relationship between people and the landscape, of culture as an object of study, have meant that not only has the indigenous world been represented in particular ways back to the West, but the indigenous world, the land and the people, has been radically transformed in the spatial image of the West. In other words, indigenous space has been colonised (Smith 1999, p. 53).

For the four Parihaka girls the prospect of performing with an orchestra in a large two-thousand-seat auditorium was both daunting and exhilarating. None of them had any experience of formal theatre or stage performance techniques. Learning how to own and define their own physical space and how to fully embody who they were and who they represented were new goals to aspire towards. Fortunately the girl's perspective and appreciation of the world was deeply seated in their experi- ences of growing up on the Parihaka papa kāinga. Like many rural-based Māori children, they were raised in a community where participating in ritual and other forms of cultural and spiritual expressions were natural and routine occurrences. On the papa kāinga they regularly witnessed members of their community perform karanga (ceremonial call of welcome), deliver whaikōrero (formal speeches), sing waiata tawhito (traditional songs) and recite karakia (prayers). Their teacher, Whaea Ngapera had taught them many waiata poi and other aspects of the performance traditions of their forebears. When the girls started to prepare for *Witnessing Parihaka* we turned to these powerful and tangible understandings for insight and inspiration, to help build their confidence and to contribute depth and meaning to their performance.

+ + + + + + + + + +

Eight: April 16, 2011: Opunake High School: Taranaki

Rangiawhina, Jameco, Courtney and Tatijana sit in a small circle near an upright piano at the front of the local school hall. Ngapera, Kiri and I are preparing the girls for the first performance of *Witnessing Parihaka*. We have selected the largest local hall to rehearse in. Maata and Ngapera chose the girls—they are now an integral part of piece.

Together we discuss big spaces and how people through their thoughts and actions can fill them with their voice, their presence and their sense of being. I ask the girls to be really quiet, to close their eyes and listen. "Open up your ears, further ... and further. What can you hear?" We wait for a minute; they listen intently. When they have finished, they tell us; "We heard the sounds from outside—birds, the wind, a squeaky door somewhere..." We talk more about their singing and I ask; "Do you think the sound of your voices can fill this big hall, can it reach into every corner, every space?" I then ask. "How far do you think your voices can carry? Can they reach back in time? Who will be listening?"

+ + + + + + + + + +

13   A Tradition of Collaborative Composition

Parihaka's musical tradition is a testimony to the strengths and benefits of community composition. Waiata were often written collaboratively involving an extended process of refinement and selection, in particular, the search for the most evocative text, and in the case of waiata poi or waiata ā-ringa, physical gestures that supported and added meaning and nuance to the views expressed in the text. Compositional practices such as these would have probably taken longer but the end result would have had the backing of the wider community, confirming its broad appeal and ensuring its ongoing use.

From 1860 through to 1881 the core philosophy and community approaches at Parihaka were formed. Passive resistance tactics became a larger feature of their strategy from 1878 and in 1880 Parihaka's position increasingly came under attack from the state. This tension gave rise to newly established forms of composition and performance including the use of poi becoming particularly prominent between 1881 and 1900. These new waiata provided a way of voicing their principles, experiences and position in the conflict. They also acted as a means of communication in getting messages out. They were statements of philosophy where people presented their ideas and tested their perspective of the issues. If they weren't responded to well by their audience then they fell from use and other ones were composed. Waiata that were appropriate or resonated with the people were the ones that were retained. They were shared with others and taught to successive generations, continuing to be performed. Other waiata were retained because they conveyed the shared identity and narrative of a specific group of performers. These were not shared but were sung only by those hapū or descendants (R. Hond, personal communication, December, 2010).

The qualities found of the text in *E rere rā*—the waiata performed in *Witnessing Parihaka*—are typical of Parihaka waiata. The words are multifaceted; they include double meanings, irony and innuendo. They are candidly outspoken and uplifting, capable of reviving the spirits of the performers and encouraging feelings of kotahitanga (togetherness in purpose) among the community. Waiata such as this ensured the maintenance of integrity and they inspired people to uphold the tikanga of Parihaka, even against insurmountable odds.

14 Te Puapua—Parihaka's Ceremonial Drum

Te Puapua, one of two Parihaka ceremonial drums is nearly as old as Parihaka itself. It is a large Western bass drum made of calfskin, rope and wood—it is thought to originally be an instrument from a nineteenth century Pākehā fife and drum band. One of the early strategies employed by the people of Parihaka was to appropriate Pākehā objects, imagery and narratives. These were decontextualized and reused by the community for the purposes of affirming authority over the government and communicating their strategies of assertion and survival. The use of a Pākehā designed drum was as much a political statement as a musical one, its performance confirming their declaration of rangatiratanga (sovereignty).

The experience of witnessing Kui Whero playing Te Puapua at Te Miringa's tangihanga (funeral) had a powerful effect on me. I learnt then what an iconic part of Parihaka's musical legacy it was and I was entranced by her subtle and expressive performance skills. A few weeks before the premiere, kui confirmed that she was able to travel to Tāmaki-makau-rau[17] and join us on stage. At the rehearsals and performances she skilfully improvised throughout set sections of the piece—as she had done during the informal speeches at the tangihanga. At these points in the orchestral score I left rhythmic space for her to be able to extemporise, and the piece ended with her final improvised solo accompanied by a single delicate sustained orchestral chord. This ending ensured the audience's focus remained with Parihaka—and not the orchestral music. Kui Whero's solo provided a riveting and poignant finish.

We were very fortunate to have Te Puapua and Kui Whero onstage with us at both public performances, in 2011 and 2013. Musical instruments such as Te Puapua are live entities, they are independent living figures; people cannot control them. They have their own mana (prestige, authority, spiritual power) and their own mauri (life principle, vital essence), spanning both time and place.

---

[17] Tāmaki-makau-rau—Auckland City.

15   Ko te Rā Tapu—the Sacred Day

The Parihaka descendants have maintained a tradition of remembrance that dates back nearly 150 years. The rā tapu (sacred day), held on the 18th and 19th of each month, are set aside for all to gather at Parihaka, visitors and tangata whenua (local people) alike. It is a time of commemoration, celebration and discussion about Parihaka's history and tikanga. It is also a time for collective consideration of any requests or proposals made by residents or visitors. The format—after the whakatau (official welcome) and whaikōrero (formal speeches)—is an open forum where consultation is highly dynamic and very public; all can contribute, all can listen.

+ + + + + + + + + +

Nine: April 19, 2011: Mahi Kuare, Toroanui, Parihaka: Taranaki

It is 11.30 am on the rā tapu, the 19th of the month. We are assembled inside the wharenui Mahi Kuare. Maata, Ngapera, Kiri and I have been preparing for this opportunity to explain to those living on the papa kāinga about the planned trip and performance of *Witnessing Parihaka*. The other two marae confirmed their support yesterday. Seated on the pae (the speaker's bench) are the pahake who have been advising us. Looking on from the many whakaahua (photographs, paintings, drawings) hanging on the walls are the tūpuna of this marae. "Ngā mihi nui ki a koutou katoa. Ka huihui mai tātou katoa." I finish my speech, sing a waiata and sit down. What will their response be? Will the community support the forthcoming performance?

   Koro Len Robinson, an elder at Toroanui stands. "Kororia ki te Atua i runga rawa, maungaarongo ki runga i te whenua, whakaaro pai ki ngā tangata katoa (glory to God on high, peace on earth, goodwill to all mankind)". He continues, speaking with intensity, vigour and passion. He supports the new piece and performance; he believes this is an opportunity for the mokopuna (grandchildren) to be heard outside the papa kāinga, for them to represent Parihaka. Suddenly, without warning he stops and he sits down abruptly, collapsing in his chair. People rush to him. Is he all right? I tēnei wa, ka rere te piwaiwaka kei roto i te whare—at this moment a small bird (a pīwaiwaka) flies into the wharenui. It flits around above our heads in a wide circle—then departs as quickly as it arrived. Time seems to stop. I watch Koro Len to see how he is doing. Someone says he is OK—we breathe a sigh of relief.

   Others stand—they support the project too. At the end of Ngapera's kōrero, the four girls perform *E rere rā*; the support of the community is confirmed. The bell is rung—the food is ready.

+ + + + + + + + + +

16   The Guardianship of Knowledge

Before presenting our proposal at the rā tapu we followed a process of informal consultation across the whole papa kāinga lasting many months. This was to ensure we had observed Parihaka tikanga and had the support of the elders from the three active marae. Publicly discussing the merits of *Witnessing Parihaka* at the rā tapu seemed a daunting prospect at the time as debate at this type of community forum can be intense and sometimes confrontational, and yet, presenting the project in this way was essential as confirmation guaranteed we had the full support of the community. The public performance of a new creative work like this, away from the home papa kāinga, is open to claims of misrepresentation. Everyone needs to be given the opportunity to question and be assured that the work will uphold the mana (prestige, authority, spiritual power) of the community.

Traditionally Māori observed strict oral traditions for learning and maintained rigorous processes of selection to ensure matauranga (knowledge) was only passed on to those who had the prerequisite skills and understanding as well as an appreciation of their collective responsibility to use knowledge wisely. To care for the people and to care for the knowledge is one in the same therefore whoever is entrusted with the knowledge has a responsibility to consider the needs of the people, the needs of the collective group. Parihaka matauranga is unique and it needs to be protected and treasured. By presenting our proposal at Parihaka's monthly open forums we were acknowledging a vital community practice that ensured its ongoing guardianship.

+ + + + + + + + + +

Ten: May 10, 2011: Main stage, Aotea Centre, Tāmaki-makau-rau (Auckland)

It is the day before the premiere of *Witnessing Parihaka*. Kui Maata, Paora Joseph and I stand before three very large bound rolls of hand painted cloth. Each one depicts a raukura (feather, plume, treasure) and measures several metres in length. Janine, Paora's partner has painted them. They will be elevated to stand like tall pou (poles) among the performers on stage. Ka whakatū ngā raukura—stand tall raukura!

Soon the orchestral stagehands will arrive to set up stands, chairs and percussion instruments for the orchestra. We unravel the panels, rolling them carefully out across the wooden stage. Paora speaks quietly; the words of the karakia (prayers) drift and then hover above the images. He acknowledges the tikanga they represent; he speaks to the past, to the people of Parihaka. As he finishes we notice one of the feathers lies in the opposite direction to the others, not because it was painted this way but because of the direction the panel was rolled. I wonder what to do. Maata smiles, "This is how they've revealed themselves to us, so this is the way we'll hang them." We carry in the tall three-metre-high wooden frames, attach the panels, two facing the sky—ko Ranginui—one facing the earth—ko Papa-tū-ā-nuku.[18]

+ + + + + + + + + +

---

[18] Papa-tū-ā-nuku—Earth, Earth mother and Rangi-nui—*atua* of the sky. All living things originate from them.

17 Consultation and Observing Protocol

Every hapū and every marae follow their own distinctive set of protocols and although there are common customs, the differences can be significant. For *Witnessing Parihaka* we took advice from the Parihaka community at every phase of the project. I soon learnt who was happy for me to approach them for guidance and when I needed to understand more important issues I asked the advice of three or more people or pahake (learned elders). Throughout the project I tried my best to listen carefully, remain flexible and be free from any personal agenda. I was fortunate to be patiently guided through numerous decisions by many elders and overtime began to observe and appreciate the continuity of understanding that shaped the advice.

+ + + + + + + + + +

18 Responsibilities to Indigenous Communities

Being part of this project highlighted what it feels like for Māori communities to have their cultural identity and knowledge misunderstood and misused by others. I witnessed firsthand the distress caused to members of the Parihaka community by the unsanctioned appearance of their taonga (treasures) on YouTube and other digital platforms. Composers, writers, artists and the arts communities have a responsibility to support indigenous people "to protect themselves from further misrepresentation, misinterpretation, fragmentation, mystification, commodification, and simplification" (Louis 2007, p. 132). Educators need to encourage their students to take the time to undertake an in-depth study of the origins and deeper values contained within an indigenous story and urge them to always meet and learn firsthand from the authentic knowledge holders. Learning the associated forms of cultural expression that accompany a narrative—such as an indigenous language, dance or music—is critically important. Similarly it is essential arts organisations consider how best to support collaborative projects that hand back control to indigenous communities and what constitutes best practice methodologies. Likewise creative artists can contribute much by discussing and considering the implications of how they engage with indigenous communities and what short and long-term effects this engagement has on them.

> Indigenous methodologies are not merely "a political gesture on the part of Indigenous peoples in their struggle for self-determination" (Porsanger 2004, p. 8). They are necessary to "reframe, reclaim, and rename" (Steinhauer 2002, 70) the research process so that Indigenous people can take control of their cultural identities, emancipate their voices from the shadows, and recognise Indigenous realities (Louis 2007, p. 133).

19   Cross-Cultural Exchange

The final phase of this project brought together the Parihaka performers and the Auckland Philharmonia Orchestra.[19] The intersection of these two divergent cultural outlooks, musical traditions and performance practices produced unexpected and moving exchanges. Members of both groups were personally enriched and inspired by the opportunity to work and perform together.

Lee Martelli, the orchestra's education manager supervised our relationship with the orchestra and did so with care and sensitivity. Due to her understanding and assistance, significant adjustments and considerations were made to accommodate the bicultural nature of the piece—for example, karakia particular to Taranaki and Parihaka were said at the start of every orchestral rehearsal and before the first performance began, whaikōrero took place onstage.

For a project such as this it is important to have in place mechanisms and people that are able to respond and negotiate with the leaders of the professional Pākehā arts organisations. For Māori, the prioritisation of principles and processes that ensure transparent representation and collective decision-making are crucial. These often run counter to Pākehā values and systems that are founded on hierarchical management structures and processes that prioritise efficiency and the quantification of time.

20   Whanaungatanga—Interconnectedness

Three days before the premiere—almost a year since the project began—a convoy of vehicles from Parihaka arrived in Tāmaki-makau-rau carrying both performers and supporters. The next day we started our final preparations. The whanaungatanga (kinship, close friendship) felt by all was unmistakable; we were connected by our collective commitment to the project and months of preparation together. Our excitement and anticipation was high. From the first orchestral rehearsal through till the time we gathered side-of-stage to perform, we all felt the presence of ngā tūpuna o Parihaka—the ancestors of Parihaka—the people who, with dignity, courage and determination had upheld the principle of passive resistance and opposed the taking of their ancestral land 130 years ago.

+ + + + + + + + + +

---

[19] The Auckland Philharmonia Orchestra is a publicly funded professional orchestra with a long record of supporting contemporary composition through the commissioning, performance and recording of new work.

Eleven: May 11, 2011: Main stage: Aotea Centre: Tāmaki-makau-rau

It is 6.30 pm. Rangiawhina, Jameco, Courtney and Tatijana are almost ready; Kui Maata and Whaea Ngapera have been helping them. At the orchestral rehearsal the girls performed their moves and singing with great skill: the waiata poi, the pūkana, and the 'prisoners walk'. Outside the dressing rooms, Koro Len Robinson and I stand in the brightly lit corridor. He is elated—these girls have such confidence and composure and they are about to represent their tūpuna on stage. They symbolise the future of Parihaka.

It is 9.15 pm. All the Parihaka performers are gathered side of stage. We have completed our preparations, our karakia. It is time. Our bare feet feel the coolness of the wooden floors. From the darkness we walk through the orchestra into the light of the main stage, into the gaze of the audience waiting—the past is in front, the future behind us. The orchestra begins. A high-sustained chord sounds, steadfast and resolute. As it grows in volume Kui Maata starts the karanga (ceremonial call of welcome). Each wahine (woman) joins in, one after the other, voice upon voice, layer upon layer. The actors Te Kohe and Stuart begin, expertly capturing each character's gesture and tone, "Maungaarongo, mountain of peace, e tu Taranaki". The girls stand confidently—their singing fills the theatre. As the performance nears the end, all ears are transfixed—the ceremonial bass drum Te Puapua rings out for the last time as Kui Whero strikes the coarsely textured skin. The audience stand. They acknowledge us and applaud—on stage, we bow and hongi each other.

+ + + + + + + + + +

21   Being Heard

For the performers from Parihaka, to plan, create, and then perform their own story in this way was a compelling statement to the world and to themselves. At the end of the performance, as they stood side-by-side in front of the orchestra, they witnessed firsthand the audience's response. This was an opportunity to be heard and acknowledged by those outside their immediate community. As for the audience, their reaction was immediate, heartfelt and sincere. Their response confirmed that narratives told by the descendants of original storytellers do have the capacity to engage the wider public in a meaningful conversation with the past—to transcend cultural gaps in understanding. The positive benefits of creating and performing *Witnessing Parihaka* were undeniable, for the storytellers and audience alike. Perhaps if more people were to hear stories like these, discussions that foster greater understanding of past injustices would follow, encouraging tangible acts of reconciliation.

22   Discovering Our Ancestral Past

It is my hope that this account will encourage others to collaboratively engage and work with communities to tell their ancestral stories. Currently 40% of my tertiary songwriting students' whakapapa to Māori or Pacific Island genealogical lines, while others have ties to a wide variety of other ethnicities: Russian, Dutch, Chinese, Korean, English, Scottish and Irish among others. After working on this project I started teaching a new songwriting module where students compose a song about their forebears, about someone who has personal significance to them. They begin by researching their wider ancestral past and they frequently uncover fascinating family stories—stories about conflict, love and loss, as well as ones that tell of overcoming adversity. This investigation has provoked them to consider further who they are and who their forebears were. Because of this work they produced some of their most personally revealing and poignant songs.

+++++++++++

Twelve: June 18, 2011: Parihaka: Taranaki

As Kiri and I arrive at Parihaka I reflect upon all the people we have met in the past twelve months—sons, granddaughters, nieces and nephews of the people I had known all those years before. It feels like the first part of the journey is now over—we have returned and again feel close to the community. At the premiere in May I was deeply moved by the expressions of aroha (love) and acts of generosity—by the fact that so many had made the long trip to Tāmaki-makau-rau to perform and tautoko (support) our new piece. The circle is complete.

23   The Journey's End

The experiences of this yearlong journey reaffirmed to me the importance of honouring the communities we live in and acknowledging our connections to the people that surround us, to the places that hold significance to us. This project has informed my work as a composer and educator, reinforcing the indisputable power of the narrative to communicate and transcend cultural barriers as well as the capacity of ancestral knowledge to cultivate and strengthen a deeper understanding of who we are and where we come from.

Acknowledgements *Being Heard: A Māori Community Narrative* would not have been written without the generous support, guidance and contributions made by the people of Parihaka. Ngā mihi aroha ki a koutou katoa. Special thanks to Kiri Eriwata, our son Te Awanui Matthews, Maata Wharehoka, Ruakere Hond, Ngapera Moeahu and Whero Te Rangi Bailey. The *Witnessing Parihaka* performers were: Whero Te Rangi Bailey, Rangiawhina Hohaia, Courtney Ngaia-Pompey, Jameco Ngaia-Pompey, Tatijana Smith, Maata Wharehoka, Ngapera Moeahu, Kiri Eriwata, Makere Pike, Agnes Wharehoka, Whakaarahia Koroheke, Len Robinson, Te Kohe Tuhaka, Stuart Devenie, Kenneth Young, Hamish McKeich and the Auckland Philharmonia Orchestra.

Music study guide

A *Witnessing Parihaka* secondary school music study guide is available by contacting the Education Manager at the Auckland Philharmonia Orchestra, http://apo.co.nz, or the author at http://stephenralphmatthews.com

Glossary (He Papakupu)

The following translations were referenced from *Te Aka Online Māori Dictionary* (Moorfield 2003–2015).

Hongi	(verb) to press noses in greeting.
Karanga	(verb) to call, call out, summon
	(noun) formal call, a ceremonial call of welcome to visitors onto a marae, or an equivalent venue, at the start of a pōwhiri.
Karakia	(verb) to recite ritual chants, say grace, pray, recite a prayer, chant.
	(noun) incantation, ritual chant, chant, intoned incantation, charm, spell.
Kaumātua	(noun) adult, elder, elderly man, elderly woman—a person of status within the *whānau*.
Koro	(noun) elderly man, grandfather—term of address to an older man.
Kui	(noun) elderly woman, grandmother—a term of address for an older woman.
Marae ātea	(noun) courtyard—the open area in front of the *wharenui*, where formal greetings and discussions take place. The word *marae* is often also used to include the complex of buildings situated around the *marae ātea*.
Mana	(noun) prestige, authority, control, power, influence, status, spiritual power, charisma—*mana* is a supernatural force in a person, place or object.
Mātauranga	(noun) knowledge, wisdom, understanding, skill
	(noun) knowledgeable person, sage, scholar, intellectual, academic.
Mōteatea	(noun) lament, traditional chant, sung poetry—a general term for songs sung in traditional mode.
Pākehā	(noun) New Zealander of European descent. Also English, foreign, European, exotic—introduced from or originating in a foreign country.
Pahake	(noun) a Taranaki regional word for learned elder, similar in meaning to the more widely used word, kaumātua.
Papa kāinga	(noun) original home, home base, village, communal Māori land.

Poi	(verb) to toss up, swing the poi, toss up and down, toss about. (noun) poi—a light ball on a string of varying length which is swung or twirled rhythmically to sung accompaniment.
Pūkana	(verb) to stare wildly, dilate the eyes. Done by both genders when performing haka and waiata to emphasise particular words.
Tangihanga	(noun) weeping, crying, funeral, rites for the dead, obsequies—one of the most important institutions in Māori society, with strong cultural imperatives and protocols.
Tikanga	(noun) correct procedure, custom, habit, lore, method, manner, rule, way, code, meaning, plan, practice, convention, protocol—the customary system of values and practices that have developed over time and are deeply embedded in the social context.
Taonga	(noun) treasure, anything prized—applied to anything considered to be of value including socially or culturally valuable objects, resources, phenomenon, ideas and techniques. Also property, goods, possessions, effects.
Tapu	(stative) be sacred, prohibited, restricted, set apart, forbidden, under *atua* protection.
Tūpuna	(noun) ancestors, grandparents—western dialect variation of tīpuna.
Waiata	(verb) to sing. (noun) song, chant, psalm.
Waiata poi	(noun) song performed with a *poi*—modern songs are usually set to European-type tunes.
Waiata ā-ringa	(noun) action song—a popular modern song type with set actions and European-type tunes.
Waiata tawhito	(noun) old, ancient, traditional song.
Wairua	(noun) spirit, soul—spirit of a person which exists beyond death. It is the non physical spirit, distinct from the body and the *mauri*. Also attitude, quintessence, feel, mood, feeling, nature, essence.
Whaea	(noun) mother, aunt, aunty.
Whaikōrero	(verb) (–tia) to make a formal speech. (noun) oratory, oration, formal speech-making, address, speech—formal speeches usually made by men during a *pohiri* and other gatherings.
Whakaahua	(noun) photograph, illustration, portrait, picture, image, shot (photograph), photocopy.
Whānau	(verb) (–a) to be born, give birth. (noun) extended family, family group, a familiar term of address to a number of people—the primary economic unit of traditional Māori society. In the modern context the term is sometimes used to include friends who may not have any kinship ties to other members.

Whanaungatanga	(noun) relationship, kinship, sense of family connection—a relationship through shared experiences and working together which provides people with a sense of belonging. It develops as a result of kinship rights and obligations, which also serve to strengthen each member of the kin group. It also extends to others to whom one develops a close familial, friendship or reciprocal relationship.
Wharenui	(noun) meeting house, large house—main building of a marae where guests are accommodated.
Whenua	(noun) land—often used in the plural, country, nation, state, ground, territory.
	(noun) placenta, afterbirth.

References (He Rārangi Pukapuka)

Hohaia, T. M., O'Brien, G., Strongman, L., City Gallery Wellington, Parihaka Pā Trustees. (2001). *Parihaka: The art of passive resistance.* Wellington: City Gallery Wellington/Victoria University Press/Parihaka Pā Trustees.

Louis, R. P. (2007). Can you hear us now? Voices from the margin: Using Indigenous methodologies in geographic research. *Geographical Research, 45*(2), 130–139.

Moorfield, J. C. (2003–2015). *Te Aka online Māori dictionary.* From http://www.maoridictionary.co.nz

Smith, L. T. (1999). *Decolonizing methodologies: Research and indigenous peoples.* New York/Dunedin: Zed Books/University of Otago Press.

Sullivan, R. (2005). *Voice carried my family.* Auckland, Auckland University Press.

Wendt, A. (1987). Novelists and historians and the art of remembering. In A. Hooper, S. Britton, R. Crocombe, J. Huntsman, & Macpherson (Eds.), *Class and culture in the South Pacific* (pp. 78–91). Auckland: Centre for Pacific Studies, University of Auckland/Suva: Institute of Pacific Studies, University of the South Pacific.

Stephen Ralph Matthews works in Auckland as a composer, lecturer, multi-media artist and performer. Many of his works reference image and sound drawn from the land, river and sea, and incorporate mōteatea (traditional Māori song) and taonga pūoro (traditional Māori instruments). His creative interests embrace instrumental and electroacoustic music, song, text and moving image as well as the intrinsic values and worldview of the people and communities he collaborates with.

Cross-Cultural Education in Dance and Song in Aotearoa and Sāmoa

From the Cultural Roots Will Grow the Tree

Olivia Taouma

Abstract I have been teaching dance over 23 years in New Zealand and Sāmoa. I have taught people dance from many different ethnicities but the majority have been Pacific Island students. I come from a strong Sāmoan mixed heritage myself and a personal history of many dance forms. These elements have helped mould the type of educator I am today and my personal pedagogy. This chapter is a personal narrative about the pedagogy I have developed and am constantly working on in my life. Specifically looking at how I endeavour to develop in my students a sense of identity, family, individual voice and community with critique in dance. Pacific values of respect, family, co-operation, support, generosity, sharing, humility and reciprocity, in summary 'relationships' are developed alongside Western values of individuality, self-motivation, criticism, ambition, competition and equality. Thus a term I like to use in teaching is 'cross-cultural education', taking the best of both worlds with a foundation in and reflection on our Pacific students growing up as Pacific Islanders in a Western country, New Zealand.

Keywords Pacific dance • Education • Cross-cultural • Performing arts • *Va* • Culture • Indigenous dance • Contemporary • Community • Identity

1 Background

In this chapter Linda Ashley interviews dance educator Olivia Taouma about some of the background within which her narrative approach to the chapter is contextualised. In providing an explanation why her approach of telling stories is an integral part of Oceanic culture the short interview also provides some complementary Western theory placing the chapter at a cross cultural intersection that is highly appropriate for this book. This interview is followed by Olivia's story.

O. Taouma (✉)
60 Matata St. Blockhouse Bay, Auckland 0600, New Zealand
e-mail: oliviataouma@hotmail.com

© Springer International Publishing Switzerland 2016
L. Ashley, D. Lines (eds.), *Intersecting Cultures in Music and Dance Education*, Landscapes: the Arts, Aesthetics, and Education 19,
DOI 10.1007/978-3-319-28989-2_14

As mentioned in the introduction to this book, as editors David and Linda were aware that the book should be inclusive of a range of different voices and writing styles from the Oceania region. Personal narratives were one of the approaches that we were keen to include. In support of the inclusion of personal stories, some theoretical underpinnings are provided to that frame Olivia's chapter within Jerome Bruner's (1987) emphasis on the importance of exploring narrative because stories reveal how both meaning and power are structured and play out in people's lives. By way of this rationale, Bruner (1996) drew attention to how narratives are significant enough to warrant attention. Olivia's narrative provides the reader with an opportunity to understand how personal stories can bring to light particular ways of responding to socially significant situations such as pedagogical development (Goodson 2012).

Bruner (1996) emphasised that narrative should draw attention to people's beliefs, desires, intentions and actions, so the voices of Olivia and her students in this chapter act as "both a mode of thought and an expression of a culture's worldview" (p. xiv). In telling her story about the ways in which she developed her pedagogy, an autobiographical timeline is followed. This timeline and her reflections on her experiences reveal how her teaching supported her Pacific tertiary students, helping them to deal with living at the intersections of Polynesian and Western cultures in Aotearoa/New Zealand through dance and music. Their beliefs, desires, intentions and actions surface in the story as ways in which they are supported pedagogically to explore their identities. As revealed in her story, in engaging students to develop their understanding of the arts as experienced through dance and music, Olivia's pedagogy empowers and helps them to structure social meanings as played out within their lives and communities. Olivia's and her students' worldviews, however, incorporate and interface with the cross currents of intersecting cultures. In so doing, as found in Olivia's story, multiple and overlapping layers resulting at the intersections can lead to some cultural complexities and pedagogical challenges.

In the interview that follows, the theoretical framework is explored and seen to be in the cross currents of cultural flow. In these currents some of the students' stories, as experienced through learning in the performing arts, surface and tell of crucial educational issues such as identity formation, creativity and Pacific culture growing within a Western educational environment. It becomes clear how stories, glued together by Olivia's own story of developing pedagogy within a tertiary education setting, form a cultural hub for the chapter.

Linda *In telling your stories, Olivia, I imagine you swimming in Bruner's "sea of stories" (1996, p. 147). He envisaged stories as being at the core how we make sense of, and learn about, the world. Can you explain the importance of telling stories in Oceanic culture?*

Olivia *Pacific culture is made up of living traditions of oral history and rituals. Traditions and meanings are passed down through the generations via narratives and stories that remain a vital part of the culture and are constantly evolving. Stories are often presented physically through poetry, music compositions and* *songs, dances and myths and legends. The combination of these is manifested in dance. Poetry is composed with music into song and physically enacted through movement to create a dance. Queen Salote of Tonga was a great example of this. She was a poet, especially of love poems (hiva kakala), which were composed with music into song, and she also choreographed the movement thus creating new dances, like her famous lakalakas.*

In today's world young people growing up away from their Pacific cultural heritage are placed in the predicament of living two worlds, a Westernised world and a Pacific cultural world. Their stories often reflect the conflicts and complexities of these two worlds, and the struggle in finding their identity. Being able to express themselves through their Pacific traditions of poetry, song, music and dance has enabled many of them to create a balance of sorts between the two worlds, where they utilise Pacific cultural compositions and movements with Western theatre forms, structure and framework.

Sesilia Pusiaki, a past student of mine whom I continue to mentor, is a great modern Tongan example of this. She created a cross-cultural Tongan work Sei 'O Fafine which developed in a series of events from her training in the performing arts and different Western dance forms, as well as life-long learning of Tongan performance. It was important for her to tell her story and express how she makes sense of the world as a New Zealand born Tongan girl growing up in a Tongan traditional family in Auckland, struggling to come to terms with her identity and the balancing act between the two worlds as well as living with a large family and the complexities and dynamics of that. It was a first for New Zealand audiences to be allowed a rare inside view of Tongan life for girls in New Zealand. It allowed these people not only an experience from inside a large Tongan family but also to taste the values that they live by and install in the children. It allowed people to see the beauty, the struggles, the humour and the hope. It allowed Tongan audiences a rare chance to see themselves, reflected, on stage. They saw their own families and teachings and recognised their own successes and failings. It allowed people the opportunity to discuss Tongan culture, values, arts and especially Tongan dance and music. The importance and value of such stories are untold, like a ripple in a pond made by a pebble it will keep having an affect into the future.

Linda *I feel that that your story's descriptions of creative process and student learning can help the reader to understand how you or your students were brought to reflect on their own dance-lives and the type of challenges that were faced. In relation to meeting challenges as you developed your pedagogy, I found* Bruner's *(1996) notion of dialogue, as associated with building mindful practice, to be integral to structuring the learning process. Bruner envisaged dialogue as producing "… cultures that operate as mutual communities of learners, involved jointly in solving problems with all contributing to the process of educating each other" (81). As a reflective teacher, your reflections can sometimes remain unseen. Can you describe any memorable moment perhaps in relation to a dialogue with students and building a community of mutual learning?*

Olivia *Dialogue and communication within a community is key to how I teach students to develop a work. Pacific culture is about the 'we' not the 'I'. I liken it to the saying that it takes a village to raise a child, so to does it take a village to create a work. A student of mine who was fakalaiti (transgender) was struggling with creating a work that had strong Tongan and Samoan foundations. She and her dancers felt vulnerable about the possibility of being told off or offending people from these cultures. I held a private showing of her work where I invited other emerging and established choreographers, who were from these cultures, including elders of high cultural esteem. The feedback they gave her was not only supportive and encouraging but the Tongan elder even stated that she could tell people how much he supported her work and to take courage as he loved her story and can see how important it was for people to experience it and to never doubt herself as she knows within her what is right. This is how I encourage all my student choreographers to work, by creating an environment of a community with the work, not only with the dancers, singers, musicians etc. but also with feedback and input from peers and established artists as well as cultural elders, all of whom will support, push, challenge, encourage and inspire the work to evolve with strong supported foundations.*

Linda *I am always struck by how your students' dance works look different from most other tertiary dance in New Zealand. Their dances highlight Polynesian ways of moving and being. They seem to have a signature trait in the lack of Western contemporary dance vocabulary that can be common in intercultural fusion dance. Can you give an example of the special movement characteristics or themes that produce a distinct Polynesian style and look?*

Olivia *I believe Pacific dance comes from within, the movements are taught usually within families, churches or cultural groups but the spirit of the movements that go hand in hand with the song and music lies within the person's ancestry and blood ties to it, and connects to that person's spirit. Others can copy the movements but often I have seen this come off plastic, touristy or just plain awkward. There have been very few occasions where I have felt a non-Pacific person has truly connected spiritually with Pacific dances, as it is the spirit that brings the dances to life. It is the va[1] that connects the person, their bodies and spirit, to others on the dance floor, to the music and song and to the audience. The va must be strengthened from a spiritual/cultural place first for Pacific choreographers, before layering Western theatre and dance forms/elements into it. It is where I believe Pacific choreographers need to understand the value, uniqueness and need for their Pacific movement and stories in today's dance world. Once they have those strong cultural foundations their stories spring more easily onto the floor and with their dancers. It is not about comparing how untrained they may come across in Ballet and other Western forms of dance, as they are only movement vocabularies to use as tools to express your*

---

[1] Conceptually in Tongan language *va* represents the spaces in which secular and spiritual relationships with self and others are connected. It is, however, a concept that is close to many Polynesian cultures (Anae 2007).

stories, it is about having belief in yourself and value that your stories need to be told, and what movement vocabulary you choose to express it with is completely up to you. The audience feedback, dance reviews and industry feedback to my graduate students choreographing in New Zealand today, e.g. Sesilia Pusiaki, Amanaki Prescott-Faletau, Leki Jackson-Bourke, Troy Tu'ua, Antonia Stehlin, Katerina Fatupaito, all show that it works very well, and that these choreographers stories are not only important but are moving, inspiring, unique, challenging and innovative to the people they come in contact with. The va has been strengthened and grown.

Linda *If you were asked to give one key reflection on sustaining Pacific dance and/ or song in your teaching from when you were developing your pedagogy what would it be?*

Olivia *I once had an argument with another dance teacher about if students needed more Western dance training and provision of more ballet in the programme. The belief was that only by learning Western forms of dance you got anywhere in the world, as a professional dancer. They did not understand that I was not interested in the whole focus being about creating professional Western-style dancers. My focus has always been about the students at hand, namely our Pacific students who were studying for a Diploma in Pacific Performing Arts and did not have many dance classes a week. Most come with no Western dance training or experience, or interest in it. My focus has always been to introduce how wonderful and amazing dance is, how important it is, and how valuable their stories are culturally, and also how connected they are to it through their identity and ancestry. This in turn develops a love and appreciation of the art, a connection to it, as well as producing some great, new, innovative choreographers and dancers. It is about the majority, the 'we', not the individual, the 'I', and I saw the majority of every class graduate with a love, appreciation and spiritual connection and understanding of dance. I see them at most Pacific dance shows in Auckland in the audiences cheering and loving the dance works.*

Now we see all the wonderful choreographers and dancers that have come out of PIPA and hopefully better understand why my focus was different, not a typical mono-cultural Western one, and that is partly why they are succeeding today as part of the dance world. If we do not value our Pacific selves, through our cultural movements, and the way we tell our stories in dance, then we are failing as dance teachers and will only end up producing the same type of students, with the same movements and the same techniques of story telling and choreographing as every other Western dance trained student in the world.

Linda *Thank you Olivia. Our conversation has confirmed for me why including your oral history in a written form is culturally appropriate and vital to the ethos of the book. In this way, your chapter is also set, aptly, at an intersection of Western and Pacific culture. So let's hear your story.*

2 Introduction

As Helu-Thaman (as cited in Airini et al. 2010) states:

> Because the cultural identity formation of most Oceanic people is relational rather than individualistic, it follows that the spaces or *vā* between and among persons, or between a person and his/her environment, together with the frameworks that determine such relationships, must be nurtured and protected. Understanding the significance of the notion of *vā* and educating for its continued nurturance and maintenance are central to any discussion about education for inter-cultural understanding in Oceania, if not globally. (p. 4)

A Pacific student is connected in so many complex ways to their ancestors, *aiga* (family), church, community, ethnicity and culture. They connect on a relational level to people and concepts, which have to be taken into account in their education. Thus, a term I like to use in teaching is 'cross-cultural education', taking the best of both worlds with a foundation in and reflection on our Pacific students growing up as Pacific Islanders in a Western country, New Zealand.

3 My Story

Coming from a large artistic family, with a Sāmoan family history of dance teachers and musicians, I don't think I fell far from the tree. I came to New Zealand from Sāmoa at the age of four not speaking English in 1979. Being a new migrant and having to learn a whole new language and culture impacted on my life and in later years the way I teach.

During this time growing up in Auckland my mother, of course, enrolled me into the first ballet class aged four saying: "Copy that woman in the front". This was the start of my long relationship with Western forms of dance from ballet to jazz, hip-hop and contemporary dance. I loved it all and spent most of my afterschool days, and holidays, at the now defunct *Limbs*[2] and *Auckland City Dance*[3] studios. Here my passion for dance movement and expression through the body developed in different styles and ways. I hid my insecurities of feeling 'different' and 'other' through an indifference in classes where my teachers didn't know how to reach me, to push my natural dance potential, as they couldn't relate to me and I still couldn't relate to that woman up in the front I had to copy.

I recall seeing and meeting my first brown dancers of Western dance forms in class when we got to watch the *Limbs* dance company in rehearsal, and I was transfixed by two stunning male dancers, Taane Mete and Taiaroa Royal, who are still stunning the world today. I could not take my eyes off of them as it was the first time

---

[2] New Zealand's first professional contemporary dance company 1978–1989.

[3] Auckland City Dance is now called City Dance Auckland, after it was taken over in 1994 by a charitable trust.

I had seen someone up there on the dance floor I could identify with and see that there was a place for people like me in Western dance.

I was taught Sāmoan dance by my stern and strong tempered grandmother, Italia Meleisea Taouma, who did not suffer fools easily and taught in the old ways with a tight rod in hand. She was one of the members and dance teachers of the now famous Western Sāmoa Teachers College,[4] who are famed for their dances, song recordings and performances, so she had a high level of expectation in Sāmoan dance of her grandchildren.

My father, Dr. Papalii Pita Taouma, was next as I toured schools and universities with him as a demonstrator and assistant, teaching people about Sāmoan dance. This was my first hand experience teaching 'other' ethnicities about my culture and art form. It was the start to a long career in teaching.

In 1996 I choreographed, danced, directed and produced my first full-length dance show entitled 'Words Unspoken', which was based around 'identity' and its many different forms that impacted on my life. It was a 'cross-cultural' contemporary work that fused my Samoan dance movements and culture with my *palagi* (Caucasian) side and contemporary dance. It was the first time I started to develop a way to express this feeling of being 'other' and who I am as a person and as an artist. A time where I felt the need to express myself through my identity as a cross-cultural person, experimenting with mixing my Sāmoan cultural movements with my Western dance training, creating cross-cultural movement. Reflecting reflexively on where I fitted into this Western world and how I identified myself there, I was a part of a new generation of Pacific Islanders growing up in New Zealand and experiencing such things as culture and language clashes.

4 Cross-Cultural Education, the Beginning

When I first started teaching dance, in 1997 as a trained teacher,[5] it was at a decile 1 Secondary school, Hillary College.[6] This school was in the heart of south Auckland, where a high proportion of Pacific Islanders live and where there was also a high rate of low achievement in school. I loved it. I recognised myself here, through the students. It was the first time for these students to 'study' dance and, as a lot of them had experience and ability, they found something they were not only good at and loved but also they could study and pass up to a high level at school. It also helped being Sāmoan and being able to relate to a lot of them culturally. It was again a time of experimenting and using different techniques but something that I always worked into the programme was recognising, acknowledging, respecting

---

[4] Western Samoa Teachers College is now part of the National University of Samoa, since 1997, and is referred to as the Faculty of Education.

[5] BEd., Massey University and Dip Tchg., Auckland College of Education.

[6] In New Zealand decile 1 schools are the 10 % of schools with the highest proportion of students from low socio-economic communities.

and supporting their cultures. *Fa'aloalo*, respect in Sāmoan, was always the number one rule. This cultural connection and reflection helped create a sense of 'family' and 'safety' in class. This is what I would call *teu le va*. Dr. Melanie Anae (2007) explains that *Va*—or *vā, va'a, vaha*—can be loosely translated as a spatial way of conceiving the secular and spiritual dimensions of relationships and relational order, that facilitates both personal and collective well-being, and *teu le va* as the valuing, nurturing and looking after these relationships to achieve optimal outcomes for all stakeholders.

Another major part of successfully teaching cross-cultural dance at the school, which is a part of Pacific socialisation, was laughter and fun. You can go anywhere in the world and as soon as you find a group of Pacific people hanging out you will often hear loud raucous laughter. This intermixing of cultures within the teaching environment encouraged the students to feel recognised, valued and a part of the education culture, the class became another 'home'.

The main goal of mine in dance was not to develop professional dancers, even though a few of them did become this, but was to create robust, holistic, culturally cognisant students. Learning was connected to fun experiences where the students would see and experience dance as a tool to express who they are and what they want to say and it aimed to develop a sense of appreciation for, knowledge about and love of dance for the rest of their lives.

Dance, especially popular social Western dance forms, were a characteristic of these students' social lives and also a big part of their culture that you performed on special cultural occasions e.g. school socials, church fundraisers, twenty-firsts, weddings. You didn't lie on the floor and slither across it like a snake or 'contract' and 'release'[7] your body into different shapes as dancers do in modern dance. These new ways of moving were always met with resistance and apprehension by my students. For them modern, creative or theatre dance felt awkward, different, foreign and strange. They felt 'out of place', an 'other' and self-conscious about looking at, feeling and being aware of their bodies in this new light as their identity and culture was displaced.

One of my biggest achievements at this school was having such a high success rate of students achieving, and student demand for the classes that the school turned the programme into a performing arts academy, making it into a major programme of the school. My reflection on milestones such as when the majority of the school rugby first 15 team chose to take my dance classes as a subject because they loved it, became pivotal in developing my pedagogy. A few students went further and studied dance at tertiary level, two going on to dance for New Zealand's contemporary dance company *Black Grace*.

After 6 years there I decided I needed a change and travelled. This opened my eyes to what was out there in dance, in choreography, but also more importantly culturally. I watched the Alvin Ailey dance company live in a theatre in Harlem and had a new cultural experience which made their show and movements that much deeper and moving. From New York, to Chicago, to New Orleans to Los Angeles, to

---

[7] Martha Graham technique.

London and Amsterdam dance changed my view of the world and also my cultural understanding of what dance can be to the person performing it and also to the audience.

5 Cross-Cultural Education in Samoa

The next stop was Sāmoa. After travelling through other people's cultures I wanted to then live in my birth home Sāmoa; to breathe it for a while. Dance in Sāmoa is an integral part of life and cultural practice not only in the villages but also at school, in the nation's celebrations, any social function and for any formal occasion. It is such an integral part of life it has the honour of being the finale of any event and formalities, called the *Taualuga*. When this dance occurs it indicates to everyone present that it is the end of that function. Western dance forms were not taught and I found a handful of people had experienced being taught modern dance a long time ago through different visiting people. There is no theatre as such in Sāmoa or dance companies, just a few young hip-hop dance crews who enter different competitions when they come up. At that time there was no study of dance as a subject in schools or as part of any curriculum. This changed and I was one of the advisers for the new Sāmoa Secondary Schools Performing Arts Curriculum[8] and also co-writer for the teachers' guides.

In my teaching I wove basic Western dance exercises, themes, and topics with Sāmoan cultural themes and movements such as the *se'e* (Sāmoan movement of the feet) and sāsa movements (a sitting dance where hand/arm actions strike out and express everyday activities and life in a Sāmoan village). I taught trainee secondary and primary school teachers at the National University of Sāmoa. Here trainee teachers learnt to have fun while moving their bodies in very different ways. They soon realised they could not only perform these movements, but they could explore movement and their traditional actions. They became more confident in themselves and less apprehensive, recognising that they not only enjoyed it but that their students would love to experience this. They loved that I was Sāmoan and could talk to them, even in my limited Sāmoan, and understand them when they spoke in Sāmoan but also understand their culture and their lives to a much deeper extent than other foreign teachers there. They felt understood, respected and supported and they always knew it would also be fun. This time, I observed how creating experiences in which students could develop a sense of appreciation and love for dance is an approach that may not produce necessarily excellent dancers but it is important in terms of advocacy for including dance in education, especially in school classrooms.

---

[8] Sāmoan Ministry of Education, Sports and Culture. (2004). *Performing Arts: Sāmoa Secondary School Curriculum.* Auckland: Auckland Uni Services.

6   Shaping My Pedagogy: Reflections on Constructing Identity – Past, Present and Future

In 2007 I moved back to New Zealand, now with a husband and child, and started as the Head of Dance at the Pacific Institute of Performing Arts (PIPA), a new tertiary course in Auckland that offered a Diploma in Performing Arts (Pacific). Here students learnt Pacific Studies and Pacific Performing Arts as well as Western forms of acting and dance. It was the first time I had come across a tertiary institute directly focused on Pacific achievement and cross-cultural development taught in the performing arts.

In 2009 I became the Head of Pacific Studies as well as Dance. This is where I started to really build and shape my personal pedagogy into a cross-cultural educational, holistic programme and environment for students. The student was not seen as just another number or a blanket 'student' label, where everyone is treated 'the same'. Instead I actively tried to build a culture of *va*, developing the students' senses of belonging, acknowledging, understanding, community, self belief, respect, identity, appreciation and encouraging experience of awareness and love as individuals, as a group and cross-culturally. I created a curriculum and planned learning experiences in a 2 year programme for the students across their subjects that would support these underlying values, and help create a 'family' environment of acceptance, respect and support for cultural roots.

A group of students discussed the educational culture I had created in my classes. Sesilia Pusiaki described it as "family orientated – a home away from home. Classmates are brothers and sisters. When one person falls the whole group falls". Critchley explained how he felt valued, and Maika described how he felt in touch with his ancestors, seeing the then and now (Ashley 2013a, b, p. 17).

Students with gender identity struggles thrived in this environment as they found acceptance, self-value, respect and a sense of being part of a family that loved and supported them for who they are and not what they were born with. They often shone as dancers and choreographers. A great example of this was a group of PIPA Lesbian, Gay, Bisexual, Trans and Queer (LGBTQ[9]), graduates who formed the dance group *Fine Fatale*. They have been creating innovative, cutting-edge cross-cultural works in Auckland since 2010, and are a shining success that a lot of younger LGBTQ performers look up to.

It became very clear after teaching here for a while, that unlike the students I had previously taught the majority of these students struggled with their cultural identity. It became imperative to me that the students start their journey at this school learning about themselves and their identity before they started learning about other people's stories. The first topic became 'identity'. Through their genealogy, students would learn about themselves, their ancestry and their family stories. This helped shape their perception and understanding of self, growing cultural roots

[9] A community of people whose sexual or gender identities can create shared political and social concerns. Defining LGBTQ – Liberate Yourself www.liberateyourself.co.uk/lgbtq/what-is-lgbtq/

to help develop strong foundations from which to create and explore. The students also learnt about each other on a very personal, deeper level, which helped create more connection, understanding, appreciation and respect for each other and their cultures: the *va* was strengthened. It was cathartic as many students here would state they felt 'plastic' and 'lost' about their Māori or Pacific culture before undertaking this project. There was a disconnection which they felt, and this project helped start a reconnection to not only their cultures but also their families and peers; a lot of them had family issues and social problems. An example of this was where a young very thin and under fed, shy, unconfident unkempt boy started the year stating he didn't know anything about his Māori side and that it was 'plastic'. By the end of his second year he was standing tall, proud, and confident performing a beautiful dance work wearing a stunning *Korowai*,[10] expressing his Māori cultural heritage and identity. Importantly, immersing the students in their own culture and learning of other Pacific cultures, gave the students a sense of pride, identity and place in the world.

Through lessons by Pacific elders, historians, writers, artists and teachers, these cultural seeds were fed from deeper roots. One elder I always brought in was my father, who taught me and gave me the confidence and approval to explore. He explained quite simply that Samoan *siva* (dance) has evolved like every other dance form over time, and that when you use the word 'traditional' it is only a particular point of time you are choosing to slice from its history, as before that time the dance form had many variations and will continue to do so through its relationship with people, time and place.

Having Pacific elders or Pacific specialists come in and teach our students, encouraged and gave students belief in their own voices and work, that they are valued and what they want to say is important. Such visits helped the students find themselves artistically and have the confidence to explore and experiment in their cultural foundations. When it was time for the students to explore their own creativity and voices to express what they wanted outside of the safety and confines of school many looked to their cultural roots and experiences to develop exciting, innovative and culturally layered works. Examples of this can be seen through the work of graduates such as Sesilia Pusiaki, Troy Tu'ua, Leki Jackson Bourke, Katerina Fatupaito and Antonia Stehlin to name but a few.[11]

In dance I encouraged them to find and express their identity, especially in choreography. Beginning with exercises that were stripped back to movement at its simplest. One of their favourites was walk-the-catwalk, whereby you have to walk the length of the room and back with the attitude and expression of your culture and your life, show us who you are just by walking. Another involved eyes closed, lying on the floor, thinking about what the music or sounds make you feel and allowing

---

[10] Māori feather cloaks. Korowai are highly prized of all traditional Māori garments and are regarded as family and personal heirlooms.

[11] Pusiaki's Tongan traditional dance work can be found online at https://www.youtube.com/ watch?v=dSii2Ktpv4o. Extracts from other dances can be viewed online: https://www.youtube. com/watch?v=56HODYalDmQ https://www.youtube.com/watch?v=O1V5k1GXYAg

the body to naturally move to the sounds. These gave students shared experiences of awkwardness, apprehension, shyness and fear, due to being completely physically aware of yourself and your feelings in a raw state. The more exercises of self-discovery through movement the more they trusted, discussed, shared and laughed, and saw and developed real connections and relationships, again the *va* was strengthened.

In developing a sense of safety, trust and community through shared experiences of 'awkwardness', they also learnt to 'let go' of any defense walls in class, and when they got into learning new and different techniques the more they would participate openly. The more they participated and practiced, the more these new movements became part of their bodies' dance vocabulary that they could execute well and perform in confidence. Combining this with an equal dose of cultural satire, respect and much laughter created an environment where the students saw a way they could express themselves through exploration of not only Western movement but also their own cultural dances. Cross-cultural dance was new, exciting and unique to each of them, it allowed them the freedom to just be.

There were always a few students who shied away from dance and were not confident enough in their bodies to fully open up. One of my biggest hurdles with teaching Pacific Island students was to create an environment whereby everyone felt comfortable to dance no matter your weight or size, especially for the girls. Young girls are age appropriately self conscious, throw into that Pacific Island culture of religious humility and modesty and you will see why contemporary dance could have some barriers.

After lessons of teaching them correct alignment, softening through the ground, landing through the feet into the ground, contracting and release and falling techniques, the dance students soon realised, especially in the floor work, that having some natural cushioning really helped. Once you have a bigger person in the class landing softer than half the class just through technique you have the whole class engaged. I once brought back one student who was overweight but he could dance beautifully, with flowing floor work and leaps which landed so softly, demonstrating that weight and size is not a barrier and that in fact in some cases can be your strength. Interestingly, a few of these students went on to develop their dance-selves through acting jobs where they were required to move and dance. I meet up with them still today and they often laugh about those shy days and running away from themselves, but now see the importance of it all and appreciate everything they were taught.

Cross-cultural fusion in dance however, can cause offense for some traditional gatekeepers, which is why having cultural advisors is important. Therefore, having visits from established Pacific choreographers, such as myself, Charlene Tedrow, Neil Ieremia and Lemi Ponifasio, to act as role models and mentors inspired the emerging creatives, showing them a future pathway for themselves in this industry and world. For instance, PIPA graduate Amanaki Prescott-Faletau choreographs work so unique and boundary-less that she is forging quite a career already in Auckland. She pushes the boundaries not only in her movement vocabulary and stories, but she also creates dance for non-theatre spaces like the botanical gardens, galleries and for digital art works and television. Throughout her choreographic work she retains her cultural roots and connects to them seamlessly. She has experienced first hand the real value in the industry through her cross-cultural dance works. An example of this can be understood better through this review of choreography with her dance group *Fine Fatale*:

> The complex and furious co-ordination of measured arm gestures and hip sways, the affirmative attack in their movement, and the predatory sassy catwalk sashays smashed quite a few conventional boundaries. In fact the combination of siva and Voguing, and whatever else is on fire in this clash of tradition, masculine, feminine, past, now and future brings a brave new world of dancing in Polynesian Vogue. (Ashley 2013b)

Although this is fusion dance what this review highlights is how characteristic Polynesian movement vocabulary such as hip sways and articulate arm gestures feature predominantly in the overall look of the performance. Whereas, Western vocabulary dominates in some contemporary indigenous dance. I remember New Zealand choreographer, Douglas Wright visiting PIPA in 2012 and saying to the students: "In the Western world they don't want to see my work, they see that everyday over there, they want to see all of your work because it is different, unique and something they have most probably never heard of or seen before". This helped students see value in their stories and creative work outside their micro-worlds.

7 Dance and Music in Pacific Cultures

A part of my story that would be helpful for the reader is to outline two key ways in which dance and music function in Pacific culture, because it was crucial to include them within my pedagogy.

First, Pacific ownership of traditional songs and dances are connected to the person, their families, villages and country. There are very different rules for each country let alone composer, but there is some leniency granted in rearranging Samoan songs if the recording information states the name of the original composer. Tonga and Niue is a very different matter, so learning your history of these Pacific songs, who composed them and why, what do you need to do to gain culturally appropriate permission to use them, is very important.

Cultural appropriation, acknowledgement and intellectual property are other matters students had to learn a lot about when dealing with Pacific cultural dance and song. Learning about their own cultures was not without its surprises for the students, and this became clear in a specific incident when a television crew wanted to film our students singing a Pacific song. The students had been taught many songs from different Pacific Islands but had decided to sing one they loved for television, which one of them who was not the ethnicity of that Pacific song had recomposed into a funky pop version. The students concerned didn't have a staff member guiding them or present during this filming. When the episode went to air the students were proud and excited which soon turned to sad and apologetic. The

Pacific family who had composed the original song complained to the television programme about the terrible composition of their song that was sung and filmed without their permission and which they found culturally offensive. This brought up great issues for the students to not only learn from but to discuss and understand so that this mistake would not be repeated.

Young people assume that many of our Pacific songs are just out there for anyone to do what they want, but in fact in some cases they are written, composed and published by people/families in the Pacific Islands and in Western countries today. Just like the Australia Performing Rights Association[12] in New Zealand copyright music, Pacific communities have the Pacific grapevine where anything on television, on the internet or in the paper gets across very fast to the people who actually own the song, more so if it is shown in the same country they live in. In this instance, the students', PIPA's and the programme's apologies, along with withdrawal of the song on its online episodes, was enough to appease the family and a great lesson learnt for all of our students.

Second, a Pacific approach to the relationship between dance and music can be found in the word *faiva*. I use *faiva* to describe the relationship between song, music and dance in Pacific cultures. It is Tongan and represents the interweaving of the poet (song composer), music and dance through more than just performance it also is a cultural reinforcement of Tongan values (Shumway 1977).

Students at PIPA and emerging Pacific performers in dance use *faiva* in the form that the song, music and dance are integral to each other and are performed together. A great example of a contemporary version of this is Sesilia Pusiaki's (PIPA graduate 2010) dance-theatre work *Sei 'O Fafine* in which every dance scene is supported by three on-stage singers who come in and out of the show like a Greek chorus. Sesilia uses Western theatre techniques interchangeably with traditional Tongan *faiva*. The songs are picked specifically because of their lyrics and musical compositions; dialogue at times is poetic prose, all to support the scenes taking place through dance movement in the show. This ground breaking Tongan contemporary dance-theatre work is a great example of an artist who has very deep cultural roots and cultural support – she knows who she is. So when she tells her stories she can interchangeably move between both her Tongan and Western worlds, as well as interweave these worlds around each other on stage without causing controversy or cultural offense.

What is so surprising to many is the fact that Sesilia sees this work as Tongan first and as a contemporary Western work, second. Sesilia pointed out that her work is first and foremost grounded in Pacific traditions, but it is also "about you and the work you want to create" (Ashley 2013a, p. 17). Because of the cultural roots Sesilia has found supportive roots from which to create and explore, especially when she was breaking new ground and creating history in the Western theatre space through Tongan cultural foundations. This work has been developed over 4 years, with eight showings, and in all that time there has not been one complaint or cultural offense

---

[12] Australia Performing Rights Association license organisations to play, perform, copy, record or make available their members' music, and they distribute the royalties to their members.

taken of the cross-cultural works use of Tongan cultural song, music and dance (*faiva*).

Leki Jackson Bourke (PIPA graduate 2012) completed his first choreographic work through the annual Pacific Dance Choreographic Lab event in Auckland.[13] He based his work around firstly Niuean song, music and dance through his experiences and feelings of and about Niue and certain parts of Niue's history. It is a cross-cultural contemporary dance work that interweaves two worlds, Niuean dance and Western contemporary dance. This is done smoothly through Leki's Pacific foundations in Niuean, Samoan and Tongan as well as contemporary dance and choreographic training at PIPA. Explaining how his work with song, dance and music at cross cultural intersections Leki Jackson Bourke described how he had been helped to develop his own Pacific identity in the context of Aotearoa and that in "finding my foundation and my cultural heritage I also think about the people who came before me... honouring their journeys and stories", (Ashley 2013a, p. 17). His work will continue to develop, as will more emerging Pacific contemporary dance works, as artists look to choreographing more works that cross over and reflect on their two worlds of being Urbanesians.[14]

Dance works, such as those made by Pusiaki and Jackson Bourke use *faiva* and *va* successfully. In fact both *faiva* and *va* are so integral in Pacific dance works that often people do not even know they are doing it. I find when I envision dance works, or workshop a work, it comes naturally and is something I find always surprising when others analytically dissect it out in a point or reference. Today I see many young emerging Pacific choreographers writing poetry and songs, performing spoken word and combining it into their dance works thinking they are being innovative by using different inter-art forms. In fact they are following an innate sense of *faiva* and *va*, that lies within their cultural-self, that they may have been brought up with, it is in their blood and ancestry and surfaces through their artistic work and expression.

7.1 *From the Cultural Roots Will Grow the Tree*

In developing my pedagogy I have sometimes reflected on internationally recognised Sāmoan author Albert Wendt's statement from an online interview in 2012 with Maryanne Pale[15]:

> We need to write, paint, sculpt, weave, dance, sing and think ourselves into existence. For too long other people have done it for us – and they've usually stereotyped us, or created versions of us that embody their own hang-ups and beliefs and prejudices about us. So we have to write our own stories!

---

[13] Pacific Dance Choreographic Lab 2014 http://www.pacificdance.co.nz/choreolab_2015.php

[14] Urbanesia-Urban meaning city and in the Greek language *nesia* means island, reflecting the larger number of Pacific children growing up in western cities.

[15] http://creativetalanoa.com/2012/10/15/a-pacific-living-legend-professor-albert-wendt/

Immersing my students in this ethos has helped them see they have not only value and a place creatively in this world, but that there is a need out there for more Pacific creators to tell their stories.

I also align with Thelma Perso (2012) when looking at the students we teach and their cultures, we must look within and without for a deeper understanding. We must then act on this knowledge, turning our understanding into better subjects, programmes and curricula. I believe cultural roots that are acknowledged, respected, shared and experienced in a class will create a strong teaching environment whereby students will feel recognised, valued, supported and happy in their learning. This underpinning belief has helped create more success in dance for my Pacific students. Exploring cultures and learning more Pacific dance, music and history will create stronger Pacific contemporary choreographers and artists who will be able to draw not only on their Pacific cultural roots but also Western forms of dance, theatre and technique. This is an exciting time to see this being developed right now in New Zealand, telling me it is a new wave that will keep on growing and that currently has a real presence in the world of dance but has an even bigger future ahead. In the end it is up to the students to pick up the challenge to create and I am now seeing the fruit of that through graduates who are continuing to explore and push the boundaries culturally and successfully. From their strong cultural roots these Pacific artists are growing into even stronger trees, branching out into the global world of today.

References

Airini, A. M., Mila-Schaaf, K., Coxon, E., Mara, D., & Sanga, K. (2010). *TEU LE VA – Relationships across research and policy in Pasifika education. A collective approach to knowledge generation & policy development for action towards Pasifika education success.* Wellington: Ministry of Education, New Zealand.

Anae, M. (2007, November). *Teu le va: Research that could make a difference to Pasifika schooling in New Zealand.* Paper commissioned by the Ministry of Education and presented at the joint NZARE/Ministry of Education symposium, Wellington.

Ashley, L. (2013a). Diversity is celebrated here. *DANZ Quarterly, 32,* 16–17.

Ashley, L. (2013b, October 19). *Brave new worlds, future visions, spirits let loose.* [Review of Pacific Dance Triple bill, Tempo Dance Festival]. http://www.theatreview.org.nz/reviews/review.php?id=6433

Bruner, J. S. (1987). Life as narrative. *Social Research, 54,* 11–32.

Bruner, J. S. (1996). *The culture of education.* Cambridge, MA: Harvard University Press.

Goodson, I. (2012). Investigating narrativity. In I. Goodson, A. M. Loveless, & D. Stephens (Eds.), *Explorations in narrative research* (pp. 1–10). Rotterdam: Sense Publishers.

Pale, M. (2012). *A Pacific living legend-Professor Albert Wendt,* Creative Talanoa. http://creativetalanoa.com/2012/10/15/a-pacific-living-legend-professor-albert-wendt/

Perso, T. (2012). *Cultural responsiveness and school education, with particular focus on Australia's First Peoples: A review & synthesis of the literature.* Menzies School of Health Research, Centre for Child Development and Education, Darwin Northern Territory.

Shumway, E. B. (1977). *Ko E Fakalngilngi: The eulogistic function of the Tongan poet.* Laie Hawaii: The Brigham Young University, Hawaii Campus.

Olivia Taouma Olivia Taouma   founder and Director of LIMA Productions in 2009 (a non-profit organisation for emerging Pacific Performing Artists), has been a freelance Dancer/Choreographer/Producer/Teacher in New Zealand and Samoa for many years. In Samoa she co-wrote the Secondary schools Performing Arts Curriculum, and wrote and taught the Diploma and Bachelor papers in Performing Arts at the University of Samoa. She moved back to Auckland in 2008 and took up the position of Head of Dance at The Pacific Institute of Performing Arts (PIPA), choreographing many of PIPA's plays, productions and dance shows up to 2012, and also choreographed for the highly acclaimed play 'Passage', for Four Afloat Productions in conjunction with The Edge (2010).

Musicultural Identity and Intersecting Geographic Contexts in Oceania

Trevor Thwaites

Abstract In discussing the impact of intersecting geographical contexts in Oceania, I will consider the phenomena of cultural and subcultural difference in music through local, national and globalised contexts. I will examine these phenomena at the points where they intersect, what we might call borderlands—regarded as a 'third space' (Bhabha H, The location of culture. Routledge, London, 1994)—where hybrid identities can be formed that shape meaning and learning in culturally inclusive ways. In this essay I propose that musical identity allows for cultural and artistic perspectives to be revealed across the broad palette of genres in music education. In the New Zealand context I use Māori popular music as a specific example. I use the term *musiculture* in an attempt to break down the tensions between function, status, and taste in order to reveal commonalities between musical forms and new ways of hearing and enacting music. Blacking (How musical is man? University of Washington Press, Seattle, 1973) reminds us that "in any society, cultural behaviour is learned" (p. 103). I suggest that when culture is framed within a geographical context, it takes on different perspectives within the geographical space and in music education it becomes a pattern of interconnected musicultural traits.

Keywords Musiculture • Cultural geography • Music education • Musical identity

1 Introduction

Music might be regarded as a form of culture because it shapes how we see and hear our world and acts as a kind of filter through which we interpret our daily experiences. The effect of music shapes the way in which our perceptions of the musical 'real' are a product of our negotiated and socially created meaning. The styles of music we might engage with can also influence the clothes we wear, the food we eat and even the way we speak: think of punk, gothic, hip hop, reggae, country,

T. Thwaites (✉)
Faculty of Education and Social Work, University of Auckland, Auckland, New Zealand
e-mail: t.thwaites@auckland.ac.nz

© Springer International Publishing Switzerland 2016
L. Ashley, D. Lines (eds.), *Intersecting Cultures in Music and Dance Education*, Landscapes: the Arts, Aesthetics, and Education 19,
DOI 10.1007/978-3-319-28989-2_15

bebop (jazz), to name only a few. These music-based cultural habits and artistic responses have sometimes been categorised as subcultures.

I propose the term *musiculture* in an attempt to by-pass the clumsy integration of terms such as *subcultures* and *music-based cultures*. Butts (2007) has also used this term and with the same intended meaning. I endorse Butts' definition of musiculture as an "affiliation with a subculture based on a musical genre" (2007, abstract), adding to her definition *subcultures and cultures which have developed into robust communities throughout the world*. I use the term musiculture in the sense of an affiliation with the broader musical forms or styles, such as art music or popular music. What the term musiculture does is to regard all musicultures as equal, and it also "places music and culture on an equal footing" (2007, p. 3). These musical cultures, whether ancient or modern, are not simply unchanging traditions which have been inherited wholesale from the past; each is a dynamic form that has the capacity to absorb change if its members allow it to. Importantly, a musiculture is not necessarily linked to the age of its members. Finnegan's significant 1989 study showed the wide generational age range of individuals participating in music subcultures (and those of rock musicians in particular).

Culture gives sense to the world and offers a vision while undertaking the organisation of thought processes. Any culture is a system of representation, and these representations find their expressions in acts and discourses. Cultures contain cultural traits or cultural elements to ground their myths and ideologies and, importantly, cultures also need to believe in themselves and shape cultural identities. They need a place or space in which to dwell. The music classroom need not favour just one musiculture. The classroom can accept a type of cultural mosaic inside its walls and perhaps even establish a metaculture of music in its programmes, one which is encompassing and empowering and where fertile cross-breeding can be allowed to generate new musical forms.

There is no one kind of art music, just as there is no one kind of pop or rock music. There are stylistic variations that might come from encounters with other cultures, religions, genders, or other forms of music, and all can have an impact in education. One solution for music education that not only considers society and music in history, but also culture and music in geography, draws upon the concept of cultural geography—a human geography that explores human differences and spatial sensibility while taking into account the emotional dimension.

We live in the world and our practical relation to space requires an explanation of the self and practical understanding. To advance this argument I draw on the theory of culture and space framed by the French geographer Joël Bonnemaison in his study of Melanesian cultures (2005). I will apply his theory of cultural geography to music and music education in New Zealand.

2   Musiculture and Cultural Geography

A cultural system is different from a social system in the sense that it is more expansive. Bonnemaison reminds us that "cultures create the diversity of the world, thereby making it more interesting. At one level differences separate; at another they are a gathering force" (2005, p. 58). The space the culture occupies as cultural space differs from one's subjective experience or perception of space, but when *affective space* and *space as experienced* coincide, the resultant cultural space becomes a collective history (p. 77). Rather than being an enclosed space, we should see cultural musical space as musicultural elements, material or non-material, which can be isolated and, therefore, investigated. Gestural traits, performance practices, and the particular ways in which a musical instrument is used are all musicultural traits that can be studied in terms of their originality and their diffusion from a specific source. To fit with this definition there must be an audible and visible musicultural element to the trait.

In his research into what he calls "a new cultural geography", Bonnemaison outlines his key terms (2005, pp. xvi–xvii), some of which provide us with a methodology for an examination of cultural spaces in music: *islandness, reticulated space, iconology, geosymbol, ante-world* and *networked society* (see Table 1). I see this construct as being especially useful for music teachers working across various fields and forms of music as they endeavour to treat each style equitably and on its own merits. It helps us get to the essence of a musical style and to delve more deeply into its roots, what we might perceive as a founding place.

The value put on a founding place creates a frame or boundary, rather like an island or region, within which a musiculture operates. Metaphorically, *islandness* narrows down our focus to the spatial perceptions involved in the relating of land to sea that comes from living on an island, or perhaps as musicians working in a specific style, genre or context. Both a founding place and islandness require some form of horizon. This horizon frames our perspectives and sense of place. Bonnemaison notes that Melanesian cultures tend to look inland from the shores of their islands, while Polynesians tend to look outwards over the sea, framing how each group sees the world.

An island always represents a separateness, a limit, a shore or border of anxiety, even though joined by the sea and under the sea with other islands. Once on land in our musical territory one's link to the great movement of music in time is severed. What remains is space, "narrow, closed and bordered … It becomes the one and only value" (Bonnemaison 2005, p. 84). This suggests that it is the spatial sensibilities of different groups that are at the root of their cultural differences and that a particular musical space becomes a founding space, whether that be Liverpool, Vienna, Weimar, New Orleans or the Bronx. A *founding place* differs from a *central place*. While the central place makes the rest of the structure converge towards itself, the founding place pushes out the forces that rise up within its core, replicating itself in similar places. But instead of creating a periphery, the founding place carries the power of the musiculture, or a fragment of it, farther away, "in chain-like fashion" (ibid, p. 85); it initiates distribution.

The cultural space termed *reticulated space* acknowledges its origins, which could be a town or city, a country or region, a belief or function. Reticulated space is a network of spatial links that has no evident centre or periphery and where each group is the equal complement to the group before or after it on the road. Power is gained through competitive distribution and relations of exchange as the flow of information and goods. "It is not structured by a centre but by a founding place with

Table 1 Summary of key musiculture concepts

Islandness	Origins	Where did the unique qualities of a musiculture originate and/or develop? Generally inward looking, with protected borders, and contained in a central place
Reticulated space	Communicative distribution	How is the music distributed? Takes the values of the musiculture and forms networks out from its origins (founding place) to distribute its musicultural values
Iconology	Appearances and representations	How is the music recognised and how does it appear? The symbols, musical beliefs and identity of a musiculture. Iconology presents the vision of a musiculture through cultural meanings and musical standpoints, including musical elements, features and other representations
Geosymbols	Ecology of the style	External shaping influences, contemporary parallel influences, and performance contexts. What style came before? How does the music emerge in different settings? Its manifestations. Ecology as the relationship between the music and its environment. Geosymbols link the musicultural space to the belief system and show how musicultural values and beliefs shape the ways of being of a musiculture
Ante-world	Links to other musical styles	Includes what came before musically, either from within the musiculture or from other musicultures, perhaps even running parallel to the musiculture. It is open to ideas that might be oppositional, different, or adjacent to its own. It encompasses both historical and contemporary influences and residual musicultures
Networked space	Hybrid musical unions (milieu culture)	New concepts that help shape new forms of musiculture. Makes the links within and between musicultures, is open to change, perhaps forming a 'third musical space' between two musicultures
Metaculture	Overarching aspects of style and genre	Can be likened to the generic culture of music beyond specific musicultural systems—for example, rock, orchestral, jazz—but which incorporates all available musicultural possibilities

several interrelated focal points … a spatial differentiation. Culture cannot live outside its space" (Bonnemaison 2005, p. 68), and without a reticulated space a musiculture would lose most of its value. Here the founding place still has value, but is no longer constrained as in islandness; it seeks to expand its borders. A musicultural reticulated space represents an open area where the glory and the power of great musicians is set in motion.

Musical representation, vision, and values fix identity, produce icons, and define a specific musiculture. *Iconology* refers to the cultural meanings invested in specific features of the musical landscape. Icons carry a particular meaning which they bestow on the places and features and provide roots for a people. They seek to make intelligent the musical world as a whole. They offer an image of the musical world as much as an image of the individual self in the musical world. They represent a particular standpoint and vision. This means that both teacher and student are associated with personal factors and beliefs, myths, and life history. Iconology is the cultural meanings and musical standpoints that make a collective vision intelligible. Once we have established the musical territory we are to explore, we need to examine the musical landscape, its shapes and forms, and how this might inform the specific musical environment. We might then require knowledge of a territory's history, its significant musical leaders, music works, and performance practices—the symbolic representations and technologies that shape the cultural identity of those who dwell within its boundaries.

The things that tie the beliefs, values, and symbolic representations of a specific musiculture to a particular spatial location, which could be musical, categorical, or physical, Bonnemaison calls *geosymbols*. A *geosymbol* is the spatial indicator. It is the specific association between a particular spatial location and a cultural or subcultural belief system. It is a sign in a space that mirrors and shapes identity. *Geosymbolism* is the symbolic structure of a geographical setting—its signification. Human beings inscribe and illustrate their values in the musical landscape.

Geosymbols might indicate the boundaries of a musical territory, but they also animate it and give it meaning; they express a common set of values. As such, geosymbols both produce and construct musical territories. Territories are powerful markers within which symbols become visible. These spatial symbols, or geosymbols, include symbolic places that are meaningful signifiers—Nashville, Detroit, Vienna, Jamaica, Woodstock, or specific recording studios (Abbey Road, Muscle Shoals, Capital Studios, Sun Records) for example; these are identity-bearing symbols. Musicultural identity is the marrying of a musical style and a territory. The territory fills a number of musical, geographical, social, and political functions that are in keeping with the universe of memory, representations, and values.

Musicultures establish territories that embrace beliefs, symbols, and signs and these might be involved in establishing musical heroes or perhaps challenging an entrenched status quo. *Ante-world* signifies either a previous social world, a current rival, or an oppositional world. Ante-world regards the concept of territories, not as political regions but as more abstract places, perhaps even as a frame. These territories contain the myths and celebrities of their specific musical type, as well as the institutions, corporations, and followers that support them. No musical identity exists without a space that sustains it, or without a territory marked by symbolic representations which give strength to the specific belief system of that identity. It is important to remind ourselves that territories usually embrace territorialism, implying the potential desire to defend musical beliefs and values. We might see the musiculture as a kind of "dynastic realm" which organises its world and ensures sustainability (Anderson 1991, p. 19). The stars have names that resound across the realm of the musiculture, such as Elvis, Hendrix, Santana, Zappa, Prince, Bird, and Beethoven. Bonnemaison speaks of an *ante-world*, or anti-world, that always revolves underneath the accepted world system, a sort of world in reverse (2005, p. 115), which is defined and perceived in various ways. It is both an ante-world, in the sense of an earlier, anterior world, and an anti-world, in the sense of a rival or opposite world.

Networks make links to the various musical expressions and structures within the reticulated space. *Networked society* refers to a society bonded through musical nodes, tied together in a spatial network. Here the notion of islands and island-hopping springs to mind. Each musicultural island might contain its own forms of natural elements, but the essence of music *as* music is the ocean on which the peda-gogical canoe navigates the in-between spaces in order to connect and allow fertile cross-breeding. Musical forms of expression are not frozen in time, and an essen-tialist view of a musiculture is avoided by the incorporation of the notion of net-worked societies. In this way the music classroom becomes a space of interdependent links within a broader musical system that spreads well beyond the limits of the curriculum. It operates by consensus. The focus at any one time might be on a spe-cific category of music, but a series of road-like links enables both teachers and students to jump from one link to the next and even to change routes.

Networked space is the network that acknowledges the presence of interdepen-dent links within a music curriculum and that allow us to make connections between styles and genres, perhaps through harmonies, scales, forms, technologies, etc. We can regard our classroom as an open area where we can explore, examine, and test each style or genre to ascertain its specific musical character, not unlike so-called network societies. For Webb (2007), "time and space may well be informed and temporally affected by distant sounds and voices, networks and space-time connec-tions that are way beyond the local, but the local is the hub of experience, percep-tions and articulation of the musical world" (p. 260).

Cultural representations in music become more vivid and meaningful when they are embodied in specific spaces by the music educator. Cultural space is a geosym-bolic space "laden with emotions and meanings: in its strongest expression it becomes a sanctuary-like territory, that is to say, a space of communion with an ensemble of signs and values" (Bonnemaison 2005, p. 47). In their discussion on the economies of signs and space, Lash and Urry (1994) suggest contemporary cultural spaces are spheres which operate in the contemporary cultural industries, such as systems of production, cultural artefacts, and communication structures, and these become the reality of everyday life, a reality that fans help to build. As members of various musicultures, our students need a territory, a space that allows some founda-tion to its geosymbols and solidifies the space-as-experienced which the students are familiar with. For the teacher, the space unfolds along successive levels of per-ception, musical values, and human consciousness. A musical space allows for self-identification based on musical feelings and vision. The space can be a place for ritual, or a resonance, even. For the student, territory is a political stake, and its affective and symbolic forces become the nexus of power; its landscape is identified as a personal environment and as a resource and an identity.

This equitable geographic approach leads us to regard musicultures "as a con-stant process of becoming as a result of discovery, invention, innovation, evolution and diffusion" (Bonnemaison 2005, p. xviii). Cultures require systems to make them comprehensible, so that the spaces in which they operate have horizons as well as buttresses. We might also consider the notion of indigenous and perhaps apply it to the authentic musician in a particular musical culture, suggesting spaces where the educated, bilingual (in a musical sense), or multilingual musician from outside the territory might enter and either colonise or appropriate the music, perhaps even inscribing on it the horizon of a new musical community. Adopting an approach of cultural geography allows us the potential to look at collective musical identities and their spatial territories and to modify our pedagogy. I suggest that this approach will bring about a musical open-mindedness, not just in our students, but also in ourselves.

Incorporating a *metacultural*, musicultural perspective within contexts of cultural geography allows me to identify some pedagogical applications for music education. The root word *meta* addresses the idea that there is a hidden aspect beyond the word itself and a still deeper connotation. *Meta* addresses that which lies beyond, that which incorporates. *Meta* signifies the fundamental feature—that which is beyond, that which touches on the very essence of things. In terms of pedagogy and research, *meta* represents the ultimate questioning as the classroom becomes *musicultural*.

3   Reggae and the Collective Identity

Music can produce notions of collective identity and this works both with diaspora as well as groups of disaffected peoples unrelated by race or ethnicity. The impact of dub reggae on British youth of West Indian origin (African-Caribbean) origin during the late 1970s was highlighted by Hebdige (1979). Hebdige sees dub as providing a "communication with the past, with Jamaica and hence Africa considered vital for the maintenance of black identity" (p. 83), although it seems that the West Indian identity formed a stronger bond.

In the case of Māori, the impact of both reggae and hip hop was particularly powerful, bridging the geographical spaces between Jamaica in one case and the Bronx in the other, providing a collective identity and a symbolic sense of community. While reggae and hip hop, together with their distinctive facets, have been re-rooted and assimilated in diverse locations and musical genres, and at the same time generating a commercial viability, they are particularly embedded in cultures that are "largely depoliticized and/or alienated from the dominant culture" (Whiteley et al. 2004, p. 9). Reggae music, despite its island roots, has spread around the globe and is especially popular with groups of people who feel culturally disenfranchised. Reggae has had a profound impact on the music of Oceania, possibly because groups who feel disenfranchised have adopted its laid back insistence on political change. In New Zealand, Māori and Pasifika young adults have been attracted to reggae music since its inception, with Herbs, in the 1970s, and Katchafire being a more recent example.

Table 2 shows, in note form, how a musicultural model might be applied to reggae.

Table 2 Key musiculture concepts applied to Reggae

Islandness (origins)	Jamaica colonised by Spanish in 1494; the indigenous Arawak population disappeared after 70–80 years. British captured Jamaica in 1655 and imported slaves from Africa to work the sugar plantations. Slaves emancipated 1838
	Rastafarianism emerged as a religion in 1930s Jamaica. Rastafarians took the crowning of the Emperor of Ethiopia, Prince Regent Ras Tafari, in the 1930s as the coming of the new black Messiah; he was later known as Haile Selassie
	Mento becomes the dominant street music in Jamaica from the late nineteenth century and up to the 1930s: mento made fun of current events or were suggestive in nature. Rhythmically similar to the Cuban *son*. Instruments included banjo, kalimba (or rumba box playing bass notes), hand drums, sometimes the penny whistle. 'Ethiopia', a mento recording by Lord Lebby, was one of the first expressions of Rastafarian consciousness on record. Bunny Wailer later made minor modifications to this song in his 1980 hit 'Back in Jamaica'. An example of mento being used for the tourist market is the song 'Yellow Bird' by Jamaica Duke and the Mento Swingers in 1970
	Quadrille: the earliest music Bob Marley heard live was believed to be his uncle's band playing quadrille tunes based on Jamaican melodies. Quadrille song and dance groups are still part of the Jamaican musical heritage. The European diatonic scale was combined with recalled complex African rhythms to produce a version of the quadrille, which was very popular with the slave communities
	Junkanoo originated in a West African fertility ritual associated with the yam harvest and was incorporated with Christian elements (such as the Devil). Some of the rhythms were eventually included in ragga (raggamuffin) recordings. Another audible heritage is found in the press rolls of percussive accents used by Jamaican drummers generally
	Black American music had an impact on local music during the 1940s and 1950s, also music from neighbouring Cuba, Haiti, the Dominican Republic and Panama. Movements drove for independence from Britain, even as large-scale emigration to the US and Britain, taking place in a time of post-war reconstruction and economic expansion. Political independence granted to the colony of Jamaica in 1962
	Sound systems: a large number of speakers, rather like a mobile disco, used for street parties by the poorer Jamaicans who could not afford the plush venues
	By the mid-1960s a distinctly Jamaican sound had been established which used fast rhythm and blues (R&B) as its model but having its rhythmic stamp as an abrupt series of off-beats; this was named ska. The Skatalites seen as the masters of ska (Ernest Ranglin, legendary reggae session guitarist, was a member). By 1966 some musicians were moving to slow the music down to a more 'rock-steady' tempo, laid back feel with bold bass lines
	Revival Zion and Pocomania combined African and Christian religious elements and involving hand-clapping, foot-stamping, bass drum, snare drum, cymbals, and rattles. The Pocomania church influenced Toots and the Maytals, and also Lee Scratch Perry (who heard the rhythms as he passed by the church on his way to a session)

(continued)

Table 2 (continued)

Reticulated space (Distribution)	Networks formed quickly with Jamaicans living overseas, especially Britain, then later globally, especially the rest of the West Indies, the United States, New Zealand and Australia
	Chris Blackwell lived in Jamaica and started Island Records. In 1962 he moved to London and in 1964 produced Millie's 'My Boy Lollipop', which became ska's greatest hit (although the heavy shuffle feel was given the stylistic description 'blue beat'). Blackwell's most famous signing was Bob Marley. Blackwell was a clever marketer and much of reggae's international popularity is due to his great foresight
	Reggae has the power to speak to marginalised groups internationally (often indigenous or immigrant) and Bob Marley's message has been used by diverse groups around the world: Chinese students in Tiananmen Square (1989), both sides in the Nicaraguan civil war, also used when the Berlin Wall fell ('Three Little Birds'). 'Redemption Song' has been an important source of motivation for many disenfranchised groups
	Films: *The Harder They Come* (1972) featuring the music of Jimmy Cliff, Desmond Dekker, Toots and the Maytals, the Slickers, and the Melodians ('Rivers of Babylon'); *Rockers* (1977) starring Gregory Isaacs, Burning Spear, Robbie Shakespeare; *Countryman* (1982) an adventure story with sound track music by Bob Marley and the Wailers, Steel Pulse, Aswad, Dennis Brown, Toots and the Maytals, Lee Perry; *Dancehall Queen* (1997)
Iconology (Representations)	Babylon, Western imperialism and oppression
	In 1968 ska artists The Maytals recorded 'Do the Reggay', which had an even stronger bass. The guitar played bright chords on the up-beat, with a tempo even slower than rock-steady
	'One drop': the single strong beat on beat three, stylistic drumming. Laid back feel with bass lines weaving in and out of the drum beat. Example: Sly Dunbar and Robbie Shakespeare (Sly and Robbie), who played on countless recordings by Jamaican and international artists
	Bob Marley (and the Wailers); Skatalites; Jimmy Cliff; Toots and the Maytals; Peter Tosh; Burning Spear; Lee Scratch Perry (Producer)
Geosymbols (Contexts)	Rastafarian colours: in the flag, green represents the beauty and vegetation of Ethiopia, gold the wealth of the homeland and the sun, and red, for blood and the church. Ganja, the marijuana leaf symbol. Lion's head for the Lion of Judah (Bible: Genesis). Dreadlocks, in contrast to the straight, blonde look of the white man's thin hair. The term *natty dread* used to describe a Rastafarian with dreadlocks. *Rude boy*: young men discontented with the unemployment and their general existence in the shanty towns and slums of west Kingston
	'One drop': common throughout South American and Caribbean music
	Reggae bass lines almost drag the beat but are very melodic and provide both the anchor and focal point as they weave in and out of the drum rhythms. The spaces are as important as the notes
Ante-world (Sustaining spaces)	Black American dance parties (idea brought back by Jamaicans returning from working in the US)
	American rhythm and blues (R&B) (Fats Domino, Bill Doggett, Chuck Berry, Ernie Freeman, Louis Jordan)
	Latin music, meringue, calypso
	In the US the contemporary jazz album *A Twist of Marley* (2001) brought together international artists and singers in a tribute to Bob Marley

(continued)

Table 2 (continued)

Networked space (Hybrid formations)	Dancehall developed from the experimental sound of the DJs. Characterised by its raw energy, the DJ is the star and not the singer
	Dub – in the 1970s many records (e.g., 45 s) were put out with the song on one side and the backing only (sometimes slightly electronically enhanced) on the other (King Tubby, Lee Scratch Perry). Late twentieth-century dance music owes a debt to reggae. Pioneering hip hop DJ of the 1970s, Kool Herc, was born in Kingston, Jamaica
	Dub poetry speaks of hypocrisy and social repression (Benjamin Zephaniah: Jamaican-born, raised in Birmingham, UK)
	Ragga, short for ragamuffin, was Dancehall music which had been gradually overtaken by digitised renditions. Claimed to still be in touch with the original sound system style
	UK reggae group Steel Pulse modified reggae music in response to Britain's different environment and lifestyle
	Jungle: a reggae-influenced techno fusion
	UK bands drawing on reggae in the 1980s: The Specials, Sting and the Police, The Clash, Madness, Finlay Quaye, UB40
	Later artists: Eddy Grant, Ziggy Marley, U-Roy, Third World. In New Zealand: Katchafire, Salmonella Dub, Three Houses Down, Black Seeds, House of Shem

4 New Zealand as a Luminal Space for Cultures in Contact

Over time a culture makes contact with other cultures and shares ideas, technologies, and music and dance representations—the spread of the ukulele around the Pacific Islands, for example, or the adaptation of popular songs by Māori which have been adapted to generate new expressive purposes throughout the twentieth century. These adaptations and changes are outlined in Table 3. Of course, some dance and music must remain unique and unchanged because it is steeped in cultural grounding, for example, waiata tangi (funeral lament). The point here is that music and dance are a means of cultural transmission and exchange in the luminal space where the cultures meet, with the exception being those forms that signify life and death, rites of passage, and ceremony.

McLean (1996) urges us to realise that song loss among Māori, in common with other Polynesian cultures, was not entirely the result of the impact of the missionaries and their English hymns and colonisation in general. Before colonisation there was already in place a "vigorous composing tradition with new songs regularly displacing the old" (p. 276). The decline in compositions, or the loss of functions for some categories (paddling songs and food-bearing songs, for example) contributed to the decline caused by colonisation and new technologies. Tapu[1] also played its part, and McLean refers to waiata tangi (lament) which must only be sung on the

---

[1] Tapu relates to the power and influence of the gods. Everything has an inherent tapu because everything was created by the Supreme God, Io. Tapu has also been extended to include prohibitions and restrictions, such as making an error in the performance of a waiata.

Table 3 Key musiculture concepts applied to contemporary Māori music

ORIGINS *Islandness* Unique original qualities.	The first Polynesian settlement in Aotearoa/New Zealand, approximately 1000 years ago, saw a period characterised by the use of song and dance for a variety of purposes, including spiritual, ceremony, genealogical memory, war. Mnemonic and verbal devices for memorising matters of cultural significance were embedded in the songs and incantations (takutaku) through auditory means. Song types included moteatea (ancient songs), oriori (lullabies referring to genealogy),waiata (more commonplace songs) and haka (a noble posture dance)
	With the arrival of the first Europeans in the seventeenth (Abel Tasman, 1642) and eighteenth centuries (Captain Cook, 1769), various influences emerged, such as the sailor's musical instruments—concertina and violin (fiddle), the rough way the sailor's used their voice, which fascinated Māori (Barrow 1965, p. 24), Christian hymn singing (from around 1820), and familiarity with the Western musical scale. Introduction of Western harmonies, especially through shanties, hymns, popular and folk music (English, Irish and Scottish). This period saw a significant transformation in Māori music
DISTRIBUTION *Reticulated space* Distribution networks	A more secular period occurred from the late nineteenth to early twentieth century with the popularisation of Māori songs and dances (via concert parties), and the advent of tourism enabled individual performers to emerge
	Canoe songs and poi performance developed, for example, representing the Arawa canoe (Maggie Papakura and her sister Guide Bella around 1905)
	Māori concert party from Whakarewarewa toured England in 1911 and comprised a large troupe of Arawa led by Maggie Papakura (Barrow 1965, p. 28)
	World War I: military service produced Māori concert parties and Māori composers, as well as inspiring love songs, laments and songs of home
	Influences from Polynesia: adoption of guitar as a favourite instrument
	World War II: music used to boost the morale of Māori at home and at war. At dances, big band swing and their use of saxophones appealed to Māori sensibilities
	The post-war move from rural communities to urban brought traditional values to the city
	Showbands working in Australia, England, Hawaii, the United States

(continued)

Table 3 (continued)

REPRESENTATIONS *Iconology* How the music is recognised, the symbols and musical expression	Cultural meanings invested in specific features of the music from waiata-a-ringa through both world wars, showbands, and on to contemporary music
	The move to revive Māori music in the early twentieth century was led by such prominent figures and former Te Aute College students as Sir Apirana Ngata, Sir Maui Pomare, Dr Wi Repa and Sir Peter Buck who, as members of the Young Māori Party, sought the revival of Māori cultural life (Barrow 1965, p. 30). This was a significant transitional period. Ngata, first secretary of the Party, guided the cultural revival and, in music, encouraged action songs as waiata-a-ringa with stylised body movements synchronised with the singing. This form often used adapted European songs but remained Māori in essence and spirit and embodied Māori pride. There are earlier records of Māori songs (lyrics) sung to English tunes, perhaps as early as the 1860s (Mclean 1996, p. 312)
	From the 1920s, Māori performers and leaders became significant in the promotion of the music from Sir Apirana Ngata and Princess Te Puea
	The showbands: Maori Hi Five, the Quin Tikis, the Maori Volcanics; former showband stars such as Dalvanius Prime, Prince Tui Teka, John Rowles, Rim D Paul; Howard Morrison (solo and with Quartet), Hirini Melbourne; and later performers such as Mahinurangi Tocker, Moana Jackson (Moana and the Moahunters), Whirimako Black, Hinewehi Mohi, Tiki Taane, Maisey Rika
CONTEXTS *Geosymbols* External shaping influences, values and beliefs	Sets of values that produced and constructed musical territories that are distinctly Māori
	Pasifika-ness from heritage places value on gods or guardians of the natural world. Princess Te Puea was inspired by a visit by Pacific Island performers to her marae in Ngaruawahia and from this developed a style of action song
	The 1970s Royal Tour produced a more formal design of the action song, often designated as waiata-a-ringa (hand-songs)
	Identity-bearing symbols, such as the use of traditional instruments, were used in new contexts (Moana and the Moahunters, Hirini Melbourne); the inclusion of haka (Tiki Taane)
	Political function of keeping the *mana* of the music alive in memory and in performance
SUSTAINING SPACES *Ante-world* Musical influences, running parallel to the style	Big band jazz around the time of World War II, and the appeal of the saxophone to many Māori
	Influences of reggae seen in groups such as Herbs, Salmonella Dub, Katchafire, Trinity Roots
	Influences of hip hop emerge in artists such as Upper Hutt Posse, DLT (in the 1980s), who were able to challenge the status quo of music in their reconceptualisation of musical territories to a New Zealand-influenced territory where Māori values and beliefs were the norm

(continued)

Table 3 (continued)

HYBRID FORMATIONS *Networked Space* New concepts arising from the music, combinations create the emergence of 'third musical spaces'	Ngata's waiata-a-ringa using popular songs from overseas
	Music of both world wars drew on music heard while on active duty
	Pasifika influences
	Rock 'n' roll, soul, funk, reggae and hip hop all powerful influences
	Choral music: National Māori Choir
	Whirimako Black singing jazz in te reo[a] Māori

[a]*Te reo* is the name Māori give to their language. Sometimes it is referred to (for example, Barlow 1991) as *Reo Māori* (Māori language)

occasion of death, and to sing on other occasions is to invite death. This meant that too few singers were willing "for fear of the consequences, either to teach or record songs" (McLean, p. 277). Strict conditions were observed where songs were endowed with a sacred tapu, and McLean cites the story of the karakia 'Tena tapu nui' and how Tuuhoro, son of Tama-te-kapua, the captain of the ancestral Arawa canoe, died as a result of reciting it incorrectly.

In many cultures, what is most important about music or dance representation is that it "aspires to repeat the time-honoured idioms rather than develop them in new ways" (Crowther 2007, p. 59). As an example, when heard out of context, the compound-rhythm haka can sound nursery rhyme-like, but the unknown quantity of the haka makes a new sense of rhythm in the collective life of Māori. Essentially, the movements of the haka include foot stamping, arm thrusts, quivering hands, body and head movement, out-thrust tongue, and distorted eyes. Here is a description of the haka as observed by M. de Sainson who came to New Zealand with d'Urville in 1827 and witnessed a haka on the deck of the *Astrolabe*:

> Little by little their bodies are thrown back, their knees strike together, the muscles of their necks swell, and the head is shaken by movements which look like convulsions; their eyes turn up, so that, with horrible effect, their pupils are absolutely hidden under the eyelids, while at the same time they twist their hands with outspread fingers very rapidly before their faces. Now is the time when this strange melody takes on a character that no words can describe, but which fills the whole body with involuntary tremors. Only by hearing it can anyone form an idea of this incredible crescendo, in which each one of the actors appeared to us to be possessed by an evil spirit; and yet what sublime and terrible effects are produced by this savage music! When by a final effort, the delirium of howls and contortions is borne to a climax, suddenly the whole group utters a deep moan and the singers, now overcome by fatigue, all let their hands drop at the same moment back on to their thighs ... (as cited in McLean 1971, pp. 16–17)

McLean (1971) adds that the haka as a war dance took two forms. The first was the peruperu, designed to frighten the enemy and demonstrate a gesture of mass defiance. The second was the tutungarahu or whakatuwaewae, whose purpose it was to find out whether the troops were ready for battle. During this dance "the entire party leaped high in the air with both feet off the ground. Old men, who acted as judges, crouched low and looked along the ground. If only one man in 500 was out of time, his feet would be seen to be down when all the others were up and this would be taken as an omen against success. In such a case, the war party would not set out..." (p. 17).

Some Māori had a much more open mind when encountering and engaging with European dance than their Pākehā counterparts had of their own dance. Miss Isa Outhwaite writing for *The Graphic*, 29 March 1879, tells of Christmas Day in the Bay of Islands:

> An invitation came in, written in Maori, on mourning paper, asking us to tea and a dance at the neighbouring settlement ... and then to the schoolroom where the dance was to take place, and which was the only room in the building that would allow any one standing erect in all its parts ... The girls were very shy, but we said we would not look on all night, and when we each took a partner, they seemed to gain a little confidence - waltzes, mazurkas, and Varsoviennes were danced well and with spirit. In the middle of the evening we prevailed upon the natives to give us some of their "Hakas" or old posture dances, and very quaint weird performances they were, given with wonderful time and rhythm, and accompanied by a peculiar chant. Overhearing two of the young men "egging each other on" to the point of asking the "white girls" to dance, we intimated that we would dance "Sir Roger" with them, which, perhaps, some of our English readers will think was very bold; but then you see we manage things better in New Zealand. They danced, however, in a very statuesque and classical style, which was not in accordance with my notion of how "Sir Roger" should be danced. So I created a diversion by going my very fastest. The old men applauded, the women choked with laughter, and the young men called out "Ahi! Ahi! Like the wind, like the wind she goes; not a sound, not a sound!" My example was contagious, and the room was very soon in a glorious uproar. (as cited in Barber 1985, p. 109)

There is no doubt that cultural boundaries overlap, and they have done so for centuries, but nineteenth-century colonisation, and more recently globalisation, changed the cultural sensibilities of all parties involved. In the previous quoted example it is the European ladies who are intent on preserving their own cultural dance form by taking the dance much faster than Māori, who were content to move from haka to the middle-class dances of the Pākehā colonisers, while adding the stateliness more attributable to upper-class British culture.

Christian hymn singing in Oceania was enacted with cultural overlays, for example, the various ways of approaching the voicing and selection of the harmony, and which vary between island nations. In New Zealand, Sarah Selwyn, the wife of Bishop Selwyn, writing in 1845, commented with dismay on the way the Māori congregation approached hymn singing, without her acknowledging that the congregation were applying their own cultural norms to the interpretation. Note that most Māori chants were performed by groups of singers who are started off and kept together by a song leader, or precentor.

> The hymns were sung, not with English tunes but after their native notions which are peculiar. The scale did not seem to contain more than three or at most four notes, the precentor holding fast to one of them as each verse was ended. The choir, which was the congregation, after he had howled his first note for the first few words of the next verse, all struck in simultaneously and sang to the end, breaking off suddenly, all but the precentor who howled on. (Selwyn, as cited in McLean 1971, p. 23)

In a similar manner, forms of music from the European Classical Period (approximately 1750–1825), such as sonata or rondo forms, are often spoken of as "fixed identities, moulds or templates into which composers pour music in accordance with which compositional ideas are forced to conform" (Campbell 2013, p. 6). This common practice reduces the music to formulas as in, for example, the exposition, development and recapitulation of sonata form. This identity has been noted by Deleuze (1984/1994) in the sense that difference is excluded in favour of a fixed 'identity'; difference is embedded in the concept as conceptual difference but not as a concept of difference (p. 32). We can also see this tension between fixed and dynamic cultural identities happening within the rhetoric of human cultures as well.

Where certain forms of physical and sonic articulations are extended, rather than constrained to remain in specific cultural contexts, then they may become instrumental in extending an expressive medium's logical development. What this means for Crowther (2007) is that "if a culture focuses on a medium's logical scope (in terms of semantic [the meaning of the representation, which may relate to words, perhaps in a story or myth] syntactic [the formal properties of signs and symbols including words], and phenomenal [perceptible to the senses] structure) then what develops in that respect has a genuine transhistorical and transcultural validity through opening up new ways for the [cultural] code to be applied" (p. 60). Music and dance can thus be viewed as intra-cultural—essential and protected—and inter-cultural—containing transcultural and transhistorical cognitive and affective (or aesthetic) significance. How we think about the music and dance and how our senses and emotions are affected by it depends on the cultural codes we apply to our interpretation.

4.1 Māori Entertainers

The development of Māori Showbands in the 1950s and into their heyday in the 1960s can be seen as having been influenced by the eclectic approach represented by Princess Te Puea's band and concert party of the 1920s, Te Pou o Mangatawhiri (Bourke 2010, p. 328), and the waiata-a-ringa initiated by Sir Apirana Ngata, which adapted Māori sensibilities to globally popular songs. Like Te Puea's concert party, which incorporated traditional kapahaka and poi routines with Hawaiian dancing, comedy, and popular instruments such as the guitar and ukulele, the showbands wanted to both entertain and educate. "The showbands were unashamedly in show business, with their Māori culture being a point of difference from their competitors" (Bourke, p. 328). They were heavily influenced by music hall traditions and also by the Las Vegas style of Louis Prima and Keely Smith, both of whom were *mestizos* (part Spanish).

In one sense, the Māori showbands carried on a tradition started by the concert parties some 50 years earlier. In another, the showbands carried the action song with dance into the contemporary realm of the day, where floor shows from the local club or dancehall through to the big Las Vegas acts (such as Frank Sinatra, Sammy Davis Jnr, Bobby Darin, Louis Prima and Keely Smith) set the standard for incorporating songs, action and dance—the complete entertainment package. We can also see a link to black American performance sensibilities, enhanced by Louis Jordan in the 1940s, through to Fats Domino and Chuck Berry in the 1950s, and the soul singers of the 1960s, such as James Brown, Solomon Bourke, Wilson Pickett, and The Drifters.

With names like Maori Hi-Five, Maori Volcanics, and the Quin Tikis, the show-bands toured the world and were very popular in England, Hawaii, the United States, and Australia. Ironically, they came to have a mythical status in New Zealand where they were rarely seen or heard, and there is virtually no recording or film footage of the bands at their peak. Their legendary status paved the way for the acts that followed, some of which contained former showband members, such as members of the newly formed Howard Morrison Quartet, Prince Tui Teka, John Rowles, Rim D Paul, Little Hector Epai, and Dalvanius Prime.

Perhaps an enduring legacy of the showbands is that key members of the various groups went on to influence Māori entertainers back home in New Zealand as well as to raise the profile of Māori overseas, especially in Australia and Hawaii. Some band members forged solo careers overseas (such as John Rowles and Rim D Paul), with most eventually returning to New Zealand where they continued with their musical careers as well as mentoring and influencing local musicians. It should be apparent that the key aspects presented in the musicultural model outlined in this paper—islandness, reticulated space, geosymbols, iconology, ante-world, networked space, metaculture—usefully describe the musical ways in which showbands and their successors developed their style while retaining links to their Māoriness. These connections are made more explicit in the notes on musiculture concepts as applied to contemporary Māori music in Table 3.

4.2   Music as Protest and Empowerment

In contrast to the previous example, some Māori bands engaged not in entertainment as such, but in protest and empowerment, for example the song 'Poi-E' by Dalvanius Prime and Ngoi Pewhairangi. The song was developed in 1982 after the linguist Pewhairangi asked Prime, the musician, how he would teach the younger generation to be proud of being Māori and a 'Kiwi'. Prime responded that he could do it by giving them new language and culture through the medium they were comfortable with. What developed was a kind of opera which told the story of the small Māori community of Patea and what happened when the town's meat freezing works closed and how the people were affected. The closure itself caused significant social disruption, forcing many of the young to leave their close-knit marae and move to the cities to look for work. One song from the opera, 'Poi-E', became a hit for the Patea Māori Club in 1984, even though some record companies had originally turned it down. It featured poi,[2] chant, rapping, breakdancing, and a catchy beat.

---

[2] *Poi* describes the performance art of swinging soft balls attached to flax strings (poi) in a rhythmic manner, accompanying song and dance.

The lyrics, in telling the story, are assisted by use of the twirling poi. Pewhairangi likened the effect of the poi to that of a fantail that flies through the forest, analogous with Māori youth trying to find their way in the cities of the Pākehā. Just as the fantail has to flit between trees and leaves, Māori youth when they move to the city have to flit between skyscrapers, both concrete and cultural, in search of identity (New Zealand Folk Song 2005). The music of Prime and Pewhairangi was a powerful symbol for Māori, as it showed how the use of cultural music and dance practices could be brought into play as both protest and cultural restoration.

5 Conclusion

Music is a powerful agent for the development of knowledge and understanding, the nurturing of sensitivity and imagination and as a rubric for sociocultural representations of meaning. Inclusive music education must acknowledge the culture, identity, and needs of all students, and this makes for a complex pedagogical web.

In this chapter I have drawn on various perspectives of culture and subculture to establish a theory of musiculture based on, in particular, the Melanesian fieldwork-based theories of cultural geographer Joël Bonnemaison. Cultural systems can also be examined scientifically, as studies in anthropology have shown, or aesthetically, as typically exemplified by music to be admired for its uniqueness of structure and setting and idealised as an inspiration for further expression. The alternative model I have outlined here is that of cultural geography, which implies a merging of the two. I see cultural geography as offering a specific approach to investigating the relevance of musiculture in the students' world—it deals with symbols and with meaning, with emotions and reason. It is also a means through which to understand the music of the various cultures in New Zealand and in the bicultural relationship between Māori and Pākehā. The application of cultural geography to the study of musicultures clearly prioritises the beliefs and knowledge of specific groups and the musical spaces they occupy. Technique, while essential for the communication of these beliefs and knowledges, is likely to differ depending on the need and context, and a technique that suits one musiculture may be entirely unsuitable for another.

Whiteley et al. (2004) suggest that "artistic ideals of originality and romanticism form part of the technological advances to musical production, not least in commercial pop music where sets of values surrounding taste promulgate notions of authenticity" (p. 16). Production values and marketing might also, I would argue, blur the distinction between cultural values and representations (including language and instruments), the production values of the recording, and the commercial aspirations of the artists and record label. This may well be the case with some Māori artists, such as Moana and the Moahunters, Herbs, and Katchafire. My point is less about commercial success and more about the blurring of the cultural aspects.

I have demonstrated how new definitions of culture have moved beyond expressing only the identity of, for example, a musical community, to expressing how such communities are rendered specific and differentiated in the spaces and territories they occupy. If the key to understanding musicultures is to ask *how* they are different, we can see the way in which musicultures represent and use signifying systems as having new importance. Any kind of artistic collection inevitably embodies hierarchies of value and exclusion, the rule-governed and the free. The tension between cultural totemism—elevating a form of music to such a level of reverence that its immutability is unquestioned—and the access to musical cultural forms for exploration and innovation by all is what I have sought to resolve. Great musical minds can flourish in whichever musiculture they choose to settle. All music has symbolic meaning, and the need for musical artists to challenge existing traditional structures is very strong. This means that, educationally, our students should interact with other cultural forms of music or they may be left in an environment of collected musical artefacts to be revered and left historically static.

We can regard all music, however diverse, as a valuable global and national resource in terms of our musicultural identities, cultural diversity and international connectedness. Through this discussion I have suggested that music educators consider incorporating the concepts of cultural geography in which various forms of music reside in spaces whose boundaries are negotiable. This approach would mean we can use the language of both popular music, music of Māori and art music (and of all the other musics in-between) and incorporate their cultural concepts and artistic practices as modes for creative expression in education. This model of critical questioning, which draws on cultural geography, allows musicultural identities to be constructed in both a discursive and a material sense, interrogating and disrupting patterns of existence in spaces of teaching and learning and allowing for a mediation of the curriculum.

Cultural traits, such as the audible, create areas of preferential communication among musicians of the same style, heirs to the same musical legacy, or followers of certain composers or performers. Visible musicultural traits are often rendered into audible and visible signs that serve to mark out a territory with an array of significant works, dress and ways of performing. All musicultures create the symbols and representations that sustain their perceived identity and which have the potential to transform musical identities from fixed to fluid and to foster the creation, communication, and interpretation of newly revealed spaces in music education.

References

Anderson, B. (1991). *Imagined communities*. London: Verso.

Barber, L. (1985). *Sketches from early New Zealand*. Glenfield/Auckland: David Bateman.

Barlow, C. (1991). *Tikanga whakaaro: Key concepts in Māori culture*. Auckland: Oxford University Press.

Barrow, T. (1965). *Traditional and modern music of the Māori*. Wellington: Seven Seas.

Bhabha, H. (1994). *The location of culture*. London: Routledge.

Blacking, J. (1973). *How musical is man?* Seattle: University of Washington Press.

Bonnemaison, J. (2005). *Culture and space: Conceiving a new cultural geography* (J. Pénot-Demetry, Trans.). London: I. B. Tauris. (Original work published 2000.)

Bourke, C. (2010). *Blue smoke: The lost dawn of New Zealand popular music 1918-1964*. Auckland: Auckland University Press.

Butts, A. (2007, August 11). *Musiculture affiliation and the adult elite*. Paper presented at the annual meeting of the American Sociological Association, TBA, New York City. Retrieved from http://www.allacademic.com/one/www/research/index.php

Campbell, E. (2013). *Music after Deleuze*. London: Bloomsbury.

Crowther, P. (2007). *Defining art, creating the canon: Artistic value in an era of doubt*. Oxford: Oxford University Press.

Deleuze, G. (1994). *Difference and repetition* (P. Patton, Trans.). New York: Columbia University press. (Original work published 1984.)

Finnegan, R. (1989). *The hidden musicians*. Cambridge: Cambridge University Press.

Hebdige, D. (1979). *Subculture: The meaning of style*. London: Methuen.

Lash, S., & Urry, J. (1994). *Economies of signs and space*. London: Sage.

McLean, M. (1971). *Maori music: A bulletin for schools*. Wellington: Department of Education.

McLean, M. (1996). *Maori music*. Auckland: Auckland University Press.

New Zealand Folk Song. (2005). *Poi-E*. Retrieved from http://folksong.org.nz/poi_e/index.html

Webb, P. (2007). *Exploring the networked worlds of popular music: Milieu cultures*. London: Routledge.

Whiteley, S., Bennett, A., & Hawkins, S. (Eds.). (2004). *Music, space and place: Popular music and cultural identity*. Aldershot: Ashgate.

Trevor Thwaites (PhD) is a Senior Lecturer at the Faculty of Education, University of Auckland. He has been involved in secondary music education for 41 years as a classroom teacher, lecturer, supervisor, curriculum writer, examiner, assessment developer and National Moderator. He is also a busy musician, playing a range of jazz-based styles and genres in Auckland-based groups and ensembles.

Tama Wātea:
Integrating Māori Perspectives into Dance Education: A Tertiary Example

Ojeya Cruz Banks

Abstract This chapter explores the complexities and possibilities of intercultural dance education through reflecting about a project carried out by the Dance Studies programme housed in the School of Physical Education, Sports and Exercise Sciences located at University of Otago in Aotearoa/New Zealand. The ethnographic reconnaissance examines the challenges and potentials of integrating Māori perspectives into dance education; and how Māori worldview(s) can stimulate critical-cultural-gender understandings. The politics of asserting indigenous worldview within education extend beyond the parameters of dance pedagogies and the New Zealand context. Dovetailing into global education conversations, this study provides insights into the following: the intricacies cultural diversity, the problems arising from multicultural tokenism, the need to confront official school knowledge and curriculum; and the importance of recovering indigenous meaning and realities within postcolonial societies.

Keywords Dance education • New Zealand • Gender • Indigenous worldview/ knowledge • Postcolonial context • Curriculum

"This is very colonial curriculum", I said to my colleagues. We were discussing the content of (a)dance course and I was frustrated. I had recently migrated to New Zealand to start working as a lecturer at the University of Otago. Looking back now I think I was way too confronting and defensive. Plus, I was just beginning to understand the historical-political context of racism and the 'bicultural' identity of the nation. However, at that time a glaring discrepancy was that there was no Māori or Pacific Island dance in the syllabus. When I asked why, I was told it's because we don't have the skills and students get those subjects in other classes. However, the curriculum included dances which the tutors including myself were unqualified to

O.C. Banks (✉)
School of Physical Education, Sport and Exercise Sciences – Te Kura Para-Whakawai,
University of Otago – Te Whare Wānanga o Otāgo,
12 Gorman, MacAndrew Bay Dunedin, Dunedin 9014, New Zealand
e-mail: Ojeya.cruzbanks@otago.ac.nz

© Springer International Publishing Switzerland 2016
L. Ashley, D. Lines (eds.), *Intersecting Cultures in Music and Dance Education*, Landscapes: the Arts, Aesthetics, and Education 19,
DOI 10.1007/978-3-319-28989-2_16

teach. I had questions about the curriculum decision- making process. Why were some dances included and others not? Over the years, I have continued to raise the debate and explore how to develop the programme in culturally relevant ways and particularly how to integrate Māori epistemologies into the curriculum and my own teaching.

In July 2012, I invited the founder, dancer and choreographer Jack Gray (Ngati Porou, Puhi and Te Rarawa) of the Atamira Dance Company, an internationally acclaimed and nationally celebrated Māori Contemporary Dance Theatre. He spent a week working with three of our male students, who showed a special interest in dance. With Gray they explored Māori contemporary approaches to dance and issues of masculinity. The residency with Gray developed choreographic material that the students and I would develop toward a performance.

Above are tensions, observations, and aspirations I have had working at the University of Otago as a Lecturer for the Dance Studies Programme in the School of Physical Education, Sport and Exercise Sciences. Exploring the complexities of the intercultural dance education, this chapter reflects upon a project carried out and funded by the Dance Studies programme housed in the School of Physical Education, Sports and Exercise Sciences located at University of Otago in Aotearoa/New Zealand; and examines the challenges and potentials of integrating Māori perspectives into dance education. How these perspectives can invigorate dance pedagogy and stimulate critical-cultural-gender understandings is considered. The politics of asserting indigenous worldview within education extend beyond the parameters of dance pedagogies and the New Zealand context. Dovetailing into global education conversations, this study provides insights into the following: the intricacies cultural diversity, the problems arising from multicultural tokenism, the need to confront official school knowledge and curriculum; and the importance of recovering indigenous meaning and realities within postcolonial societies.

Conceptual encounters between Māori and Western paradigms of dance and dance education struggle with incompatibility. Not to mention, the philosophies and approaches of dance education imported from England and then later United States brought particular ideologies and practices. Dance education is a western construct that can often clash with indigenous Pacific understandings and aesthetics of dance (see Ashley 2013). Another postcolonial conundrum is that indigenous dance in New Zealand and worldwide have experienced deliberate oppression during early colonial-Christian missionary times. Eurocentric models of dance described as creative and contemporary have become a norm across the globe. While, efforts toward intercultural dance education come with challenges, reflections and strategies that address the erosion of our ethnospheres are needed; each culture and landscape is a branch of the human imagination, poet anthropologist Wade Davis (2007) says.

Currently there is minimal research on the integration Māori perspective into dance education literature; however there are artists, scholars and educators making contributions in this regard such as: Gaylene Sciascia, Tanemahuta Gray, Janinka Greenwood, Liz Melchior, Cathy Livermore, Cat Ruka, and Louise Potiki Bryant; also the workshop Tu Moves held at the New Zealand School of Dance and the dance summer intensives hosted by the dance companies *Okareka* and *Atamira Dance Company* should be acknowledged. This reconnaissance recruited three third-year male Physical Education students with Māori heritage to participate in the residency with Jack Gray. Members of the local Māori community made contributions to the project as well. Katrina Potiki Bryant (Ngāi Tahu), who developed Toi Ora, a practice that fuses physiotherapy concepts with traditional Māori habits of posture, alignment and rākau/warrior stick skills. In addition, kaumatua/tribal leader Huata Holmes (Ngāi Tahu) was consulted about relevant southern Māori cosmologies. The dance piece was named *Tama Wātea* by theatre practitioner Rua McCallum, (Ngāi Tahu), who attended a rehearsal and gave the young men feedback on their performances. "Tama is the word for boy, but the word wātea contains several metaphors" alluding to time, space, knowledge, and women, said McCallum in an email correspondence. These partnerships guided the development of choreography performed at 2012 Tempo Dance Festival and in particular the show *Tertiary Colours*.

Ruminating about this dance pedagogy is done through reflecting upon what I observed from watching the students work with Gray and what I learned from local iwi/tribe consultation. The research is written from my perspective as a Pacific Islander of Guam/Guāhan-African- American born in the United States and viewpoint as a dancer, dance anthropologist, and dance educator. Participant- observation field notes were logged and excerpts of dance sessions were video recorded. Student reflections about the residency were collected but are not featured in this paper. Key authors such as Hokowhitu (2004a, b, 2008), Burrows (2004), Broomfield (2011), Cheesman (2009), Risner (2007a, b, 2008), Whitinui (2010), Royal (2007, 2009, 2010) and others will be considered to deliberate the postcolonial context and pedagogical possibilities. Below is a description of the social history of dance education -the milestones and issues unique to New Zealand.

1   A Brief Social History of Dance Education: The Challenges and Opportunities

Dance education "has a long tradition of expert practitioners and dedicated advocates that dates well back before the emergence of mass schooling and far into antiquity" (Robinson 2015, xvi) across many cultures. However, the social history narrative of dance education in Aotearoa/New Zealand often begins when the subject was transplanted from England and established as a part of a Physical Education (PE) curriculum (Buck 2007; Bolwell 2009). Starting in the 1900s, many of the PE teachers from England and other European countries trained in Laban techniques and Swedish gymnastics employed to teach. The transferred dance curriculum focused on folk dance and was gender specific (Ashley 2012; Buck 2007; Hong 2002). One of these teacher migrants was Phillip Smithells, the first dean of the School of Physical Education, Sport and Exercise Science at the University of Otago in 1948. A strong advocate for dance, and creative arts, Smithells argued all learning was kinesthetic (Smithells 1974). He founded the first New Zealand modern dance company and implemented a 'Māori inclusive curriculum' at the University of Otago (Bolwell 2009; Booth 2013). However, decades later this effort was dubbed tokenistic. Hokowhitu (2004b) and Burrows (2004) note Smithells' use of Māori movement and rhythm was divorced from a holistic philosophy and was not tikanga/correct cultural practice. While Smithell's approach was culturally inappropriate, his effort and interest created an important platform within the PE programme for stimulating critical debates and much needed reforms.

However, as Renner (2011) has stated, navigating bicultural and multicultural diversity is still a huge challenge for dance education because many teachers lack confidence in Māori skills and knowledge (see also Bolwell 1998). Tolich (2002) would argue this problem has to do with 'pākehā paralysis' or how many European New Zealanders shy away from studying Māori culture for fear being labelled wrong or disrespectful. He argues this situation needs to be critically examined and suggests there need to be in place cultural protocols and safety for pākehās who do want to engage with things Māori. This is particularly important for teachers who need to be adept cultural brokers with regards to curriculum and teaching. Without these efforts, academic programmes and schools might be perpetuating 'pāhekā paralysis'. On-going professional development in Māori worldview could bring about a "renewed look at our heritage", which is important for teacher education, Renner states (2011). Another requirement is a rethinking of curriculum in ways that is sensitive to diversity and respectful of the unique place of things Māori, Burrows (2004) urges; and adds, disciplines such as dance within PE have the ability to interrogate dominant theories and practices. However, I want to add that dance studies need to go beyond confronting hegemonic thinking in PE toward becoming more culturally responsive to Māoritanga/Māori culture and viewpoints. This is dilemma that has been going on since Smithells' time; it's old baggage.

Many changes have occurred since the Smithells' era. Gaining momentum in the 1980s, advocacy for dance across the industry was occurring and in the year 2000 dance became a part of the arts curriculum and deemed a unique discipline (Hong 2002; Whyte et al. 2013). At this time, the dance subject was no longer just a part of the PE curriculum and became a mandatory subject for primary schools. After the curriculum success of 2000, there was some disappointment with the 2007 curriculum revision by the Ministry of Education that reduced the definition of dance to one paragraph (see Cheesman 2009). Weary of the implications of the paring down of the description of dance and cultural identity; Cheesman also feels strongly more time exploring dance in teacher education is necessary. Other issues indicated by recent research states there is very little dance being taught in the schools by generalist teachers. Authors are concerned about sustainability of dance, teacher's lack of dance and cultural competence and funding limitations; there is a need for pedagogical collaborations, and ongoing professional development for teachers (Ashley 2012; Melchior 2011; Renner 2012; Snook 2012; Snook and Buck 2014).

Dance is also included in the Māori performing arts curriculum, Nga Toi Roto Te Marautanga Aotearoa and taught as a separate subject from the arts such as dance in the schools (Whyte et al. 2013). This subject kudos both Māori and dance content, however, the silo curriculum model does have consequences. For example, Bolwell (1998) calls for more interdisciplinary and intercultural links between subjects so teachers can see the how individual subjects feed into one another. Research found that a significant number of teachers did not see the importance of kapa haka/Māori group dance (Whitinui 2010). Recommendations made by Whitinui, include collaborations between schools, teachers and Māori communities to identify schemes for incorporating Māori language, culture and customs as a valid part of the curriculum. Implored from his research is a need to ensure teacher education strengthens the transactional potentials between subjects and Te Ao Māori. Kopytko (2006) would agree and has suggested school partnerships with community-based cultural dance festivals for bringing about innovative pedagogies that demonstrate the country's bicultural/multicultural identity, knowledge and skill-sets.

Both Whitinui and Kopytko suggest cross-cultural pollinations that make way for sharing "decision making power" with local iwi/tribes (Hokowhitu 2004b: 76). Dance education is implicated in the need to address issues of equity and a striving to fulfill the legal obligations we have as a bicultural nation (Bolwell 1998; Burrows 2004). Additionally, East (2014) reminds us that the national, bicultural dance identity of New Zealand is young, evolving and learning to consolidate. The above research signals a demand for culturally- rounded teachers in New Zealand.

Over the last few years there have been improvements towards integrating Māori dance viewpoints into the Dance Studies curriculum at the University of Otago but it is still quite minimal compared to the ideological influence of Rudolf Laban and Gymnastics. While Jack Gray's residency was short term and extra-curricular, it did jump-start my thinking about Māori approaches to dance education; in addition to providing some strong male role modeling for the dance students. Gray is a luminary of the Atamira Dance Company, a cultural think and performance tank for issues of indigenity and dance. Snook and Buck (2014) talk about how "dance education artists" contribute to professional development in dance for teachers; moreover, dance experts such as Gray can also help to support and develop possibilities for integrating Māori perspectives of dance into curriculum. Gray and other company members are important educational facilitators for exploring intercultural dance knowledge and making. Their mission reads, "our work embodies the essence of our unique landscape shaped by the cultural identity of our people and their stories". The company is described as reflecting "a multitude of performance styles and techniques... (and) cultural upbringings and influences have also had their effect" (Werner 2008, p. 290). Māori worldviews, Western theatre aesthetics and other cultural perspectives explicitly guide the creative processes, performances and their teaching.

Te Ao Māori perspectives unearth different epistemologies of dance (Cruz Banks 2009; Royal 2007), it can also challenge pigeonhole thinking about dance and the social world. Māori worldviews activate spiritual and political dimensions of dance and enunciate problems of gender dichotomies (Cruz Banks 2013; Hokowhitu 2014; Royal 2007, 2010). For example, the social construction of gender in Western European culture often perceives dance as a 'female art form'; and this has interrupted male participation because boys often fear the labels: effeminate or gay (Risner 2007a; see also Soriano and Clemente 2010). Risner notes how the homophobic prejudice and social stigmas discourage both heterosexual and homosexual male dancers. Calling for a critical examination of models of masculinity and gender roles in dance, Risner says we need to look at how dance education might perpetuate what Pollack calls 'gender straightjacketing' or narrow perceptions of masculinity (in Risner 2007b, 2008). Broomfield (2011), says we need pedagogical interventions that "offer students critical perspectives... that challenge stigma and prejudice" (p. 128). Dance education needs to foster different consciousness about what it means to be human (Risner 2007b).

Risner (2007a) does acknowledge that not all nations or cultures view dance as inappropriate male activity. However, I would add that this point needs more than recognition because cultural counterpoints can be poignant informative material for thinking about dance. Viewing masculinity from other cultural standpoints presents important strategies for confronting gender norms (see Kerr-Berry 1994). Intercultural contrasts can expose the way gender is a socio-cultural product, and that gender and culture should not be inspected separately.

The following is a portrait of the Tama Wātea dance project illustrating my discoveries into Te Ao Māori perspectives of dance and masculinity.

2 Project Tama Wātea

On day one, I welcomed Jack Gray to our school and invited the students to introduce themselves. My inspiration for bringing them together was to provide the young male dancers with an opportunity for professional development and help them set intentions and goals for their practice. I wanted to expose them to different ways of thinking about and generating movement. The three male student participants were recruited from my dance education course. Two of them self-identified as Māori and one was not so sure about his Māori genealogy. The students had slim training in 'contemporary dance' but two of them had strong kapa haka/Māori performing arts backgrounds. All showed a passion for learning dance.

Gray's week long residency included four workshops that were three hours long. The students volunteered their participation; and this was a big responsibility for it added to their University course load. Gray facilitated playful workshops that welcomed laughter and introduced them to a wide range of dance and performance tools that included breathing, walking, partnering/contact work, and choreographic exercises. The sessions culminated into solo dances the young men composed based on conversations and their kinetic experiences. I did some observing, filming and dancing with them.

On the second day, the boys seemed less nervous and looked like they were starting to enjoy the physical research. An exercise that stood out to me was one that involved learning to move in unison while improvising and using peripheral vision. It felt like a game. The task went like this. One person would step out of the room until invited back into to identify who was the guiding dancer. The rest would stand in a cluster, Gray would non-verbally assign one person to be the movement leader and he danced with them. Moving as one, the group slipped, undulated, flicked, and crept with a sense of solidarity and connection. Similar to the contemporary dance exercise known as flocking, however, this exercise was about making it invisible who was directing the movement. It meant you had to maintain a collective focus and constant sensing of the group spirit. When it was my turn to identify the lead dancer, I realized it was not that easy. The young men displayed an ability to move seamlessly as a collective. I asked Gray about the purpose of this exercise and this is what he said:

> The exercise was just about how peripherally we can own our wairua. Even though not necessarily leading there's a whole range of presence indicators – ie: keeping eyes centered, following spirit by feel and energy, translation and interpretation in the moment. We're able to do these things. (Gray 2013, email conversation). Later he elaborated, "By 'own' I mean feel instinctively assertive and to trust these ways of "keying" into that space of indigenous awareness" (Gray 2014, email conversation)

Turukei Pere (1997) translates wairua as a spiritual dimension "that governs and influences the way one interacts with other people and her or his environment" (p. 16); it is spirit, soul that exists from birth to beyond death (Moorfield 2011). In 2009 Gray commented that working with wairua is what makes the Atamira Dance Company unique and counting through a dance was not necessary for them (Cruz Banks 2011). Recently he said to me when Dolina Wehipeihana was creative producer, this was the norm and part of the chemistry of the original dancers and choreographers of the company. Gray (Informal email conversation, 7 February 2014) wrote, "the conscious incorporation of wairuatanga as a cultural value is realised through our tikanga practices – prayer, ritual, song, story and acknowledging our ancestors" (email correspondence). Learning how to activate and utilize this wairua is fundamental to Māori knowledge, and for making sense of the customs; it is believed that youth need to be spiritually nurtured in ordered to be prepared for healthy adult lives (Moko Mead 2003; Durie 2011).

On the last day of the residency, the young men worked on their solos, they all seemed focused and kept reviewing their notes; the room was quiet. Working individually in separate corners of the room, I was impressed with their diligent inquiry and the moments of uninhibited movement exploration. One student, moved in the middle of the room rolling his body like water, shifting his torso, arms swinging above his head in a circle, body shifting in different directions; he moved from his hips. He glided, covering little space as his hand curved, and swivelled with momentum; and his head tilted away from his long extended right arm. He stopped, body stiffened and awkwardly found his way to the floor, dragging his body with his hands, he curled and paused incrementally until he was standing. His energy changed, he found his sternum, arms flung open and relaxed, from his hips up into his chest, the middle body rippled, face open and bright, he looked in awe.

While the boys continued to work, Jack reminded them "Be clear about what you are expressing. Don't forget stillness, a beginning, middle and end, character and changes of energy". I was touched by the innocence of their movement studies, and noticed their bodies had softened since the first day. They looked vulnerable and strong. I also sensed fear but they were confronting apprehension as they danced.

For most of their sessions, I left Gray in charge and I would pop in from time to time; thinking it might be beneficial to give the boys private time with him without a female in the mix. Dance Studies currently has no male dance lecturers, and I think this might make it a bit intimidating for some interested male students to study dance beyond the compulsory first year dance curriculum.

During project Tama Wātea, I spoke with Kaumatua Huata Holmes, a respected elder and orator of the Otago, Ngāi Tahu tribe. I shared with him my interests in the Tāne mahuta creation story as a springboard for exploring masculinity with my students. Tāne mahuta is the courageous son of Ranginui (Father Sky) and Papatūānuku (Mother Earth) who brought light and life. Holmes said, "that story is unique to the North Island, down south we have a different one". He went on to tell me about Tuterakifanoa (Tu), who dug out lakes, valleys and harbours and clothed the earth with plants and creatures prior to the coming of mankind.[1] He sent me something to read prepared by Waitaki Valley Community Committee with contribution from the Te Maiharoa family via email. When I told him I wanted to explore ideas of Māori masculinity, he said to me that a concentration of masculinity is "out of balance" and that male energy feeds from the feminine. Pay attention to Tu's helpers in the story Holmes emphasized. In this cosmology, male energy is not in conflict with female energy. Tuterakifanoa is an amalgam of energy. He suggested, "Tu might provide a clue to the kind energy you might want to create in the dance." Rua McCallum also advised in an email "male energy can never be separated entirely from female because we as humans contain the energy of both even though we are born either male or female". After the Gray residency, we developed upon the choreography composed with him and used the imagery of the Tuterakifanoa story to explore movement quality, intention and character. However, that part of the pedagogy is not discussed in the scope of this paper.

Holmes' and McCallum's comments above interrupt the dominant discourse about gender identified by Risner (2007a, b) and Broomfield (2011), and provide another worldview of masculinity that debunks the dichotomy of feminine and masculine. Holmes analysis of the Tuterakifanoa cosmology contrasts status quo notions of masculinity. This is particularly relevant because Māori men are often stereotyped in the media as macho and aggressive (Hokowhitu 2004a, 2008). Colonial genealogy of masculine pigeonholing in New Zealand has taken a toll on Māori identity. However, Holmes' point about the feminine and masculine 'not being in conflict' challenges the dominant paradigm and discourse. Learning to live beyond these Western constructs of manhood is vital to bring forth tikanga Māori values such as *wairua* (spirit), *aroha* (love) and *manaakitanga* (support and concern for others) (Hokowhitu 2004a).

Reconceptualising masculinity in culturally plural and relational terms transforms dominant archetypes and can yield what Jolly (2008) calls 'moving masculinities' that divest colonial constructions of the indigenous man. For example, Te Ahukaramū Charles Royal's (2007, 2009, 2010) research and revitalization of whare tapere or Māori houses of storytelling, music, dance and games fell out of use in the early nineteenth century and is undergoing a revival (see also Potiki Bryant 2014); a central theme is to balance the attributes of masculine and feminine

---

[1] Retrieved September 11, 2013, http://www.doc.govt.nz/Documents/science-and-technical/SfC244b.pdf

in dance. Jack Gray has been a key participant and an associate choreographer for whare tapere research and performances, writes this trajectory provides an opportunity to embody a different kind of masculinity through the mythical paragon Tanerore. He says, unlike common Māori male haka/dance qualities of anger or intimidation, Tanerore is not to be feared for he radiates warmth, illumination, and strength. The tradition seeks to enliven more fluid expressions of femininity and masculinity that offer somatic tools for developing indigenous Māori theatre and performing arts.

Whare tapere research invigorates analytical trajectories of gender. In the culturally diverse societies we live in, it is important to teach "a reflexive view of dance from different cultures" (Ashley 2013, p. 5)". This is why our interpretations of dance need to be world rounded (Foster 2009). However, Norridge (2010) warns that often-intercultural discussions on dance tend to be reduced to conversations about ethnic identities. The above scholars call for conceptualising different worldviews of dance and dance education to provoke intercultural paradigm shifts for teachers and students.

Conversations with Holmes, McCallum and Gray, as well as the observations and participation in workshops introduced me to epistemology of masculinity and dance. Through the Tama wātea project I discovered qualities and definitions man and woman as two parts to a whole; and dance was conceptualised as a spiritual journey, a ceremony and the embodiment of authentic self.

The following is an additional description of the dance residency.

For the last hour of the workshop, they performed their work and Gray accompanied their dances with percussion. They presented their solos consecutively as if it was one dance; and live music added texture to their movement. You could see the dancers interacting with the drumbeats passionately. The space felt very charged up and I found their choreographies riveting, and even the boys seemed astonished by their dancing.

Dancer one commences in the middle of the room in a squatted position, his head bowed down as he unfolds onto his back, slowing extending his legs and arms, slogging his body, arms flop and swing relaxed against the floor as he moves to the wall and flips over onto his belly in sync with the drumming. He pushes up to standing and plunges against the wall as if frightened. He skips with the beat of the drum while contracting his centre, swinging head side-to-side as he travels to the other side of the room. Dancer two also starts in the middle of the room on the floor, with is torso resting on his thighs, his face is buried. The rhythm matches his energy, slow and tense. He undulates his body slowly and suddenly stretching out one leg and one hand stiffly and repeats this three times with audible breath and then holds the position. Then slowly glides his arms across the floor and as drum thumps become more fluid, he spirals up to standing. Dancer three, begins in the far corner of the room, he coiled on his side, and its silent. His arms and legs gently uncurl and curl and the music begins. Top arm sways open and feet extend. Rolling onto his back, he suddenly sits up, and exhales as arms and legs extend. As he lays carefully back down on the floor, head vibrates. He pivots toward the wall and climbs it with his feet and pushes his body away and slides onto his belly. His hand tucks in and then motions

fluidly away and back in a circular pattern, eyes follow and head undulates. He does
this with the other arm and then repeats as he plants his feet firmly on the floor, head
lifts up and one arms sweeps over his head as the drumbeat becomes more pro-
nounced. Both hands swish down the length of body, down the thighs and one leg as
he smoothly stands up as the rhythm crescendos. Once upright, he quickly hangs
over his supple body, pulls up through his hands and a strong ripple pops out of his
chest.

As the final dancer concludes, the last drumbeat is played. We all remain quiet.
With his eyes, Gray motions all of us towards him, and we hongi and naturally move
into a circle formation.

Hongi is vital element to Māori ceremonies; and involves the touching of noses
to sniff and exchange the breath of life. A common practice within Māori ritual
encounters, hongi normally marks the end of speeches (Moko Mead 2003) but in
this case it concluded the dancing. Reflecting about the above moment, Gray said "I
wanted to recalibrate the sheer intimacy of what was shared by the dancers"; they
demonstrated an acute sensitivity to wairua. The sharing of their life force was as
visible as speaking" (email correspondence).

3   Evolving Aotearoa/New Zealand Dance Education

Project Tama Wātea provided opportunities for students to engage in dance experiences that were guided in Māori philosophies of wairuatanga/spiritual dimension of
life. Based on observations of the above compositions, the students transcended
dominant qualities of masculinity; they made expressions of gentleness to strength
visible. All three choreographies unfolded like a koru/fern, subtly and spiraling out
from the center. As they emerged from their cocoons, they embodied an unleashing
of life, emotions, conviction and power. An ownership of their mana/authority/spiri-
tual power was revealed full force in their dancing. I was really impressed with the
performance skills the students were developing with Jack Gray.

His didactic tools borrowed from Māori values and ways of doing things in addition to Western theatrical dance. Being a contemporary dancer trained in ballet,
Western contemporary techniques, as well knowledgeable in kapa haka, whare
tapere, and tikanga Māori, Gray's approach bodes well for fostering models and
intercultural dance education relevant to dance education in Aotearoa/New Zealand.

My observations of the pedagogy get me wondering about how Western theatrical concepts that dominant dance education such as how Laban's 'dance elements'
can interact with Te Ao Māori perspectives in deep meaningful ways. For instance,
by centralising the practice and awareness of wairuatanga/spiritual dimension in his
teaching, how might Gray's pedagogy conceptually inform and guide understandings of dance, dance teaching, somatic experiences, dance analysis, definitions of
techniques, choreography, community experiences, collaborations, and performance for cultivating a culturally relevant dance education? If dance can grow more

equal encounters between Māori and Western knowledge, it will undoubtedly aid the nation in what East (2014) calls the 'evolutionary journey' of dance in Aotearoa.

Acknowledgements I want to thank Linda Ashley for her support on this paper. Jack Gray for the wonderful student mentorship, teaching inspiration and constructive feedback on this research. I also want to express gratitude for the project guidance given by Kaumatua Huata Holmes and Rua McCallum. Lastly, I want to say many thanks to the students for embracing the journey.

References

Ashley, L. (2012). *Dancing with difference: Culturally diverse dances in education*. Rotterdam: Sense Publishers.

Ashley, L. (2013). Dancing with cultural difference: Challenges, transformation and reflexivity in culturally pluralist dance education. *Dance Research Aotearoa, 1*(1), 5–23.

Bolwell, J. (1998). Into the light: An expanding vision of dance education. In S. Shapiro (Ed.), *Dance, power and difference* (pp. 75–95). Champaign: Human Kinetics.

Bolwell, J. (2009). Dance education in New Zealand schools 1900–2008. *Tirairaka Dance in New Zealand, 2009*, 1–47.

Booth, D. (2013). Remembering Smithells: Past, present, future. *Quest, 65*(4), 394–411.

Broomfield, M. A. (2011). Policing masculinity and dance reality television: What gender nonconformity can teach us in the classroom. *Journal of Dance Education, 11*(4), 124–128.

Bryant, L. P. (2014). Whakaahua: Coming to form. *DANZ Quarterly: New Zealand Dance, 37*, 6–8.

Buck, R. (2007). INTERNATIONAL COMMENTARY 7.2 New Zealand. In *Springer international handbook of research in arts education* (Vol. 117). Dordrecht: Springer.

Burrows, L. (2004). Understanding and investigating cultural perspectives in physical education. In J. Wright, D. Macdonald, & L. Burrows (Eds.), *Critical inquiry and problem solving in physical education* (pp. 105–119). London: Routledge.

Cheesman, S. (2009). *Sustaining dance education in New Zealand: Some issues facing pre-service, primary teacher educators*. Retrieved from http://ausdance.org.au/?ACT=73&file=1006

Cruz Banks, O. (2009). Critical postcolonial dance recovery: An international literature review. *Journal of Pedagogy, Society and Culture, 17*(3), 355–367.

Cruz Banks, O. (2011). Dancing te moana: Interdisciplinarity in Oceania. *Brolga: An Australian Journal about Dance, 35/2*, 75–83.

Cruz Banks, O. (2013). Espritu tasi/the ocean within: Critical dance revitalization in the pacific. *Dance Research Aotearoa, 1*(1), 24–36.

Davis, W. (2007). Dreams from endangered cultures. *Tedtalk*. http://www.ted.com/talks/wade_davis_on_endangered_cultures?language=en. Retrieved August 2, 2014.

Durie, M. (2011). *Ngā Tini Whetū: Navigating Māori futures*. Wellington: Huia Publishers.

East, A. (2014). Dancing Aotearoa: Connections with land, identity and ecology. *Dance Research Aotearoa, 2*(1), 101–124.

Foster, S. (2009). Worlding dance – An introduction. In S. Foster (Ed.), *Worlding dance* (pp. 1–13). New York: Palgrave Macmillan.

Gray, J. (2009). Whare Tapere: Te Kairohirohi-the light dances. *DANZ Quarterly: New Zealand Dance, 17*, 16.

Hokowhitu, B. (2004a). Tackling Māori masculinity: A colonial genealogy of savagery and sport. *The Contemporary Pacific, 15*(2), 259–284.

Hokowhitu, B. (2004b). Challenges to state physical education: Tikanga Māori, physical education curricula, historical deconstruction, inclusivism and decolonisation. *Waikato Journal of Education, 10*, 71–84.

Hokowhitu, B. (2008). The death of Koro Paka: "Traditional" Māori patriarchy. *Special Issue, Pacific Masculinities, The Contemporary Pacific, 20*(1), 115–141.

Hokowhitu, B. (2014). Colonised physicality, body-logic and embodied sovereignty. In L. Graham & H. Glenn Penny (Eds.), Performing indigeneity: Global histories and contemporary experiences. Lincoln: Board of Regents of University of Nebraska.

Hong, C. M. (2002). *Dance in the school curriculum of Aotearoa New Zealand.* Retrieved from http://portal.unesco.org/culture/en/files/40498/12668598913school.pdf/school.pdf

Jolly, M. (2008). Moving masculinities: Memories and bodies across Oceania. *The Contemporary Pacific, 20*(1), 1–24.

Kerr-Berry, J. A. (1994). Using the power of West African dance to combat gender issues. *Journal of Physical Education, Recreation & Dance, 65*(2), 44–48.

Kopytko, T. (2006). *A focus on dance in schools: Innovative and successful learning through dance!* Retrieved from http://www.danz.org.nz/Magazines/DQ/June06/dance_in_schools.php

Mead, H. M. (2003). *Tikanga Māori: Living by Māori values.* Wellington: Huia Publishers.

Melchior, E. (2011). Culturally responsive dance pedagogy in the primary classroom. *Research in Dance Education, 12*(2), 119–135.

Moorfield, J. (2011). *Te Aka dictionary.* Auckland: Pearson.

Norridge, Z. (2010, September). *Dancing the multicultural conversation? Critical responses to Akram Khan's work in the context of pluralist poetics!* Retrieved from http://fmls.oxfordjournals.org/content/46/4/415.full.pdf+html

Renner, S. (2011, March 17). *Lecture on the history of dance education in New Zealand.* University of Otago.

Renner, S. (2012). *Primary teachers' efficacy beliefs in dance education.* Retrieved http://ausdance.org.au/uploads/content/publications/2012-global-summit/education-dance-teachers-artists-rp/primary-teachers-efficacy-beliefs-in-dance-education.pdf

Risner, D. (2007a). Critical social issues in dance education research. In *International handbook of research in arts education* (pp. 965–984). Dordrecht: Springer.

Risner, D. (2007b). Rehearsing masculinity: Challenging the 'boy code' in dance education. *Research in Dance Education, 8*(2), 139–153.

Risner, D. (2008). When boys dance: Cultural resistance and male privilege in dance education. In S. B. Shapiro (Ed.), *Dance in a world of change: Reflections on globalization and cultural difference* (pp. 99–115). Champaign: Human Kinetics.

Royal, Te Ahuharamū C. (2007). Ōrotokare": Towards of model of indigenous theatre and performing arts". In M. Maufort & D. O'Donnell (Eds.), *Performing Aotearoa: New Zealand theatre and drama in an age of transition* (pp. 193–208). Germany: P.I.E. Peter Lang.

Robinson, K. (2015). Foreword. In C. Svendler Nielsen & S. Burridge (Eds.), Dance education around the world (pp. xv–xvii). London: Routledge.

Royal, Te Ahuharamū C. (2009, October 17). *Te Whare Tapere: Ōrotokare".* Lecture at Aitanga: Māori contemporary dance summit.

Royal, Te Ahuharamū C. (2010, June 29). Whakaahua – An approach to performance. Keynote address presentation at *Dancing across the disciplines: Cross currents of dance research and performance throughout the global symposium.* Dunedin, New Zealand.

Smithells, P. A. (1974). *Physical education: Principles and philosophies.* Auckland: Heinemann Educational Books.

Snook, B. (2012). *Someone like us: Meanings and contexts informing the delivery of dance in New Zealand primary classrooms.* Unpublished doctoral dissertation, University of Auckland. Retrieved from https://researchspace.auckland.ac.nz/bitstream/handle/2292/19824/whole.pdf?sequence=2

Snook, B., & Buck, R. (2014). Artists in schools:"Kick Starting" or "Kicking Out" dance from New Zealand classrooms. *Journal of Dance Education, 14*(1), 18–26.

Soriano, C. T., & Clemente, K. (2010). Movement for men: A course challenging the notion that male students don't dance. *Journal of Dance Education, 10*(2), 59–61.

Tolich, M. (2002). "Pāhekā paralysis": Cultural safety for those researching the general population of Aotearoa. *Social Policy Journal of New Zealand, 19*, 164–178.

Turukei Pei, R. (1997). *Te Wheke*. Wairoa: Ao Ako Gobal Learning NZ Ltd.

Werner, T. (2008). *Dance: The illustrated history of dance in New Zealand*. Auckland: Random House.

Whitinui, P. (2010). Indigenous-based inclusive pedagogy: The art of Kapa Haka to improve educational outcomes for Māori students in mainstream secondary schools in Aotearoa, New Zealand. *International Journal of Pedagogies and Learning, 6*(1), 3–22.

Whyte, R., Melchior, L., & Cheesman, S. (2013). Looking back: Dance education in schools. *Dance Research Aotearoa, 1*(1), 86–111.

Ojeya Cruz Banks Ojeya Cruz Banks   (PhD) works as a senior lecturer and choreographer for the Dance Studies program in the School of Physical Education at the University of Otago in Aotearoa/New Zealand. Her research includes dance anthropology, pedagogy, choreography, post-colonial studies, and indigenous perspectives of dance; and she specializes in sabar and djembe dance traditions from West Africa, and contemporary dance. She was selected for the esteemed 2008 Professional Choreographer's Lab at the Jacob's Pillow School of Dance, 2011 Pacific Dance Choreographic Laboratory (Aotearoa) and was the keynote speaker and choreographer for the award-winning 2012 BlakDance festival in Australia.

The Ocean Swim: Rethinking Community in an Early Childhood Education Performing Arts Research Initiative

David Lines

Abstract This chapter describes a community research project called MAPS (Move, Act, Play, Sing), which involved community artists in music, dance and drama working with three early childhood education centres in Auckland, New Zealand. The MAPS project developed a programme that focused on stimulating and encouraging performing arts teaching and learning through a community-inspired, practice-based research approach. The pedagogy enabled the three early childhood centres with different cultural dispositions to respond to arts provocations from community artists and develop their own cultural focal points, decisions and directions. This chapter describes the project's aims and philosophy of practice and discusses how they can be viewed as alternatives to individualistic approaches to performing arts teaching and learning. A working metaphor of the 'ocean swimmer' provides a backdrop for rethinking community in performing arts learning in this context.

Keywords Working metaphor • Community • Music • Dance • Drama • Performing arts pedagogy • Early childhood

1 Introduction

The ocean swimmers enter the ocean at the beach, dive in, and begin to move through the oncoming waves. The water is smooth near the beach, but as the swimmers get further from shore they move with the changes in the waves as they come at them from different angles and with different intensities. Sometimes the swimmers feel they are being pushed to the side, off course, and in another direction. Their swimming movements adjust to the pushes and pulls of the currents and

D. Lines (✉)
Faculty of Creative Arts and Industries, University of Auckland, Auckland, New Zealand
e-mail: d.lines@auckland.ac.nz

© Springer International Publishing Switzerland 2016
L. Ashley, D. Lines (eds.), *Intersecting Cultures in Music and Dance Education*, Landscapes: the Arts, Aesthetics, and Education 19,
DOI 10.1007/978-3-319-28989-2_17

waves. Further out the swimmers get into a regular swimming action but with each stroke and kick they continue to adjust and respond to the intersecting waves. Sometimes the troughs and valleys of the waves make their swimming motion easy and smooth. Sometimes the waves become too intense, forcing some swimmers down beneath the surface. Eventually the productive power of the ocean together with the swimmers' movements guides them to another island and a new beach.[1]

The ocean swimmers' story is a working metaphor (Richardson and St. Pierre 2005) for this chapter about a community inspired performing arts project in early childhood education in Aotearoa/New Zealand—called MAPS: Move, Act, Play, Sing.[2] Working metaphors are productive in that they provoke ways of thinking. The swimmers in this short story carry out a swimming journey through the ocean to a new island and beach. While they swim, the ocean directs, engages and changes their journey—a journey that is meaningless and, in fact, impossible without the presence and invitation of the ocean itself. Putting the metaphor to work, I invite readers to think of the ocean as an early childhood centre community—a community that is diverse like the ocean, with many intersecting parts and components—both animate and inanimate. Similarly, the swimmers can be compared with the people in the early childhood centre—the children, teachers and parents—who choose to engage in performing arts experiences in, with and as part of their community. The actions of the swim are meaningless without the ocean, as are the actions of performing arts without the intersections of the centre community and environment.

This chapter discusses the particular 'ocean swim' of the MAPS project. MAPS involved three early childhood centre communities in Auckland: a semi-rural centre on the fringes of the city (Helensville Montessori), a central city centre (St Andrew's, Epsom Early Childhood Centre), and a Māori immersion centre (Te Puna Kōhungahunga). Each centre had its own diverse community made up of parents from varying socioeconomic groups, teachers, children, and helpers. In addition each centre had their own 'oceanic environment': geographic, physical, environmental, social, philosophical and spiritual places and spaces that enabled them to function as a community. The MAPS project sought to bring performing arts experiences into centre spaces through community-inspired pedagogies over a period of 18 months. MAPS was primarily an exploratory practice-based research project that employed ethnographic techniques (interviews, observations and online blog reflections) to gather data on each case study early childhood centre. Ethical approval was sought so that teacher interviews and online teacher blogs could be used to report on teacher perceptions and perspectives of each experience. This chapter elaborates on

---

[1] The ocean swimmer analogy is also used by French theorist Gilles Deleuze (1994, p. 165) in a discussion on learning.

[2] The MAPS project report is on the Teaching and Learning Research Initiative web site at http://www.tlri.org.nz/tlri-research/research-completed/ece-sector/move-act-play-and-sing-maps-exploring-early-childhood. The project's research team included the following researchers: David Lines, Chris Naughton, John Roder, Jacoba Matapo, Marjolein Whyte, and Tiffany Liao and early childhood centre teachers.

the underlying philosophy of the project and how this was realised through the performing arts experiences.

Aotearoa/New Zealand is a country that is influenced both by its oceanic locality and its colonial past. As such, its approach to arts education takes account of the complexities and influences of its past—that of its European colonisers from afar, its indigenous Māori inhabitants, recent migrants from the Pacific, and in more recent times migrants from Asia. These different cultural influences have impacted on how music, dance and drama are viewed and valued in education resulting in an intersecting means of expression: as separate domains of art as commonly experienced in the western world intersecting with collective expressions of meaning and community as experienced in traditional Māori and Pacific Island societies, with many variants in between. In early childhood education these differences are reflected in early childhood centres as teachers, parents and other community members work with young children in different experiences such as singing songs aided by recorded western music backing tracks, dancing and moving to western classical music or popular music, performing Māori waiata with traditional movements and gestures and so on.

The arts at a basic level have a close connection with community. Music, dance and drama, as 'performing' arts suggest a form of interaction or dialogue between performers (singers, actors, dancers) and their audiences. In Oceania the expression of community is very strong in the combined music and dance performances of Māori and Pacific Island peoples. This oceanic sense of community often finds its expression where music and dance become a collective and unified means of group performance that communicates meaningful community values and cultural identity. Kapa Haka, a well-known Māori performance genre, for instance, "puts into practice a key Māori tenet *whakawhanaungatanga*, which is the notion of strengthening the individual through shared community activities" (Rakena 2012, pp. 1–2). The creation of Kapa Haka initiatives and education has served to enable and inspire young Māori, rejuvenate Māori language and create a decolonised space for art-making and the affirmation of a political voice (Rakena 2012, p. 2). Thus, a notion of building, strengthening and empowering individuals through a community-minded art form can be found in Māori and Māori informed educational contexts.

This expression of community is also reflected in the early childhood curriculum in New Zealand *Te Whāriki: He Te Whāriki Matauranga Mo Nga Mokopuna O Aotearoa/Early Childhood Curriculum* (Ministry of Education 1996) which is a bicultural curriculum that utilises key community-based themes: Mana Atua (well-being), Mana Whenua (belonging), Mana Reo (communication), Mana Tangata (contribution) and Mana Aotūroa (exploration). These themes form a framework in which children's learning and participation is guided in early childhood centres throughout Aotearoa/New Zealand. The themes inform early childhood educators of the relationality of children's learning and the 'oceanic' threads that shape and construct children's learning in context. They express a view of child learning through the lens of social and cultural participation with which the performing arts can play an important role. Seen from the perspective of *Te Whāriki*, performing arts education becomes much more than staged performances or skill training but an important means of holistic learning and well-being within an interactive community setting.

New Zealand arts practices also have links with the European and British arts beliefs and influences that came from the colonial settlers from the late eighteenth century onwards to the present day. Typically, in education, as in many countries influenced by the West, this has involved more distinct training and learning of performances, arts modes and genres such as classical instrumental music or ballet—often taking on more individualistic forms of training centred on the development of individual performance techniques and skills. While out-of-hours lessons and classes in these music and dance genres have proved to be popular, in early childhood and primary music education a generalist and narrowed curriculum approach to teacher training has created issues around the sustainability of teacher expertise in the teaching of music and dance (Grierson and Mansfield 2003). In addition teachers of young children have been increasingly separated from formal music and dance knowledge due to further reduction of teaching training and direction. While some teachers are chosen as semi-specialist leaders (often due to their experience in performance art programmes outside state education) so as to redress a loss of performing arts expertise, the detachment of the teaching population from forms of music and dance teaching is an increasing concern. Despite this, primary school classrooms and early childhood centres remain as potential sites for meaningful community arts programmes and cultural enrichment. Further, recent research has indicated that Māori and Pacific Island teachers have generally higher levels of confidence and belief in their cultural identity and that this impacts positively on their musical identity as teachers (Bodkin 2004). The MAPS researchers thought these factors should be affirmed and utilised.

MAPS sought to redress problems of teaching and learning performing arts in early childhood by initiating a community approach. Rather than take an approach that relied solely on the building of performing arts skills with teachers, the project drew on the meaningful potential of community arts to ignite performing arts teaching and learning. The idea was that a community arts focus would open up areas of interest that would assist teachers in becoming more confident in teaching performing arts and enable them to utilise a more collaborative approach that took into account the needs and aspirations of the local centre environment. Returning to the oceanic metaphor, this meant making a conscious effort to raise the swimmers' awareness of the ocean as they ventured in the water to swim a new swim. The idea was that more meaningful and pedagogically relevant performing arts experiences could be enabled and achieved through a heightened awareness of community desires, wants and needs. By recovering the idea of community, centre communities could then work towards 'upskilling' in areas of performing interest that served their specific needs. This was intended to be a more sustainable model for performing arts development than random skill training in music, dance or drama.

The community focus of MAPS drew theoretical and practical inspiration from both the Italian pedagogy, Reggio Emelia and the community arts movements of recent decades in the United Kingdom. The importance of community in early childhood is one of the central tenets of Reggio Emelia practice. Reggio Emelia early childhood education is a thought-provoking example of how the arts can be a vehicle for children's experiences as active, honoured, participators in a local community. The Reggio notion, a pedagogy of listening (Rinaldi 2006), also reflects a pedagogical stance that embraces community and of the need to sense, watch and listen to diversity and difference in children's responses to arts provocations. Similarly, the Reggio idea of 100 languages (Edwards et al. 2012) embraces a diversity and intersection of modes of learning beyond speech and writing—to a whole range of symbolic languages in the arts, as reflected in the many modes of expression offered in the community. Reggio practices are traditionally known for their attention to the visual arts and MAPS was an intentional move to bring these ideas into the performing arts as well.

The community arts movements in the United Kingdom also gave the MAPS project some theoretical and practical points of reference. The community arts in the United Kingdom emerged, in part, as a reaction against a dissatisfaction with institutionalised arts education programmes—which have failed in many instances to engage with the real needs of communities. This movement has been described as "collaborative arts activity that seeks to articulate, engage and address the needs, experiences and aspirations of the participants and as such is defined by its method of work and aims rather than by any art form itself" (Higgins 2012, p. 24). One defining aspect of the United Kingdom community arts movement is its emphasis on process over product with a refocusing of arts experiences on participation and involvement rather than as curriculum or performance products as is sometimes found in specialised and elite music and dance education. The aim of this approach therefore is to promote a kind of cultural democracy—that celebrates difference (rather than assimilating difference through one dominant approach)—and that community arts programmes "must allow people to create culture rather than have culture made for them" (Higgins 2012, p. 34). Metaphorical speaking, ocean swimmers need to discover their different swimming pathways through their continued relationality with ocean waves and currents as they swim. Both the Reggio Emelia and the United Kingdom community arts movements then supported the idea of restoring the ownership of arts experiences into the hands of the community members themselves rather than from those who sought to preserve more elite, specialised notions of high-art. They also recognised the importance of embracing a kind of cultural democracy in art-making that took into account the different kinds of arts expression that were meaningful to children and youth as democratic participants in their societies. Given that a community arts ethos already existed in the Oceania context as explained previously, the Reggio Emelia and United Kingdom community arts seemed to have a certain amount of synergy and resonance with the chosen approach.

The MAPS project took these ideas and assimilated them into a project that advocated for and attempted to put into practice an early childhood performing arts initiative that embodied this community ethos. Community artists in music, dance and drama were chosen and employed to work with teachers, parents and children. They were chosen not as teacher educators in the first instance, but as artists who had a passion for their art and for working with and enabling communities through arts experiences. Adrian, the dance community artist had a background in working with disabled children in dance. Kirsten, the music community artist had experience working with mothers and babies and Molly, the drama community artist had done considerable work with process drama and the acting out of personal and collective stories with groups. Setting up the community ethos for the project took some discussion and sharing of ideas. The artists needed to be prepared to work with and negotiate arts ideas with the early childhood centre teachers and parents. This meant taking into account the intersecting cultural and philosophical interests of each centre—these were quite diverse ranging from Montessori and Reggio concepts through to Māori beliefs and understandings. From a pedagogical point of view, this meant looking for opportunities of co-authorship in arts experiences where the participants could respond to the invitations of the community artist and feel free to contribute with their own suggestions and ideas of cultural interest. This amounted to what Higgins describes as "working *with* the people not *on* the people" (Higgins 2012, p. 30). What was increasingly obvious too was that the centres themselves could not be seen as single unified 'cultures' as such but that through arts experiences many intersections of interest would emerge within centre cultures. In these cases the waves would be pushing from many different directions and the community artists had to find ways in which their arts practices could embrace those changes. To this end, a rhizomatic (Deleuze and Guattari 1987) way of thinking about performing arts experiences in centres was preferred as it took into account the different impulses, shifts and changes of interest of centre teachers and children the moment they occurred.

2 Community Arts Practices in MAPS

In what follows is a brief description of some of the community based arts approaches that were adopted through the MAPS project. With three early childhood centres involved, the research team was keen to build a sense of community with the whole group from the onset. With this in mind, cluster day workshops were held in the weekends where centre teachers, researchers and community artists met together to share performing arts ideas in a safe and friendly environment. Many of the teachers were initially afraid of performing arts activities—perhaps due in part to the perception that performing was for experts only. The community artists worked hard on these days to break down any such perceptions and enable the teachers to feel comfortable with their contributions. This was done through the setting up of an open, improvisatory type of session inviting responses from participants that they felt comfortable with. In dance this amounted to ideas such a building group movement shapes or making simple responses to partner movements and shapes. In music, the teachers participated in a playing-by-ear percussion 'jam' where beats and rhythms shifted and changed through gradual changes in timbre and rhythm entry. In drama, the teachers were invited to act out meaningful story ideas in short vignette pieces that were supported with audience participation and suggestions. Gradually, through these and many other games and actions, the teachers began to feel more ownership of performing arts and 'jump in' to the action without feeling embarrassed or self-conscious.

In another phase of community arts practice, the community artists visited the early childhood centres to talk to teachers and work directly with the teachers and children with performing art-making. The teacher discussions were important for these were times when the specific characteristics, desires, beliefs and aims of each centre were shared. It was also important that the community artists got to know the teachers personally and that a sense of trust was established. At Helensville Montessori, the semi rural centre, a strong desire for community relevance was made clear. This centre was very interested in making sure that their teachers and community took on board performing arts teaching and learning in a very proactive way. To this end, they made a performing arts space available in the centre in a 'gazebo'. This creation of a dedicated space helped established a sense of importance and ritual to doing the performing arts. Here, the community artists took sessions with the children with teachers and interested parents also participating. Community artists were asked to come every other week so the teachers could have time to explore the performing arts ideas directly with the children themselves on their own terms.

Slowly the centre teachers began to take on more responsibility as initiators of performing arts experiences with children. Some teachers discussed this in terms of a "ripple effect"; a kind of movement of desire between community artist, teacher and child, spreading out from an initial provocation. Centre teachers began to take on their own improvised drama story experiences with children through an inclusive approach that involved children's choices and story ideas. Children responded to community artist provocations through the exploration of sounds, through both engaging in spontaneous sound making and through watching others and then responding in their own time. Arts sessions in the gazebo at Helensville stimulated the interest of other children who would come to stare at the action, taking in the experiences as 'listeners'. At the St Andrew's Early Childhood Centre the ripples extended to include visual art connections. This Reggio-inspired centre has a rich history in making visual art and they had a strong desire to make a connection between these experiences and learning in the performing arts. Here, graphic representations of sounds were drawn through an exploration that took into account the children's previous work in community inspired art. These spin-off experiences were identified as "rhizomes" (Deleuze and Guattari 1987), or expressions of emergent community desire that led to an increased sense of ownership and an acknowledgement of difference within each group.

Parent evenings were an important aspect to the project, as parent involvement was seen as critical in making the community ethos clear and real to each centre. These evenings not only included talking about and discussing the project, but the parents particularly enjoyed participating in the community arts experiences themselves. The evenings helped the parents feel a sense of ownership about community performing arts and how they could support their children and the teachers. There were many instances of children sharing daily MAPS experiences with parents at home and this made much more sense to them following these evenings.

One interesting feature of the work of the community artists with teachers and children in centres was the way in which they adapted their pedagogical approaches to suit the community ethos of the project. In one music lesson guided by the music community artist, teachers and children were encouraged to explore sounds through the mediums of imagined stories, costumes, and found sounds. Here, once again Kirsten, the community artist set up opportunities for intersections of desire to emerge, and this was supported through the encouraging of sound exploration through stories. The energy of the lesson shifted from Kirsten's initial provocations as she pulled out costumes and sound making devices with lots of interactive suggestion, through to children taking on playful sound interactions through times of free play. The emphasis was on culture-making, of the creation and sharing of the children's own sonic discoveries and choices—and making these listenable through teacher guidance. This openness of pedagogy similarly extended into dance and drama provocations too. The dance improvisations were particularly remarkable due to the opportunities that Adrian, the dance community artist, created through invitational movement and the way in which the young children took on rhizomatic directions through moments of intense interest and sharing.

These performing arts experiences culminated in a community event, which was planned by each centre at the end of the MAPS project. Each centre needed to create a community event that brought together their performing arts interests and the different intersections and threads that they embraced through the project. The Māori immersion centre, Te Puna Kōhungahunga, chose to perform a *maunga* (mountain) journey to represent and celebrate their journey with the performing arts. Te Puna Kōhungahunga has a close spiritual and physical connection with its nearby maunga—Maungawhau, a small volcanic cone a half hour walk away. Their community event journey took the children, teachers and whānau (families) up the mountain with resting spots along the way to reflect on and perform playful rituals of music, dance and drama. The journey included enactments of food gathering performed by their Māori ancestors, waiata (song) performances, and chanting across the crater rim at the top of the volcano—where the children's musical calling intersected with the physical presence of the mountain to create a moment of intense pleasure and fun. The mountain journey was a community experience that developed from the desires and beliefs of the local centre and opened out into a meaningful experience that was supported through the performing arts.

3   Conclusion

The MAPS project was an effort to rethink community performing arts, not by simply performing in the community, but by bringing a community philosophy into a performing arts pedagogy. This amounted to helping the ocean swimmers to learn to swim by experiencing the ocean. In doing so, MAPS allowed children, teachers and parents to engage in performing arts processes that were—on the whole—right and timely for them as a diverse community of interest. MAPS fostered an emergent kind of pedagogical approach that was sensitive to the needs and desires of the community, and that could respond in kind through the expressive resources available to them. It utilised an inclusive and responsive pedagogy (Rohan 2011) that looked for ways of drawing in the needs and desires of not only the teachers and children, but the parents and wider community too. This led to pedagogical forms of transmission such as improvisation, games, cross-arts, nature—outdoor experiences, storying, playing by ear-or jamming, and child-centered, open and inviting teaching styles. Attention to process was an important ingredient—even the community events became unfolding processes rather than staged performances. This was particularly apparent in Te Puna Kōhungahunga's arts journey up the mountain. The community-minded performing arts experiences allowed for different intersecting cultures to come together in a form of expressive and meaningful rituals of music, dance and drama. Further, as a Māori centre, Te Puna Kōhungahunga's perspective of community was enhanced by the holistic and community-minded view of the performing arts they embraced.

The MAPS project sought what Gablick (1992) has called "a reenchantment of art", a fresh approach to what is meaningful in art—through the lens of community. Performing arts like music, dance and drama face many challenges in post-colonial societies like New Zealand where competing concepts of 'performance', 'art' and 'community' intersect, often through educational circumstances. These differences were apparent in MAPS, and the process of negotiating different points of view sometimes took time and patience—the researchers and artists needed to learn to become good listeners. However, the community approach taken by MAPS made some progress towards identifying an alternative performing arts pedagogy that was informed by a community ethos. And, in some ways, the geographical location of the project—in Aotearoa/New Zealand—allowed for the project to be accepted and affirmed, perhaps this was partly due to the strong influence of community in Oceanic performing arts. MAPS sought to find pedagogical approaches that could contain the different and intersecting cultural communities of each centre—taking into account the complex interests and desires of the children, teachers and parents, and the ethnicities, beliefs, philosophies, and values held by each group. The community arts approach taken was not looking for cultural sameness—the production of similar forms of music and dance performance—but of cultural diversity that reflected the visions, desires, needs and interests of the centre communities.

References

Bodkin, S. (2004). *Being musical: Teachers, music and identity in early childhood music education in Aotearoa/New Zealand*. Unpublished doctoral thesis, University of Otago, New Zealand.

Deleuze, G. (1994). *Difference and repetition* (P. Patton, Trans.). New York: Columbia University Press.

Deleuze, G., & Guattari, F. (1987). *A thousand plateaus: Capitalism and schizophrenia* (B. Massumi, Trans.). London: University of Minneapolis Press.

Edwards, C. P., Gandini, L., & Forman, G. E. (2012). *The hundred languages of children: The Reggio Emilia experience in transformation* (3rd ed.). Santa Barbara: Praeger.

Gablick, S. (1992). *The reenchantment of art*. London: Thames and Hudson.

Grierson, E., & Mansfield, J. (2003). *The arts in education: Critical perspectives from Aotearoa New Zealand*. Palmerston North: Dunmore Press.

Higgins, L. (2012). *Community music: In theory and in practice*. London: Oxford University Press.

Ministry of Education. (1996). *Te Whaariki: He Whaariki matauranga mo nga mokopuna o Aotearoa/Early Childhood Curriculum*. Wellington: Learning Media.

Rakena, T. (2012, July). The voices of warriors: Decolonising the Māori voice. Paper presented at the *ISME Community Music Activity Commission*, Korfu, Greece.

Richardson, L., & St. Pierre, E. (2005). Writing: A method of inquiry. In N. K. Denzin & Y. S. Lincoln (Eds.), *The handbook of qualitative research* (pp. 923–949). Thousand Oaks: Sage.

Rinaldi, C. (2006). *In dialogue with Reggio Emilia: Listening, researching and learning*. New York: Routledge.

Rohan, T. (2011). *Teaching music, learning culture: The challenge of culturally responsive music education*. Unpublished doctoral thesis, University of Otago, New Zealand.

David Lines David Lines (PhD) is Associate Dean (Academic) at the Faculty of Creative Arts and Industries, University of Auckland. David's research interests include music education philosophy, improvisation, early childhood arts education and intercultural arts education. He is a jazz pianist and he regularly performs and records with his band in Auckland and around New Zealand. He is editor/author of *Music Education for the New Millennium: Theory and Practice Futures for Music Teaching and Learning* (Wiley, 2005) and numerous other research articles.

CPSIA information can be obtained at www.ICGtesting.com
Printed in the USA
LVOW09*1350120616

492248LV00008B/35/P